The Art of Executing Well

THE Art OF Executing Well

Rituals of Execution in Renaissance Italy

Edited by
Nicholas Terpstra

Early Modern Studies 1
Truman State University Press

Cover: Detail of miniatures demonstrating the stages of comforting, ca. 1480. Illuminated manuscript, Compagnia del spedale de la morte, Bologna, Italy. The Pierpont Morgan Library, New York. Gift J. P. Morgan (1867–1943), 1924. Ms. M 188, fol. 5r. Reproduced by permission.

Cover design: Teresa Wheeler
Type: Warnock Pro © 2000 Adobe Systems Inc.; Minion Pro © 2000, 2002, 2004 Adobe Systems Inc.
Printed by: Edwards Brothers, Inc., Ann Arbor, Michigan USA

Library of Congress Cataloging-in-Publication Data

The art of executing well : rituals of execution in Renaissance Italy / Nicholas Terpstra, ed.
    p. cm. — (Early modern studies ; v. 1)
Includes bibliographical references and index.
ISBN 978-1-931112-87-1 (hardback : alk. paper) — ISBN 978-1-931112-88-8 (pbk. : alk. paper)
1. Executions and executioners—Italy—History. I. Terpstra, Nicholas.
HV8551.A75 2008
364.660945'09031—dc22

                                                                2008034780

For Adriano Prosperi
Mentor, colleague, friend

Contents

Contexts

Contemporary Texts

Graphs, Illustrations & Tables

Acknowledgments

The first seeds for this project were sown in conversations that Kathleen Falvey and I had at Kalamazoo in 1990. Both of us were intrigued by the manual that Bolognese comforters had used to prepare themselves for their trip into the cells to comfort prisoners condemned to death, and we had already begun presenting papers on it at conferences. Little happened for a decade, until Pamela Gravestock began casting about for a primary source on which to base a graduate essay. The idea for a translation revived, and soon more contributors began joining the project. Their emergence was usually unexpected, often serendipitous, and always added new dimensions to the project. A chance phone call from Falvey, retired in Hawaii, led to an exchange of letters and she immediately signed on for an expanded version of the original project. At an early point, Sheila Das agreed to translate the two books of the manual, and at our regular meetings to discuss and debate chapters and *laude*, we exchanged verbs and insults in equal measure and ended up having more fun than either the subject or the text warranted.

Das was working with an early transcription, but in the spring of 2004 Alfredo Troiano sent a message out of the blue asking whether, as a historian of Bologna, I knew anything about a new manuscript that Yale's Beinecke Library had recently purchased. The Beinecke manuscript of the manual had also come out of the blue. No earlier scholars had been aware of its existence, but it became an important element in Troiano's dissertation and Troiano became a key collaborator in the team. He produced an expanded critical transcription of the manual based on a wide reading of copies found in Italy and America, and during an extended period of research in Italy in 2005 and 2006, he broadened the circle of collaborators further. Troiano's lengthy conversations with Mario Fanti, the author of the first study of the Company of S. Maria della Morte and its manual, brought Fanti into the work as a vicarious collaborator. Troiano also contacted Adriano Prosperi, the author of an authoritative early article on the Italian *conforterie*. He learned that Prosperi had just launched a seminar at the Scuola Normale Superiore in Pisa bringing senior scholars and graduate students together around this very text, not unlike the one he had conducted with Carlo Ginzburg around the *Beneficio di Cristo* some years before. We invited Prosperi to join our collaborative effort, and he reciprocated by inviting Troiano and me to offer seminars in Pisa in the spring of 2006. It was on the steps of the Scuola Normale, heading into that seminar, that I first met Massimo Ferretti, who chatted about his work on early *tavolette* and immediately offered to contribute an article. A few weeks later, Alison Frazier and I talked over lunch at Villa I Tatti about her work on the 1512 plot against the Medici, and soon she too had brought her translation of the della Robbia account into the project. Over the course of these years, members of the group gave papers individually or together at McGill University, the University of Toronto, the Biennial New College Conference in Medieval and Renaissance Studies in Sarasota, and at meetings of the Sixteenth Century Studies Conference (2006), the Society for Renaissance Studies (2008), and the Renaissance Society of America (2007, 2008). It was after one such session at the RSA meeting in Chicago in the spring of 2008 that Meryl Bailey came forward to talk about her work on the *conforteria* of Venice and also about the sixteenth-century ballads by Giulio Cesare Croce that she had come across. Soon Bailey too was in the volume.

I have never been involved in a project that expanded so unexpectedly, and yet so naturally, without any particular outline or foresight. Sometimes following your nose just makes more sense than engineering a plan. Yet this only works if others are around to pick up pieces and offer impromptu aid. Apart from its nine authors and translators, this volume grew through the energies and contributions of a host of collaborators. Graduate and undergraduate research assistants from both the University of Regina and the University of Toronto came in at various stages from building databases to copyediting bibliographies. I would like to thank in particular Corina Apostol, Winston Black, Jason Kelln, Cynthia de Luca, Sarah Mantel, Colin Rose, and Jenea Tallentire. Filomena Calabrese and Sarah Melanie Rolph translated the Italian articles in the collection. Students in History 443H took the translation of the manual itself for a test run in seminar and their discussions generated many helpful ideas for the project.

When expansion in one area opened gaps in another, colleagues in America and Italy volunteered to go to the archives to chase down documents or references, usually on very short notice. Shortly after arriving at Yale, Jennifer De Silva headed to the Beinecke Library to transcribe the "Authorities" found in the manuscript there. Federica Franceschoni picked up more "Authorities" with a digital camera in the University's manuscript reading room while in Bologna between flights. Mauro Carboni checked an obscure but vital reference in one of the *Libri di Giustiziati* when he too had much else on his mind.

Beyond this very practical help, other friends and colleagues have given appropriate measures of hospitality, critique, suggestions, and wine over the years. I would like to thank in particular Mauro Carboni, Giancarlo Angelozzi, Armando Antonelli, Titzia di Dio, Konrad Eisenbichler, Mario Fanti, Olga Pugliese, John Roney, Anna Maria Scardovi, Larissa Taylor, Don Dino Vannini, and Lynn Welsh. Most special thanks above all to Mary Posthuma, who appreciates the unexpected and is the most generous of friends.

Michael Wolfe, General Editor of the Early Modern Studies series, and Nancy Rediger, Director and Editor-in-Chief at Truman State University Press, have supported the project strongly, while the suggestions of the Press's two anonymous readers helped bring the manuscript into shape. Barbara Smith-Mandell has been an extraordinarily sharp-eyed and efficient editor.

Beyond moral support, funds from various sources have allowed the project to move ahead in fits, starts, and a final burst. A research grant from the Social Sciences and Humanities and Research Council of Canada (SSHRCC) funded the first archives trip to Bologna in 1990 and also the work of two research assistants in setting up an early database of executions and comforters. More recently, SSHRCC funds administered by the History Department at the University of Toronto have allowed research assistants to transcribe, tabulate, and translate materials. Victoria University underwrote the work of research assistants with a series of Senate Research Grants, including a particularly generous grant to cover the costs of photographs, editorial work, and publication.

It may seem odd to dedicate a volume to one of its contributors. Yet Adriano Prosperi's 1982 article in *Quaderni storici* was for many of the rest of us the first guide and inspiration for our own work on the *conforterie*. Through conversation and publication, Prosperi has mentored many of those who work at the intersection of politics, religion, and reform in the sixteenth century. I first came to know him as a graduate student embarking on dissertation research in Bologna. He offered guidance freely and helped me navigate through one of those particularly delicate and difficult situations that could arise for foreign students in the archives. While we had little contact in the years following, one of the great privileges of this project has been the opportunity it has afforded to work together as colleagues. He has sought with characteristic generosity of spirit to promote the work of scholars in Italy and North America who over the past decade or so started comparing their notes, their ideas, and questions about comforters, comforting, and the comforted, and the tragic framework in which this activity took place. That collaboration has made this volume, and much else, possible.

Nicholas Terpstra
Toronto
May 2008

Introduction
The Other Side of the Scaffold

Nicholas Terpstra

In Renaissance Italy a good execution was both public and peaceful—at least in the eyes of authorities. Yet how could one be sure that the prisoner and crowd would cooperate? Studies of early modern executions often focus on the means by which authorities kept public order or how executioners did their work. They say little about a feature that was unique to Italy: the presence in prisons and on scaffolds of laymen who worked intensely with the prisoners themselves to prepare them spiritually and psychologically for execution. In most parts of Europe, clergy accompanied those condemned to death through their final hours. In Italy this was largely the work of the laity, often men from the highest social ranges, who gathered in confraternities called "companies of justice" or *conforterie* to undertake this charitable work. Lorenzo de' Medici was a member of Florence's *conforteria*, S. Maria della Croce al Tempio, commonly known as the The Blacks (Neri), and Michelangelo Buonarroti belonged to Rome's S. Giovanni Decollato (St. John the Baptist). Italy's first *conforteria* was Bologna's S. Maria della Morte, known colloquially as the Company of Death, and it inspired imitators in Florence, Rome, Naples, and other major cities. These confraternities produced a rich literature of works aimed at helping comforters to prepare for and carry out their work with condemned prisoners through the night before execution and on the difficult journey to the scaffold. From at least the fourteenth century, authors across Europe had been penning sermons and treatises on how to prepare oneself for death, articulating a form of spiritual discipline known as the *Ars moriendi* or "Art of Dying Well." The confraternities dedicated to helping prisoners drew heavily on this literature as they developed a customized literature that would train them in how to use persuasion and argument, stories and prayers, images and songs to divert a condemned man's attention from his impending death and so reconcile him to his fate. The literature they developed thereby helped them

1

achieve the goal of a "peaceful" public execution.

This volume offers a sampling of some of the tools comforters used, and sets the stage for approaching them with a series of essays that expand on the theatrical, artistic, theological, musical, and historical contexts of comforting. The primary sources move us directly into the wrenching process of executions by including rare first-person accounts that convey vividly the prisoners' experience of their final hours. While there are numerous studies of the official public theater of execution, none examine executions from "the other side," and ask how things looked from the point of view of the prisoners themselves or of those who assisted them. Most of the documents here are translated for the first time into English. The longest is a manual produced in Bologna by and for those who comforted prisoners through their last night and up to the point of execution. Two anonymous authors wrote books 1 and 2 of this *Comforters' Manual,* passing on the experience they had gained through many executions. Their two books highlight the distinct approaches of laymen and clergy to the condemned. The other extended text in the volume is a riveting eyewitness account of the last hours of two patrician Florentines who were executed for conspiracy in 1513. In the anguished chaos of this cell, all manual-driven prescriptions get thrown aside. Yet the prisoners, steeped in the same religious culture as the comforters, seek the same peace, reconciliation, and consolation as they cry out against their fate and huddle with friends. Their conversation shows how alive they are to the differences between classical humanist and Christian approaches to death, but also how they want desperately to intertwine the two at a critical point in Renaissance Florentine history. This poignant account also became a manual of sorts for later comforters who wanted to understand the anguish of prisoners before they entered any individual cell, and who thus sought out anything that prisoners had either written or from which they had taken comfort. Included here are poems written by prisoners on the eve of their execution, songs sung by the condemned and their comforters in those last hours, sayings from various classical and Christian authorities on how best to approach death, and illustrations of the small panel paintings called *tavolette* that were thrust into the prisoners' faces to distract them as they made the public journey to the gallows. Finally, a pair of broadsheet ballads from the early seventeenth century show how executions became sources of popular entertainment, complete with violence, romance, and moralizing messages.

Book 1 of the *Comforters' Manual* of Bologna's Company of Death was written in the early fifteenth century, and book 2 in the later fifteenth century. There is no sure information on either the dates or the authors. The *Comforters' Manual* is unique among Renaissance literary texts in opening a window onto the contrasting attitudes of Italian laity and clergy towards the theological, spiritual, and psychological dimensions of punishment and death. Although it was widely copied across northern and central Italy, there is no complete published Italian edition and no part of it has ever been available in English translation. Beyond books 1 and 2, the manual also sometimes incorporated a section of songs and prayers and a set of sayings about death and dying; no single extant manuscript has all four of these parts together. It was, above all, a working document. There are variations between particular copies that reflect the needs and interests of different comforters at different times. The translation offered in this collection has been prepared by Sheila Das, working with a base text edition prepared by Alfredo Troiano, and drawing elements from some of the best available manuscripts in Italian and American libraries.

The different parts of the *Comforters' Manual* present different views of the execution rituals. Book 1, written by a priest or friar, is more formal and overtly theological, while book 2, written by an educated lay comforter, is more practical and pastoral. Both deal directly with the questions that must have overwhelmed those taking on this charitable work for the first time: How do you prepare yourself? What can you possibly say? How do you deal with other prisoners crowding round as you try to pray with a prisoner, or with family members who protest the injustice of the sentence? How do you deflect awkward theological arguments. Where do you position yourself as the prisoner moves up the gallows ladder or kneels at the block?

Some copies of the *Comforters' Manual* include selections of prayers and the popular songs called *laude* that prisoners and comforters sang together in order to allay the dread of the impending execution. Some of these songs were very old and others quite new. It is a sign of how popular they were that no manuscript has quite the same collection of them. This suggests that the songs a comforter included in his own copy of the manual reflected what he heard sung most often on the streets or in the churches and to which the prisoner could most readily sing along. Similarly, some copies of the manual include pages of brief sayings drawn from biblical, classical, and early Christian writings called "Authorities." No manual has the same collection—some emphasize Christian authors while others emphasize classical ones, and some offer the same sayings in Latin and in Italian. This very idiosyncratic approach reflects the sayings that students would pick up in their studies of history, literature, or moral philosophy, and that they would collect in personal notebooks.

Beyond the *Comforters' Manual,* the next major document in this collection is Luca della Robbia's (1484–ca. 1519) *Narrative on the Death of Pietro Paolo Boscoli and Agostino Capponi* (1513), a memoir of the last night of two patricians arrested for conspiracy. Both the translation and the introduction have been prepared by Alison Knowles Frazier, working with older Italian published editions and manuscripts in Florentine and Roman libraries; the version presented here marks its first complete translation into English. Della Robbia's gripping account takes us from the time when Boscoli and Capponi first realize to their horror that they will not be pardoned and released, and includes their frantic efforts to put their affairs in order while also preparing themselves psychologically for what is to come in a few hours. The memoir highlights the tensions between the patricians' classically oriented approach to death and the more theologically oriented approach of the comforters who, frankly, do not come off particularly well in the account. The divide here is not between classical and Christian, because the humanist Boscoli is also a disciple of the radical cleric Savonarola, who had been burned as a heretic over a decade earlier. What Boscoli finds hard to take is the thoughtless rote droning of *laude* and prayers that his confraternal comforters from the Company of the Blacks offer. He engages instead in a more learned spiritual discussion with della Robbia and demands that a friar associated with the still-vibrant Savonarolan movement come in to give him spiritual comfort. Is this a "true" account? All our manuscript copies date from at least a century after the executions, when it had become a comforters' manual of sorts in Florence and, as Frazier notes, a deeply politicized document. Frazier traces the disputes about its "reliability" and situates the text in larger debates about republicanism, civic humanism, and the aims of the Savonarolans. Certainly della Robbia nudges the characters into somewhat stereotypical frames: the comforters are anonymous, unlearned, and ignorant, while Capponi is verbose and self-absorbed. Boscoli is thoughtful, humble, and articulate, demonstrating both classical virtues and Christian convictions as he courageously faces his *fortuna* with *virtù.*

Finally, a pair of ballads by the Bolognese poet Giulio Cesare Croce (1550–1609) shows how public executions returned to the street as popular literature and song. Self-taught and immensely popular, Croce had a keen ear for the popular mood and a sharp eye for profit. He produced hundreds of ballads that spanned the range from comic to tragic and that remained in print long after his death. Meryl Bailey has translated two ballads that demonstrate a different emotional range and hint at shifts in how executions were being received. The first, *The piteous case and tearful lament of two unhappy lovers*, recounts the execution in 1587 of a young patrician Bolognese woman and her lover who had murdered the father who stood in the way of their happiness. The other, *The lament and death of Manas the Jew*, refracts these same themes of love and murder through the lens of anti-Semitism. A Jew in Ferrara helps a Christian woman murder her brother-in-law and both are executed for the crime in 1590. Yet in this second ballad, Croce makes all references to the crime—and even the woman—oblique, and concentrates his verses on the protracted torture of the Jew and his cries for mercy. Bailey shows that while classical allusions, a romantic tone, and composition in *terza rima* turn the first ballad into a sympathetic account, the violence, scorn, and catchy rhythm of the second render it mocking, vengeful, and callous. Both hit the market as broadsheets aimed at a popular audience, and so inevitably they too joined the evolving library of moral literature that aimed to shape how the condemned, the comforters, and the citizenry thought about the meanings and rituals of public executions.

These Renaissance texts make up the second half of this volume. In place of a single introduction, six essays offered in the first half explain the contexts and meanings of the primary sources and of execution rituals generally. They explore the spiritual and theological issues around public executions in the Renaissance, the relation of execution rituals to late medieval public theater, the use of art to comfort the condemned, the literature that issued from prisons by the hand of condemned prisoners, the psychological dimensions of the comforting process, and social, political, and historical dimensions of executions and comforting in the city of Bologna, where the lay confraternities dedicated to this work first emerged and where the manual that was to influence many others across Italy was first written.

The comforters were well aware of the theatrical dimension of executions generally and of their work in particular. But they saw drama in two dimensions—both the drama of the execution as a public event, and also their own work with the prisoners as a scene in the eternal drama of salvation. Kathleen Falvey demonstrates that comforters' awareness of both dimensions was sharpened by the passion plays and *sacre rappresentazioni* that were staged by confraternities in Italian cities and squares. Their counseling aimed to help prisoners imagine themselves in the role of martyred saints or of biblical characters like John the Baptist, a dramatic parallel highlighted when passion plays were staged on the same piazzas used for executions and when players borrowed props like an axe or a chopping block from the executioners. Falvey sets both the Bolognese *Comforters' Manual* and della Robbia's account of the execution of Boscoli and Capponi into the context of late medieval and Renaissance religious street theater, noting how the demands and values of drama shaped both forms of literature.

The *Comforters' Manual* details the process by which members of Bologna's Company of Death were to comfort condemned prisoners in their charge. Comforters used biblical texts, *tavolette,* and *laude* to prepare themselves, and then took these same tools in hand to assist prisoners in their final hours. Pamela Gravestock examines how these tools, and in particular the *laude,* were used to prepare both the prisoner and the comforters psychologically and emotionally. Comparing the content of the *laude* to the themes and issues raised in the manual proper allows us to see how comforters might have employed them together. Beyond that, examining the use of *laude* in other contexts shows how this popular art form can be understood as the "voice" of the prisoner.

Some of the *laude* translated here do indeed represent a particular prisoner's voice. On 12 August 1469, a minor bureaucrat Andrea Viarani was beheaded in Ferrara after taking part in a plot launched by his employers, the Lords of Carpi, against Duke Borso d'Este of Ferrara. While in prison, Viarani wrote a number of poems that survive in eight manuscript copies. Alfredo Troiano takes three that have received almost no attention in modern scholarship and reads them in conjunction with the *Comforters' Manual.* We know the manual was used by the Ferrara *conforteria* of S. Maria dell'Ascensione, known locally (as in Florence) as "The Blacks"—and the comforters who assisted Viarani very likely consulted it. Troiano focuses on explaining the content of the poems and exploring different aspects of their political context: the rapid conversion of a condemned man and his behavior in face of an imminent death penalty, the reconciliation between capital criminals and the societies that condemned them, and the transformation of Viarani's verses into models for contrition, piety, and dying well that were used when comforting other condemned prisoners.

A key part of comforting on the final journey to the scaffold lay in keeping the prisoner focused by obliterating the sounds and sight of the crowd. Comforters achieved this by singing and whispering constantly in the prisoner's ear and holding the *tavolette* directly in front of his eyes. As Massimo Ferretti shows, the few surviving panels include some that were used in Bologna by the very comforters who employed the *Comforters' Manual* translated here. These *tavolette* featured images of Mary, Christ, and martyred saints with whom the prisoner was to identify as he faced his death. Ferretti expands on the physical condition of remaining *tavolette* and explores their iconography and meaning.

Comforting took place in a Catholic framework and used the promise of salvation to bring the criminal to confession, communion, and an acceptance of his fate. But what of those who refused to acknowledge their crime or seek forgiveness? Adriano Prosperi looks at the ambivalent responses of both religious and secular authorities to the question of whether such criminals should be given last rites. Synods of the early medieval church held that hard-hearted criminals should receive neither sacraments nor prayers, and this disciplinary view held sway until the fourteenth century. There gradually emerged a more generous approach that aimed to bring criminals to conversion, an approach that demonstrates the expanding recognition of human individuality in the Renaissance period. Yet there continued to be authorities, ecclesiastical and political alike, who advocated a more punitive approach, particularly with regard to heretics. Prosperi explores the resulting debates and the complicated intertwining of humanism, orthodoxy, and absolutism that they demonstrate.

Why did politically engaged men in Italy take on the work of accompanying criminals to the scaffold when other European cultures assigned this work to priests and friars? Bologna's Company of Death commissioned the *Comforters' Manual* and its members took it with them into the prisons. Nicholas Terpstra examines the historical and political dimensions of their work, looking first at the crimes and criminals the Bolognese prosecuted and how comforting and executions took place, before turning to ask who these men were, what other roles they played politically, and how the *conforteria*'s standing in the network of local charitable institutions shifted as Bologna's political situation changed. More than two hundred men assisted the nearly one thousand men and women Bologna executed through the latter half of the sixteenth century; most were "disciples" who served at a few executions for a few years in their youth, but roughly 20 percent became "masters" who served at literally dozens of executions over a lifetime of service. These were the men who studied the manual at home and carried it along into the prison, using its suggestions, memorizing its prayers, and singing its songs. Reviewing the social class and political profile of the comforters shows that both rise steadily through the sixteenth century. As the Company of Death identified ever more closely with Bologna's political fortunes and political elite, it identified less closely with the prisoners whom the elite had marked for death. Comforters moved gradually to the other side of the scaffold, that is, closer to those political authorities who aimed for peaceful executions as a means of securing peaceful rule. With this the art shifts from "dying well" to "executing well."

The rituals of comforting were deeply pious and deeply political. Some authors here emphasize one element and some the other, though the dovetailing of religious and political orthodoxy in late Renaissance and early modern cities should relieve one of any urge to put these into opposing categories. Order was order, on earth as in heaven, and comforters believed they were called to be agents of that divine order. The religious rituals they laid around the harsh realities of prison and scaffold in their pursuit of the "art of executing well" aimed to bring peace and order to the cities they lived in and above all to the souls of those whom these cities executed.

⋅   What is perhaps more significant is the enduring pull the *Comforters' Manual* had on those who assisted prisoners. This was less the case with book 1, written by a cleric and reflecting that cleric's grasp of abstract theology and the complicated hierarchies of saints, martyrs, and angels in heaven. The harsh editing of this book by later copyists is silent testimony to how unhelpful many comforters found it to be. Book 2, on the other hand, was often copied out and always in full—eloquent testimony to how much it spoke to comforters long after it had been written. It breathed the values of fifteenth-century imitative piety and brought comforters into close brotherly relation with those they assisted—a metaphor pictured graphically by manuscript illustrations that show a prisoner together with two or three comforters, and also underscored by della Robbia's account. By the mid-seventeenth century, comforters were less interested in that close one-on-one relationship and were packing the prisons with friends and allies curious for a close-up look at the prisoner and the process, particularly when a criminal notorious enough to engage the attentions of a balladeer like G. C. Croce was in the cell. One might think that the hierarchies of book 1 would now resonate more loudly with these *magnifici* and *illustrissimi*. Yet in fact they still used book 2, still used *laude,* and still read della Robbia—telling signs of how directly those Renaissance values addressed the hard realities of prison and scaffold and met the immediate needs of the prisoners and comforters who walked through them together.

Patrician comforters certainly acted as advocates of the judicial system and not of the prisoners, aiming to secure prisoners' quiet acquiescence even to unjust sentences. They were unapologetic proponents of the death penalty. And yet one wonders about longer-term effects of this charitable activity, particularly on those thousands of men who assisted as disciples at a handful of executions for a year or two before moving on in their political and professional careers. One should recall that it was *only* in Italy that social and political leaders through their *conforterie* sat with criminals through a long night, marched with them through the streets, and positioned themselves no more than an arm's length away before the executioner did his work. Did this shared experience create an influential audience ready to hear the views of the Milanese author Cesare Beccaria (1738–1794), whose *Essay on Crimes and Punishments* (1764) was the first sustained critique of capital punishment? In shifting the basis for punishment from divine justice to social utility, Beccaria moved to a paradigm the authors of the Renaissance manuals would have found foreign and even heretical. And in rejecting capital punishment altogether as lacking either utility or even legitimacy, he envisioned a state where a *conforteria* would be pointless.

Although his views were antithetical to those of the Renaissance *conforterie,* one has to wonder whether these brotherhoods in some way created an audience for Beccaria's work two centuries later. Those lining the streets of eighteenth-century cities may have found the sight of black- or white-robed comforters holding up tablets and singing in a criminal's ear to be bizarre relics of an antiquated and arbitrary system of justice. Certainly Enlightenment reformers swept the *conforterie*—and indeed all confraternities—out of the way in the new legal codes of the late eighteenth century. But might one also trace effects within the *conforterie* themselves? The master comforters who had moved from the theological abstractions of book 1 to the spiritual realities of book 2 demonstrated a preference for the practical over the abstract in religious terms. This in itself could represent the first step of a movement intellectually towards a more secular model of punishment based on practical utility. More than that, the rapid turnover of disciples suggests that at least some of those who left the work would have agreed, on the basis of direct and intense personal experience, with Beccaria's argument that capital punishment was inconsistent with humane values. The very institution of the *conforteria* ensured that for many of Italy's political and cultural leaders, the execution of criminals by the state was not an abstraction, but a vivid, concrete, and horrific reality that they had witnessed at close hand. This was unique in Europe. It may help us understand why Beccaria's book gained such a wide readership and following in Italy, and why two decades later, the Duchy of Tuscany could be the first European state to formally abolish capital punishment.

The Art of Executing Well
Contexts

Chapter 1

Scaffold and Stage
Comforting Rituals and Dramatic Traditions in Late Medieval and Renaissance Italy

Kathleen Falvey

From the fourteenth to the mid-sixteenth century, the practice of ministering to prisoners about to be executed became institutionalized and regularized within some Italian lay confraternities.[1] Many of these were penitential confraternities and their devotion to Christ's Passion took on a participatory quality that influenced their delicate mission to those facing the shame and terror of public execution. This was also a period when vernacular religious plays flourished throughout Italy, with plays of Christ's Passion and of saints' martyrdoms becoming common in the very areas where the confraternal comforting of prisoners was established and well known.[2] It was usually confraternal laymen who mounted the plays and performed the parts. And in fact, these Passion plays were sometimes performed in the same civic spaces that on other occasions were sites of public executions. Audiences of the faithful flocked to outdoor stages on religious feast days to see dramatizations on the themes of death and martyrdom, and then a few days later might return to the same place to witness the rituals that accompanied a prisoner's final hours. The first "staged" drama of Christ and the saints would clearly have colored their reactions to the second "real-life" drama of the prisoner going to his death with piety and dignity. It was possible that a single layman could take a role as an actor on the Passion play stage and as a comforter in the prison and on the

---

[1] An earlier and shorter version of this paper was published as "Early Italian Dramatic Traditions." It is republished here with permission. See also Cutini, "I condannati"; Parisini, "Pratiche"; and Prosperi, "Il sangue e l'anima."

[2] A guide to the widespread popularity of Passion and Martyrdom plays for the period in question may be found in my "Italian Vernacular Religious Drama."

scaffold. This powerfully emphasizes a fundamental spiritual reality: *confratelli* and prisoners were "brother penitents" seeking intimate union with Christ in his redemptive sufferings.

Yet the relations are even more complex. Because of the complex inter-weaving of religious and civic institutions, a single lay confraternity member might be a member of city council charged with formulating civic statutes and ordinances; he might be a magistrate charged with using these same laws to pursue criminal proceedings against a defendant; he might be a comforter charged with assisting prisoners condemned under capital sentence; and he might be *confratello* who had a hand in composing, producing, and acting its Passion and martyrdom plays. And of course, this individual citizen might also run afoul of the law and find himself in need of either pardon or comfort-ing. Dramatic and penal forms interpenetrated each other and, given the im-manence of symbolic actions in the tightly knit society of Renaissance Italian towns, both were animated with religious and secular themes.

This essay will explore these interpenetrations and themes using the Bo-lognese and Florentine texts translated in this volume, and comparing these to religious dramas staged by confraternities in northern and central Italy. It will offer some initial considerations about the profound correspondences that existed between dramatic traditions and the efforts of dedicated laymen to transform a brutal penal event, public execution, into a ritualized and very "real" re-enactment of the death of Christ or one of the martyrs.

The *Comforters' Manual* of the penitential confraternity of S. Maria della Morte in Bologna that is translated in this volume offers a good way to ap-proach an understanding of the nature of the *conforteria* during the period under consideration.[3] As noted in the introduction to the edition translated here, the manual is composed of two books. Book 1 prepares the comforter for his mission by furnishing him with explanations and arguments to move the prisoner to receive the sacraments of penance and the Eucharist. Book 2 is more practical, instructing the comforter how to act, and what to say, from the moment he enters the prison on the eve of the execution, through the night, and up to the very moment of the prisoner's death. Most manuscript copies include either the texts or titles of "*laude* and prayers," which were verses and/or hymns that may have been sung or merely recited during the

---

[3] *Comforters' Manual*, PML ms. 188. I wish to express my thanks to the authorities of the Pierpont Morgan Library for permission to consult this manuscript and pertinent catalogues; I have employed the original folio numbers in the footnote citations rather than the later penciled pagination. For an extended discus-sion of the manuscript and its tradition, see Fanti, "S. Maria della Morte."

comforting process. This repertory of *laude* and prayers was available to the comforter to use at his discretion during the various steps in the process according to the needs and dispositions of the condemned. Among them was Jacopone da Todi's *Dona del Paradiso,* one of the most dramatic and almost theatrical treatments of Christ's Passion to come down to us from early Italian poetic traditions.[4] During the comforting ritual, the prisoner was urged to conform his humiliation and suffering to that of Christ and to comport himself with love and dignity as Christ himself did—to "perform," so to speak, in an all-too-realistic Passion play.

Within this metaphorical Passion play, book 1 constituted a kind of model script for the comforter. This script was principally suggestive, to be used at the discretion of the comforter in individual situations. The tone and diction are familiar, gentle, and loving, as indicated by the first words to be spoken on entering the prison and meeting the prisoner for the first time:

> My dearest brother and friend, God and the Virgin Mary who accompany me know well that we belong to that blessed charitable company [of S. Maria della Morte] and that we would rather come to visit you in any manner but this, wearing any other habit, and for any other purpose. (bk. 1, ch. 1)[5]

The comforter regrets the situation in which he finds the prisoner, but asserts it is the will of God and no one may go against it. God does not will the violent death of anyone, but he "lets it happen" and allows the world to inflict suffering on the body in this life so that the soul may not suffer in the next. And since the brother prisoner is at the end of his days, he needs to understand very clearly that his sufferings will not be meritorious unless he accepts voluntarily the providence allotted him and a divine sentence that cannot be appealed. The prisoner must humble himself and avoid nurturing resentment or self-pity about his bodily state and sufferings since his flesh is destined to rot anyway, and to raise his mind to God.

Book 1 details the miseries of the body before and after death, and of life in this world in general. It highlights the example of Christ, specifically his Passion, and it praises his patience in suffering. This is the model for the prisoner. When the condemned man hears the bell summoning his fellow citizens for the ritualized drama of the execution, he knows that he will soon

[4] For a discussion of how this work might figure in theatrical traditions, see my "The First Perugian Passion Play," 135–37.

[5] *Comforters' Manual,* fol. 2r, PML ms.188.

be bound and led to the public reading of his sentence and then through the crowded streets and squares. He must then especially remember how Christ was likewise bound and led away like a thief and how the people of Jerusalem heaped scorn on him. Christ was innocent, yet was as meek as a lamb during his ordeal and offered no defense. The martyrs were also innocent and did not seek to excuse themselves. The prisoner is to take these examples and, like them, must not speak in his own defense during the public rituals. It would do neither his body nor his soul any good. The sentence cannot be changed; no one was ever saved at this point in the penal process by offering excuses, whether or not those excuses were valid.

The prisoner is assured that if he accepts his sufferings and death in the spirit of Christ and the martyrs, the heavens will open to him at the end of his ordeal and he will find himself at once welcomed into paradise by the vast and delightful company of the blessed. Fully twelve chapters evoke the various orders of this company, with a special chapter dedicated to John the Baptist, traditional patron of condemned prisoners because the manner of his death—decapitation—was still a common means of public execution. The prisoner is reminded of this correspondence and is exhorted to humility and patience: "You know that you are not as just and holy as John; so, you must be patient about the fate that has overtaken you."[6]

Again and again the prisoner is urged to think intently upon the torments of the various martyrs, and these are enumerated in detail. Included are some the prisoner may have himself already experienced (such as flogging) or may have to look forward to (such as being torn with heated pincers, having a member cut off, being hanged, burned, or beheaded). "So," the comforter reasons, "my brother, you must fight, and get your strength from the examples of the glorious martyrs." Imitating the martyrs can transform his own sufferings into the same sweetness that they experienced. They were so inflamed with the love of God that they were often oblivious of the torments inflicted on them. But a warning is added. At this extreme hour, when the prisoner has the opportunity of soon entering into the company of the "cavaliers of Christ," he may also lose his soul just as he is about to lose his body. So he must pray to the martyrs for strength and constancy. Whatever the state of the prisoner's soul at the moment of death—that is, his human and spiritual disposition—will remain the state it is fixed in for all eternity. This will determine whether he is saved or damned.

Book 1 concludes with a heady Neoplatonic *lauda* and prayer that the

---

[6] *Comforters' Manual*, bk. 1, chap. 22, fol. 23r, PML ms. 188.

comforter should have the prisoner recite along with him in order to raise his soul's state as he goes to his death. The poem is full of spousal images and themes, and promises intellectual glory to the redeemed person,

> who bears fervent love to beloved Jesus,
> and who ever seeks, wholly enamored
> the spouse of his soul who is a perfect lover
> and who transforms him into transforming love....[7]

This concluding stanza warns that human imperfection can never be put aside except by tasting deeply of Christ incarnate. Whoever wishes to find this beloved Jesus will experience a "spousal immersion" that is to be tightly embraced with pure will and longing heart.

Book 2 seems almost another, more practical version of the first book, the two having been composed separately and copied into the manuscript in question. The anonymous work was written in the first person, probably by an official or spiritual director of the confraternity. Throughout, the author, addressing the comforter directly, tells him how to act, what gestures to employ, what sentiments to foster in the prisoner, and, as in book 1, supplies him with an actual script of exhortations and prayers. The comforter is urged to keep the prisoner's mind occupied with consoling words and prayers and not to abandon him, for as morning dawns with the bustle of various officials setting about the business of the day, the prisoner will realize that the moment of his death draws very near and will experience the struggles of his flesh. He must mince no words, but tell the prisoner that in the next two or three hours that remain to him he will enter into the fiercest battle of his life, and he may lose it. His enemies are the devil, the world, and his own flesh. The devil will tempt him to despair, the world will mock his humiliation, and his flesh will fear the coming pain.

Together with words, prayers, and songs, the comforter focuses the prisoner's attention with a *tavoletta*, a little board painted with the instruments of the Passion, a depiction of the Crucifixion of Christ or of the martyrdom of a saint such as John the Baptist. These are the prisoner's spiritual models, and the comforter keeps the board immediately in front of the prisoner's face once they exit the prison so he cannot see anything else. While the prisoner is on public display during the reading of his sentence, the comforter gives

---

[7] *Comforters' Manual*, bk. 1 (*lauda* and prayer), fol. 38r, PML ms. 188; my translation. For an alternate reading, see page 245 below.

him no rest, keeping his attention fixed either on himself, the comforter, or on the *tavoletta,* lest he look around or even hear the accusations proclaimed against him. After this reading of the sentence, the procession in Bologna moves through crowded streets to the church of St. John the Baptist, adjacent to the place of execution, where the prisoner kneels in the doorway for the elevation of the consecrated host. The comforter encourages him to make a final confession, saying, "See, my brother, Death is right behind you." As they approach the block or gallows, the manual gives detailed instructions concerning the way the comforter is to deal with the technical aspects of the two usual forms of execution: decapitation (for which Bologna employed a special brace called a *tagliadura* while other Italian cities used a small guillotine-like apparatus called the *mannaia*) or hanging. In either case, he is to keep the *tavoletta* directly in front of the prisoner's face until the very last moment and to continue to suggest to him that he should repeat the same words with which Christ died: "Lord, into your hands I commend my spirit."

The *Passion of Revello*

The traditions of presenting Passion plays need to be considered in attempts to understand the phenomenon of the late medieval and Renaissance *conforteria.* Yet it is also important to discover if the energy also operated in the opposite direction. Did the rituals of comforting influence the composition and performance of Passion plays? This seems to be the case for the three-day *Passion* of the small Piedmont town of Revello, composed, in the form that has come down to us, in circa 1479 to 1490. In her magnificent edition of this work, Anna Cornagliotti makes no mention of such an influence, but the portrayal of the sufferings and deaths of both Jesus and John the Baptist offer significant possibilities for consideration.[8]

The *Passion of Revello* is actually a dramatization of the life of Jesus with a separate Mary Magdalene play appended. During the first day of performance, a curious stage direction marking a necessary change of actors highlights the passage of time from Jesus' infancy until he enters upon his public life. After scenes of the Slaughter of the Innocents and a brief Council in Hell, this stage direction reads: "And little Jesus does not appear any more, and big Jesus, he who has to be piteously crucified, takes leave of Mary and Joseph" (part I, lines 3458ff). It is both striking and fitting that as soon as the actor portraying "big

---

[8] Cornagliotti, *La Passione di Revello.*

Jesus" enters the play, the brief commentary embedded in the stage direction refers to his death. This thematic orientation is soon borne out in action and text. Upon leaving Mary and Joseph, Jesus goes to John to be baptized, and at the end of the ceremony withdraws alone to another part of the acting area. Immediately the angel Uriel comes to announce his redemptive mission to him and already comforts him for his death: "Sta' forte" ("Be strong"; I.3846). Jesus acknowledges, "You have been sent to comfort me, / true angel and my friend" (1.3847–48), before he goes alone into the desert to pray.

Uriel's "Sta' forte" is especially effective, because it indicates succinctly the whole point of the comforting effort. It appears in other contemporary plays as well. Christ himself gives this same loving imperative to John the Baptist in a Florentine beheading play when he appears to him in prison in the guise of comforter: "Ista' forte, Giovanni."[9] St. Catherine of Alexandria offers the same comforting command in the three-day Sienese *Feast and History of St. Catherine, Above All Others Devout and Beautiful.*[10] This young philosopher and martyr had converted many of the emperor's court, including the empress herself. When the emperor sentences them to death soon after conversion, Catherine comforts the other woman about to die, saying, "O Empress, be strong and constant." Comforting scenes like this that echo the Bolognese manual occur frequently in Passion and martyrdom plays, and invite further study for their relationship with actual comforting rituals.

The *tavoletta* painted with an image aimed to strengthen the prisoner for his ordeal, keeping him from being distracted, or perhaps from seeing a loved one or an enemy along the route, or the instruments of torture, if these were to be employed. The article by Massimo Ferretti in this collection expands on the production and use of these images painted on portable panels.[11] Up to the moment of death, the comforter would keep this image before the eyes of the prisoner according to explicit and detailed instructions. For the one being comforted, the *tavoletta* became at once an object of intense devotional concentration and a kind of ritually reflecting mirror in which he was urged to see himself strengthened, consoled, and ultimately transformed. However, when such an image is presented to Christ himself in the *Passion of Revello*, it has a disturbing effect and seems at first not to comfort him but to terrify him.

[9] Newbigin, "La Rappresentazione," in *Nuovo Corpus.*

[10] *Feast and History of St. Catherine*, BCIS ms. I.II.33, fols. 12–45v. I am grateful to the authorities of the Biblioteca for the opportunity to consult this manuscript and others pertinent to its study.

[11] See also Edgerton, *Pictures and Punishment*, chap. 5; and Feinberg, "Imagination All Compact."

The scene in question is in the garden of Gethsemane just before Jesus' arrest, and it embellishes on the action of Luke 22:43: "And there appeared to him an angel from heaven, comforting [*confortans*] him." It is the second day of the performance. Annas and Caiaphas have just dispatched Judas accompanied by a centurion and his knights to the garden where Jesus is known to be. As they move through the acting area towards the garden station, Jesus offers his first prayer: "*Abba Pater,* if it is possible for you to do it, / Let this death pass me by. / Do it, my Father, for I am greatly suffering" (II.561–63). Rising, he goes to find his disciples sleeping, and, returning to pray a second time, expresses himself willing to "drink from this chalice" if it is necessary. Although stage directions are quite explicit in the Passion sequence, none here indicates whether or how "this chalice" is offered to him. Instead, after he goes once again to find his friends asleep, an unusually long stage direction mentions that something else is offered to him by his original comforter, the angel Uriel. It is an image of his imminent sufferings and death, and the stage direction emphasizes that when he sees it, Jesus sweats blood.

> And, as he is positioned to pray, let the angel Uriel come to show him the Passion painted on a cloth. And then Jesus lies down on the platform, and underneath let there be someone to paint his face and hands red, as if he sweated. And when he will have been thus a little while, let him get up. And let one of the angels come without saying anything and dry his sweat. And, that having been done, Jesus prays piteously saying,

> O my Father in heaven.
> I see well, and clearly understand
> that I need to die.
> This is heavy for me.
>   (II.578 [stage direction], 579–82)

The action then moves to the heaven station where God the Father summons the angel Michael and orders him to go down to comfort Jesus, for the day has come for him to accomplish the redemptive mission:

> He needs to suffer a cruel death
> and drink vinegar mixed with gall.
> At a column he will be beaten,
> for thirty coins he will be sold.
>   (II.589–92)

The Father wants Michael to know that no one ever suffered so cruel a death as that prepared for Jesus, who is experiencing such great fear that he has just sweat blood:

> Go at once
>
> .   .   .   .   .
>
> Say to him: "Don't be at all discomforted.
> This has been ordained from all eternity."
>
> .   .   .   .
>
> Beg him to take courage
> and not go against his death
> because without fail I will be always with him
> and never in those sufferings will I abandon him.
> Tell him not to be afraid of Satan,
> because I will hold his soul in my hands.
> He is my only child,
> and above all others I will exalt him,
> for I love him with all my heart.
>
> (II.599, 604–5, 615–23)

The Father again urges Michael to hurry since the Jews are already on their way to arrest Jesus. With their declarations of love and care, the Father's speeches express his insistence that he will not abandon Jesus in his sufferings. Yet later developments undercut this. In line 1230 of the third day of the play, the audience will hear Christ's crucifixion cry: "My God, my God, why have you abandoned me?"

Michael descends to the garden, delivers the Father's message, and encourages the agonizing, bloody Son:

> Now be comforted, and be courageous
> in accepting your death and torment.
> This is how it has to be,
> There is no other way....
> Now watch yourself, if you should be afraid.
>
> (II.655–58, 665)

Jesus retorts:

> If I should be afraid!
> O Michael, say whatever you want—
> it is not the head of the good comforter that aches!

> How well I know that I have to die....
>
> . . . .
>
> But if you were now in my place....
>
>   (II.666–69, 673)

Jesus describes the struggle he is experiencing and exclaims that, in spite of the rebellion of his body, "I will *make* it die!" He concludes by sending Michael back to tell his Father that he is ready, but to beg him, in courtesy, not to allow Satan to be near him when he is dying: "I am very much afraid of him" (II.698).

Michael now seems to understand somewhat the terror Jesus is experiencing and urges him to "Sta' forte" and not to lose his way. However, the angel's words on leaving are anything but comforting: "Be constant and do not be troubled. / I see that your friends are running away!" (II.706–7).

The Revello *Book of St. John the Baptist*

Scholars believe that the *Passion of Revello,* a massive work, was composed by making use of shorter preexisting plays, among them dramatizations of the conversion of Mary Magdalene and the beheading of John the Baptist. And, in the case of the latter, there is evidence that the dramatization of John's martyrdom was later extrapolated from the *Passion* text and repeatedly printed as a separate *Book of St. John the Baptist*.[12] Reproductions of the woodcuts illustrating the 1522 edition were used by Anna Cornagliotti to illustrate pertinent details in her edition of the *Passion*; she supposes that they bear some affinity with staging practice.[13] In these woodcuts John is shown being beheaded not with the usual swing of the sword familiar from so many near-contemporary representations but anachronistically with the *mannaia* (see fig. 1). This is an unusual detail, the only such illustration I have encountered so far. One wonders whether a local comforting group employed an image of John being martyred by the same instrument that awaited the condemned prisoner at the end of the ritual procession to the place of justice. Or, was the actual *mannaia* used for public executions lent to the players for the production of a drama that called for wide cooperation and involvement in its production?

Ten years after the appearance of Cornagliotti's edition of the *Passion*, Marco Piccat published a companion volume studying the background and context of the play based on extensive research he had carried out as he had

---

[12] Cornagliotti, *La Passione di Revello,* xix, xxiv, xxvi.
[13] Ibid., xc.

put the Revello town archives in order.[14] He documents the preparations made in August 1461 for a *ludus* of Mary Magdalene, and notes that the local nobleman, the Marquis of Saluzzo, lent drapes and tapestries for the production. Piccat also studies evidence for the production of a three-day Passion play beginning on Easter, 22 April 1481, in the square in front of the Church of the Magdalen. A number of scaffolds were constructed, the timber being lent by various persons and institutions and later returned or paid for. In the context of such widespread lending and cooperation at all levels for the production of a play that would include the dramatization of John the Baptist's beheading, the question arises: Since the actual instrument employed for public executions would not be in use during such celebrations, might it have been lent to the group of actors putting on the play? In such a small, tightly knit community, the answer might possibly be yes, but neither Cornagliotti nor Piccat addresses the question.

The Remarkable Case of Two Catherines in Siena

It is in late fourteenth-century Siena that we find one of the most memorable instances of the practice of the *conforteria* transposed to the stage. The possible complex dramatic connection here is with a play depicting the martyrdom of the legendary philosopher-saint, Catherine of Alexandria.[15]

The year is 1375, and the comforter is another Catherine, whose surname is Benincasa, and who is familiarly known as St. Catherine of Siena. In a letter to her confessor, mentor, and future biographer, Raymond of Capua, Catherine Benincasa describes her conversion and comforting of the condemned political prisoner Niccolò di Toldo, and her own visionary participation in the events surrounding his execution.[16] Catherine transforms Niccolò's final moments into the closing actions of a sacred play portraying a saint's martyrdom.

On the morning of the execution, Catherine waited for Niccolò at the place of justice, just as she had promised him, "with continual prayer and the presence of Mary and of Catherine virgin and martyr." Before Niccolò arrived, she got down and stretched her own neck on the block, filled with a strong desire for martyrdom. Rising, she felt herself inwardly assured by

---

[14] Piccat, *Rappresentazioni popolari*. I am grateful to Nerida Newbigin for bringing this work to my attention.

[15] *Feast and History of St. Catherine*, BCIS ms. I.II.33, published in part, with some errors, by Giuseppe Rondoni, "Il mistero di S. Caterina in un codice della Biblioteca Comunale senese."

[16] S. Caterina da Siena, *Epistolario*, 1298–1302.

Mary that Niccolò, in his last moment, would receive light and peace of heart. Catherine continues her description:

> Then he arrived, as a meek lamb, and seeing me,
> he began to laugh, and he wanted me to make
> the sign of cross. When he received the sign,
> I said, "Come on! to the nuptials, my sweet brother!
> for soon you will be in life without end." He got down
> with great meekness, and I stretched out his neck, and leaning down,
> I reminded him of the blood of the Lamb. His mouth said nothing
> but "Jesus" and "Catherine." And, as he was saying thus, I received
> his head in my hands, closing his eyes on divine goodness and
> saying, "I want this!"[17]

It is quite clear what Catherine wanted: her own martyrdom. She had seen her saintly namesake in Ambrogio Lorenzetti's fresco in the local Augustinian church—Catherine of Alexandria bearing her own severed head as an offering to the Virgin and Child. She desired to imitate the martyr, to accompany Niccolò in his bloody passage, or to take his place so that she too could assume the iconographic epithet *cephalophorous*. Catherine had comforted Niccolò twice before his execution: in the evening before and earlier that same morning. On the second occasion the prisoner, already converted, begged her to stay a little longer. She states, "And I held his head on my breast. And then I felt a jubilation and sensed the odor of his blood; and it was not without the odor of my own, which I desire to shed for the sweet spouse Jesus." So strong was her desire for martyrdom that once Niccolò had been executed and she had seen his soul ascend to heaven, as in the final scene of a martyrdom play, she remained where she was on the ground "with the greatest envy." Dealing with her personal disappointment in her letter, she exclaims, "Ah! miserable misery! I do not want to say any more."[18]

The parallels between the lives of the two Catherines are well known: the early refusal to marry, the mystic nuptials with Christ, the recourse to hermits for spiritual advice, the reputation for learning and the ability to dispute with the great ones of this world, the practice of the *conforteria*, martyrdom.[19] The biographer of the later Catherine repeats with great emphasis that her life of

---

[17] S. Caterina da Siena, *Epistolario*, 1300.

[18] S. Caterina da Siena, *Epistolario*, 1301.

[19] See the learned and beautiful chapter entitled "The Invisible Companion" in Brown, *Cult of Saints*, 50–68.

penance, labor, and sleeplessness was a long drawn-out process of martyrdom.[20] In a real sense, one may assert that not only did Catherine Benincasa pray to, imitate, and dwell "in the presence of" her patroness, but she actually lived the other's life to a significant degree and deliberately assumed her iconography. Perhaps one might also add that she acted out the drama of her martyrdom— with the assistance of the unfortunate Niccolò di Toldo.

A unique play survives from late fourteenth-century Siena that portrays scenes from the life and passion of Catherine of Alexandria, including all the elements just mentioned that parallel the life and suffering of Catherine Benincasa.[21] It is a long play divided into discrete parts designed for performance on three successive days, and is contained in a manuscript collection that probably belonged to a confraternity with which Catherine Benincasa was intimately connected.[22] In parts 2 and 3 of the play, the legendary Catherine on several occasions comforts those about to be executed: the judges summoned from all over the world, those whom she disputes with and then converts, the empress herself who visits Catherine in prison and is converted by the encounter, several courtiers dear to the emperor. So extensive is the converting, comforting, and dying, that the emperor finally summons Catherine once more before him: "Come here, enchantress who caused so many to die—even my empress died because of your spells." Strangely, the emperor concludes his chiding of Catherine with a proposal of marriage. If only she will adore his idol he will make her his empress. Catherine answers that she is already married—to the eternal God. The emperor presses on, insisting that as *his* bride she would have no equal among women. Catherine tells him to be quiet, and he orders her decapitated.

Catherine goes to her death uttering a lyric prayer: "O my sweet spouse; O Jesus Christ, my sweet Lord," and an angel appears to assure her that at her departure from this life, she will have a legion of angels in attendance. Stage directions are missing here in the manuscript and it is not clear what business is involved in the execution and ascent of her "soul" to heaven. Perhaps, as in other plays, the actor himself is raised up by means of some mechanical "cloud," or perhaps a small baby is raised up to represent the soul. The executioner expresses astonishment that milk, not blood, pours forth from both trunk and severed head, and the overseeing emperor attributes the phenomenon to black

[20] Raimondo de Capua, *Santa Caterina da Siena,* 8.

[21] *Feast and History of St. Catherine,* BCIS ms. I.II.33.

[22] de Bartholomaeis, *Origini,* 384, 421 no. 1.

magic. The play concludes as angels carry Catherine's body to Mount Sinai "with great reverence and devotion."

One can only speculate what influence such a dramatization of the martyrdom of her patron saint may have had on the conduct of Catherine Benincasa. She knew the legend and iconography from other sources, to be sure. When she passionately merges her readying of Niccolò for execution with her own desire to imitate her patroness in martyrdom, in ecstatic anticipation she senses that the odors of both their bloods mingle. Later, "in the presence of" this same patroness she rehearses her own decapitation as part of the public spectacle at the actual place of justice. Yet in the end, it is the "martyr" Niccolò's head she holds in her hands and not, like Catherine of Alexandria, her own.

Two Plays of the Beheading of John the Baptist: Perugia and Florence

The "saint play" developed in Perugia in the middle of the fourteenth century, and among early examples is found a work that portrays the beheading of John the Baptist, contained in a book of *laude* prepared for the confraternity of St. Andrew.[23] It is a spare, elegant composition that seems to constitute a kind of bridge between scriptural plays dealing with the life, Passion, Resurrection and Second Coming of Christ, and saint plays, often dealing with martyrdom, that were to flourish as a separate genre in the next century. The beheading play shares the characteristics of the so-called gospel laud composed for each day of Lent, brief dramatizations of the scriptural passages assigned in the liturgy as gospel readings, probably performed in close connection with the celebration of Mass. Few liberties were taken with the basic narrative outline. The Perugian play was composed for the ancient feast of the Beheading of John the Baptist (29 August) and dramatizes mainly the narrative of Mark 6:17–29.

Yet this same play contains all the elements of a martyrdom play: the mission of the saint that conflicts with the evil plans of a tyrant; his arrest and imprisonment; his accusation and trial in an unjust court; his torment; his prayer or vision in prison; his martyrdom, burial, and passage into the other world.

The play provides room for what one might term the development of spectacle "between the lines of the text," and perhaps more interestingly suggests connections with other local events and practices. These include public outdoor

---

[23] *Laudario della Compagnia di S. Andrea*, fols. 63r–64v, BAP ms. 955.

receptions accompanied by instrumental music, singing, and dancing; festive and imploratory civic processions; funerary processions and the emotional public *corruptio* or *corrotto*; the funeral rituals of the flagellants themselves. Yet most important for our purpose here is the fact that the confraternity of St. Andrew comforted prisoners condemned to death. The members of the confraternity also saw to the dignified burial of those just executed. Little is known of early Perugian confraternities' ritual, life regimen, statutes, participation in guild and civic affairs, works of charity and assistance, and theater. The St. Andrew confraternity had its oratory near the gate through which condemned criminals were led out to the place of execution, and had adopted the practice of the *conforteria* by at least 1458, the earliest date for which the activity is documented.[24] In other cities, the confraternities performing this charitable work were often dedicated to the beheading of the Baptist and even took their names from it (e.g., S. Giovanni Decollato in Rome and in Ferrara). It may well be that the St. Andrew confraternity comforted prisoners earlier than the date for which documentation survives, and that this special aspect of their civic mission influenced the composition of the play.

In the Florentine *Beheading of John the Baptist* play, it is Christ himself who visits John in prison to comfort him just as armed men dispatched by Herod's seneschal conduct the executioner "through straight streets" to the prison where—trembling all over, begging the saint's pardon, and making clear that he is forced to do the act—he will behead John. Direct prison references mark Christ's comforting message. For John himself death will mean both paradise and a special mission to the church fathers held in limbo to inform them that Christ will soon come to release them and bring them to share the eternal feast with singing and laughing. They will see Christ coming in glory and justice, with strength to break down the gates that confine them and to crush Satan under his feet, binding him forever in the same prison he once ruled. Christ's final exhortation begins "Istà forte, Giovanni" (Be strong, John) as he assures the Baptist that his sufferings will bear great fruit and urges him not to be afraid. John's response is to tell Christ to look at his face: it is happy and dry; he is tormented by neither sorrow nor tears. He even has the courage to tell Christ to leave: "Go now, Lord, for my time is coming."

It was possibly this beheading play, and certainly one similar, that was presented in a grandiose production just outside the walls of Florence on Sunday,

---

[24] Marinelli, *Le Confraternite di Perugia*, 97n498.

29 August 1451, the feast day of John's martyrdom.[25] Contemporaries estimated the audience for the play at 50,000, which would be more than the city's entire population at that time. What is remarkable is that the site chosen, the Meadow of the Gate of Justice, was the actual place of public executions. On other days, large crowds came to witness real criminals being beheaded or hanged on a raised stage after their ritualized comforting by Florence's confraternity of S. Maria della Croce al Tempio, commonly known as The Blacks.[26] The dramatic presentation of John the Baptist facing death with the calm serenity of faith provided onlookers with valuable models for the successful outcome of the comforting process. According to the Bolognese *Comforters' Manual,* when things really "worked," the prisoner's very cell could become radiant with spiritual light and consolation—the presence of Christ himself—and the procession to the place of execution would be suffused with joy and even anticipation.

This optimistic ethos informs Luca della Robbia's account, translated in this volume, of the last hours of two young Florentine men, Pietro Paolo Boscoli and Agostino Capponi, who were condemned for plotting against the newly restored Medici regime and executed 23 February 1513. On the eve of Boscoli's execution, comforters from The Blacks passed the night with him in prison. Luca joined them and describes how, as Boscoli arrived at the place of execution, he kept his eyes on the *tavoletta* and, echoing the intensely spiritual poetry of the *laude,* said, "Lord, you are my love. I give you my heart. I love only you and yet I love everything, for I love all out of love for you. Here I am, Lord. I come willingly; grant me strength and vigor…. Make me, I beg you, like to your passion." Boscoli continued praying, "Into your hands, Lord, I commend my spirit."

Even this brief and tentative examination of disparate materials suggests the profound correspondences that existed between the rituals of public execution and the performance of Passion and martyrdom plays. In the case of the penitential confraternities, it seems clear that a sense of brotherhood in sinfulness and need for mercy informed the efforts of the truly devout comforter during the last hours of the condemned—as well as an impulse towards

---

[25] Newbigin, "La Rappresentazione," 109. See the excellent illustrated discussion in Edgerton, *Pictures and Punishment,* 126–64.

[26] Eisenbichler, "Lorenzo de' Medici," 85–98.

spousal union with Christ. The discovery of the latter aspect may seem surprising, for it indicates that the comforting process held open to the prisoner the possibility of achieving in a very short period of time the sweetness and ecstasy of mystical union. When I first read the heady *lauda* or prayer that concludes book 1 of the Morgan manual, I dismissed it as an example of inferior poetry replete with inelegant repetitions and imprecise formulations. But when I reexamined it in the light of Catherine Benincasa's invitation to Niccolò di Toldo as he approached the place of justice laughing, "Come on! to the nuptials, my sweet brother!" and of Pietro Paolo Boscoli's repetitious and intoxicated "Lord, you are my love," I realized that this verse, inferior poetry though it might be, corresponded with common and widely known formulations of mystical elation. In numerous plays staged by confraternities across Renaissance Italy, martyrs go to their stage deaths singing similar verses. Perhaps none does so more memorably than the Alexandrian Catherine in the Sienese play discussed above:

> O my beloved spouse,
> O Jesus Christ, my sweet Lord,
> You know with what affection
> I have always carried you in my heart. Receive my soul
> With love within your arms.
>
> (fol. 45r)

Such examples, on the stage or on the way to the scaffold, took on deep meaning in an audience urgently concerned with the art of dying well.

Works Cited

Archives

BAP   Biblioteca Augusta, Perugia
BCIS Biblioteca Comunale degli Intronati, Siena
PML   Pierpont Morgan Library, New York

Printed Sources

Brown, Peter Robert Lamont. *The Cult of the Saints: Its Rise and Function in Latin Christianity.* Chicago: University of Chicago Press, 1981.

Cornagliotti, Anna, ed. *La Passione di Revello: Sacra rappresentazione quattrocentesca di ignoto piemontese.* Torino: Centro di Studi Piemontesi, 1976.

Cutini, Clara. "I condannati a morte e l'attività assistenziale della Confraternita della Giustizia di Perugia." *Bollettino della Deputazione di Storia Patria per l'Umbria* 82 (1985): 173–86.

de Bartholomaeis, Vincenzo. *Origini della poesia drammatica italiana.* 2nd ed. Torino: Società

Editrice Internazionale, 1952.

Edgerton, Samuel Y. *Pictures and Punishment: Art and Criminal Prosecution during the Florentine Renaissance.* Ithaca, NY: Cornell University Press, 1985.

Eisenbichler, Konrad. "Lorenzo de' Medici and the Confraternity of the Blacks in Florence." *Fides et Historia* 25/1 (1994): 85–98.

Falvey, Kathleen. "Early Italian Dramatic Traditions and Comforting Rituals: Some Initial Considerations." In *Crossing the Boundaries: Christian Piety and the Arts in Italian Medieval and Renaissance Confraternities,* edited by Konrad Eisenbichler, 33–55. Kalamazoo: Medieval Institute Publications, Western Michigan University, 1991.

———. "The First Perugian Passion Play: Aspects of Structure." *Comparative Drama* 11, no. 2 (1977): 127–38.

———. "Italian Vernacular Religious Drama of the Fourteenth through the Sixteenth Centuries: A Selected Bibliography on the *Lauda drammatica* and the *Sacra rappresentazione.*" *Research Opportunities in Renaissance Drama* 26 (1983): 125–44.

Fanti, Mario, ed. "La Confraternita di S. Maria della Morte e la Conforteria dei condannati in Bologna nei secoli XIV e XV." In Fanti, *Confraternite e città a Bologna nel medioevo e nell'età moderna,* 120–74. Italia Sacra 65. Rome: Herder Editrice, 2001.

Feinberg, Larry J. "Imagination All Compact: Tavolette and Confraternity Rituals for the Condemned in Renaissance Italy." *Apollo* 161, no. 520 (2005): 48–57.

Marinelli, Olga. *Le Confraternite di Perugia dalle origini al secolo XIX: Bibliografia delle opere a stampa.* Perugia: Edizione Grafica, 1965.

Newbigin, Nerida. "La Rappresentazione di San Giovanni Battista quando fu decollato." In *Nuovo Corpus di Sacre rappresentazioni fiorentine del Quattrocento,* edited by Nerida Newbigin, 109–33. Bologna: Commissione per I testi di lingua, 1983.

Parisini, Alessandra. "Pratiche extragiudiziali di amministrazione della giustizia: La 'liberazione dalla morte' a Faenza tra '500 e '700." *Quaderni storici* 23, no. 1 (1988): 147–68.

Piccat, Marco. *Rappresentazioni popolari e feste in Revello nella metà del XV secolo.* Torino: Centro di Studi Piemontesi, 1986.

Prosperi, Adriano. "Il sangue e l'anima: Ricerche sulle compagnie di giustizia in Italia." *Quaderni storici* 51 (1982): 959–99.

Raimondo de Capua. *Santa Caterina da Siena.* 5th ed. Translated by Giuseppe Tinagli. Siena: Edizioni Cantagalli, 1978.

Rondoni, Giuseppe. "Il mistero di S. Caterina in un codice della Biblioteca Comunale senese." *Bullettino senese di storia patria* 3–4 (1895): 231–63.

Siena, S. Caterina da. *Epistolario.* Edited by Umberto Meattini. Roma: Edizioni Paoline, 1979.

Chapter 2

Comforting with Song
Using *Laude* to Assist Condemned Prisoners

Pamela Gravestock

In addition to relevant biblical stories, exempla, prayers, and meditations that comforters could draw upon to perform their difficult task more effectively, they also had at their disposal collections of *laude* or devotional songs that are included in confraternity manuals.[1] These texts echo the themes found throughout the manual proper—the Passion of Christ, the suffering of Christian martyrs and saints, and the role of the Virgin Mary as an intercessor—and were used by the *confortatori* to help prepare the prisoner for a good death.

This review of the *laude* focuses on the titles and texts of 141 incipits found in seven fifteenth- and sixteenth-century manuscript copies of the Bolognese *Comforters' Manual*.[2] The Morgan manuscript (ca. 1470) has the highest number of *incipits* (87), although the texts of all but one are lost.[3] The Beinecke manuscript contains the largest number of *laude* texts (49), while a manuscript that was once owned by Bolognese comforter Giovanni Francesco Cattanio (AAB ACCU ms. I.XI.B) has 39.[4] While all of these manuscripts incorporate *laude*, there is significant variation among them. It was possible to identify forty-one identical or similar incipits for *laude* that appear in more

---

[1] For more on comforting confraternities, see Black, *Italian Confraternities*; Edgerton, *Pictures and Punishment*; Henderson, "Religious Confraternities and Death"; and Gravestock, "Comforting the Condemned." See also Terpstra, "Death and Dying"; "Piety and Punishment"; and "Confraternal Prison Charity."

[2] These are PML ms. 188 (87), YBL ms. 1069 (48), AAB ACCU ms. IX.B.1 (43), BAB ms. 4880 (20, with 2 versions of 4), BAB ms. 4824 (4), BUB ms. 702 (11), BUB ms. 858 (5). BAB ms. 4824 is an early sixteenth century manuscript and the remainder are fifteenth-century manuscripts; see table 2.1 for a comparison of *incipits*. I am grateful to Alfredo Troiano for providing me with details and a complete transcription of all of the *laude* contained within the Yale manuscript (YBL ms. 1069).

[3] Only the title page of the Morgan *laudario*, with 86 *incipits*, survives; there is one *laude* in the text of the manual: PML ms. 188, see pages 244–45 below. See also L'Engle, "Compagnia dell'Ospedale."

[4] For more on Cattanio, see "Comforting by the Books" below, page 185 note 8.

than one version of the manual. "Alta Regina de stelle incoronate" and "Misericordia, O alto Dio Soprano" appear in five of the seven versions, while "Christo
mio dami fortezza" and "Misericordia Padre omnipotente," are among the sev-
en texts that appear in four of the manuals. Only one, "Misericordia o sommo
eterno Dio," by Gregorio da Rovorobella (1458–88), a notary in the court of
Giovanni II Bentivoglio, de facto *signore* of Bologna from 1463 to 1506, appears
in all seven editions[5] (see table 2.1 on page 44 for a complete listing of the *laude*
found in these seven manuscripts and the chapter "*Lauda* and Prayers" below
for the texts of the ones noted above). It is also important to note that among
these manuscripts, the *laude* are not exact copies of one another. There are slight
variations in terms of spelling and grammar and at times more significant differences occur that may involve deviations in individual verses or more substantial passages. Such variation indicates that there was not a standard set of
laude associated with S. Maria della Morte's comforting ritual and suggests the
choice may have been at the discretion of the individual(s) or the confraternity
who produced the copies of the manual.[6]

   In spite of the descriptive and often prescriptive nature of the comforting manual, there is no clear indication of how the *laude* should, or could, be
used. It may be that their widespread use and popularity led to a general understanding of their role and purpose. When these manuals were produced,
laude had been in use across Italy for some two hundred years, during which
time they had become the principal genre of nonliturgical religious songs.[7]
Laude dating from the medieval period through to the sixteenth century include poems of praise, invocations, meditations, exhortations, descriptions of
sacred scenes, narratives, monologues, and dialogues. Originally cultivated
by medieval mendicant orders during their spiritual exercises, they were subsequently adopted throughout Italy as part of the devotional practices of both
the *laudesi* and *disciplinati* confraternities.

   In Bologna, *laudesi* and *disciplinati* confraternities developed from the thirteenth century, with the former adopting worship based on praise and the latter
focusing on penitential exercises that included the practice of flagellation. As elsewhere in Italy, these companies provided charity to the community, offering alms

---

[5] Troiano, "Un laudario per condannati a morte," 40–41.

[6] The *laude* appear in different parts of individual manuscript manuals (in some they form a third section
of the text, in others they are placed between the first two books, and a few are also scattered throughout
the first two books).

[7] For a general history of the *laude*, see Prizer, "Lauda spirituale"; and Barr, *Monophonic Lauda*. For the *laudesi*
companies, see Henderson, *Piety and Charity*, esp. chap. 3. For the development and musical setting of the
laude, see Alaleona, "Le laude spirituali italiane"; and idem, *Storia dell'Oratorio Musicale*.

and burial assistance, and erecting hospitals. In their devotional services each also employed the *laude,* which were sung during their regular services, for special religious holidays, and at various stages of funerals (including at the service, during the procession to and at the cemetery).[8]

Laude employed by the *laudesi* and *disciplinati* confraternities across Italy focused on themes similar to those of the comforting manual and their *laude*—the Passion of Christ, the Virgin Mary, and the saintly martyrdoms.[9] For these groups, the *laude* served multiple purposes. Those penitential in tone were used during flagellation and as devotions related to the Passion; while those of a praising nature were perceived as having the ability to release a soul from purgatory. They were considered a particularly effective means of veneration that had the ability to strengthen relationships between human beings and the divine. As Blake Wilson has pointed out,

> A closer look at lay company activities reveals what they considered to be one of the most effective means of persuasion—song. The *lauda* of the *laudesi* companies were deemed strong spiritual currency, for as sung prayer it passed swiftly up the ladder of carefully cultivated sacred connections, from deceased members, through the saints, small and great, to Mary and Jesus to join the eternal *canto celestiale.*[10]

By the late fourteenth and early fifteenth centuries, the activities of both the *laudesi* and the *disciplinati* were increasingly familiar to the general public through frequent civic and religious processions. Moreover, in Florence, *laudesi* companies held weekly lessons at which *laude* were taught to members of the confraternity and quite possibly the wider community.[11] At this time, *lauda* singing also began to move outside the services of these companies and entered other forms of popular devotion. They were used in association with sermons, found in contemporary *sacra rappresentazione* (sacred plays), and formed part of the services of youth confraternities. They made their way into

[8] Wilson notes that "thematic links between *lauda* and sermon suggest the possibility that *laude* were sung or recited in conjunction with sermons, and that some *laude* may have been composed for that purpose"; *Music and Merchants,* 26. See also Terpstra, *Lay Confraternities*; Macey, "The *Lauda* and the Cult of Savonarola"; Wilson, *Music and Merchants*; and Henderson, *Piety and Charity.*

[9] Although *laudesi* and *disciplinati* companies originally focused on praising and penitential *laude* respectively, by the fourteenth century each was using both types in their devotions and services; Prizer, "Laude di Popolo, Laude di Corte," 171.

[10] Wilson, *Music and Merchants,* 7.

[11] This practice continued into the fifteenth century; Wilson, *Music and Merchants,* 70–73.

public performances by contemporary musicians[12] and were often used in private devotion, frequently in times of sorrow, such as at the deathbed of a loved one, or to console a grieving family member. With such widespread use during this period, it is clear that *laude* would have been increasingly familiar to contemporary audiences. The fact that they were based on popular secular songs, typically learned by ear, certainly helped to ensure their adoption and long-standing success.

The *laude* contained within the separate manuscripts of the Bolognese *Comforters' Manual* appear to have been carefully selected for their purpose, combining both praising and penitential songs. The manuals say nothing of attributions or sources for the *laude*; however, a preliminary review of contemporary *laudarii* from other regions reveals some commonalities. The thirteenth-century Cortona *laudario* composed for the Fraternità di S. Maria delle Laude (Biblioteca Comunale di Cortona, ms. 91) includes over forty *laude*; at least two have titles identical or similar to those found within the Bolognese manuals ("Ave, regina gloriosa" and "Spiritu Sanctu, dolçe amore"). Similarly, the thirteenth-century Florentine *laudario* (Biblioteca Nazionale Centrale di Firenze, Magl II.I.1222, Banco Rari, 18) shares at least one ("Ave Maria Diana stella") with our manuscripts. In addition, there is a strong possibility that some of the Bolognese *laude* may have been penned by the Venetian poet Leonardo Giustiniani (ca. 1383–1446) and one, "Dona del Paradiso," was written by Jacopone da Todi in the thirteenth century.[13]

The appearance of texts from Cortona, Florence, and Venice speaks to their popularity and suggests that they may have migrated across Italy with various groups or individual confraternity members.[14] The fact that *laude* were typically simple vernacular songs sung to popular tunes would have made this an easy transition. Furthermore, there is evidence from *laudesi*

---

[12] The followers of Savonarola brought the *laude* to the streets in fifteenth-century Florence, singing them as they marched in processions at Carnival or on Palm Sunday; Macey, "The *Lauda* and the Cult of Savonarola," 442. They were also sung by improvisers in Florentine piazzas during the fifteenth century; Prizer, "Laude di Popolo, Laude di Corte."

[13] Luisi's edition of the *Laudario Giustinianeo* aimed to identify the entire corpus of Giustiniani's *laude*; however, Patrick Glixon and others have questioned these attributions. Glixon argues that "Spirito Sancto amore," "O gloriosa vergine Maria," "Maria, del ciel regna," "Maria, madre di Dio," "Salve regina o germinante ramo," and "Stella matutina" can be attributed with certainty to Giustiniani. He also identifies Feo Belcari as the author of "Salve regina de misericordia." Other late medieval and early modern authors of *laude* include St. Francis of Assisi, the Florentine poet Feo Belcari, Lorenzo de' Medici, his mother, Lucrezia Tournabuoni de' Medici, and Girolamo Savonarola; Luisi, *Laudari Giustinianeo*.

[14] *Laude* may have been disseminated via mercantile channels as *laudesi* confraternity members were frequently drawn from the merchant classes; Wilson, *Music and Merchants*, 38.

and *disciplinati* confraternities that *laudarii* were shared and loaned among groups, which may have contributed to their widespread use. And, by the late fifteenth century printed texts of *laude* were being produced and were circulating outside of the regions for which they were originally produced.[15]

While comparable examples can be identified for some of the *laude,* others were likely written locally.[16] This would not have been unusual, as many *laude* were in fact composed for local use or for particular situations and audiences.[17] A local confraternity member may have penned (or revised) the *laude* contained in the manuals prepared for comforters; however, without attributions or further evidence, it is impossible to say with certainty. While the thought of identifying the lineage and authors of these *laude* is intriguing, this may be an impossible task. Even in regions for which there is extensive documentation and continuing research, there are disagreements about the attributions of particular *laude.* For the present purposes, it may be enough to know that the *laude* included in the various editions of the Bolognese *Comforters' Manual* combined locally written texts alongside popular versions from other regions. They were selected at the discretion of the individual(s) who developed the manual. The variation seen within the four versions produced for the Bolognese confraternity suggests that contemporary trends or personal preference shaped the final decisions.

Given their focus, simplicity, "spiritual currency," widespread use, and popularity, it is no surprise that the *laude* found a place in comforting rituals. They were an integral part of comforting, and a necessary and useful tool for comforters. *Laude* offer hope to the prisoner, work to alleviate his fear of dying, and remind him of the glory that awaits. Their themes focus his mind on his salvation and offer comfort in his final hours. Through their vivid and affective language, they work to draw the condemned into a devotional state of penance or praise. Incorporating responses required of the prisoner, and employing parallel and repeating lines, the *laude* help to ensure that the prisoner gave his full attention to the comforter. As aural tools, they help to divert his attention from distractions while functioning as a form of ritual exchange, offered by the prisoner to Christ, the Virgin Mary, and the saints.

---

[15] Giustiniani's *laude* were printed and circulated beginning in the last quarter of the fifteenth century and the works of Innocentius Dammonis were printed by Venetian publisher Petrucci in 1507 and again in 1508.

[16] Bologna had its share of *laude* composers, among them Giovanni Spataro (ca. 1460–1541), choirmaster at San Petronio in the early sixteenth century.

[17] This led to both regional variations and differences when *laude* were produced for use by patricians at court or for confraternities; Prizer, "Laude di Popolo, Laude di Corte."

This exchange is personalized through frequent use of the "tu" form that the individual reciting the *laude* adopts in his appeals.

The *laude* may have been sung—as they typically were outside the context of the comforting ritual—or recited as a prayer.[18] Given how they were typically used outside the context of the comforting ritual, one could assume that they were sung by the comforters and/or the prisoners. But given the structure of these texts, this was not necessary.[19] Many, and particularly those that appeal to Christ, the Virgin Mary, and the saints for intercession or forgiveness, can certainly be read as prayers. How they were used—recited as prayers or sung as devotional songs—might have depended on the stage of the ritual, the spiritual or emotional need of the condemned, or the preference of the prisoner or comforter. Whatever the use, they would have served the same purpose and worked towards the same goal.

Although the manuals do not specifically state when and how the *laude* should be used, the very structure of the comforting ritual suggests numerous possibilities. An examination of the *laude* in relation to both the comforting ritual and the confraternity manual will help to demonstrate this.

Before meeting with the condemned prisoner, the comforter must begin the process by preparing himself physically, mentally, emotionally, and spiritually. *Laude* would certainly help here and comforters may have sung a praising *lauda* (such as "Ave regina virgo gloriosa," "Christo mio dami fortezza," or "Ave Maria") collectively or alone to ask for divine assistance: guidance, strength, or the ability to perform their duty effectively. As the prayer that closes the opening chapter of the manual asks, "and make my tongue serve me adroitly...."

This entreaty is a reminder that the comforter's most valuable tool is his rhetorical skill. For the most part, it is his words—and his voice—that will carry him and the prisoner through the long night. He must work carefully and quickly to bring the condemned to a state in which he can accept his fate willingly, relinquish his ties to worldly possessions, family, and loved ones, and repent and confess. The comforter must be well prepared in order to put the prisoner at ease and move him steadfastly through this process. His success relies upon his familiarity with the guidance provided by the manuals and his ability to call upon and utilize relevant examples. He is advised to

---

[18] The manuscript frequently counsels "oracione" and "preghiera," which may distinguish different types of prayer, and the collections of verses are frequently designated "laude e oracione."

[19] Jennifer Fisk Rondeau ("Prayer and Gender") argues that the ritual of *lauda* singing is itself a form of prayer.

approach the prisoner cheerfully, to refrain from using harsh words, and to avoid demonstrating pity for his plight. He must instill a strong sense of hope while persuading him to devote himself to God, and in this the comforter must choose his words carefully. The manual recommends,

> Familiarize yourself with the preaching of experienced men since in those places one sometimes often hears many beautiful things and usually very subtle arguments concerning this matter. And when you hear a nice saying or a particularly interesting argument that you like, write it down so that you can keep it in mind. (bk. 2, Prologue)

And so, as the comforter relies most heavily on words to aid him in his task, the *laude* are yet another valuable tool. When recited or sung to or with the individual, their subject matter and incantational tone would help to bring about a state of calm, enabling the prisoner to proceed through the stages of penance, repentance, confession, and devotion.

Once fully prepared, the comforter made his way to the prison. The manual is unequivocal and resolute about the need to divert the prisoner's attention away from worldly matters to those concerning his salvation. This constant emphasis on the *contemptus mundi* resonates through both the manual and the *laude,* providing a useful means of redirecting the prisoner's attention in this way. Many of the *laude* are entreaties to Christ, the Virgin Mary, or the saints asking for forgiveness, mercy, and assistance in seeking salvation. These *laude,* and the overall comforting process, help to dispel the prisoner's fears. They underline God's willingness to forgive those who repent, and give the condemned hope as he approaches his death; for example, "Merciful Omnipotent Father" (Misericordia Padre omnipotente) begins:

Merciful Christ our Saviour
On the cross you died for humankind
Great beneficent Christ, hear my call
God exalt me in your clemency
By not looking at my great error....[20]

A *lauda* such as this helps to focus the condemned's mind on matters of the soul and the afterlife and helps him to leave behind his family and friends and

---

[20] *Comforters' Manual,* fol. 56, BAB ms. 4880. This also appears in PML ms. 188, YBL ms. 1069, and AAB ACCU ms. IX.B.1.

earthly possessions. The *lauda* and the words of the comforter work together to remind the prisoner of the glory of salvation.

The manual and the *laude* emphasize the Virgin Mary's role as intercessor, and many in the Bolognese manuals appeal directly to the Virgin, including "Salve Regina, e germinante l'amo," "O alta regina de stelle incoronata," "Alia oratio ad virginem Mariam," "Ave Maria," "De se tue brave, O Vergine Maria," "Vergine gloriosa alma Regina," "Ave regina sempre dico," "Alta regina pollete e benegna," "Ave Maria regina madre de dio e sposa," "Dona del paradiso," "Salve regina de misericordia" (see table 2.1 for a complete list). These songs adopt a praising tone and focus on Mary's ability and willingness to act as an intermediary on behalf of the dying individual. They position her as a source of hope and comfort as in "Maria, Salve regina Misericordia," "O alta regina de stele incoronata," and "In le tue bracce Vergine," which includes the graphic lines:

> If your helping hand does not reach
> To my tired and battered little boat
> Then every effort, that to the depths of my soul I have endured,
> will be lost and in vain.

The saintly martyrs also play a key role in the comforting manuals and the *laude* and their deaths are to serve as an example to the condemned. The comforter reminds the prisoner that these men and women, many of whom suffered deaths much more tragic than he is about to experience, gracefully accepted their fates, without protest and in full devotion to God. Therefore, the prisoner should model his own death on theirs. Some of the *laude* reflect this notion of calling upon the saints through the repetition of their names, as in "Father of the Heavens, the Son, and the Holy Spirit" (Padre de cielo, figlio e spirito sancto), which reads,

> Oh St. Stephen, major martyr
> St. Bastian, Fabian, and Lawrence
> You Christopher who carried our Saviour
> Oh St. Cosimo, Damian, and Vincent
> St. Cervasio and Prothasio and Polo
> John and you, advocate, St. Morenzo.[21]

[21] *Comforters' Manual*, fols. 79–83, BAB ms. 4880. This *lauda* may in fact take its shape from the litany of saints. The service book of the Florentine company Gesù Pellegrino records that their office of flagellation included the litany of the saints followed by a series of invocations (addressing the Virgin Mary, the archangels, patriarch, prophets, apostles, evangelist, martyrs, popes, confessors, doctors, monks, hermits, Levites, and female saints). See Henderson, "Religious Confraternities and Death," 124.

This incantational tone helps to focus the prisoner's attention.

The strong emphasis on the Passion of Christ throughout the comforting ritual reinforces the contemporary notion of *imitatio christi* (something advocated for by the contemporary *ars moriendi* tradition in preparation for death). Given the salvific nature of Christ's death, individuals were encouraged to meditate on the events of the Passion. Contemporary devotions on the Passion emphasized knowing through experience and viewed the body as the locus of experience. The condemned were to view their executions as cathartic, a means by which they could share in Christ's suffering and achieve redemption. Their deaths would be the ultimate *imitatio christi*. Moreover, Christ's death was to serve as an example on which the prisoner should model his own end as book 1 chapter 9 ("Which deals with the first prescription to have your sins pardoned") instructs, "and so you should do the same, imitating him, because all the actions of Christ are instructions to us." This notion is mirrored in the *laude,* such as "Misericordia Padre omnipotente" (cited above), in a set of *laude* that focus on Christ's last words on the cross: "La prima parola che voy dixisti," "La seconda parola per dixisti," "La terza parola dipista con gran dolo," "La quarta parola che dixisti," "La quinta parola dipisti con sospiri," "La sesta parola dipisti pendendo," and "La septima dipisti con dolore,"[22] in "O croce sancta de opire dolore coperta," or "Cristo mio dami fortezza" (found in "*Laude* and Prayers" below at page 276).

The comforter used the *laude* at his discretion while attending to the prisoner in his cell—which he deemed most effective and when. While the manual gives no explicit directions, there are particular sections that might have led the comforter to rely on *laude* as a tool. In book 2, the manual refers to those who are willing to listen and say prayers, stating "You must not tire of those who are inclined to listen and pray with you.... And I tell you that nothing ignites the devotion of the hearer as much as prayer" (bk. 2, ch. 5). One chapter later, it notes, "For those who are inclined to read and so comfort themselves, and who do not care to listen much, be sure always to have with you the Hospitals' *Book of the Passion* or some other book, be it the *Life of the Christ* or *of the Holy Fathers* or other devout things. And let him read as much as he likes." With a wide selection of relevant *laude* at his disposal in the manual, it would be easy

---

[22] These seven *laude* contained in BAB ms. 4880, fols. 52–55, might have been most useful during this final stage of the ritual. This set refers to and draws directly on Christ's last words from the cross ("Father, forgive them, for they do not know what they are doing" [Luke 23:34]; "Amen I say to thee this day thou shalt be with me in paradise" [Luke 23:43]; "Woman, behold thy son. Behold thy mother" [John 19:26–27]; "I thirst" [John 19:28]; "It is finished" [John 19:30]; and "Father, into thy hands I commend my spirit" [Luke 23:46]).

to select one for these circumstances.

Prior to departing the prison, the comforter would have reminded the condemned that he need not be concerned about the shame of public execution. Yet his efforts would be severely tested en route to the gallows. Bolognese prisoners were first led from their cells to the second-floor loggia of Palazzo del Podestà, overlooking the Piazza Maggiore, to have their sentences read aloud. The manual instructs the comforter to use the prayers and *laude* to comfort him and divert his attention:

> Have him praying continually until you reach the place where the condemnation is read.... When you are at the orator's stand and his condemnation is read, then you should be very daring in your speech and never let him be still because then he would be greatly transformed due to the multitude of people that he sees. And always make sure that he looks you in the eye and at the tablet, so that he does not look around. Always make him say some prayers so that he does not think and so that he does not listen to what is being read. (bk. 2, chs. 21–22)

As the prisoner processed through the streets of Bologna, perhaps stopping to hear Mass before proceeding to the field of the Mercato del Monte where public executions were often held, he would inevitably face members of his community and family and perhaps even the victims of his crimes. Here again, the *laude* would serve to drown out and distract the prisoner from the gathered crowds. They were frequently sung during public processions, including those for funeral services, and their effectiveness in this instance would increase dramatically when used in conjunction with another of the comforter's tools: the *tavoletta*. As noted elsewhere in this volume, these panels painted with scenes from the Passion of Christ, or of saintly martyrdoms, were held in front of the prisoner's eyes to focus his attention and to block out the images of those he passed in the streets.

Samuel Edgerton has described these images as "a visual narcotic to numb the fear and pain of the condemned criminal during his terrible journey to the scaffold."[23] The *laude* would likewise ensure the prisoner's focus, and,

---

[23] Edgerton's research is based on a set of ten *tavolette,* dating to the sixteenth and seventeenth centuries, that survive from San Giovanni Decollato in Rome. It has been suggested that the scenes chosen for the *tavolette* were based specifically on the type of punishment to be enacted with images of St. John the Baptist used for prisoners who were beheaded, and those focusing on the removal of Christ from the cross used to comfort those about to be hanged. This second association has been made based on the presence of the ladder in these images—a symbol commonly associated with contemporary hangings. See Edgerton, "Little

used in conjunction with the *tavolette,* would serve to effectively minimize the impact of seeing family or friends and hearing the shouts of community members who often lined the procession route to shout at the condemned and decry their acts. At the gallows, as the comforter continued to speak to the prisoner, the words of the *laude* would ensure that in his final moments he was comforted by the death and salvation of Christ and the hope that he too would be saved. Together, the *laude* and the *tavolette* provided a complete sensory diversion in the final wrenching stages of the comforting process.

While the manual instructs the comforter to use prayer throughout the ritual, this advice intensifies in the final chapters of the manual, appearing more frequently and with a greater sense of urgency. This is no surprise, since the comforter's task became increasingly difficult with every step away from the prison. He is to say to the prisoner "At every one of these stages I will be with you and I will remind you of what you should do" (bk. 2, ch. 19). And further, "For those who you find do not lose strength at the tolling of the bell and who do not seem to care about it, never stop praying at their side nor talking about miracles" (bk. 2, ch. 19). As his hands are tied, as he leaves the prison, as his sentence is read, as he is led through the streets, en route to and at the site of his execution—the prisoner has a comforter praying constantly beside him. "Always make him say some prayers so that he does not think"; "begin some beautiful prayer, the most beautiful one that you know"; and so on. Here again, he may call upon the *laude,* perhaps employing those that incorporate responses to actively engage and focus the prisoner. Or he may use those that recall Christ's last moments in an effort to ensure that the crucified saviour is a model for the executed criminal's own death. And in a final act of *imitatio christi,* he instructs the prisoner to repeat Christ's last words as his own, "Into your hands, oh my Lord, I commend my spirit and soul."

The simplicity and affective nature of the *laude* contributed to their ongoing popularity from the late Middle Ages through the early modern period. These attributes also made them a particularly valuable resource within the context of the comforting ritual. Devotional songs, whether penitential or praising in nature, would have served the *confortatori* well. They were an effective tool in

---

Known 'Purpose of Art,'" 47, 49, 72–73, 188. See also his *Pictures and Punishment* and "*Maniera* and the *Mannaia.*" See also the article by M. Ferretti in this volume.

preparing the comforter for his difficult task. More importantly, their structure and thematic focus helped to alleviate a prisoner's fears, to direct his attention away from earthly matters, and to ensure he was well prepared for his ensuing fate. And in the most difficult final moments, the calming words of the *laude* might echo in his mind, ensuring that his last thoughts were of salvation.

Works Cited

Archives

AAB   Archivio Arcivescovile, Bologna
ACCU   Archivio Consorziale del clero urbano
BAB   Biblioteca Arcivescovile, Bologna
BUB   Biblioteca Universitaria Bologna
PML   Pierpont Morgan Library, New York
YBL   Yale University, Beinecke Library, New Haven, CT

Printed Sources

Alaleona, Domenico. "Le laude spirituali italiane nei secoli XVI e VII e i loro rapporto coi canti profane." *Rivista musicale italiana* 16 (1909): 1–54.

——. *Storia dell'Oratorio musicale in Italia.* Milan: Bocca, 1945.

Barr, Cyrillia. *The Monophonic Lauda and the Lay Religious Confraternities of Tuscany and Umbria in the Late Middle Ages.* Kalamazoo: Medieval Institute Publications, Western Michigan University, 1988.

Black, Christopher F. *Italian Confraternities in the Sixteenth Century.* Cambridge: Cambridge University Press, 1989.

Edgerton, Samuel, Y. "A Little Known 'Purpose of Art' in the Italian Renaissance." *Art History* 2, no.1 (1979): 45–61.

——. "*Maniera* and the *Mannaia*: Decorum and Decapitation in the Sixteenth Century." In *The Meaning of Mannerism.* Edited by F. W. Robinson and S. G. Nichols Jr., 67–105. New Hampshire: University Press of New England, 1972.

——. *Pictures and Punishment: Art and Criminal Prosecution during the Florentine Renaissance.* Ithaca: Cornell University Press, 1985.

L'Engle, Susa. "Compagnia dell'Ospedale di Santa Maria della Morte." In *Haec Sunt Statuta: Le corporazioni medievali nelle miniature bolognesi,* edited by Massimo Medica, 194–95. Modena: F. C. Panini, 1999.

Gravestock, Pamela. "Comforting the Condemned and the Role of the Laude in Early Modern Italy." In *Early Modern Confraternities in Europe and the Americas: International and Interdisciplinary Perspectives,* edited by C. Black and P. Gravestock, 129–50. Aldershot: Ashgate, 2006.

Henderson, John. *Piety and Charity in Late Medieval Florence.* Oxford: Clarendon Press, 1994.

——. "Religious Confraternities and Death in Early Renaissance Florence." In *Florence and Italy: Renaissance Studies in Honor of Nicolai Rubinstein,* edited by P. Denley and C. Elam, 383–94. London: Committee for Medieval Studies, Westfield College, University of London, 1988.

Luisi, F. *Laudario Giustinianeo: Edizione comparata con note critiche del ritrovato laudario Ms. 40 attribuito a Leonardo Giustinian.* Venice: Edizioni Fondazione Levi, 1983.

Macey, Patrick. "The *Lauda* and the Cult of Savonarola." *Renaissance Quarterly* 45, no. 3 (1992): 439–83.

Prizer, William. "Laude di Popolo, Laude di Corte: Some Thoughts on the Style and Function of the Renaissance Lauda." In *La Musica a Firenze al Tempo di Lorenzo il Magnifico,* edited by P. Gargiulo, 167–95. Firenze: L. S. Olschki, 1992.

———. "Lauda spirituale." In *New Grove Dictionary of Music and Musicians,* edited by Stanley Sadie, 14:367–73. New York: Grove's Dictionaries, 2001.

Rondeau, Jennifer Fisk. "Prayer and Gender in the Laude of Early Italian Confraternities." In *Gender Rhetorics: Postures of Dominance and Submission in History,* edited by R. Trexler, 219–33. Binghamton. NY: Medieval and Renaissance Texts and Studies, 1994.

Terpstra, Nicholas. "Confraternal Prison Charity and Political Consolidation in Sixteenth Century Bologna." *Journal of Modern History* 66, no. 2 (1994): 217–48.

———. "Death and Dying in Renaissance Confraternities." In *Crossing the Boundaries: Christian Piety and the Arts in Italian Medieval and Renaissance Confraternities,* edited by K. Eisenbichler, 179–200. Kalamazoo: Medieval Institute Publications, Western Michigan University, 1991.

———. *Lay Confraternities and Civic Religion in Renaissance Bologna.* Cambridge: Cambridge University Press, 1995.

———. "Piety and Punishment: The Lay *Conforteria* and Civic Justice in Sixteenth Century Bologna." *Sixteenth Century Journal* 22, no. 4 (1991): 679–94.

Troiano, Alfredo. "Un laudario per condannati a morte: Il ms. 1069 della Beinecke Library di Yale." *Studi e problemi di critica testuale* 72 (2006): 31–70.

Wilson, Blake McDowell. *Music and Merchants: The Laudesi Companies of Republican Florence.* Oxford: Clarendon Press, 1992.

Table 2.1. *Laude* in Manuscripts of the Bolognese *Comforters' Manual*

	Title	Translation	PML 188	YBL 1069	BAB 4880	BAB 4824	BUB 702	BUB 858	AAB IX.B.1
						Archives[a]			
1	Al nome sia del glorioso Padre	To the Name of the Glorious Father	x						
2	Al Padre al Figlio al sprito Sancto	To the Father, Son, and Holy Spirit	x						
3	Alta regina possente e benegna	High Queen, Powerful and Kind	x	x					x
4	Anchora non era gionto al luoco tristo	Once Again Arriving at a Sad Place	x						
5	Anima benedeta	Blessed Soul	x		x				x
6	Anima che guardi	Soul That Sees	x						x
7	Anima peregrina	Pilgrim Soul	x						x
8	Ave del cielo lucifera stella	Hail Shining Star from Heaven	x						x
9	Ave diana stella lucente e serena	Hail Diana, Shining and Serene Star	x	x					x
10	Ave Maria d'ogni chiareça luce	Hail Mary, Light of All Clarity	x	x					
11	Ave Maria matutina stella	Hail Mary, Morning Star	x	x					
12	Ave Maria o vergine sacrata	Hail Mary, Oh Consecrated Virgin							
13	Ave Maria regina madre de Dio e sposa	Hail Mary, Queen Mother of God and Spouse	x	x					x
14	Ave Maria, salutata da l'angelo	Hail Mary, Saluted by the Angel		x					
15	Ave regina di superni cieli	Hail Queen of the Highest Heavens	x	x					
16	Ave regina imperadrice sancta	Hail Queen, Holy Empress							x
17	Ave regina sempre dico sancta	Hail Queen, I Always Call Holy	x						
18	Ave regina, virgo gloriosa	Hail Queen, Glorious Maiden	x						
19	Ave stella lucente e ancora serena	Hail Star, Shining and Yet Serene			x				

	Title	Translation	PML 188	YBL 1069	BAB 4880	BAB 4824	BUB 702	BUB 858	AAB IX.B.1
			Archives[a]						
20	Ave tempio di Dio, sacrato tanto	Hail Temple of God, So Greatly Consecrated		x					
21	Ben ti possiamo lodare, o dolce legno	Good That We Should Praise You, Oh Sweet Wood			x	x			
22	Benedeto sia el giorno	Blessed Shall Be the Day	x						
23	Chi inançi a tutte le cose vole essere salvo	Who Before All Things Wants to Be Saved	x						
24	Chon desiderio vo cerchado	I Seek You with Desire	x						x
25	Chon pura fede e gran contricione	With Pure Faith and Great Contrition	x						
26	Christo mio, dami forteça	My Christ, Give Me Strength	x	x	x				x
27	Christo sanctifica me	Sanctify Me Christ				x			
28	Come che per vento foglia treme	As in the Wind the Leaf Trembles	x						
29	Croce sancta, dogni dolore coperta	Holy Cross, Covered with Every Anguish	x						x
30	De le sue braze, O vergine Maria	From/Of your Arms, Oh Virgin Mary				x			
31	Deffedate peccatore	Be Wary, Sinner	x						
32	Deus, in auditorium meum intende	Lord Bend to Hear Me	x						
33	Di tuto chio facto al mio viventi	Of All I Did to My Living Ones				x			
34	Dio ve salvi altissima alegrezza	God Secure You the Highest Happiness	x						
35	Dolce Madona, altissima salute	Sweet Madonna, Highest Salvation	x						
36	Domine Iesú Christo salvatore	Lord Jesus Christ Savior	x	x					
37	Dona del Paradiso	Lady of Paradise	x						
38	Done amorose, pelegrine e bele	Loving Women, Beautiful Pilgrims		x					

Table 2.1: *Laude* in Manuscripts of the Bolognese *Comforters' Manual*, cont'd

	Title	Translation	PML 188	YBL 1069	BAB 4880	BAB 4824	BUB 702	BUB 858	AA B IX.B.1
					Archives[a]				
39	Eterno Padre, Idio sumo Signore	Eternal Father, God Highest Lord		x					x
40	Fonte abondante per la quale vegiamo	Abundant Fountain, by Which We Stand Watch	x						
41	Gloria superna del celestiale choro	Supernal Glory of the Celestial Choir	x						x
42	Gloriosa Vergene Maria	Glorious Virgin Mary	x						
43	Gratia ti rendo, Ihesu crucifiso	Grace I Give You, Jesus Christ		x	x		x		x
44	Gratia vi domando	Grace I Ask of You	x						
45	Guardatami o noi che al mundosite	Look at Me, or Us, That to Purity							x
46	Hostia sacrata preciosa e degna	Consecrated Host, Precious and Worthy							x
47	Iesù spiendore de la prima luce	Jesus, Splendor of the First Light	x						
48	Iesù verace ardore	Jesus, Burning Truth							x
49	Imperatrice de quelo sancto regno	Empress of That Holy Kingdom		x					x
50	In gemiti e suspiri io me nutricho	With Sobs and Sighs I Feed Myself		x					
51	In le toe braça Vergene Maria	In Your Arms, Virgin Mary	x	x					
52	In lo initio di sancti evangelij	In the Beginning of the Holy Gospels	x						
53	In lo recorro a voi, Signor mio caro	In Running Back to You, Oh Lord my Beloved	x						
54	Io credo in uno Dio Padre a chi è possible	I Believe in One Father God, to Whom All Is Possible	x	x					
55	Io recoro da voi, o Signore caro	I Run From You, Oh Beloved Lord		x					
56	Io sono quella spietade e crudele morte	I Am That Impious and Cruel Death		x					x

	Title	Translation	Archives[a]						
			PML 188	YBL 1069	BAB 4880	BAB 4824	BUB 702	BUB 858	AA B IX.B.1
57	L'anima mia da christo s'è smarita	My Soul from Christ Has Wandered	x						
58	L'ultimo dolore dispone in Christo	The Ultimate Grief Settles in Christ			x				
59	L'ultimo volere dispono in Christo	The Ultimate Will Settles in Christ	x						
60	La nocte e 'l di si è vintiquatro hore	Night and Day Are Twenty-four Hours	x						
61	Le piaghe mie de doglia se renfresca	My Tears of Grief Renew Themselves	x						
62	Madre di Christo, gloriosa e pura	Mother of Christ, Glorious and Pure							x
63	Madre de Christo, alta imperatrice	Mother of Christ, High Empress			x				
64	Madre de Dio, misericordiosa e sancta	Mother of Christ, Merciful and Holy	x	x					
65	Magnifica signore l'anima mia	Magnificent Lord, My Soul . . .				x			
66	Maria lucente e fragrante rosa	Mary, Luminous and Fragrant Rose			x				
67	Mi raccomando a voi, Signore mio caro	I Recommend Myself to You, Lord My Beloved				x			
68	Mirati, o peccatore, la tua serpe	Behold, Oh Sinner, Your Serpent	x						
69	Misericordia a noi, Signor mio caro	Have Mercy on Us, Lord My Beloved							x
70	Misericordia, dulcissimo Dio	Have Mercy, Sweetest Lord	x						
71	Misericordia, o alto Dio soprano	Have Mercy, Oh High Supreme Lord		x		x	x	x	x
72	Misericordia, o sommo eterno Dio	Have Mercy, Oh Highest Eternal Lord	x	x	x	x	x	x	x
73	Misericordia, Padre omnipotente	Have Mercy, All-Powerful Father	x	x	x				x
74	O Alta regina de stelle incoronate	Oh High Queen, Crowned with Stars			x		x	x	x
75	O Christo mio, dami forteça	Oh My Christ, Give Me Strength	x						

Table 2.1: *Laude* in Manuscripts of the Bolognese *Comforters' Manual*, cont'd

	Title	Translation	PML 188	YBL 1069	BAB 4880	BAB 4824	BUB 702	BUB 858	AAB IX.B.1
			Archives[a]						
76	O Christo mio, te chiamo di cuore	Oh My Christ, I Call to You from My Heart					x		
77	O Christo omnipotente	Oh Christ All-Powerful	x						
78	O croce gloriosa d'onore degna	Oh Glorious Cross, Worth of Honor							x
79	O croce gloriosa e trionfale	Oh Glorious and Triumphant Cross	x	x					x
80	O croce sancta, d'ogni dolore coperta	Oh Holy Cross, in Every Sorrow Covered	x			x			
81	O croce sancta del pio Salvatore	Oh Holy Cross of the Pious Saviour	x						
82	O Dio eterno, tu m'ai creato	Oh God Eternal, You Created Me		x					x
83	O dolcissimo Signor, clemente e pio	Oh Sweetest Lord, Merciful and Pious				x			
84	O donna intemerata in eterno	Oh Lady, Undefiled in Eternity	x						
85	O fonte piena d'ogni humilità	Oh Fountain, Full of Every Humility	x						
86	O glorioso Signore, che su la croce	Oh Glorious Lord, Who on the Cross	x						
87	O glorioso Vergine, piglia cura	Oh Glorious Virgin, Take Care		x					x
88	O gratiosa Vergine Maria	Oh Gracious Virgin Mary							x
89	O Iesú Christo, mio dilecto	Oh Jesus Christ, My Delight	x		x		x		x
90	O Iesú Christo, nostro salvatore	Oh Jesus Christ, Our Saviour		x					x
91	O illibata Vergene Maria	Oh Pure Virgin Mary	x						
92	O in excelsis, o tua doglia	Oh in the Highest, Oh Your Anguish	x						
93	O Padre eterno, vero, iusto e pio	Oh Father Eternal, True, Just, and Pious		x					

	Title	Translation	Archives[a]						
			PML 188	YBL 1069	BAB 4880	BAB 4824	BUB 702	BUB 858	AAB IX.B.1
94	O Padre nostro, che nei cieli stai	Oh Our Father, Who Is in the Heavens	x						
95	O Padre nostro, del mondo redemptore	Oh Our Father, Redeemer of the World	x						
96	O Padre nostro, sempre Dio chiamo	Oh Our Father, I Always Call You Lord	x	x					x
97	O Padre nostro, uno Dio vivente	Oh Our Father, A Living God	x						
98	O Padre pieno de misericordia	Oh Father, Full of Mercy	x	x					
99	O Padre, o Figlio, o Spirito Sancto	Oh Father, Oh Son, Oh Holy Spirit	x						
100	O precioso sancto sangue giusto	Oh Precious, Holy, Righteous Blood	x						
101	O sacro sangue, giusto e benedeto	Oh Holy Blood, Righteous and Blessed	x	x					x
102	O sancti e sancte martiri de Dio	Oh Holy Men and Women Martyred for God	x						
103	O Signore beato et in croce crucifixo	Oh Lord, Blessed and on the Cross Crucified	x						
104	O signore iesu xpo salvatore	Oh Lord Jesus Christ Saviour							x
105	O Signore mio benigno, che gran pena portasti	Oh Lord My Gentle One, Who Bore Great Penalty	x						
106	O Signore mio, chi fusti legato	Oh My Lord, Who Binds You Closely					x		
107	O Signore mio, che 'l tutto governi	Oh My Lord, Who Governs All	x	x					
108	O Signore mio, io te chiamo di core	Oh My Lord, I Call to You from My Heart	x				x		x
109	O summo eterno et infinito bene	Oh Highest, Eternal, and Infinite Good	x				x	x	x
110	O summo redentore, eterno Idio	Oh Highest Redeemer, Eternal God		x			x	x	x

Table 2.1: *Laude* in Manuscripts of the Bolognese *Comforters' Manual*, cont'd

	Title	Translation	PML 188	YBL 1069	BAB 4880	BAB 4824	BUB 702	BUB 858	AA B IX.B.1
			Archives[a]						
111	O vergine pietosa	Oh Pious Virgin							x
112	O voi i quali in gloria gaudeti	Oh You Who Are Enjoyed in Glory							x
113	Padre de cielo, Figlio, e Spirito Santo	Father of Heaven, Son, and Holy Spirit				x			
114	Per acquistare lo santo paradiso	To Gain the Holy Paradise			x				
115	Per fugire ocio chom animo francho	To Flee Sloth with a Free Spirit			x				
116	Piangiti, cieli, che de l'alto gremio	Weep, Heavens, That From on High Come Close	x						
117	Primo principio de la nostra fede	The First Origins of Our Faith	x	x					
118	Qual è quello che pare al puncto extremo	This Is What Appears at the End Point	x						
119	Quando te sguardo in croce, Signore mio	When I See You on the Cross, My Saviour	x						
120	Regina eterna, se mei preghi mai	Queen Eternal, If My Prayers Ever …			x				
121	Salve Iesú Christo, salvadore superno	Hail, Jesus Christ, Saviour Supreme	x	x					
122	Salve regina, salve, salve tanto	Hail Queen, Hail, Hail So Much	x						
123	Salve, regina de misericordia	Hail, Queen of Mercy	x	x					
124	Salve regina, e germinante amore	Hail Queen, and Blossoming Love				x			x
125	Se il ciecho traditore mondo fallace	If the Blind, False, and Treasonous World							x
126	Se io feci mai, Signore, in alcun lato	If I Ever, Lord, in Any Side …			x				
127	Se io me confesso e glorioso padre	If I Confess Myself, and Glorious Father …	x						
128	Signore beato, in croce crucifisso	Blessed Lord, on the Cross Crucified			x				
129	Signore mio, Jesu Christo salvador	My Lord, Saviour Jesus Christ				x			

	Title	Translation	Archives[a]						
			PML 188	YBL 1069	BAB 4880	BAB 4824	BUB 702	BUB 858	AAB IX.B.1
130	Sommo inventore de tutta la natura	Highest Creator of All Nature	x						
131	Sommo principio e Glorioso padre	Highest Origin and Glorious Father	x						
132	Spandi la luce tua verso oriente	Spread Your Light to the East	x						
133	Spirito sancto d'amore	Holy Spirit of Love	x						
134	Sposa de Dio, io me ve racomando	Bride of God, I Commend Myself to You	x						
135	Te fu Christo salvatore	You Were Christ Saviour					x		
136	Tu padre eterno, tu signore benegno	You Father Eternal, You Gentle Lord	x	x					
137	Tu sei el mio vivo e vero Idio	You Are My Living and True God		x					
138	Veniti, o fonte tutte, al mio soccorso	Come, Oh Fount of All, To My Aid	x						
139	Vergine gloriosa, alma Regina	Glorious Virgin, Nurturing Queen				x			
140	Vergine alta regina	Virgin High Queen							x
141	Vergine regina intemerata	Virgin Fearless Queen	x						

[a]Archival Abbreviations

PML   Pierpont Morgan Library, New York
YBL   Beinecke Library, Yale University
BAB   Archdiocesan Library, Bologna
BUB   University Library, Bologna
AAB   Archdiocesan Archive, Bologna

Chapter 3

Mirror of a Condemned
The Religious Poems of Andrea Viarani

Alfredo Troiano

> *He said, "What is the source of such a grace*
> *for me, that my soul's sweetness will wait*
> *for me at the holy place of execution?"*
>
> Catherine of Siena, Letter to Raymond of Capua[1]

From the late medieval period through the Renaissance, Italian culture witnessed a deepening concern with the fate of the soul in the face of death. The severe and ascetic vision of the *contemptus mundi* intensifies with a sharp religious-existential anxiety of the kind that can be seen, for instance, in Francesco Petrarca's poetry. Treatises on the "art of dying well,"[2] devout poems on the "thoughts of death" (*memento mori*),[3] and frescoes and paintings that elaborate on themes like Triumph of Death and the Dance Macabre[4] powerfully express the conviction that the things of this earth are frail and transitory, that deep penance is a vital instrument of salvation, and that death itself marks a short transit through which one rejoins the Creator.

Born in and shaped by this cultural environment, the lay confraternities

---

I would like to express my thanks to Sheila Das for translating Viarani's poems into English and for making her translation of the manual available to me. I would also like to thank Nicholas Terpstra and Anna Graniero for assistance in the translation of this article.

[1] Catherine of Siena, *Epistolario*, ed. Duprè, 1:31. For a translation, see Catherine of Siena, *Letters*, trans. Noffke, 1:87. See also Scudder, *Saint Catherine of Siena*, 112.

[2] O'Connor, *Art of Dying Well*.

[3] Varanini et al., *Laude cortonesi*, vol. I*, no. 36; vol. II, nos. 73, 75, 78; vol. III, nos. 61, 71, 72; O'Connor, *Art of Dying Well*; Tenenti, *Il senso della morte*, 121–27; and Vigo, *Le danze macabre*, 91–131.

[4] Tenenti, *La vita e la morte* (the appendix contains the edition of a treatise, "Art of Dying Well," 113–55); and Scaramella, *L'Italia dei Trionfi*, 57–58.

called *conforterie* drew up manuals of the kind translated in this volume in order to assist those condemned by public justice to death. Is it possible to determine what hearing they received from these prisoners? Through the Middle Ages prisoners themselves frequently wrote spiritual texts—almost exclusively poems—as a cathartic response to their situation, and in their poetry they frequently reflected on their condition and fate.[5] Moving ahead to the fifteenth and sixteenth centuries, more than one condemned prisoner wrote poems while awaiting execution. It is a genre, still largely unexplored, that one could call "scaffold literature."[6]

The three religious poems presented in this article were composed by Andrea Viarani of Faenza before he was beheaded for treason in Ferrara in 1469. They demonstrate how Viarani absorbed and personalized the comforting messages offered to him by Ferrara's *conforteria*. Familiar themes from the "art of dying well" are put into verse and into the first person, with the result that the condemned prisoner himself may become a comforter, and not only for himself. Bologna's *conforteria* of S. Maria della Morte copied Viarani's poems into its *Comforters' Manual,* with the result that comforters could adopt the voice of the prisoner when speaking to those awaiting death. Viarani's poems also reach deeper into the spiritual literature composed in the shadow of the scaffold. They reflect St. Catherine of Siena's symbolism about the cruel rituals of human justice and Viarani's own echo of her wish to die as a crusader-martyr of Christ.

Little is known of Andrea Viarani's life before his involvement in the conspiracy against Borso d'Este, Duke of Ferrara, in 1469.[7] He was born into a noble family in Faenza, near Ravenna. His father, Ugolino, was a jurisconsult and at one time served as ambassador in Venice for Guidantonio Manfredi, Lord of Faenza (1439–48). Lord Guidantonio was succeeded by his brother, Astorgio II, in 1448, and for many years Andrea followed his father's example of allying with the ruling family by serving as Astorgio's secretary.

---

[5] Meneghetti, "Scrivere in carcere," 197–99. See also *Le loro prigioni*.

[6] Finkenstaedt, "Galgenliteratur: Zur Auffassung des Todes." On the phenomenon of prisoners' writing, recall François Villon's *La Ballade des pendus* (1462), the eleven poems of Viarani's master and co-conspirator, Giovanni Marco Pio, noted below, and Jacopo da Diacceto's Latin 44-line-long poem; Piccolomini, "Ultimi versi."

[7] Rossi, *Andrea da Vigliarana,* 71–72. On the Viarani family, see Campana, "Civiltà umanistica faentina," 305–10, 312–13, 316, 328.

The Viarani family played an important role in Faenza's cultural life, and not simply because of their work in the court of the Manfredi lords. Their own cultural formation was deeply influenced by Ambrogio Traversari (1386–1439), the monk and general of the Camaldolese Order, who was a great humanist and who wrote warmly about his friendship with Ugolino and his brother Bartolomeo.[8] Other members of the family who rose to prominence locally included Stefano Viarani, who taught both astrology and practical medicine in Bologna (1407–27) and Pavia (1427–46), and Bartolomeo's son (Andrea's cousin), Taddeo, a jurist and professor in Bologna from 1464 to 1465, who also wrote a poem of nineteen couplets in praise of Traversari.[9]

On 2 May 1468, Astorgio II died and was succeeded by his son Carlo. Both Ugolino and Andrea Viarani moved into opposition and began conspiring against Carlo in alliance with one of Guidantonio's sons, Taddeo Manfredi, who had become Lord of Imola. The Viarani were discovered and sent into exile in Imola, where Andrea served Taddeo as secretary.[10] While living in Imola, Andrea became involved in another and more dangerous plot that Giovanni Ludovico Pio and his brother Giovanni Marco, together the Lords of Carpi, had been organizing against the Duke of Ferrara, Borso d'Este (1450–71).[11]

Carpi was at that time under the authority of the Este dukes. The Pio brothers Giovanni Ludovico and Giovanni Marco were nephews of Duke Borso, their mother's brother, but became hostile towards him for family reasons. When one of their sisters was raped by Borso's trusted secretary Ludovico Casella, the duke failed to respond and his nephews launched their conspiracy in revenge.[12] They obtained support from Milan and Florence, and counted on the complicity of Borso's brother, Ercole. Andrea Viarani joined the conspiracy when Giovanni Ludovico Pio reached to Imola and recruited his sister, Marsibilia, who was wife of Viarani's employer, Lord Taddeo Manfredi. The spreading plot took them both into its vortex.

On 17 July 1469 the conspiracy was foiled when Ercole revealed the plot

---

[8] Campana, "Civiltà umanistica faentina," 307–10. Traversari himself tells us about his friendship with the brothers Ugolino and Bartolomeo Viarani; *Hodoeporicon,* chap. 11; and *Epistolario,* bk. 10. For biographical notes on Traversari, see Tamburini's introduction in *Hodoeporicon,* 1–20.

[9] Campana, "Civiltà umanistica faentina," 310, 312–13, 342nn305–10.

[10] Zama, *I Manfredi,* 227.

[11] Cappelli, "La congiura dei Pio signori di Carpi," 377–93. On the plot in general, see Gundersheimer, "Crime and Punishment," 123–27; and Chiappini, *Gli Estensi,* 154–57.

[12] "Cronaca della città di Ferrara," BCAF, ms. Classe I, 67 (16th century, fol. 181v). According to Carlo's account, there was hostility because Borso broke the promise of marriage between Pio's sister Bianca and Galeotto I Pico from Mirandola.

to Borso in Modena. The Pio brothers were arrested together with their secretary, Andrea Viarani, transported to Ferrara, and imprisoned in the prison
called Torre dei Leoni in the Castel Vecchio at the heart of the city. After a
rough trial, they were found guilty of treason (*crimen lesae maiestatis*) and
sentenced to death. Giovanni Ludovico and Andrea Viarani were regarded as
more guilty of the crime, and so Borso was particularly determined to make
an example of them. He had a scaffold erected in Ferrara's main square for
the first time in a dozen years in order to make their public execution all the
more prominent.[13] The scribe of Ferrara's *Book of the Condemned* (*Libro dei
giustiziati*) penned the usual terse entry:

> On 12 August [1469], the magnificent Giovanni Ludovico Pio from
> Carpi and a certain Andrea from Viarana, his chancellor, were be-
> headed. A scaffold was raised for them in front of the law court [*pe-
> zol di corte*] in order to let the people watch well. They dared betray
> our Most Illustrious Sir Borso, Duke of Ferrara.[14]

Giovanni Marco Pio died a little over a month later on 22 September,
though he was treated more honorably with a private execution at night in the
Castel Vecchio courtyard. All three conspirators had been comforted by Ferrara's *conforteria*, S. Maria Annunziata, who, like their counterparts in Florence,
were commonly known as The Blacks because of the black robes they wore.[15]

Literary tradition ascribes three religious poems to Andrea Viarani, composed
while he sat in the Ferrara prison awaiting execution. Oddly, they are not found

---

[13] The piazza became the regular place of execution only after 1481; Mazzi, *Gente a cui si fa notte,* 43–44,
75–82.

[14] *Libro dei giustiziati,* fol. 6r, BCAF ms. Classe I, 404, according to the edition by Mazzi, *Gente a cui si fa notte,*
109. Plate 1 of Mazzi's volume shows Ferrara's main square with the scaffold in front of the law court.

[15] Ferrara's Compagnia di S. Maria Annunziata (the Battuti Neri) emerged in August 1366, devoted particularly to taking condemned people to the scaffold "with discipline, litany, laud and prayer and silence." The
brothers drew up their statutes in 1366 and in 1381 built a hospital for poor pilgrims. These charitable works
earned them the attention of the public authorities, and they received some rooms in the public palace so
as better to assist the condemned. An early matriculation list of 1378 shows that the members were largely
craftsmen and merchants, but from 1529 to 1545, noblemen, prelates, learned men, and even, for the first
time, women joined; Prosperi, "Mediatori di emozioni," 279–92. See also Mazzi, *"Gente a cui si fa notte,"*
66–74. The Neri's manual goes back to the second part of the fifteenth century, and its first part is an expanded
version of book 1 of the Bolognese *Comforters' Manual*; Nobile, "Il libro della vita beata." The *Libro dei giustiziati* contained the names of the condemned that they had assisted; Mazzi, *"Gente a cui si fa notte,"* 130n90.

in any of the records of the Ferrarese *conforteria* of S. Maria Annunziata. All extant copies are within the records of Bologna's *conforteria* of S. Maria della Morte, and they begin appearing in that *conforteria*'s manuscripts from the later fifteenth century, suggesting that Viarani's poems moved very quickly into broader circulation.[16] In one of the early Bolognese manuscripts, BBU 157, Viarani's three poems follow eleven others that were written by his co-conspirator, Giovanni Marco Pio. All fourteen poems follow a copy of the *Comforters' Manual* that is translated in this volume, and they are copied as part of a large collection of vernacular prayer-songs in verse (*laude*) that were recited by the comforters along with the condemned.[17]

Giovanni Marco Pio's poetry is written in a variety of forms and meters—specifically the ballad, tercet, sirvente, and sonnet—that speak to Pio's education and culture. While at an earlier point in his life he may have written of love or loyalty, the topics that enter the verse he writes in prison awaiting execution are more limited: the single ballad and most of the tercets are in praise of and commitment to the Virgin Mary. Most of the sirventes deal with contempt of the world, Pio's wish for detachment from the past and from evil, and his wish to trust in God in the precariousness of the present. A further sirvente directs a plea for forgiveness and mercy to Duke Borso d'Este: "may you forgive…without spectacle of cruelty," though it is not known whether it was in response to this plea that Duke Borso secured a more discreet and private execution for the man who had plotted to unseat him.[18]

Andrea Viarani wrote one sirvente and two sonnets. The sirvente was a lyric verse named after the medieval Provençal troubadours (*sirventes*) who had developed it, and who usually used it to offer satirical, political, or moral commentary. Viarani's sirvente "If the blind, false, and treasonous world" ("Se 'l cieco traditor mondo fallace") is a devout and moral meditation 137 lines long whose topics are the detachment from the world and repentance.[19] One of his sonnets, "Eternal Father" ("Eterno Padre"), stresses the effectiveness of

---

[16] Degli Innocenti, "I volgarizzamenti italiani," 243–47; and Luisi, *Laudario giustinianeo*, 146–48. Two contemporary manuscripts of the same confraternity also contain Viarani's poems: AAB ACCU ms. IX B 1; and YBL ms. 1069. Another copy of the poems (ms. 177) at the Biblioteca Classense in Ravenna belonged to the Urbino *conforteria*. Finally, ms. 2274 in the Biblioteca Angelica in Rome is a collection (fifteenth to sixteenth century) of devout poems and prose that includes Viarani's poems.

[17] Fanti, "S. Maria della Morte," 122–73: and Prosperi, "Il sangue e l'anima." On the genres and topics of the *laude* in particular, see Troiano, "Un laudario per condannati a morte," 31–70.

[18] Ravagli, *Rime edite ed inedite*, vol. 4 (1907) fasc. X-XII: 178–87; vol. 5 (1908) fasc. I–III: 34–41; fasc. IX–XI: 129–37, 162–70.

[19] Viarani's sirvente is a quatrain chapter (three hendecasyllables and one seven-syllable) with the rhyme structure ABbC CDdE…XYyZ Z; Beltrami, *La metrica italiana*, 277–78, 364.

Christ's blood, while in the other, "Eternal Queen" ("Regina eterna"), the poet asks the divine Mother forgiveness for his sin. The balance of this article will focus on Viarani's sirvente "If the blind, false, and treasonous world" because it most clearly develops the themes found in the comforting manuals, and most nearly brings the reader into the mind and emotions of a man who is at once both the comforted and the comforter.

All the anxiety of the moment is contained in four opening verses that pour out in a long rushed breath.

> If the blind, false, and treasonous world,
> full of injustice, betrayal, and deception
> has held you many years
> far from your Maker and the Supreme Good,
>
> Shows now both the shadowy and the fleeting nature
> of hoping for vain pleasures, which
> that foolish desire inclines towards
> never thinking of its true salvation:
>
> Now that heaven has given you much grace
> and you are brought back to the point,
> Andrea, that God has made you
> repentant of the wrong committed.
>
> Lift your mind to God, move your hard heart
> and do not be so obstinate with him
> but with devout tears,
> repentant of having erred, ask for forgiveness.
>   (lines 1–16)

The first two quatrains work out the ascetic theme of the *contemptus mundi*. Andrea Viarani's poetic meditation notably begins with his strong affirmation of the comforters' first lesson, which is that one must move beyond the concerns of this world because it is all ultimately vain, empty, and transitory. The Bolognese *Comforters' Manual* is quite explicit on this point:

And for certain, take note of this, that given the many adversities, the many trials, the many burdens that nowadays reign in the world, and that we are always subject to and wrapped up in, the saner side is to elect to die than to always live in this misery and in this world which is so *false* and so unfair and so *full of deceit*…for that reason you must be sorry for having loved this vain and fleeting world so much…everything of the world is vain, pompous, and haughty, and it passes like a shadow and like sleep. (bk. 1, chap. 2; italics mine)[20]

In these first four verses, the adverb *hora* (now) is emphatic, and its position at the center of the four verses and at the beginning of line 9 marks critical changes in mood. It puts an end to the world's illusions. One immediately notices that the style and content of the passage deepen. The analytical and pensive mood of stanzas 1 and 2 where Andrea signifies an awareness of and detachment from the world becomes suddenly more agitated and personal. The interaction with himself has now become closer—the vocative "Andrea" is used first only at line 11. It is a privileged time, because the assurance of God's grace in this context inspires contrition. But that time—*now* (hora) —is much more privileged because it is also the point of death (the "puncto de la morte" in the Bolognese manual).[21]

Adriano expresses his agitation much more directly in stanza 4, lines 13 through 16:

Lift your mind to God, move your hard heart
and do not be so obstinate with him
but with devout tears,
repentant of having erred, ask for forgiveness.

As he follows one imperative closely on another in this verse, Andrea reminds himself that "there is no time to lose"; this echoes the warnings of the comforter, who says:

[20] *Comforters' Manual*, fols. 7ra, 9rb, PML ms. 188. "Et per certo nota questo, che a le molte adversità, a le molte fadighe, a li molti affani che ogi dí regnano al mondo et a li quali ci convene sempre essere sugietti et avolupadi, più sana parte si è ad ellegere de morire che sempre vivere in questa miseria et in questo *mondo* tanto *falso* e tanto *iniquo e pieno* de tanti *inganni*…imperció tu dèi essere dolente de havere tanto amato questo vano e *caduco mondo*…perché ogni cosa si è *vanità* e pompa e superbia, e passa come *umbra*." See sirvente, lines 1–2, 5–6: "mondo *fallace*, / *pien* de *niquizia*…e *inganni* … mostrando [il *mondo*] hor *umbra* et hor *caduca* spene / de piacer *vano*." Italics mine.

[21] During the seventeenth century, a man at the end of his life was called "uomo al punto" (man at the point), as seen in a pamphlet published in Bologna in 1668 (*L'huomo al punto cioè l'huomo in punto di morte considerato dal Padre Daniello Bartoli*) cited in Battistini, "'Guardare fissamente la morte."

Aim therefore to lift all your soul to God and put it in his hands...you should concentrate your thoughts during the little time you have left in this life, putting all of your devotion in God and in being contrite for all your sins.[22]

When then did Andrea compose this meditation? He was arrested on 17 July (although other sources give the 26th or the 30th), imprisoned on the 21st, tried quickly, and finally beheaded on 12 August. The Bolognese manuscript containing the poems notes generally that the sirvente was written at the time of the imprisonment, while another manuscript in a Roman collection more specifically identifies it as having been written "after the notification of the sentence" (post latam sententiam).[23] The process of comforting a condemned normally took place after the sentencing to death, and particularly through the night before the day of execution. In Viarani's case, it is clear from the internal records of the Ferrarese conforteria that comforters did enter the prison to sit and talk with him, although it is not clear when in fact they began their charitable work. This leaves us wondering about the origin and specific motivation for the poems. Did they rise from a dormant faith that was suddenly reawakened by anxiety in face of an impending death? Did the comforting service of the Ferrarese conforteria trigger this reawakening?

Certainly the poems of both Andrea Viarani and Giovanni Marco Pio present remarkable cases of the quick conversion of a condemned man within the very political-judicial system that was making a scapegoat of him. That system required that someone effect the prisoner's transformation from sinner to martyr in a very short time.[24] The poems themselves are models of repentance and piety. Yet the idea that either man could have composed them in one night seems implausible. Given the nature of their crime, the death sentence was virtually a given from the time that the two were thrust into prison, and as a result both the comforting and also the poems themselves could have emerged over the course of the three weeks that Viarani and Pio sat in prison.

It is striking that the first request Andrea addresses to himself is "Lift your mind to God" (Leva la mente a Dio, line 13). This echoes the instruction that comes at the end of the chapters on the "contempt of the world" in book 1 of the

---

[22] Comforters' Manual, bk. 1, chap. 6, fols. 9vc–10ra, PML ms. 188.

[23] "Miscellanea," BAR 2274, 17n1.

[24] Prosperi, "Il condannato a morte," 201–7. The comforting service of St. Catherine of Siena shows a similar case; Galletti, "'Uno capo nelle mani mie.'"

Bolognese *Comforters' Manual*. The comforter is to encourage the condemned prisoner with the words, "Lift up your mind" (Lieva*re* la mente). The expression is in fact a leitmotif in the manual, recurring frequently from its earliest pages.[25]

The comforters emphasized three "perfect and good" (perfecte e bone) rules when helping a condemned man through his last hours. First, forgive the offenses suffered and caused. Second, ask mercy of God. Third, be devoted to the Eucharist.[26] Andrea privileges the second one, and this is no surprise. One can suppose that the infinite mercy of God must have been one of the most effective topics in the comforting process precisely because it recurs so frequently and is expressed so memorably. The Ferrarese manual used by Andrea's comforters elaborated that even if the condemned man's sins "are multiplied much more than the sand of the sea, the stars of the sky, the drops of the rain" (sono multiplicati più che non è l'arena del mare, le stelle del cielo, le goze de la pioza), then he ought to be reassured that the mercy of God is much greater than them.[27]

Andrea's verse sets this out just as directly. While prayerful meditation recalls a host of sins vividly to mind, the assurance that there is no fault that exhausts God's forgiveness must be just as vivid. After the necessary detachment from the past and evil, the poem takes the form of an exhortation: weep for and repent of the very sins that you have committed.

> but with devout tears,
> repentant of having erred, ask forgiveness.
>
> . . . .
>
> Be absolutely certain that an hour
> of bitter tears is enough for your salvation,
> being as contrite
> as accords your serious failing.
>
> . . . .
>
> …weep your heart with your eyes and your voice.
> (lines 15–16, 37–40, 112)

---

[25] "Lift your mind and understand well what I want to tell you" (*Lieva la mente* tua et intende bene quello che io te voglio dire). *Comforters' Manual*, bk. 1, chap. 6, fol. 10v, PML ms. 188. "And for that reason, my brother, I beg you for the love of God that you lift your mind away from earthly things and put it in the things of God…you must lift your mind, commending your soul to the Lord Jesus Christ." *Comforters' Manual*, bk. 1, chap. 14, fol. 17r–v, etc. PML ms. 188.

[26] *Comforters' Manual*, bk. 1, chaps. 8–9, 13–14; and Fanti, "S. Maria della Morte," 167.

[27] Nobile, "Il libro della vita beata," 58; and Prosperi, "Il sangue e l'anima," 973–74.

In stanzas 11 through 22, the meditation ceases to be only a personal matter. The *you* (tu) being addressed moves from the particular individual to "everyman," or from Andrea himself to whoever has lost hope of being forgiven by God (see in particular lines 81–84). This is the point at which Andrea the condemned becomes Andrea the comforter. And not only of himself; Viarani aims with this prison poem to persuade others of the effectiveness of sorrowful contrition, even at the point of death.

Five adjectives describe confession in the *Comforters' Manual*: complete, ashamed, sorrowful and contrite, open, and private.[28] The manual makes clear that the third characteristic of sorrow and contrition is, in accordance with the teaching of the church fathers, the most significant feature of confession. Whatever led a person to sin, whether ignorance or malice, God does not disdain the "contrite and humble" heart (contrito et humiliato); here the comforter uses the words of the psalmist David from Psalm 51, the "Miserere mei."[29]

Weeping and repenting, tears and contrition. Viarani says more than once that these are the medicines that heal the soul:

This is that saving medicine
that can heal your weakness

.   .   .   .

The medicine that I speak of is that
of tears, which saved Mary Magdalene

.   .   .   .

This is medicine which made perfect
the good Peter…

.   .   .   .   .   .

And the thief on the cross…
(lines 53–54, 57–58, 61–62, 65)

Like a skilled comforter, Andrea reaches to the Bible for examples of contrite sinners who can serve as his pastoral models: Mary Magdalene, Peter, and the good thief crucified beside Christ at Golgotha. Devotion and bitter tears saved the first two; a confession and cry for mercy, the third. These characters are included among the examples of repentant and forgiven sinners to whom the comforter could point as he taught the condemned prisoner the

---

[28] "intiera, vergognosa, cum dolore e contritione, aperta e secreta." *Comforters' Manual,* bk. 1, chap. 12, fols. 14v–16r, PML ms. 188.

[29] "A broken and a contrite heart, O God, thou wilt not despise." Ps. 51:17.

way of attracting God's benevolence.[30]

Comforters could also reach to the church fathers for assurance that weeping as contrition was an effective sign of grief for one's sins. Many pertinent sentences drawn from the church fathers were included in the section of the Bolognese manual designated the "Authorities" (Auctoritates), a section addressed largely to those condemned who were more educated.[31] From Ambrose, they learned that "Penance is weeping for past evil, and not making evil any more," and from Jerome, "Whoever wishes at the point of death to be sure of God's pardon, should while being healthy do penance and weep for the sins committed." Isidore of Seville also associated the tears of the humble and contrite mind with the compunction of the heart.[32]

However, for Andrea Viarani, all that is not enough. May the cries of a contrite heart, at the point of death, let man obtain release from any sin whatsoever? Doubt enters and erodes the very purpose of repentance, which was to foster confidence of salvation:

> Ah! Don't wish to abandon your soul,
> being diffident of eternal grace.
> (lines 17–18)

In other words, "Don't abandon yourself to despair."

Medieval confessors had identified doubt in God's mercy—that is, the belief that one might not be worthy of salvation—as the vice of despair (*desperatio*). It was described even more precisely as the "temptation of the devil regarding faith" (temptatio dyaboli de fide), and was a very serious sin.[33] Jerome and Augustine strongly suggested that the "crime of despair" was the only sin from which one could not obtain pardon.[34]

During his preparation for dying well, the condemned must be made certain that there is no enemy but "the devil from hell." "And do you know what the devil will do to you?" the comforter warns. "He will put all your sins before you so that you suffer and ask God for forgiveness. But if you don't, he will instead do it so that you become ashamed and confused, and so you lose

---

[30] *Comforters' Manual*, bk. 1, chap. 11. This was a central element of the art of dying well.

[31] See Fanti, "S. Maria della Morte," 132–34.

[32] *Comforters' Manual*, fols. 39v, 55v, 58v, BBU ms. 702; and Nagy, *Le don des larmes*.

[33] Schmitt, "Il suicidio nel medioevo," esp. 343. In the Scrovegni Chapel at Padua, Giotto portrayed (ca. 1303–8) Despair as a woman beheaded, a suicide, whom a devil catches by the hair. In treatises on the art of dying well and in manuals for those sentenced to death, Judas is described as an example to avoid because he succumbed to despair and took his own life; see Tenenti, *Il senso della morte*, chaps. 3–4.

[34] *Comforters' Manual*, fols. 42r, 51v, BBU ms. 702.

hope that God can or wants to forgive you, as did Judas the traitor."[35] The devil will also plant the idea in your heart that your enemies are happy and that they are saying, "See, God has given that little thief what he deserved." Andrea thinks about it. For him the devil is still the one who deliberately makes human beings believe that God's justice is hemmed in by the same constraints as human justice.

> Showing that God sometimes
> cannot go against Justice
> and your great, wicked sin
> he cannot cancel without great punishment.
>
> (lines 97–100)

The devilish insinuation brings out a crucial point. "The confraternal model of assistance to the condemned," writes Adriano Prosperi, "must occupy a proper place in the picture of justice as a state repression of criminality.... It was necessary to control the results of the grand ritual so as to achieve retribution for the crime, repentance of the offender, reconciliation.... The aim of the new form of charity was to transform the condemned criminal into a saint; the detested individual whose life was being taken must somehow become a lamb ready to shed his own blood for the salvation of his own soul and for the good of the community."[36] Now looking at stanza 6, lines 21 through 24:

> But now, as you put on that blessed band
> of the true Cross, upon which God
> suffered death when he descended
> and took flesh to ransom you.

This call to one's own soul to take up the cross follows the ascetic *contemptus mundi* in the two opening stanzas, and develops naturally out of the main theme of Christianity: the incarnation and Passion of God's son. Christ was the necessary sacrifice of God's justice. His blood, Andrea reminds us, is of an infinite and universal value:

> For this the Lord God chose to die,
> so to be able to then wash away
> the stain of sin with his blood
> from whoever with a contrite heart comes back

---

[35] *Comforters' Manual*, bk. 2, chap. 19, fol. 50r a–b, PML ms. 188.

[36] Prosperi, *Dare l'anima*, 338–39.

> to contemplate the true light above.
>
>   (lines 41–45)

But now what matters most is that he understands and feels that he himself is the beneficiary of redemption.[37]

> See that God has opened the doors
> of paradise for you
>
> .   .   .   .   .   .
>
> Why don't you, poor man, consider how
> after a thousand thousands of grave offenses,
> he has his arms spread
> on the hard wood waiting still more?
>
>   (lines 29–30, 33–36)

"And do not say, 'I have but little time to make penance,'" the comforter warns while concluding his instructions on confession. "Remember the thief who was up on the cross, who had a shorter space of time than you do. God is so benevolent that he is content with the good will of the person when he sees that he is truly repentant of all his sins, and that he confesses them completely to the priest."[38] The good thief is singled out frequently in the Bolognese manual, and Andrea also focuses his attention on this gospel character (see stanzas 17–18). The good thief is the alter ego of whoever is about to mount the cross of his own death sentence. The condemned criminal sees in his mind's eye the pierced and bloodied Christ whom that thief witnessed and to whom he pleaded. Andrea recalls the model of the good thief and the assurance he offers that a condemned can pass, in an instant, from the troubles of life to the glory of heaven.[39]

> In that moment he earned,
> for every old malicious sin and wrong,
> forgiveness and by heavenly grace
> he was that very day placed in paradise.
>
>   (lines 69–72)

---

[37] For the same purpose, Viarani uses the interrogative clause in the sonnet "Eterno Padre, Idio sommo Signore" (Eternal Father, God and Supreme Lord).

[38] *Comforters' Manual,* bk. 1, chap. 12, fol.15r, PML ms. 188.

[39] St. Caterina of Siena realized the effectiveness of this example and inserted it in her intercession prayer on behalf of two condemned; see Prosperi, *Dare l'anima,* 332–33.

Stanzas 28 through 31 guide us to an intriguing conclusion. Here the religious and moral meditation becomes an invitation to contemplate Christ crucified. In the Bolognese *Comforters' Manual,* the chapter in book 1 on Christ's Passion being "for our example" follows the chapters on the *contemptus mundi*; for the condemned approaching death it is good to focus hope, devotion, and memory on Christ afflicted and suffering on the cross.[40] Having a fast and effective hold over the sentenced criminal, the chapter then shifts the emphasis from the innocence of God's son ("just lamb…clean lamb…pure lamb without vice and injustice," etc.) to the tortures of his Passion ("And still, nonetheless, he let himself be so mistreated, that, is taken and tied, beaten and flogged, his bones broken," etc.). In order to make Christ's example more vivid, immediate, and effective, the comforters brought crucifixes and *tavolette* that depicted scenes from the Passion and the Crucifixion on one side and scenes of martyrs' deaths on the reverse. Both were held before the prisoner, who was urged to kiss them during his terrible journey to the scaffold.[41]

The immediate visual image of the Crucifixion grips Viarani. And the Christ he contemplates is above all the man who, "without sin, unjustly, but willingly," let himself be scourged and killed "for your salvation" (lines 115–16). The comforters emphasized that the innocent Christ demonstrated "goodwill" in the face of an unjust death sentence, perhaps in order to avert popular rebellion against the errors and outrages of public justice in Italian cities. To the examples of Christ and John the Baptist, they added the examples of the saint martyrs who "willingly took the penalties and the suffering without being the least bit guilty." How much more should a criminal willingly accept a sentence that his own sins have earned for him?[42] But it seems that Christ's bloody torments attract Viarani's attention even more:

Contemplate the five mortal wounds
and his precious body pierced,
mocked and bloodied
from the thousand thorns of that cruel crown.

(lines 117–20)

Blood plays a prominent role in the following stanza (31) and summons up an image that places the reader at the feet of the cross: contemplate Christ's

---

[40] *Comforters' Manual,* bk. 1, chap. 7, fols. 10r–11r, PML ms 188.

[41] Prosperi, "Mediatori di emozioni."

[42] *Comforters' Manual,* bk. 1, chap. 7, fol. 10v, PML ms 188.

whole body and, "from His head to His feet you will see His pure, immaculate blood" (lines 121–22). The fascination with blood was a central facet of flagellant spirituality, and it is not surprising that *conforterie* were usually flagellant brotherhoods like Ferrara's Blacks.[43] Beyond flagellation, their devotional focus on the Eucharist, the transubstantiated body and blood of Christ in the sacrament of communion, underscored this emphasis on blood. Criminals were carefully instructed in devotion to the Eucharist, and the manual carefully stipulated how they were to receive it before their execution. Christ's blood shed on the cross redeemed their own blood shed on the scaffold, a theme of imitative piety that Adriano Prosperi has traced to the influence St. Catherine of Siena had on the symbolism of the cruel rituals of human justice.[44]

"But now, dress yourself in that holy band of the true Cross" (lines 21–22). So Andrea addressed himself as he prepared for the "spiritual fight" (pugna spiritualis). The theme of fighting plays an important role in the Christian ascetical tradition, recurring in the writings of the apostle Paul, St. Prudentius, and Bernard of Clairvaux, and also in the meditations of spiritual guides who had emerged in the late medieval period, like Pietro di Giovanni Olivi and Catherine of Siena, or others like Caterina di Vigri of Bologna or Bernardino of Siena who shaped the spiritual environment of the quattrocento when the Bolognese manual was written. War in general, and the conquest of Jerusalem in particular were metaphors for the war between Good and Evil, both a universal fight in history and a more meditative *pugna spiritualis*.[45] Comforters emphasized that there were two enemies in this spiritual fight: the devil and death. The Bolognese manual is full of military allegories that build one on the other: Christ is the primary combatant on the wood of the cross, the martyrs are engaged in an intense but triumphant military exercise, dirty from battle and stained with blood, and the condemned criminal may enter, if he wants, the company of these noble soldiers of Christ.[46] Therefore, dying by judicial sentence becomes a providential opportunity for martyrdom—a rare opportunity to be a "soldier of Christ" (miles Christi) outside of a wartime setting. The nexus of crusade-martyrdom, where death in battle would obtain forgiveness for any kind of sin, had been emphasized by St. Catherine of Siena in 1370 to 1380, when she was promoting a crusade in the Holy Land that

---

[43] Prosperi, "Il sangue e l'anima," 963–64.

[44] Prosperi, *Dare l'anima*, 331–32; and Fanti, "S. Maria della Morte," 167.

[45] See Cardini, "L'idea di Crociata"; Duprè Theseider, "Caterina da Siena, santa"; Fumagalli Beonio Brocchieri, *Cristiani in armi*; and Bernardo di Clairvaux, *Il libro della nuova cavalleria*.

[46] *Comforters' Manual*, bk. 1, chap. 25, fols. 24v–26r, PML ms. 188.

would be carried out by criminals, violent people, and transgressors.[47]

Coming back to Viarani, it is evident how much his metaphors in lines 21 through 22, combining biblical memory (Eph. 4:24) and Crusade allusions, are more than simply a spur to do penance.[48] Writing in the shadow of the scaffold, the poet makes clear what his goal is: he wishes to pass from being a condemned criminal to being a martyr of Christ. And we catch this in his metaphors ("But now, as you put on that blessed band / of the true Cross upon which God suffered / death when he descended / and took flesh to ransom you"; lines 21–24).[49] In other words, "you, too, take your death sentence as though mounting the cross."

In stanza 7 that follows, Viarani works out his conviction that salvation is based only on Christ's cross, and that this salvation is now at hand as he, too, faces execution:

> This is enough, more than in a thousand cards
> for you to firmly believe that you can save yourself,
> it is up to you alone if you want it,
> your life and death depends on you.
>
> (lines 25–28)

The verses contain a truth that begins, but at the same time resolves, the drama of every human being: death for death, or death for life. This is the hour and this is the opportunity—as comforters frequently made clear—either to earn eternal life or to lose the soul together with the body. Thus, what must I do to be saved? Imitate the "noble cavaliers of Christ"—those martyrs who suffered long and bloody tortures—and follow the hard, bitter, and sharp Passion of God's Son to victory.[50]

The bellicose language is much more concentrated in the last words that the comforter uses as he accompanies the condemned in his very last passage up the steps of the scaffold:

[47] According to Prosperi, this crusade of the criminals looked like a proposal for a mass execution; *Dare l'anima*, 332. Before St. Catherine, Venturino da Bergamo (1304–46), the Dominican preacher who had inspired the creation of *conforterie* across Italy, had also proposed a crusade of the kind (ibid., 325–31). See also Fanti, "S. Maria della Morte," 78–99.

[48] Ephesians 4:24. The sources of these suggestions about crusade may be literary (romances of chivalry and *cantari*) or historical (at the end of June 1464, the fifth crusade sailed under the command of Sigismondo Pandolfo Malatesta, Lord of Rimini).

[49] See Catherine of Siena, *Epistolario,* ed. Duprè, no. 11, pp. 48–49.

[50] *Comforters' Manual,* bk. 1, chap. 25, fols. 24v–26r, PML ms. 188.

"Oh creature of God, you have devoutly taken up the arms of the blessed Lord Jesus Christ, and you are armed with them now. So now you are transformed into a valiant cavalier and fight manfully since I tell you that you are near death and do not have much time left to live. This is your cross by which you must follow the dear Christ Jesus, who will reward you with his precious blood." And in this way you always continue to comfort him until you are on top of the hill or wherever the execution will be carried out. (*Comforters' Manual*, bk. 2, chap. 24)

Viarani picks up on this same theme at the end of his meditative poem: "In You my life, in You my death / relies, amen" (lines 134–35).

This couplet echoes the lesson that Viarani had reminded himself of earlier in the poem at line 28: "your life and death depends on you." Here is found a very intriguing variant, and what appears almost a reversal. We are now at the conclusion of the process of comforting and meditation, and have passed through the "contemplation of the cross" (contemplatio crucis) of stanzas 29 through 31. Viarani now repeats the same couplet, but encloses it in a prayer. At this point, "you" no longer represents Viarani speaking to himself—it is now Christ. Viarani's life and death no longer depend on his own will, but depend on Christ. But this is neither a paradox nor a reversal, but in fact a point of union. "Between the creature and himself—as St. Catherine of Siena explained to the mercenary Bartolomeo Smeducci—God has placed the blood of his only begotten Son," and this blood like "a cement makes one's soul unite with and conform to God's gentle divine will and charity."[51] Conformed by this blood to Christ, Andrea Viarani does not let his chalice slip by:

I am happy with your will.
. . . .
Do with me, Lord God, what you will,
as you are my good and eternal peace.
(lines 132, 136–37)

The poem ends here, with Viarani prepared to "die well." What happened at the place of execution is not known. But if he maintained this frame of mind, then in the perspective of St. Catherine and of the *Comforters' Manual*, Andrea Viarani will have become like Niccolò Toldo. Assisted by a comforter-saint

[51] Catherine of Siena, *Letters*, trans. Noffke, 1:188. See also Catherine of Siena, *Epistolario*, ed. Duprè, no. 52, p. 205; no. 33, p. 139; no. 34, p. 143, lines 25–27; no. 52, p. 206, lines 14–24.

up to the scaffold, he too will wash away his sins with his *own* blood, which through his will to imitate Christ will have become a sign of his participation in the sacrifice of the Son of God.[52]

Cited Works

Archives

AAB	Archivio Arcivescovile, Bologna
BAR	Biblioteca Angelica, Rome
BBU	Biblioteca Universitaria, Bologna
BCAF	Biblioteca Comunale Ariostea, Ferrara
BCR	Biblioteca Classense, Ravenna
PML	Pierpont Morgan Library, New York
YBL	Yale University, Beinecke Library, New Haven

Printed Sources

Battistini, Andrea. "'Guardare fissamente la morte': La retorica funebre nell'*Uomo al punto* di Daniello Bartoli." *Esperienze letterarie* 30 (2005): 151–70.

Beltrami, Pietro G. *La metrica italiana*. Bologna: Il Mulino, 2000.

Bernardo di Clairvaux. *Il libro della nuova cavalleria: De laude novae militiae*. Edited by Franco Cardini. Milano: Biblioteca di Via Senato Edizioni, 2006.

Campana, Augusto. "Civiltà umanistica faentina." In *Il liceo 'Torricelli' nel primo centenario della sua fondazione*. Faenza: Fratelli Lega, 1963.

Cappelli, Antonio. "La congiura dei Pio signori di Carpi contro Borso d'Este." *Atti e Memorie della Deputazione di Storia Patria per le province Modenesi e Parmensi* 2 (1864): 377–93.

Cardini, Frano. "L'idea di Crociata in S. Caterina." In *Atti del simposio internazionale cateriniano-bernardiniano* (Siena, 17–20 aprile 1980), edited by Domenico Maffei and Paolo Nardi, 57–88. Siena: Accademia Senese degli Intronati, 1982.

Catherine of Siena. *Epistolario di santa Caterina da Siena*. Edited by Eugenio Duprè. Roma: Tipografia del Senato, 1940.

———. *The Letters of Catherine of Siena*. 2 vols. Translated by Suzanne Noffke. Tempe: Center for Medieval and Renaissance Studies, 2000.

Chiappini, Luciano. *Gli Estensi: Mille anni di storia*. Ferrara: Corbo Editore, 2001.

Degli Innocenti, Mario. "I volgarizzamenti italiani dell' 'Elucidarium' di Onorio Augustodunense." *Italia medievale e umanistica* 22 (1979): 243–47.

Duprè Theseider, Eugenio. "Caterina da Siena, santa." In *Dizionario biografico degli Italiani*, 22:361–79. Roma: Istituto della Enciclopedia italiana, 1979.

---

[52] As St. Catherine later noted to Raimondo da Capua in a letter of June 1375 (that is, the middle of the crusade campaign), "I said, 'Courage, my dear brother, for soon we shall reach the wedding feast. You will go forth to it bathed in the sweet blood of God's Son, with the sweet name of Jesus....'" Towards the end the saint wrote, "The Son, Wisdom and Word Incarnate gave him the gift of sharing in the tormented love [crucified love, in Scudder, *Saint Catherine of Siena*] with which he himself had accepted his painful death." Catherine of Siena, *Letters*, trans. Noffke, 1:88. See also Catherine of Siena, *Epistolario*, ed. Duprè, no. 31, pp. 129, 131.

70

Alfredo Troiano

Fanti, Mario, ed. "La Confraternita di S. Maria della Morte e la Conforteria dei condannati in Bologna nei secoli XIV e XV." In Fanti, *Confraternite e città a Bologna nel medioevo e nell'età moderna*, 120–74. Rome: Herder Editrice, 2001.

Finkenstaedt, Thomas. "Galgenliteratur: Zur Auffassung des Todes im England des 16. und 17. Jahrhunderts." *Deutsche Vierteljahreschrift für Literaturwissenschaft und Geistesgeschichte* 34, no. 4 (1960): 527–53.

Fumagalli Beonio Brocchieri, Mariateresa. *Cristiani in armi: Da Sant'Agostino a papa Wojtyla*. Roma-Bari: Laterza, 2006.

Galletti, Anna Imelde. "'Uno capo nelle mani mie': Niccolò di Toldo." In *Atti del simposio internazionale cateriniano-bernardiniano* (Siena 17–20 aprile 1980), edited by Domenico Maffei and Paolo Nardi, 121–27. Siena: Accademia Senese degli Intronati 1982.

Gundersheimer, Werner L. "Crime and Punishment in Ferrara, 1440–1500." In *Violence and Civil Disorder in Italian Cities, 1200–1500*, edited by Lauro Martines, 104–28. Berkeley: University of California Press, 1972

Le loro prigioni: Scritture dal carcere. Atti del Convegno internazionale, Verona, 25–28 maggio 2005, edited by Anna Maria Babbi and T. Zanon. Verona: Fiorini, 2007.

Luisi, Francesco, ed. *Laudario giustinianeo*. Venezia: Edizioni Fondazione Levi, 1983.

Mazzi, Maria Serena. *"Gente a cui si fa notte innanzi sera": Esecuzioni capitali e potere nella Ferrara estens*. Roma: Viella, 2003.

Meneghetti, M. L. "Scrivere in carcere nel Medioevo." In *Studi di filologia e letteratura italiana in onore di Maria Picchio Simonelli*, edited by Pietro Frassica, 201–48. Alessandria: Edizioni dell'Orso, 1992.

Nagy, Piroska. *Le don des larmes au Moyen Age: Un instrument spirituel en quête d'institution (V–XIII siècle)*. Paris: Albin Michel, 2000.

Nobile, Bernardo. "Il libro della vita beata attribuito a Cristoforo da Bologna." *Memorie dell'Istituto veneto di Scienze, lettere ed arti* 43/2 (1991): 1–149.

O'Connor, Mary Catherine. *The Art of Dying Well: The Development of the Ars Moriendi*. New York: Columbia University Press, 1942.

Piccolomini, P. "Ultimi versi di Iacopo da Diacceto." *Giornale storico della letteratura italiana* 39 (1902): 327–34.

Prosperi, Adriano. *Dare l'anima: Storia di un infanticidio*. Torino: Einaudi, 2005.

———. "Mediatori di emozioni: La compagnia ferrarese di giustizia e l'uso delle immagini." In *L'impresa di Alfonso II: Saggi e documenti sulla produzione artistica a Ferrara nel secondo Cinquecento*, edited by Jadranka Bentini and Luigi Spezzaferro, 279–92. Bologna: Nuova Alfa Editoriale, 1987.

———. "Il sangue e l'anima: Ricerche sulle compagnie di giustizia." *Quaderni storici* 51, 17/3 (Dec. 1982): 959–99.

———, ed. "Il condannato a morte: Santo o criminale?" In *America e Apocalisse e altri saggi*, 219–27. Pisa-Roma: Istituti editoriali e poligrafici internazionali, 1999.

Ravagli, Federico, ed. *Rime edite ed inedite di Gio: Marco Pio di Savoia*. Carpi, 1909.

Rossi, Giorgio. *Andrea da Vigliarana e le sue rime*. Castrocaro: Tip. editrice A. Barboni, 1912.

Scaramella, P. "L'Italia dei Trionfi e dei Contrasti." In *Humana fragilitas: I temi della morte in Europa tra Duecento e Settecento*, edited by A. Tenenti. Clusone: Ferrari Grafiche, 2000.

Schmitt, Jean-Claude. "Il suicidio nel medioevo." *Ricerche di storia sociale e religiosa* 4 (1975): 339–71.

Scudder, Vida D., ed. *Saint Catherine of Siena as Seen in Her Letters*. London: J. M. Dent and Sons; New York: E. P. Dutton, 1927.

Tenenti, Alberto. *Il senso della morte e l'amore della vita nel Rinascimento (Francia e Italia)*.

Torino: G. Einaudi, 1957.

———. *La vita e la morte attraverso l'arte del XV secolo*. Napoli: Edizioni scientifiche italiane, 1996.

Traversari, Ambrogio. *Epistolario*. Edited by Lorenzo Mehus. Florentiae: Ex Typographio Caesareo, 1759.

———. *Hodoeporicon*. Edited by Vittorio Tamburini. Firenze: Le Monnier, 1985.

Troiano, Alfredo. "Un laudario per condannati a morte: Il ms. 1069 della Yale Beinecke Library di Yale." *Studi e Problemi di Critica testuale* 72 (2006): 31–70.

Varanini, Giorgio, Luigi Banfi, Anna Ceruti Burgio, and Giulio Cattin. *Laude cortonesi dal secolo XIII al XV*. 5 vols. Firenze: L. S. Olschki, 1981–85.

Vigo, Piero. *Le danze macabre in Italia*. Bologna: Arnaldo Forni Editore, 1978.

Zama, Piero. *I Manfredi*. Faenza: Fratelli Lega, 1954. Reprinted with bibliographical updating by A. Montevecchi. Faenza: Mobydick, 1998.

Poems of Andrea Viarani

Se 'l cieco traditor mondo fallace[53]

I   If the blind, false, and treasonous world,   1
      full of injustice, betrayal, and deception
      has held you many years
      far from your Maker and the Supreme Good,

II   Shows now both the shadowy and the fleeting nature   5
      of hoping for vain pleasures, which
      that foolish desire inclines towards
      never thinking of its true salvation:

III   Now that heaven has given you much grace   9
      and you are brought back to the point,
      Andrea, that God has made you
      repentant of the wrong committed.

IV   Lift your mind to God, move your hard heart   13
      and do not be so obstinate with him
      but with devout tears,
      repentant of having erred, ask for forgiveness.

V   Ah! Don't wish to abandon your soul,   17
      being diffident of eternal grace,
      for it never is tired of gathering
      he who, repentant, so asks.

VI   But now, as you put on that blessed band   21
      of the true Cross, upon which God
      suffered death when he descended
      and took flesh to ransom you.

VII   This is enough, more than in a thousand cards   25
      for you to firmly believe that you can save yourself,

---

[53] BUB mss. 157, fol. 208v c–d. Meter: sirvente with the pattern ABBC CDDE EFFG.

it is up to you alone if you want it,
your life and death depends on you.

VIII See that God has opened the doors   29
of paradise for you, those that Adam's
wickedness had closed with
the transgression of the forbidden apple.

IX Why don't you, poor man, consider how   33
after a thousand thousands of grave offenses,
he has his arms spread
on the hard wood waiting still more?

X Be absolutely certain that an hour   37
of bitter tears is enough for your salvation,
if you are as contrite
as accords your serious failing.

XI For this the Lord God chose to die,   41
so to be able to then wash away
the stain of sin with his blood
from whoever with a contrite heart comes back

XII To contemplate the true light above,   45
which lasts in eternity without end
and heeds nothing else
and disdains the world and its vain delights.

XIII These are the high and perfect thoughts,   49
all other hopes are brief and vain;
this is that smooth path
upon which no one who takes it falls.

XIV This is that saving medicine   53
that can heal your weakness
and all your wickedness purge
and make your soul more beautiful than ever.

XV   The medicine that I speak of is that   57
        of tears, which saved Mary Magdalene
        who then in full grace was accepted
        to the divine presence.

XVI   This is medicine that made perfect   61
        the good Peter, since he made his denial
        and then wept for his sin,
        that he earned the throne of our faith.

XVII   And the thief on the cross, who asked   65
        God for mercy, saying, "When you will
        be in your kingdom
        remember me, my Lord."

XVIII   In that moment he earned,   69
        for every old malicious sin and wrong,
        forgiveness and by heavenly grace
        he was that very day placed in paradise.

XIX   Who exists that thinks about these things   73
        should ever be separated from God, who
        never tires of offering his grace
        to whomever asks with a perfect heart?

XX   Oh incomprehensible God, Father and Lord!   77
        How immense and great is your mercy
        that stretches across everything
        across heaven, Earth, and even the abyss below.

XXI   Happy is the soul blind to everything   81
        outside the straight path, who hopes
        to find from your immense mercy
        forgiveness for every failing, however serious!

XXII   Provided that his contrite heart purify and cleanse   85
        his sin with devout tears,

and from his wretched state he rise
with the thought of not falling again.

XXIII   In so doing, God can only want   89
your salvation and highest good.
He never refuses who comes with
a humble and contrite heart.

XXIV   If the great ancient serpent,   93
eternal enemy of God, sometimes
detaches the proper thought from your mind
to make you, at your end, fall, wretched

XXV   Showing that God sometimes   97
cannot go against justice
and your great, wicked sin
he cannot cancel without great punishment.

XXVI   Sometimes he will come to remind you   101
of all the false vanities of the world
so to lead you to the bottom,
he will fight and pull you in a thousand ways.

XXVII   At that moment, look at that sign constantly,   105
in which the heavenly angels gaze at themselves,
where you find the fruit that
keeps whoever eats from ever dying.

XXVIII   Embrace and hold very close   109
the tree that the highest God made flower
with the blood of his true and perfect son
and repent your heart with your eyes and your voice.

XXIX   Lying prostrate at the feet of the blessed cross,   113
contemplate your Maker, nailed and dying
without sin, unjustly,
but willingly for your salvation.

XXX   Contemplate the five mortal wounds   117
          and his precious body pierced,
          mocked and bloodied
          from the thousand thorns of that cruel crown.

XXXI   From his head to his feet you will see   121
          his pure, immaculate blood,
          and not a single time did he
          ever sin nor could he.

XXXII   Then you will understand how singular   125
          and boundless was that divine love,
          and you will pray with all your heart
          that he does his blessed will for you.

XXXIII   Because no one else but he knows   129
          the true path for your salvation,
          whichever it may be, you will say,
          "Let your will be done."

XXXIV   For each wrong committed ask forgiveness: 133
          in you my life, in you my death
          relies, amen.
          Do with me, Lord God, what you will,

XXXV   as you are my good and eternal peace.   137

Regina eterna, se i mei prieghi mai[54]

Eternal Queen, if ever my prayers 1
were accepted by your divine presence,
as you have shown me many times
with sympathetic affection, that I have poorly known,

Now that at the last point in my wrongful life 5
I am reduced for my grave flaw
assist me, Mother, I who am waiting for your help,
and even late, still early you will be.

Hold out to me that loving hand, 9
lift me out of the mud and pull me towards you,
well you are able, because you are full of grace.

The spirit repentant of his error 12
whispers and asks forgiveness, do not make it in vain:
assist it and satisfy it with your clemency.

---

[54] BUB ms. 157, fol. 203v c–d. Meter: sonnet with the rhyme pattern ABBA ABBA CDE DCE.

Eterno Padre, Idio sommo Signore[55]

Eternal Father, God the highest Lord   1
if your love was so strong
that, so as to purge the first father Adam
from the grave fault of the wrong committed,

You became flesh, being the Creator,   5
and voluntarily accepted,
pure, innocent, and flawless angel,
a bitter death, great pain and suffering:

Now would you want, Lord, that the blood   9
spilt be futile for me?
And your five wounds
not manage to purge my wickedness?

Show, sweet Jesus, your goodness,   13
do not go against your custom and be chary with me
have your blood clean my sins.

---

[55] BUB ms. 157, fol. 203vc. Meter: sonnet with the rhyme pattern ABBA ABBA CDE DCE (assonance: 11–14 *piaghe* : *lave*).

Chapter 4

In Your Face
Paintings for the Condemned in Renaissance Italy

Massimo Ferretti

In recent years art historians have shown increasing interest in those paintings known as *tavolette* that were used to console convicts condemned to death and to divert their eyes as much as possible from onlookers and from the ritualized spectacles of execution.[1] What happened to these images? Where have they ended up and what light might they shed on comforting practices? Tools refined in museology for stylistic analysis makes it possible to determine the date and provenance of a group of panel paintings currently in held in European galleries. It can be demonstrated that these panels are from Bologna, and that they were likely used there for the comforting of prisoners from the middle of the fourteenth century. Certainly images from the second half of the fifteenth century include depictions of brothers holding these *tavolette*.[2] This study will aim to reach back before the fifteenth century to identify some of the earliest forms and to see how this variety of early forms shaped the later typology and functions of the *tavolette*.

This is the history of art as the history of heritage. One cannot always be

---

An expanded Italian version of this essay is published in Prosperi, *Misericordie*, 85–151.

[1] Samuel Y. Edgerton ("Maniera and the Mannaia": "A little-known 'purpose of art'": and *Pictures and Punishment*) initiated the discussion, which now boasts an impressive bibliography, the most recent of which includes Feinberg, "Imagination All Compact"; and essays by Di Lorenzo ("La Croce astile di Bernardo Daddi") and Sebregondi ("Riti, rituali e spazi") in *La Croce di Bernardo Daddi* Attention to this now common theme also emerges in Sarpi, "Il Libro dei Giustiziati," and other essays by L. Sebregondi and L. Graziani Secchieri in Mazzei Traina, *L'Oratorio dell'Annunciata*.

[2] The work by Fanti, "La Confraternita di S. Maria della Morte," is fundamental for the earlier phase while another important paper by Terpstra, "Piety and Punishment," focuses on the cinquecento phase. Both Martucci, "La 'salvifica morte,'" and Angelozzi, *Le confraternite laicali,* offer documents pertaining to the modern age. Prosperi, "Il sangue e l'anima," and "Esecuzioni capitali," are important both for references to the Bolognese situation and for studies of the companies of justice generally.

sure that works of art can overcome a function other than their original one. It is certainly difficult for them to survive a function as physically intense as accompanying condemned men and women to the gallows. There is no way of knowing how many *tavolette* were simply scattered or, for that matter, how many may have been burned in a kind of ritual elimination that can be found up until a century ago with all sacred images that were not ascribed any artistic or historical prestige. An appreciation for the uncommon might have secured the survival of some *tavolette* past the eighteenth century. Certainly the inscription applied at that time to one of the *tavolette* discussed below shows that there was a growing awareness of local artistic patrimony in Bologna, and a determination to preserve the "primitives" of local art. As attention to the rebirth of painting at the end of the Middle Ages grew, there also emerged a form of pride for the protection and restoration of older sacred images.

It is not the aim here to simply document that many tablets were painted in Bologna for condemned persons, but instead to explore their organization, iconography, and possible use, and the conditions that might have influenced their survival before being scattered across Europe in the great dispersals of the nineteenth century. Like the *Comforters' Manual* translated in this volume, the paintings used to console the condemned are a little like archaeological relics, and having both directly in front of us can shed light on meanings and developments in the activity of the *conforteria* itself. This study will not be systematic. It will first consider a set of three illustrations from the sixteenth century that act as later documentary evidence of what the *tavolette* looked like and how they were used. It will then turn to examine ten fourteenth-century panels, looking at their form, iconography, and physical state in order to understand both how they might have been used and how they managed to survive.

A famous drawing by Annibale Carracci (fig. 2) showing a Capuchin friar, face uncovered and holding a *tavoletta* at the foot of a scaffold, represents a turning point in the history of *conforterie*, marked by the stronger presence of clergymen. In 1583, Filippo II prohibited laypersons from entering the Neapolitan *conforteria*.[3] In Bologna three years later, Cardinal Legate Gaetani attempted to restrict the comforting of the condemned to Capuchins, although the intense

---

[3] Prosperi, "Il sangue e l'anima," 969. For further developments on the process of clericalism at the Neapolitan confraternity, see Romeo, *Aspettando il boia*, 126, 150, 154.

protests of the lay brothers of S. Maria della Morte forced a reversal.[4] By the seventeenth and eighteenth centuries there were numerous clergymen even in the Bolognese confraternity, yet this particular drawing seems at odds with the customs of Carracci's Bologna. One may assume that he completed it in Rome after moving there; he seems to have been surprised at the number of cases of capital punishment in Rome when he arrived for the first time in 1594.[5]

Unless this is a case of "secretive justice," typically reserved for clergymen and individuals of higher rank, the wall separating those figures glancing over it from the place of justice does not correspond to what is known about execution rituals. Instead, Annibale Carracci stages his drawing in such a way that it closely reflects examples found in some contemporary illustrated catechisms (like Giovan Battista Eliano's *Dottrina Cristiana* of 1587), where onlookers witness the punishments of murderers and thieves from beyond a wall or grate.[6]

Carracci's drawing shows the moment of climax, when the image held by the comforter is the only thing the prisoner sees. The urban scene disappears. Yet this very urban scene was very important to the rituals of execution and it figures in early confraternal manuscript illustrations. The illuminated first folio of the Pierpont Morgan Library manuscript reconstructs the urban setting of execution through the figurative topos of two buildings enclosed within an arch (fig. 3), and the public loggia called the *ringhiera* from which the prisoner's sentence was read. Any change in the place of execution—either outside the city or at its center—was significant. Florence usually executed its condemned outside the city, but authorities sometimes moved this to the windows of the Bargello prison (fig. 4) if they feared tumultuous crowds who might either assault or free the prisoner on his transit down the via dei Malcontenti to the scaffold.[7] Growing up in Bologna, Annibale Carracci would have witnessed condemned criminals hanged from the large windows of the Podestà's Palace on Piazza Maggiore, and also at the Mercato del Monte, a low hillside market square just inside the walls at the north end of the city.[8]

The latter site is seen in a drawing (fig. 5) by Giulio Morina completed circa 1594. The physical city of bricks and stone is the setting for a long procession that has reached the place of execution. Both images represent the same story, and are part of two series devoted to the life of Caterina di Vigri,

[4] Black, *Italian Confraternities in the Sixteenth Century,* 218. See also the article by Terpstra in this volume.
[5] Paglia, *La morte confortata,* graph 1 in app. 2, under the years 1592 (95 hangings), 1593, and 1594 (64 hangings).
[6] Palumbo, *"Speculum Peccatorum,"* 85.
[7] Martines, *April Blood,* 140–49; Connell and Constable, *Sacrilege and Redemption.*
[8] Masini, *Bologna perlustrata,* 435.

the Ferrarese nun who became abbess of Bologna's Corpus Domini convent, died in 1463, and later became a saint. The bizarre headgear worn by the condemned person in a later painted version is more clearly identified as a bishop's miter in the drawing: paper miters like this were sometimes imposed to mock condemned clergymen, or those accused of sodomy or heresy and burned at the stake.[9] In both versions, a cross fashioned out of tree branches, which was the insignia of the Bolognese *conforteria* of S. Maria della Morte, is visible on the cloak of the comforters.[10] More importantly, the large space in the background where the gallows are set up is a space that is neither built up nor outside the city walls; it is in fact the small hill that anybody from Bologna would have recognized as the large and open Mercato del Monte.[11] Bologna's characteristic arcades are also visible in the pictorial version, an even more telling and recognizable architectural signature than particular structures like the S. Benedetto bell tower on the left. With this topography, Morina sets the incident into the urban fabric of Bologna.

This emphasis on urban place also appears on the illuminated title folio of the 1562 statutes of the Confraternity of S. Maria della Morte (fig. 6), the large confraternity of which Bologna's *conforteria* formed a part.[12] The image has lay brothers sheltering under the outstretched cloak of the Madonna della Misericordia while in the background a procession wends its way down a hill and into a city bristling with towers, including Bologna's tall Asinelli and leaning Garisenda. Two *tavolette* are in the hands of the brothers, while another lies on the ground. The *tavolette* represent one defining activity of the Morte, while the procession represents another—its custodianship of the shrine of the Madonna di San Luca, located on a hill immediately south of the city. The confraternity accompanied the Marian image, believed to have been painted by St. Luke, as she was carried into the city from the hill. Both activities revolve around defining visual images that in fact link them. Liturgical processions commonly carried fabric banners called *gonfalone* that were painted on both sides. These provide an obvious model for the wood panel *tavolette*, also painted on both sides. The *gonfalone* flourished at the same time as the *tavolette,* and the two served equally as insignia of the confraternity. One is tempted to think that the model of the *gonfalone* contributed to the form of the *tavolette* and that

---

[9] For more on the donkey and miter as sign of mockery, see Ortalli, "…pingatur in Palatio," 124–25.

[10] Statuti della Compagnia dell'Ospedale della Morte, chap. 12, BCB ms. Fondo Ospedali 42.

[11] Alidosi, *Istruttione delle cose notabili,* 9 (the opening of the piazza for the livestock market, today's Piazza VIII agosto, dates back to 1219).

[12] For a description of the codex (cited in note 10), see Fanti, "Il 'Fondo Ospedali,'" 25–26.

both were the visual sign or message of the *conforteria*.[13] On this latter point, it should be remembered that the IHS monogram that St. Bernardino of Siena promoted as an antifactional point of identification and communication had been devised in Bologna.[14]

The *tavolette* in the 1562 illumination signify not only the company's activity but also its antiquity. Each one is divided into six scenes (possibly the Passion or the martyrdom of a saint), which seem to be repeated. The sixteenth-century illuminator has given them an archaic and even Byzantine aspect, not by a different pictorial style, but by using this composite outline in an unmistakably Greek manner. The archaic aspect of these *tavolette* aims not only to evoke the distant origins of the Company of Death but also demonstrates an awareness of the past that could have encouraged the conservation of the antique tablets—by then as much as two hundred years old—that the company owned.

Knowing this, it is perhaps no coincidence that the first Bolognese scholar to prepare a chronological listing of local artists was Ovidio Montalbini (1601–72), a professor in the university and custodian of its science museum, and a very active master of the *conforteria* in the mid-seventeenth century. While the first name in his list, that of Renghiero, came from a famous local chronicle by Gherardo Ghirardacci, Montalbini was able to associate those of other fourteenth-century painters with concrete memories of the works of art themselves.[15] The Morte confraternity, like many others, had become aristocratic and it was expected that educated and cultured noble members like Montalbini would more conscientiously assume a curatorial care for the antique and artistic originals found in its possession.[16]

The rectangular form of the *tavolette* depicted in the 1562 illumination is found across Italy, but was not the only shape used by comforters. Many late-sixteenth and early-seventeenth *tavolette* were triangular triptychs with hinged panels that folded out from the center panel and cut off the prisoner's lateral vision. This seems to have been a later development, however, and all the *tavolette* that appear in fifteenth- and sixteenth-century Bolognese images are rectangular. As will be seen below, that may have secured their adaptive reuse and indeed their survival.

---

[13] Schmidt, "Gli stendardi processionali."

[14] For the success of and reactions to this, Arasse, "Iconographie et évolution spirituelle," 444–51; and Arasse, "Art, dévotion et société," 208–9.

[15] Bumaldo and Montalbani, *Minervalia Bonon,* 238–39. On Montalbini as a teacher of *conforteria,* see Angelozzi, *Le confraternite laicali,* 185, 204, 207, 211, 215.

[16] Previtali, *La fortuna dei primitivi,* 43–46.

·✿⊙✿·

None of these *tavolette* survive in Bologna, but galleries in Perugia, Zurich, Tours, Stuttgart, and Florence contain seven panels that can credibly be placed in the hands of Bolognese comforters in the fourteenth and fifteenth centuries. The Perugian and Zurich panels are the oldest and may predate the period when the Compagnia di S. Maria della Morte took on the work of comforting prisoners.[17] Perugia's *St. Mary Magdalene with Sts. Jacob, Margherita, Francis, Domenic, Petronio, and Christopher* (fig. 7) has an eighteenth-century inscription on its reverse side claiming that it was used to comfort the condemned when justice was served near the Church of S. Maria di Mezzarata outside of the gate of S. Mamolo.[18] The inscription claims that this was the case until 1250, but the tablet itself appears to have been painted at least seventy years after that date. Art historians have identified the artist as either Francesco da Rimini or alternatively the "Master of Verucchio," also from Rimini; it has recently been proposed that this is a single artist.[19] The nuances in style can be explained by the shift from the more softened breadth of mural paintings known to be of Francesco's hand, to the more structured manner of the Master of Verucchio that fixes the eye on isolated moments of reality. This technique was easier to represent on tablets than on paintings.

The panels were painted shortly before 1335. In February of that year, Dominican friar Venturino da Bergamo passed through Bologna at the head of a devotional movement dedicated to helping prisoners. Venturino's work led directly to the foundation of the confraternity of S. Maria della Morte, devoted primarily to "those who go towards justice," in July of the following year.[20] Yet

---

[17] The identification of the queen in the upper right part of the tablet of Perugia (others believe the figure is Elisabetta or Orsola, but this is dubious) and of the bishop on the lower part, both devoid of marks, can only be conjectured; in the former case, the conjecture is based on the destination of the condemned; in the latter, on the Bolognese origin.

[18] "This *tavoletta* was used for the condemned to death when that justice was executed outside of the doors of Porta di S. Mamolo, near the church of S. Maria di Mezza Ratta [del] Monte on the grass near the Colina until 1250. // It was presented to Dott.re R. Carlantonio di Giov. Ant. Machiavelli by the PP. dell'Osservanza on Tuesday 2 March 1723, who had saved it in their Convent after it was given to them by a certain Donna de Baretti [*lapsus calami* for Barelli?], who rented a room upstairs with use of the small Oratory below S. M.a de Denti across from the above-mentioned church of Mezza Ratta, and that she had taken off the wall where it hung with others which, being very old, were already ruined."

[19] Boskovits, "Per la storia," 166–68.

[20] The quotation comes from Venturino's *Legenda*; Gennaro, "Venturino da Bergamo," 383n27, where similar initiatives by the flagellants of 1260, as then by the Bianchi in 1399, are recalled.

the inscription on the Perugian tablet refers to an even older confraternity dedicated to S. Maria della Mezzaratta, later known as the Buon Gesù, which in 1338 had its residence in the eponymous church.[21]

Not all art historians have relied on this inscription. Daniele Benati, for example, notes that "the precious character [of the two paintings] actually suggests a more learned and refined audience than victims who were to be moved *in extremis* to reformation."[22] Other historians and art historians do not trust Carlo Antonio Machiavelli, who received the tablet as a gift. A canon, lawyer, comforter, and historian of the *conforteria* of S. Maria della Morte, Machiavelli tampered with manuscripts of the *conforteria* in order to cast one of his own ancestors as the author of the manual.[23] In this case, it could equally be that Machiavelli was simply the first to be deceived by false information on the ancient origin of the tablet. Adding or omitting inscriptions on pictorial "monuments" recalls a time when the signatures of famous painters like Franco or Vitale da Bologna were routinely added to older Bolognese paintings. This was not "against the truth, but on behalf of the truth," as one authority was known to say.[24] In such cases, it was not the prestige of noble and illustrious families that was being promoted, but that of the city itself.

Yet there is no evidence that executions occurred in the area of Mezzaratta in the fourteenth century.[25] The misidentification may come from Dante's *Inferno*, where Venedico Caccianemici asks, "Ma che ti mena a sì pungenti salse?" (*Inferno* 18.51). The commentator Benvenuto da Imola identified the "salse" as the "ancient place of justice" on the slopes immediately outside the city wall and claimed that locals used it in their insult—hence, "your father was hanged at the Salsas."[26] The association between this area and an early *conforteria* of S. Maria della Mezzaratta appeared in print by 1766, in a new edition of the art historical guide written one century before by Carlo Cesare Malvasia.[27] The oratory is located in Malvasia's descriptive art historical grid and, although he himself had

---

[21] On this confraternity, see Terpstra, *Lay Confraternities*, 9, 19. In the cinquecento, various artists were part of this confraternity; Faietti, "Amico's friends," 51–69.

[22] Benati, "Maestro di Verucchio."

[23] Tumidei, *Italies*, 57. For more on the unreliability of the Machiavelli brothers, see Fanti, "S. Maria della Morte," 126–28; and Prosperi, *Dare l'anima*, 324.

[24] Bizzocchi, *Genealogie impossibili*, 210.

[25] Tumidei, *Italies*, 56.

[26] Benvenutus de Imola, *Comentum*, 11.

[27] Masini, *Bologna perlustrata*, 52. Such a reputation might have pointed to an earlier phase that was interrupted by the arrival of the comforting brothers of the Morte; Adriano Prosperi reminds me that even in Naples, before the foundation of the *conforteria* of the Bianchi, corpses were thrown into a ditch outside of the city.

never made the association, plaques found on the site provided the evidence.[28] Leaving aside the question of whether this constitutes sufficient proof, it shows that there developed a conscious tradition, connected to that particular part of the city outside the walls, that in a way reminiscent of Vasari identified the "first dawning" of a new art. The inscription on the back of the Perugian tablet, as an assertion of patrimonial transmission, is part of this tradition.

Was the Perugian painting a comforter's *tavoletta*? The Zurich companion tablet of *The Crucifixion*, identical in format, structure, and ornament, provides clearer evidence (fig. 8). In it, the Virgin Mary extends her arms towards the observer in a rather uncommon gesture that some scholars associate with comfort for the condemned.[29] While the Magdalen's gesture is one of grief, the Madonna appears instead to be offering mercy or heavenly welcome. The iconography of the Perugian tablet (fig. 7) draws on the immense popularity of the Magdalen in late medieval piety, and in fact she is one of the first examples suggested to the comforter in the early Bolognese manual. The selection of saints flanking her provides both examples of exemplary martyrs, and also a deeply local connection. Bologna's patron saint, the martyred bishop Petronio, identifies this as a Bolognese tablet, reinforced by others such as St. Dominic, who was buried in Bologna, and St. Francis, who had preached there. Both were prominent in the canon of the city's protectors, and their presence on the tablet underscores the fact that the punitive ritual of execution concerns not just an individual but an entire city.

The material condition of the tablets is telling. There is no trace of old hinges, which could join them as a diptych intended for private devotion. Moreover, while the decorations on the reverse side are of the same taste and hand, they do not match up sufficiently to allow the two halves to be seen as a single object. While contemporary Tuscan altarpieces featured illusionary geometrical structure or false marble, the incomplete symmetry of these two Bolognese tablets more closely resembled two-sided Byzantine icons.[30]

---

[28] Malvasia, Le pitture di Bologna, 376 (in the first edition [1686], Malvasia did not yet register the site of Mezzaratta, which only entered starting from the third edition of 1732).

[29] Freuler, *Manifestatori*, 126. Andrea di Lorenzo ("La Croce astile di Bernardo Daddi," 23–24) also thinks they were meant to comfort those condemned to death.

[30] The decorations on the reverse side are so naturalistic that, at first sight, it does not seem easy to imagine them before the Camera del Cervo in Avignon (1343). The difficulty can perhaps also be explained through the lack of a specific repertoire (it has only recently been shown by Schmidt in "Portable Polytychs with Narrative Scenes," 394–425; and *Painted Piety*, 44–58). The paintings "ad azzurrite" on a red base in the Perugian tablet seem to contrast with the decorations of Tuscan use. Later, at the time of Simone di Filippo, one encounters a Bolognese tablet decorated with geometric intagliatura on the reverse side; Markova, "The 'Annunciation,'" fig. 2.

Traces of a joint can be identified halfway through the lower side of the Perugia *Magdalen* tablet,[31] and something similar is missing from the Zurich *Crucifixion*. Both tablets seem modified to be carried in the hands. Their dimensions (44.5 x 31 cm) are greater than later *tavolette* that have survived in Rome, Ravenna, and Ascoli. Yet this greater size corresponds to what is seen in the 1562 image noted above (fig. 6), and these tablets are also subdivided in the same Byzantine way. One of the earliest Bolognese depictions, from a fifteenth-century copy of the *Comforters' Manual*, shows a comforter holding a *tavoletta* with both hands. It is rather large and lacks a handle, yet the brother directs the eyes of the convicted prisoner towards it (fig. 9).[32] The two vertical edges of the Perugia tablet, painted in the same vermilion as the reverse side, are the parts that are the most worn, suggesting that comforters initially held it in two hands by the sides, rather than by the handle that was added later.

The two tablets are richly lacquered and well conserved, suggesting that they were not taken regularly in processions or kissed frequently in the way that left marks on so many other paintings. These material clues point to the conclusion that while these tablets were almost certainly used from the beginning in the practice of comforting the condemned, they were most likely used in chapels and prison cells and were not brought along in the procession to the scaffold. In other words, the original *tavolette* were not always small devotional objects that were held with a handle, but could be larger images that were used to teach and comfort and that also served as identifying insignia for the *conforteria*.

While the tablets by Francesco da Rimini in Perugia and Zurich are in excellent condition, two other paired paintings completed a few decades later and now at the Musée des Beaux-Arts of Tours are in ruinous shape. In one, two condemned persons, both in sackcloth and with their hands tied behind their backs, are kneeling in front of a *mandorla* with the Madonna and Child (fig. 10). In the other, depictions of the martyrdoms of St. Catherine of Alexandria and St. John the Baptist flank the crucifix in a single pictorial field (fig. 11).[33]

---

[31] While I have to refer to the Italian edition for a description of the material state of the Perugia tablet, I would like to thank Tiziana Biganti, director of the National Gallery of Umbria, and Paola Passalacqua, restorer, for permission to further my study.

[32] Fanti, "S. Maria della Morte."

[33] Tumidei (*Italies*), well informed on their use, limits himself to judging them as Bolognese works of art from 1360. Rave (*Frühe italienische Tafelmalerei,* 166) and Lorenzo ("La Croce astile di Bernardo Daddi,"

Their damaged condition points to intense use over a long period, an evaluation made by Michel Laclotte when he first made these recently restored paintings known to the public in 1964. Laclotte noted that the small diptych had been ruined with time and that a precise analysis was not yet possible.[34] Without attributing them to any particular painter, Laclotte likened them to a pair of works by an artist Roberto Longhi had identified as the Bolognese painter Dalmasio degli Scanabecchi, active 1350 to 1370. Today, it is believed that this painter started to work at a later date. Some prefer to speak of Pseudo-Dalmasio, while others believe the identification is not definitively set and so keep the name in quotation marks.[35] The poor condition of the two tablets makes it difficult to attribute them to any one painter. Regardless of his name, "Dalmasio"'s manner of constructing images in compact, living, and luminous chromatic masses and enclosed in a graphic frame, remains characteristic of this painter from Bologna. He was influenced by Florentine forms, but does not look entirely Tuscan. And although it may be purely coincidental, the relation between the figures and the *mandorla* brings to mind the Berlin *Madonna della cintola* by Maso di Banco, the only Florentine "Dalmasio" preferred over Giotto.

One may be tempted to identify "Dalmasio" in the small traces of painting that are still decipherable: for example, in the angel on the left side who has the same lively eyes that the Bolognese painter, together with a few others, had discovered directly in Giotto.[36] The faces of the other angels are too worn and interpolated to give any indication if that manner of profiling is identical to the ones in older Bolognese paintings of the trecento. In its details, the stylistic development of "Dalmasio" allows us to date the two tablets of Tours to around the second half of the fourth decade of the fourteenth century. The surface evidence of their state of deterioration supports a dating of around 1336, the year that the Compagnia di S. Maria della Morte began its practice of *conforteria* in Bologna. Their comforting function becomes clear through the presence of the two bound and condemned persons and in the gesture of mediation and promise—the open hand turned upwards—that the Madonna and Child offer.[37]

22–23) subsequently made reference to this arrangement, while Volpe (*Mezzaratta,* 67) moves the date ahead to the fifth decade and attempts to attribute the work to "Jacobus."

[34] Laclotte, "Musée de Tour: La donation Octave Linet, I: Peintures italiennes," 186.

[35] For a summary, see Benati, "Tra Giotto e il mondo gotico," 66–67.

[36] Strehlke, *Italian Paintings,* 108. For an example of the way in which "Dalmasio" animates gazes, see Longhi, *Lavori in Valpadana,* fig. 46.

[37] Vertova, "La mano teas," 217; and Ferretti, "Una traccia di Giotto a Bologna," 47n25 (but we must not forget the tomb of Manfredo Pio in the Sagra di Carpi, sculpted in 1351 by the Bolognese Sibellino da Capraria).

One tablet offers a message of hope, and the other offers images of martyrdom. Did they form a diptych that the comforter opened like a book under the eyes of a condemned man? Since there is no trace of any hinge, it is very unlikely. Yet their small size (34 x 34 cm), substantial physical symmetry, and the addition of a ledge to the bottom side of both suggest that they were created by slicing a single work in half, and that in their original state, they were two sides of a single *tavoletta* that was held upright by a handle.

This hypothesis is supported by a tablet (45.5 x 33.7 cm), painted on both sides, that has been housed at the Staatsgalerie of Stuttgart since 1971.[38] Its two sides bear remarkable similarity to the two Tours panels, and B. Rave has traced the work to Bologna and to a comforting function. On the upper half of one side of this tablet is found the Madonna with her hand outstretched to offer grace. Two bound prisoners kneel on either side of her, one supported by St. Anthony Abbot and the other by St. James; both were saints who miraculously lifted those who were already at the gallows in order to prevent their deaths (fig. 12). The standing Child blesses them. Below this image are two others, one of the beheading of John the Baptist and the other of Catherine of Alexandria. The reverse side of the tablet is divided into four quadrants with distinct images of suffering.[39] The upper half gives two moments of the Passion, while the lower shows the martyrdoms of Sts. Lorenzo and Biagio (Blaise) (fig. 13).[40] The tablet is adapted so that it can be hanged, likely a way of preserving it after it was no longer in use. Another compelling sign of its original function is the heavily

[38] Rave, *Frühe italienische Tafelmalerei,* 180–88.

[39] The *Martirio di san Biagio* of the "Leggendario angioino" reproduced in *Bibliotheca Sanctorum* (3:162) is installed in a way that is similar to the Stuttgart tablet. Cf. Conti, *La miniatura Bolognese,* 85. See Török, "Problems of the Hungarian Angevin Legendary," for more on the codex, which today is divided in various sites, but was illuminated at the Hungarian court presumably in the fourth decade of the trecento, in part by illuminators of Bolognese origin.

[40] St. Lawrence was one of the saints who, in the Bolognese *Comforters' Manual,* was held up to those who lamented their death as young men. Regarding St. Biagio, the tool held by one of the two figures leaves no doubt that he was the bishop saint represented and not either Ippolito or Sisto; Rave, *Frühe italienische Tafelmalerei,* 181. A *Martirio di san Biagio* appears among the miniatures of the *Martirologio* of the Battuti Neri Confraternity of Ferrara, today housed at the Fondazione Cini (fol. 17v), and is described as "book, written and illustrated precisely for this purpose, that must have been used for the meditation of the brothers, but that was intended above all for the last hour of the condemned"; Toesca, *Miniature italiane,* 44, 51, fig. 75. The Ferrarese hypothesis has been progressively reinforced, though redated to the last decade of the trecento. For more on the use of illustrated books from the comforters of Ferrara, see Prosperi, "Mediatori di emozioni," 286.

worn surface and the completely repainted faces of the Madonna and Child. The repainting cannot be explained simply by the split that runs through the tablet at that point, but is more likely the result of believers intensely kissing the image, something frequently encountered in this genre of devotional paintings that are used as liturgical objects. The persistence of the icon in fourteenth century Bologna may also hold a clue.[41]

Who painted this tablet and when? The museum catalogue credits Simone dei Crocefissi in approximately 1380, but it is an unconvincing attribution. No other fourteenth-century artist is as recognizable as Simone, and here he is unrecognizable. His punch marks are not present and only an echo of his characteristic physionomic forms appears. The attribution may simply reflect his overwhelming artistic influence in Bologna at the time. Simone's roughness, as represented in the *Flagellation of Christ*, remains his best expressive trait, but here softens into something more banal. An alternative attribution to a follower of Lippo di Dalmasio would put the tablet in a stylistic line that is distinct from the late Simone, a line that begins to emerge only from the beginning of the nineties with the return of Lippo from a long sojourn in Pistoia.[42] Yet this is far too late and too indirect. The key to the style is instead the tidy and sweet manner of circumscribing the profiles, a manner that was already found in the illuminators of the 1360s and that in painting is associated with Cristoforo di Jacopo. If the tablet is indeed credited to Cristoforo, it must be dated around the time of *St. Christopher* of Montemaggiore (1395), a signed work that was his most artistically advanced, even if it was long before he died in 1410. But even if this suggestion were abandoned, it would not change the dating of the Stuttgart *tavoletta* to the final years of the fourteenth century.

Only a few years earlier, Simone di Filippo had painted two small tablets currently held in Florence by the Longhi Foundation, together with a third now-lost image of the *Baptist Taken to Jail*.[43] One depicts the Madonna and Child, flanked by Sts. Bartholomew and James who each intercede on behalf of a supplicant prisoner; Christ raises his hand in blessing (fig. 14). The other depicts St. Anthony Abbot witnessing the beheading of John the Baptist; he appears stiff and

[41] On the condemned's act of kissing the images, see Feinberg, "Imagination All Compact," 56. On the relation with liturgical peace, see Lorenzo, "La Croce astile di Bernardo Daddi," 17; and Sebregondi, "Riti, rituali e spazi," 33.

[42] Schmidt, "Recensione al catalogo di Stoccarda."

[43] Today, the whereabouts of this tablet are unknown. For this tablet and the others, see Moench, *La Fondazione*, 244–45.

placed there by chance in the manner of votive frescoes (fig. 15).[44] If this were a narrative series, there would have to be a fourth tablet, on the opposite side of the *Decollazione*. If one considers the rather reduced dimensions of these tablets (21 x 30.2 cm), the iconic presence of St. Anthony, and the presence and placement of the Madonna on the throne (she is here the central character but usually occupies the greater tablet of a polyptych), it is difficult to imagine how these tablets, alone or with others, might comprise the *predella* of an altarpiece. In general, each image of a *predella* corresponds to the life of a saint or comprises part of a continuous hagiographic narrative, but in this case the presence of St. Anthony would interrupt it. Yet his presence does not seem coincidental when one remembers that his legend had him supporting an unjustly condemned man on the gallows.

One can imagine these three small tablets as parts of a portable altarpiece or perhaps as simple steps to place on the altar table. It was probably part of the liturgical furnishing of the church of S. Giovanni Battista that S. Maria della Morte had built behind Bologna's Mercato del Monte in 1351, close to where the death sentences were carried out and where many condemned persons were buried.

Returning to Simone di Filippo's three paintings: to hypothesize that they were reassembled on the altar allows us to see that the *tavolette* used in comforting need not have been limited to a single use, and that other images could be employed in comforting. It may also be that these vertically oriented tablets (36–37.5 x 22 cm) were placed one on top of the other, flanking the side of the image of the saint, according to an old altar model. The altarpiece that Vitale da Bologna painted for the church of St. Anthony, which in one of the surviving scenes shows the saint holding the hanged man, was meant to be in a modern form and shining with gold.[45] Similar miraculous interventions are repeated with roughly thirty other saints.[46] It might be too much to see in this hagiographical narrative a recognition of the fallibility of human justice. Yet it would reflect another concern of every *conforteria*: to obtain the grace of prisoners, by exceptional means if necessary, but in a regular and stable way.[47]

---

[44] This saint also appears in the *Martirologio* of Ferrara; Toesca, *Miniature italiane,* 51, fol. 17v.

[45] Meiffret (*Saint Antoine,* 56n4) notes that the representation is extremely rare in northern Italy.

[46] De Gaifier, "Un thème hagiographique"; and Chartier, "Gli usi del miracolo," 147–48.

[47] I have extended beyond the case indicated in the title of Parisini, "Pratiche extragiudiziali."

❧✦❧

Did the paintings discussed here originate in Bologna? It is not a question of whether the paintings were by Bolognese artists (apart from the two tablets of Francesco da Rimini), but whether they were intended for this city. Recall how soon after Venturino da Bergamo's charismatic efforts for poor prisoners a confraternity dedicated to comforting the condemned was formed there— the earliest in Italy. As far as this genre is concerned, the artists Simone di Filippo and Cristoforo di Jacopo are present only in Bolognese documents. Yet it is above all a series of iconographic choices connected one to the other that reinforces the probability that these tablets were made for Bologna. It is important to consider an aspect not found in later *tavolette* or in other places: the representation of the condemned persons kneeling at the feet of those who intercede for them, the two pictured together like two at a time hanging from the scaffold. These convicts condemned to death are not represented as individuals, but as types. Yet portraying them in a lively manner contributes to the usefulness of the images when working with those prisoners who were in that ultimate and very emotional position. So these images must be considered in terms of the specific characters they represent.

These condemned persons occupy the position of donor-patron-petitioner, particularly from the thirteenth century. It is a particular individual, even if he did not show interest in having his own true portrait.[48] The representational field is much smaller than that of an altar or a votive fresco, and even this contributes to depicting the condemned on the same scale as their intercessors rather than as miniature counterparts. The generic condemned figures of Simone di Filippo and Cristoforo, who are certainly not artists of the caliber of Vitale, demonstrate an immediacy and a mood—expressionistic, irrational, and physically immediate— that was identified by Roberto Longhi more than seventy years ago as one of the primary stylistic features of trecento Bolognese painting.[49] Perhaps that manner of animating the abstract figures of condemned prisoners could have only come from Bologna, in an artistic environment where miniatures were expected to be visible examples, as though they were met in the street, of the cases encountered

---

[48] Besides Kocks, *Die Stifterdarstellung* (with the practical limits pointed out by Barrucand), the more recent ones are Schleif, "Hands That Appoint, Anoint an Ally"; and Jones, "'Visio divina'?"

[49] Despite the chronological adjustments, the opinion on the Bolognese trecentists of Longhi (*Lavori in Valpadana*) and of his student Arcangeli (*Pittura Bolognese*) remains one of the highest moments of Italian art criticism.

in the books of the jurists. In those types, one was supposed to recognize an individual destiny. Those prayerful condemned are best imagined by the means of expression characteristic of Bolognese painting of the fourteenth century.

Equally significant for this discussion, though circumscribed and later, is the comparison to Giotto's more ponderous stylistic organization, which Longhi used to distinguish Tuscan painting from that north of the Apennines. In this case, the comparison can be limited to the double-sided Crucifixion by the Florentine Bernardo Daddi, now in the Poldi Pezzoli Museum in Milan (fig. 16), which, together with those in Perugia, Zurich, and Tours, is among the oldest paintings intended for those condemned to death.[50] When the Florentine painter depicts the blood spilled by the martyrs, it may seem to prefigure the criminals' bitter end, but he does it with total control and gains energy from the calculated repetition of the theme. One need only consider how the clear Giottoesque blocks, in the kneeling saints, are made to rotate in a manner that clearly shows the repulsive effect of the beheadings. The presence of St. Peter Martyr and St. Thomas of Aquinas, together with St. Dominic himself, strongly suggests that Daddi's crucifixion was connected to the preaching of the Dominican friar Venturino da Bergamo. What contrasts even more sharply with the Bolognese paintings is the figure of the condemned person at the base of one side (fig. 16a). This figure is wearing the same clothes, but no longer has anything that is human. He is a soul in transit and now belongs to a reality different from the one in which the comforters operate. This taste for the macabre also points to origins in Dominican spirituality.[51] By contrast, in their depictions of condemned prisoners praying for deliverance, the trecento Bolognese painters better reflect the sensibility and new social experience that lies at the foundation of the companies of justice.

Works Cited

Archives

BCB   Biblioteca Comunale, Bologna

Printed Works

Alidosi, Giovanni Niccolò Pasquali. *Istruttione delle cose notabili della città di Bologna (1621).*

---

[50] Through stylistic means, this painting can be dated back to the middle of the 1330s. For the opinions on the date and the degree of autography, see Offner, "Bernardo Daddi."

[51] Schmitt, *Spiriti e fantasmi,* 60, 77. On the role that the line of Dominican thought had on the issue of the images, see Feinberg, "Imagination All Compact," 50.

Sala Bolognese, Bologna: A. Forni, 1999.

Angelozzi, Giancarlo. *Le confraternite laicali: Un esperienza Cristiana tra medioevo e età moderna*. Brescia: Queriniana, 1978.

Arasse, Daniel. "*Fervebat pietate populus*: Art, dévotion et société autour de la glorification de Saint Bernardin de Sienne." *Mélanges de L'École Française de Rome: Moyen Âge et Temps Modernes* 89 (1977): 189–263.

———. "Iconographie et évolution spirituelle: La tablette de saint Bernardin de Sienne." *Revue d'Histoire de la Spiritualité* 50, no. 3–4 (1974): 433–56.

Arcangeli, Francesco. *Pittura Bolognese del '300*. Bologna: Grafis edizioni d'arte, 1978.

Benati, Daniele. "Maestro di Verucchio: La Maddalena portata in cielo e sette Santi." In *Dipinti, sculture e ceramiche della Galleria Nazionale dell'Umbria: Studi e restauri*, edited by Caterina Bon Valsassina and Vittoria Garibaldi, 158–60. Firenze: Arnaud, 1994.

———. "Tra Giotto e il mondo gotico: La pittura a Bologna negli anni di Bertrando da Poggetto." In *Giotto e le arti a Bologna al tempo di Bertrando del Poggetto*, edited by Massimo Medica, 55–77. Cinisello Balsamo, Italy: Silvana, 2005.

Benvenutus de Imola. *Comentum super Dantis Aldigherij Comoediam*. Vol. 3. Firenze: Barbèra, 1887.

Bizzocchi, Roberto. *Genealogie impossibili: Scritti di storia nell'Europa moderna*. Bologna: Società editrice il Mulino, 1995.

Black, Christopher F. *Italian Confraternities in the Sixteenth Century*. Cambridge: Cambridge University Press, 1989.

Boskovits, Miklós. "Per la storia della pittura tra la Romagna e le Marche ai primi del '300." *Arte cristiana* 91, no. 755 (1993): 95–114, 163–82.

Bumaldo, Io. Antonio, and Ovidio Montalbani. *Minervalia Bonon: Civium Anademata, seu Bibliotheca Bononiensis, cui Accessit antiquorum Pictorum, et Sculporum onon*. Bononia: Brevis Catalogus, 1641.

Chartier, Roger, ed. "Gli usi del miracolo." In *La rappresentazione del sociale: Saggi di storia culturale*, 137–48. Turin: Bollati Boringhieri, 1989.

Connell, William J., and Giles Constable. "Sacrilege and Redemption in Renaissance Florence: The Case of Antonio Rinaldeschi." *Journal of the Warburg and Courtauld Institutes* 61 (1998): 53–92.

Conti, Alessandro. *La miniatura Bolognese: Scuole e botteghe, 1270–1340*. Bologna: Alfra, 1981.

Edgerton, Samual Y. "A Little-Known 'Purpose of Art' in the Italian Renaissance." *Art History* 2, no. 2 (1979): 45–61.

———. "Maniera and the Mannaia: 'Decorum' and Decapitation in the Sixteenth Century." In *The Meaning of Mannerism*, edited by Franklin Westcott Robinson and Stephen G. Nicholas Jr., 67–103. Hanover, NH: University Press of New England, 1972.

———. *Pictures and Punishment: Art and Criminal Prosecution during the Florentine Renaissance*. Ithaca: Cornell University Press, 1985.

Faietti, Marzia. "Amico's friends: Aspertini and the Confraternita del Buon Gesù in Bologna." In *Drawing Relationships in Northern Italian Renaissance Art*, edited by Giancarla Periti, 51–74. Aldershot: Ashgate, 2004.

Fanti, Mario, ed. "La Confraternita di S. Maria della Morte e la Conforteria dei condannati in Bologna nei secoli XIV e XV." In *Confraternite e città a Bologna nel medioevo e nell'età moderna*, 120–74. Rome: Herder Editrice, 2001.

———. "Il 'Fondo Ospedali' nella Biblioteca Comunale dell'Archiginnasio." *L'Archiginnasio* 58 (1963): 14–53.

Feinberg, Larry J. "Imagination All Compact: Tavolette and Confraternity Rituals for the

Condemned in Renaissance Italy." *Apollo* 161, no. 519 (May 2005): 48–57.

Ferretti, Massimo. "Una traccia di Giotto a Bologna." *Annali della Scuola Normale Superiore di Pisa, Classe di Lettere e Filosofia,* 4th ser., 1 no. 2 (2000): 33–51.

Freuler, Gaudenz. *Manifestatori delle cose miracolose: Arte italiana del '300 e '400 da collezioni in Svizzera e in Lichtenstein.* Lugano-Castagnola: Fondazione Thyssen-Bornemisza, 1991.

Gaiffier, Baudouin de. "Un thème hagiographique: Le Pendu miraculeusement sauvé." *Analecta Bollandiana* 13 (1943): 123–48.

Gennaro, Clara. "Venturino da Bergamo e la peregrination romana del 1335." In *Studi sul Medioevo cristiano offerti a Raffaello Morghen: Per il 90e anniversario dell'Istituto storico italiano (1883–1973).* Vol. 1, *Studio storici: Istituto storico italiano per il Medio Evo,* 83–87, 375–406. Roma: Istituto storico italiano per il Medioevo, 1974.

Jones, Lars R. "'Visio divina'? Donor Figures and Representations of Imagistic Devotion: The Copy of the Virgin of Bagnolo in the Museo dell'Opera del Duomo, Florence." In *Italian Panel Painting of the Duecento and Trecento,* edited by Victor M. Schmidt, 31–55. Washington, DC: National Gallery of Art/New Haven, CT: Yale University Press, 2002.

Kocks, Dirk. "Die Stifterdarstellung in der italienischen Malerei des 12.–15. Jahrhunderts." PhD diss., University of Cologne, 1971.

Laclotte, Michel. "Musée de Tours: La donation Octave Linet, I: Peintures italiennes." *Revue du Louvre et des musées de France* 14, nos. 4–5 (1964): 181–87.

Longhi, Roberto. *Lavori in Valpadana: Dal Trecento al primo Cinquecento, 1934–1964.* Firenze: Sansoni, 1973.

Lorenzo, Andrea di. "La Croce astile di Bernardo Daddi del Museo Poldi Pezzoli." In *La Croce di Bernardo Daddi del Museo Poldi Pezzoli: Ricerche e Conservazione,* edited by M. Ciatti, 11–30. Pisa: Ospedaletto, 2005.

Malvasia, Carlo Cesare. *Le Pitture di Bologna: Che nella pretesa, e rimostrata sinora da altri maggiore antichità, e impareggiabile eccellenza nella pittura, con manifesta evidenza di fatto, e rendono il passeggiere.* 5th ed. Bologna: 1766.

Markova, Victoria. "The 'Annunciation' from the Collection of Moskow's Pushkin Museum and Certain Aspects of Simone dei Corcefissi's Later Works." *Burlington Magazine* 120, no. 897 (1978): 4–6.

Martines, Lauro. *April Blood: Florence and the Plot Against the Medici.* Oxford: Oxford University Press, 2003.

Martucci, Pierpaolo. "La 'salvifica morte': Supplizi e tecniche del consenso a Bologna dal XVI al XVIII secolo." *Ricerche di storia sociale e religiosa* 51 (1997): 107–37.

Masini, Antonio di Paolo. *Bologna perlustrata.* Bologna: C. Zenero, 1666.

Mazzei Traina, Marinella, ed. *L'Oratorio dell'Annunciata di Ferrara: Arte storia, devozione e restauri.* Ferrara: Liberty House, 2002.

Meiffret, Laurence. *Saint Antoine ermite en Italie (1340–1540): Programmes picturaux et dévotion.* Roma: L'École Française de Rome, 2004.

Moench, E. *La Fondazione Roberto Longhi a Firenze.* Milano: Electa, 1980.

Offner, Richard. "Bernardo Daddi, His Shop and His Following." In *A Critical and Historical Corpus of Florentine Painting,* edited by Miklós Boskovits, 386–87. Firenze: Giunti Barbèra, 1991.

Ortalli, Gherardo. "…pingatur in Palatio": La pittura infamante nei secoli XIII–XVI.* Roma: Jouvence, 1979.

Paglia, Vincenzo. *La morte confortata: Riti della paura e mentalità religiosa a Roma nell'età moderna.* Rome: Edizione di Storia e Letteratura, 1982.

Palumbo, Genoveffa. *'Speculum Peccatorum': Frammenti di storia nello specchio delle immagini tra Cinque e Seicento.* Napoli: Liguori, 1990.

Parisini, Alessandra. "Pratiche extragiudiziali di amministrazione della giustizia: La 'liberazione dalla morte' a Faenza tra '500 e '700." *Quaderni storici* 23, no. 66 (1988): 147–68.

Previtali, Giovanni. *La fortuna dei primitivi: Dal Vasari ai neoclassici.* Turin: Einaudi, 1964.

Prosperi, Adriano. *Dare l'anima: Storia di un infanticidio.* Turin: Einaudi, 2005.

———. "Esecuzioni capitali e controllo sociale nella prima età moderna." In *La pena di morte nel mondo.* Atti del convegno internazionale di Bologna (28–30 October 1982). Casale Monferrato: Marietti, 1983.

———. "Mediatori di emozioni: La compagnia ferrarese di giustizia e l'uso delle immagini." In *L'impresa di Alfonso II: Saggi e documenti sulla produzione artistica nel secondo Cinquecento,* edited by J. Bentini and L. Spezzaferro, 279–92. Bologna: Nuova Alfa, 1987.

———. "Il sangue e l'anima: Ricerche sulle compagnie di giustizia in Italia." *Quaderni storici* 51 (1982): 959–99.

———, ed. *Misericordie: Conversioni sotto il patibolo tra Medioevo ed età moderna.* Pisa: Edizioni della Normale, 2007.

Rave, August B. *Frühe italienische Tafelmalerei: Vollständiger Katalog der italienischen Gemälde der Gotik.* Stuttgart: Staatsgalerie, 1999.

Romeo, Giovanni. *Aspettando il boia: Condannati a morte, confortatori e inquisitori nella Napoli della Controriforma.* Firenze: Sansori, 1993.

Sarpi, S. "Il Libro dei Giustiziati." In *L'Oratorio dell'Annunciata di Ferrara: Arte storia, devozione e restauri,* edited by Marinella Mazzei Traina, 59–61. Ferrara: Liberty House, 2002.

Schmidt, Victor Michael. "Gli stendardi processionali su tavola nelle Marche del Quattrocento." In *I Da Varano e le arti: Atti del Convegno internazionale, Camerino, Palazzo ducale, 4–6 ottobre 2001,* edited by Andrea De Marchi and Pier Luigi Falaschi, 551–70. Ripatransone, Ascoli Piceno: Maroni, 2003.

———. *Painted Piety: Panel Paintings for Personal Devotion in Tuscany , 1250–1400.* Firenze: Centro Di, 2005.

———. Recensione al catalogo di Stoccarda. *The Burlington Magazine* 143, no. 1182 (2001): 572–73.

———, ed. "Portable Polyptychs with Narrative Scenes: Fourteenth-Century *de luxe* Objects between Italian Panel Painting and French Arts *somptuaires*." In *Italian Panel Painting of the Duecento and Trecento,* edited by Victor M. Schmidt, 395–425. Washington, DC: National Gallery of Art/New Haven, CT: Yale University Press, 2002.

Schmitt, Jean-Claude. *Spiriti e fantasmi nella società medievale.* Roma-Bari: Laterza, 1995.

Schleif, Corine. "Hands That Appoint, Anoint, and Ally: Late Medieval Donor Strategies of Appropriating Approbation through Painting." *Art History* 16, no. 1 (1993): 1–32.

Sebregondi, Ludovica. "Riti, rituali e spazi dei confortatori fiorentini." In *La Croce di Bernardo Daddi del Museo Poldi Pezzoli: Ricerche e Conservazione,* edited by M. Ciatti, 31–51. Pisa: Ospedaletto, 2005.

Strehlke, Carl Brandon. *Italian Paintings 1250–1450 in the John G. Johnson Collection and the Philadelphia Museum of Art.* Philadelphia: Philadelphia Museum of Art, in association with the Pennsylvania State University Press, 2004.

Terpstra, Nicholas. *Lay Confraternities and Civic Religion in Renaissance Bologna.* Cambridge: Cambridge University Press, 1995.

———. "Piety and Punishment: The Lay *Conforteria* and Civic Justice in Sixteenth Century Bologna." *Sixteenth Century Journal* 22, no. 4 (1991): 679–94.

Toesca, Pietro. *Miniature italiane della Fondazione Giorgio Cini, dal Medioevo al rinascimento.* Vincenza: Neri Pozza,1968.

Török, Gyöngyi. "Problems of the Hungarian Angevin Legendary: A New Folio in the Louvre."

Arte Cristiana 89 (2001): 417–26.

Tumidei, Stefano. *Italies: Pictures des musées de la région Centre.* Paris: Somogy, 1996.

Vertova, Luisa. "La mano teas: Contributo alle ipotesi di riconstruzione dell'Altare di Donatello a Padova." In *Donatello-Studien,* edited by M. Cammerer, 209–18. Munich: Bruckmann, 1989.

Volpe, Alessandro. *Mezzaratta: Vitale e altri pittori per una confraternita bolognese.* Bologna: Bononia University Press, 2005.

Chapter 5

Consolation or Condemnation
The Debates on Withholding Sacraments from Prisoners

Adriano Prosperi

"I will die willingly because I will die in the grace of God." This annotation, written with a firm hand, accompanied by the name of Angelo de Angeli and dated 1633, appears on the first page of a parchment codex belonging to the *conforteria* of Ferrara.[1] It is not known what reasons led a confraternity brother to place a pen in the hand of the condemned and follow the ancient ritual of having the latter make that written declaration, but there are no doubts as to the significance of the sentiment expressed by Angelo de Angeli at the point of death. His testimony speaks to the success achieved by the confraternity in carrying out its work. The confraternity's task consisted in leading the condemned to accept his sentence as a means of dying in the grace of God and so of entering into eternal life. Many times this undertaking met with success, and the confraternity members would record in their book sentences such as "He died readily/ willingly and as wholeheartedly as a man has ever died," or "He died really prepared/willingly."[2] Yet it was not easy to achieve such a result. The condemned person struggled at length in crises of desperation. One of them, "when brought to the comforting room suddenly began to cry out and to yell and to bash his head against the wall."[3] Another, while being led to the gallows called out to the

---

This essay was translated from the Italian by Sarah Melanie Rolfe.

[1] "Moro volontieri perché moro in gratia di Dio." *Libro dei giustiziati*, FAA, Archivio dei residui ecclesiastici, Confraternita della Morte di Ferrara, Mazzo D no. 21, fol. 1. The codex contains the texts of funeral orations and of burial rituals.

[2] "Morse tanto disposto e tanto di cuore quant'huomo mai moresse" (Pasquino Ossa, hanged 3 December 1575); "morse molto disposto" (Gaspare Sinibaldi, decapitated 9 February 1577). Mazzi, *Gente a qui si fa notte,* 162.

[3] "Quando fu menato in confortaria al'improviso comincio di sclamare et gridare forte et battere la testa nel

devil and then asked Christ for forgiveness, which he did once again when the hanging failed due to a broken cord. He nurtured the hope of a pardon, which was usually granted in such cases. Yet when it was refused and he was brought to the scaffold the second time, he died "more obstinate than ever."[4] States of mind were extremely changeable, and this was normal in the dramatic context of public executions, where it took very little to trigger an explosion of the violence that hung heavily in the air. An illustration of this is to be found in the circumstances that befell a man condemned and put to death in the same year as Angelo Angeli. His name was Girolamo dalla Mano, and he had stabbed a man in the Po delta of Ferrara.

> He wanted neither to confess nor to say the name of Christ, despite the urgings of the clergy and the *conforteria* brothers. When he attempted to flee the scaffold, the crowd itself took to flight. A musket was fired, killing the barber Francesco Cremona and wounding others. Brought again to the scaffold, with his eyes uncovered, Girolamo was beaten and butchered. He died like an animal, and was buried by the roadside.[5]

People fleeing for their lives, shots fired, acts of violence—this was the setting of an "obstinate" death. The comforted and consoling death of those who died "willingly" was another thing altogether.

The great theater of death by execution was performed in city squares without any certainty regarding the outcome. Two lives were at stake: that of the body and that of the soul. Both remained in danger until the end—an end that extended beyond the execution, when the body might remain on display to the crowd, sometimes chopped up and strung or skewered on pikes. Other times the body was simply left hanging from the gallows, and yet other times it was delicately cut to pieces by surgeons during anatomy sessions at the university that were opened to the paying public. The rite was complex, and it could last for many days.[6] The theatrical character of public anatomy as practiced in Italian cities, and in Bologna in particular, is well documented. But

---

muro." Mazzi, *Gente a qui si fa notte,* 162.

[4] This was Ercole Fabri, called "il Bestiola," hanged 20 September 1570; Mazzi, *Gente a cui si fa notte,* 154.

[5] From the book containing the names of all those who were executed: *Libro di tutti li giustiziati,* p. 4, FAA Archivio dei residui ecclesiastici, Archivio della Confraternita della morte di Ferrara.

[6] In January 1523, Vincenzo di Preti wrote from Bologna to Isabella d'Este with news of a public anatomy: "Tomorrow they will begin here to undertake the dissection of one of the two who today were hanged as thieves; all the medical students will gather there because it's a thing that happens rarely and is very useful to their profession; it will take ten or twelve days." Luzio, "Ercole Gonzaga." 374–75.

from the point of view of the condemned, whose bodies were offered up to the curiosity of the crowd and to the intellectual exercise of scholars, the practice of public anatomy was little more than an intensification of capital punishment itself. It was an issue that figured in the exchanges between the comforters and the condemned, when a prisoner could play his last cards in the hope of winning a reduction of his sentence or at the very least a guarantee of a Christian burial for his body. In these conversations between the comforters and the condemned, one word echoed more loudly than the others: grace. It is an ambiguous word with a double meaning: grace on earth and the grace of eternal life came face to face. The condemned man who retained until the very end a hope that the governing authorities would grant him the grace of a judicial pardon was invited instead to *accept* his death with resignation as the cost of earning divine grace and with it eternal life for the soul. Divine grace in exchange for accepting public condemnation: this is the paradoxical argument that comforters like those in Ferrara advanced ever more determinedly in their work of counseling and conversion at the beginning of the modern age. But before settling into this form, intense debates about the larger question of grace broke out.

"To the world when it was half a thousand years younger, the outlines of all things seemed more clearly marked than to us."[7] Among those more clearly marked features of social life that Johan Huizinga evoked in the famous opening lines of his great work were those of execution. Executions of capital criminals were the most dramatic and even colorful means that governments had of achieving results. In public acts of execution, a fixed scenario with standard parts was repeated endlessly: there was the condemned man, the hangman or executioner, and the crowd of spectators. On one hand, the power that condemned—the judicial power of the regent or the magistrates. On the other, the power that saved—the redemptive power of the men of the church. Huizinga noted that the criminal Giovanna d'Arco was assisted by a famous preacher, Brother Riccardo, who could mobilize the greatest of crowds when he was preaching. Among the miracles of St. Vincenzo Ferrer is found the story of condemned people who were delivered from the sufferings of execution and sent directly to the peace of the other life. On one hand then,

---

[7] Huizinga, *Waning of the Middle Ages*, 9.

the hard and inexorable face of human justice and execution; on the other, the presence of the church as bearer of sentiments of mercy.

But were the roles in this ancient "theater of terror" really so clear and well defined?[8] Comparing the rites of execution in Italian cities with those in other western European countries, one is immediately struck by a noteworthy difference. In Ferrara, as in Bologna, Milan, Florence, Rome, and many other cities and towns, the Christian work of comforting was conducted not by members of the clergy but rather by laypeople. Men and women of the citizen population united together under the sign of a confraternity and, wearing their familiar cloaks, followed the condemned on his last journey. They prayed for him and with him, helping him in his final moments. Chronicles of Italian cities from the fourteenth century onwards are full of stories of executions dominated by the assiduous work of the comforter provided by the confraternities. The work was undoubtedly challenging. As the most extreme example of human mortality, the person sent to the gallows encountered all the major obstacles that could hinder that form of Christian devotion known as "art of dying well." In addition to the fear of imminent death, and to the immediate sufferings that would make it all the worse, there was concern for what would happen to a soul that had been stained by the gravest of public crimes and that as a result was threatened by the dreadful punishments of hell. For those around, it was particularly difficult to feel the love for one's fellow man that Christians were expected to demonstrate. The groups of people who crowded around the gallows in the majority of cases didn't feel much sympathy for the criminal. The government authority that delivered the sentence of public execution condemned those convicted to public execration, and the prospect of vindicating a wrong and eliminating a public enemy from the community stimulated collective feelings of grim satisfaction on the part of onlookers. For his part, the one at the gallows certainly would not have been nurturing feelings of meek devotion. He may have been innocent, and this could hardly lead him to thoughts of resignation or acceptance. If, on the other hand, he was guilty of the crimes for which he was condemned, he had reason to fear the judgment of God as well as that of men. Dark thoughts tormented him during the brief interval between sentencing and execution. This was normally a night spent in the confined space of the jail, while outside the curious crowded around and the sinister noises produced by the construction of the gallows entered through the window, along with the voices of the executioner and his helpers.

---

[8] Dulmen, *Theater des Schreckens: Gerichtspraxis.*

Why comfort him? What reasons motivated those who were moved to do so? What is known about the origins of the practice is that it came at the initiative of individuals or of small groups in cities of north-central Italy during the course of the 1300s. From there it spread as others imitated and elaborated on it. Where this happened, Christians expanded the recognized canon of works of mercy. The responsibility of accompanying the condemned in a brotherly manner on his final journey, and of easing his thoughts and looking after his soul and his body, were added to the six canonical works of charity that Christ named in Matthew 25:34–36. A second distinct cultural inheritance was adopted and modified during the course of this process. The classical literary genre of the *consolatio* that had passed from pagan culture to the Christian world was transformed. The *consolatio* had had its origins in the desire to bring comfort to those suffering the pain of losing someone dear to them. Christian belief in the immortality of the individual soul now brought a substantial change to the classical concept.[9] The concept of hope allowed the opening of a way beyond the limits that had hemmed in even the "ultima Dea" of the ancients. It is from this that the most important transformation introduced by the Christian culture of medieval Europe to the classical tradition of the *consolatio* was derived: the possibility of comforting the dying and of convincing them that their death was only the beginning of a new and eternal existence. Moreover, the dying themselves could choose whether they would live eternal life in the torments of hell or among the joys of heaven.

It was thus from the robust roots of an ancient tree that a new branch was born and flourished in medieval Christian Europe: comforting those condemned to death, or, as they were normally called, the "suffering" (*affliti*). In the vocabulary of the Italian confraternities that assisted prisoners, this was the term specifically used to denote the condemned. The *consolatio* that one was to bring to the suffering consisted in the first place of reconciliation with the church. The condemned had to be helped to die a Christian death by praying and having others pray to God for their souls. In exchange, the confraternity guaranteed a ritual burial of the body, and prayers and masses to intercede for the soul. This method of dying predominated for centuries in the Italian cities and from there it spread elsewhere. But even where there were no confraternities dedicated to this work, the manner in which someone condemned to death actually died was influenced by the Christian conception of the individual as a person composed of a mortal body and an immortal soul. Killing the body was something entirely different

---

[9] For classical and medieval sources, see Moos, *Consolatio*.

from killing the soul. Sources from the Bible to Dante taught that the "first death" was that of the body, while the "second death" was that of the soul.[10] The torments of capital execution were nothing compared with the pond of fire in hell. To escape this second death, one had to obtain grace—not the grace offered by a ruler, but the grace granted by God. The vehicle for grace was the sacraments. It was necessary for the condemned to want them. And they *could* have them. But it was not a simple matter.

A fundamental difficulty arose from the fact communities understood and experienced the human person as comprised of both body and soul together. In the concrete figure of the offender who was brought to the gallows, could one really distinguish between the earthly condemnation of the body (to death) and the eternal condemnation of the soul? Could the desire to eliminate evil from society combine with the desire to save the souls of those who were being excluded from society for their crimes? Was there the risk that the abstract distinction between body and soul would disappear in face of a particular and whole human being who was burdened by his crimes, hated by those in power and cursed by the community? Questions such as these must have presented themselves to the minds of contemporaries. A Venetian document from 1584 offers an example of this.

On 9 January of that year, the inquisitor Brother Angelo da Faenza recorded among his papers a deposition presented by the Augustinian Brother Giovanni da Siena in the form of the *spontanea comparitio*.[11] Brother Giovanni was giving testimony about an episode that had taken place the previous Wednesday in the kitchen of his convent. A brother who had returned from Padua where he had attended the hanging of two thieves spoke about what he had seen there. Brother Luigi da Barga, also present, made a declaration that created quite a stir: "They were executed for the damage they did. They are wicked and thieves. And for that even the holy church says that one should not pray for them. And this is said by the decrees."[12]

This gave rise to a lively discussion. Brother Giovanni replied that this seemed unbelievable; even thieves "when they repent" should be commended

---

[10] Revelation 20:14; and Dante, *Divina Commedia*, 1.1.117.

[11] APV, Inquisizione, b. 1, fols. 260–272, fasc. "fr. Aloysii Heremitani, *De non orando pro iustitiatis*" (1584).

[12] "Se sonno stati apiccati suo danno. Sono tristi et ladroni. Che perfino la chiesa santa dicce che non si debba pregare Dio per loro. Et questo lo dicono i Decreti." Ibid., fol. 260v.

to God with the prayers of the church. And everyone knew what happened on the occasion of capital punishment: it was these same condemned ones who turned towards those present asking "that they say an Our Father and a Hail Mary for them." Another man present at the discussion, Brother Zaccaria, energetically confirmed this, exclaiming, "I am old and I have always tried to pray to God for them and to commend their souls and I am astounded by this."[13] He strengthened his argument by trying to imagine himself at the gallows: "As I am here to lose my body by execution, should one not help my soul?"[14] But Brother Luigi insisted that one must submit to the authority of the canonical decrees. He added a new and dangerous argument: the accusation of heresy. Those who failed to accept the norm of the decrees or who sought to interpret them for themselves without authority, was a heretic. Brother Aloisio testified later that "if I did not want to believe what the decrees said then I was a heretic." Brother Luigi replied to Brother Andrea da Venezia, a young brother who had recalled the traditional use of administering the sacraments of confession and communion to the condemned, by saying, "God knows which confessions and communions are these."[15]

So was it the case that those who maintained that one could pray for a person condemned to death were heretics, and that sacraments administered in the shadows of the gallows were invalid? There was so much at stake that the dispute moved beyond the convent. An accusation of heresy, once formulated, could not but make its way to the Inquisition. The Augustinians were sensitive to these kinds of accusations because the Protestant Reformation had been born a few decades before from the work of one of their German brothers, Martin Luther in Wittenburg, and not a few among them sympathized with it. And yet, at that time, if there was suspicion of heresy, the rules of the Inquisition were very clear: whosoever concealed a similar accusation was suspected of being a supporter of heretics. And so legal proceedings began at the Venetian court. The brothers who had participated in the discussion in the convent were called upon to testify, one after the other. Brother Luigi was the last to speak. He was less bold before the inquisitor. He denied having accused his brothers of heresy. But he remained firm with respect to the matter of the decrees. He had already had the means to confront Brother Andrea with a volume of conciliar decrees in hand, likely the one prepared by

---

[13] "Io son vecchio et ho sempre visto a pregar Dio per loro et raccomandarli l'anima et mi maraviglio di questa cosa." Ibid., fol. 260v.

[14] "Come, sono lì per perder il corpo per la giustizia e non si debbe agitar l'anima mia?" Ibid., fol. 261r.

[15] "Dio sa che confessione et che comunione sono quelle." Ibid., fol. 262v.

Spanish archbishop Bartolomé de Carranza (1503–76), and he showed him the text of a decree of an ancient council that had prohibited the act of praying for the condemned. He also showed it to the investigator who interrogated him. It was a canon that prohibited praying "pro furibus et latronibus." But Brother Luigi had abandoned the certainty he had previously demonstrated in the discussions at the convent. He denied ever having accused those who thought differently than him of heresy, and he offered a much more cautious interpretation of the canon:

> I understand it in this way according to which it appears to me it was understood by the Holy Roman Church, that is, that one must not pray for the obstinate and impenitent who die without asking for forgiveness, nor sign of repentance for the errors for which he was presumably condemned by the church, and consequently incapable of receiving any favor in the next life. And this is my intention, and this I said…and I am sorry for having spoken these words so absolutely without gloss and without any interpretation.[16]

The matter came to a close on 19 January with a formal sentence: Brother Luigi was found guilty of having caused a controversy (literally, "scandalo") with his words and of having relayed in an inexact manner the words of the canon. For this reason he was admonished to be more cautious in his speech and was punished with a few penances. He had to eat a meal of bread and water, and give a sermon in the refectory the following Sunday, publicly correcting his affirmations and declaring that one must pray for the souls of those condemned to death. Finally, he had to celebrate a mass dedicated to intercession for the souls of those condemned to death.

Brother Luigi's punishment stemmed from the fact that the text of the canon did not say exactly what he had claimed it did. The inquisitor had checked the printed text and had discovered that the quote had been edited and mangled in the process.[17] It is enough to read the text of the canon quoted by the brother to see that the inquisitor was right. It concerned chapter 31, "De furibus et latronibus," approved by the Tribur synod, an assembly of German bishops meeting in

---

[16] "Io l'intendo in questo modo secondo che mi par l'intenda la Santa Romana Chiesa, cioè che non si debbe orar per li ostinati et impenitenti che moiono senza domandar perdono, nè segno di penitentia de suoi errori quali si presumano dalla chiesa damnati e consequentemente incapace di puoter ricever alcun suffragio nell'altra vita. Et questa è la mia intentione, et così ho detto…et me dispiace haver detto quelle parole così absolutamente senza glossa e senza interpretatione alcuna." Testimony of fra Luigi da Barga, ibid, fol. 266v.

[17] "Diminuta et manca nec declarata ut in canone apparet illa sententia." Ibid., fol. 270v.

895 under the authority of Pope Formosa and in the presence of Emperor Ar-
nolfo.[18] The chapter is dedicated to the question of whether one should pray for
the soul of a robber killed while thieving. The answer was that if the robber died
while thieving he was surely damned, because larceny is a mortal sin. If he was
only wounded and awaited capital punishment, one did not deny him the grace
of communion. These are documents from hard times. The subsequent chapter
addressed the topic of slayings by Christians during wars, specifically the killing
of infidel prisoners by Christians in the heat of battle. The murderer would do
forty days' penance and would be treated with indulgence by his bishop.

Brother Luigi da Barga had thus poorly understood the text of the canon.
But he had grasped the importance of merging sin and felony, and on this basis
considered the capital punishment of thieves as a real and true excommuni-
cation. Only the excommunicated were excluded from prayers and the sacraments, finding themselves outside the community of the church. One can make
clear the implicit reasoning that lay behind this biased reading: the robber committed a crime that was also a mortal sin. The distinction between crime and
sin, which had been discussed for a long time in theology and law, lost its preci-
sion in the mind of the Augustinian. Thus Brother Luigi must have imagined
that the judicial conviction covered both aspects—that is, it removed the guilty
one from both earthly and eternal life. This interpretation of the canon was
formally inexact, but it encompassed an essential aspect of the matter: the con-
vergence of sin and crime and also their divergence, or rather the real opposition between the salvific intervention of the sacraments and the punitive intent
of the conviction. It is true that at this time, crime and sin belonged in theory
to two distinct spheres and were the responsibility of two separate authorities:
crime was punished by criminal courts of justice and sin was the concern of
ecclesiastical tribunals of confession. But there was profound resistance to dis-
tinguishing between the life of the body and the life of the soul within the individual being punished. An Augustinian was more likely than others to see the
condemned as damned, and to ask the authorities to pass what was essentially
divine judgment. It was not for nothing that the former Augustinian Martin Luther had invoked the office of the sword to suppress the Peasant Revolt and had
promised eternal bliss to those who killed the most rebels. Power in the world

---

[18] "De furibus et labronibus," in *Conciliorum omnium,* 2:26–28. The canons of the synod come together to a
certain degree in the *Decretum Gratiani.* The decrees of the council were inspired by the criterion of securing
for the clerics an effective defense against the attacks of the laity. See Hefele and Leclercq, *Histoire des Conciles,*
697–707. This is likely a later printing of the collection of conciliar decrees compiled by Bartolomé de Carranza that Brother Luigi consulted.

derived its raison d'être from sin.[19] On the other hand, it is curious when a man of the church, who is faced with the spectacle of a judicial hanging, should be animated by a similar hatred for thieves. It is something worth reflecting on.

When chronicles and histories of the ancien régime described the scenes of executions in the piazzas, they often did so by opposing the cries for vengeance of the bloodthirsty crowd and the word of pardon brought by the men of the church. It is such a familiar image that it is thought to be typical of the time. With his concept of the "psychology of crowds," Gustave Le Bon reinforced this image of the piazza grown ferocious. Yet the image of early modern city dwellers as a ferocious collective individual is difficult to accept after the analyses of popular movements offered by Edward P. Thompson and Natalie Zemon Davis, among others. In fact, as Davis puts it, "Nowadays this hydra-headed monster has taken on a more orderly shape."[20] Closer analysis reveals, for example, that English spectators at the public hangings at Tyburn in the mid-1700s were capable of transforming the dark rite into a theater of irreverence and criticism of those in power.[21] And yet the dominant authorities wanted them to be animated with hatred for the criminals, and the formulas with which they sent the condemned to death revealed a harsh desire to wipe out the guilty ones. In the acts of criminal justice, one sometimes reads the wish for the delinquents to meet their second death in the lake of fire of hell.[22] It is necessary to focus attention on this. Where did this desire for a total punishment that with one blow struck down both earthly and eternal life come from? Was it perhaps a concession to the feelings of the crowd? Or should it rather be seen as an echo of far older rituals of punishment elaborated by arbitrary and inexorable authorities?

In the tradition of Christian Europe, the power to punish was founded on the Christian conception of sin: God placed the sword of justice in the hands of Christian princes to impede the consequences of sin. In a Germany shaken by peasant revolts, the traditional terms of the matter were reaffirmed by the hard Augustinianism of Luther who confirmed the medieval foundations of secular power. The reformer left these peasant rebels with no possibility of appealing

---

[19] Stürmer, *Peccatum und Potestas.*

[20] Davis, *Society and Culture,* 154.

[21] Linebaugh, "Tyburn Riot," 66.

[22] Assassins, miscreants, witches, idolaters "shall have their part in the lake which burneth with fire and brimstone: which is the second death." Linebaugh, "Tyburn Riot," 78.

their conviction. The ruler who killed them earned the divine prize of eternal salvation, while the rebels were considered "condemned souls" and "creatures of the devil." Luther promised them the death of both body and soul, while in dealing with the princes who eliminated them, he harkened back to the promises of salvation that preachers had made in the times of the Crusades. These promises came back into fashion in the Reformation, but this time they did not deal with relations between Christians and infidels, but rather with relations between rulers and citizens within a Christian society. The fact that Luther could return so readily to such arguments indicates that at a profound level the distinction between the life of the body and life of the soul had been lost. In the harsh conflict between the governing authorities and disobedient subjects, condemnation to death now included both body and soul.

It is also true that the same Luther, before the crisis of the Peasant Revolt and recalling the passage in Matthew 22:21, welcomed the distinction that Christ had made between what citizens owed to Caesar and what they owed to God.[23] And even before the Peasant Revolt, many in authority felt a pressing need for divine sanction of their earthly power. Yet not everyone was willing to follow Luther down this path. Erasmus of Rotterdam offered an indirect but very clear expression of dissent in his *Preparatio ad mortem* composed in 1533 for Thomas Boleyn. According to Erasmus, an abyss separated divine justice from its earthly counterpart and no one had the right to deduce the fate of the soul from the forms of [physical] death. According to him, it could in fact happen that "those killed for having incited a revolt flew to live with the angels."[24] On the other hand, Erasmus also disagreed with the Catholic obsession with the necessity of providing sacraments to the dying and he sought to check the anxiety of those facing death who were denied confession and communion. These he invited to seek peace in trust in God. They should abandon a way of reasoning that was founded on human appearances. In fact, one could be sent to hell even if one had died with sacramental unction; and conversely, an ardent faith could save anyone. The examples that Erasmus cites bring us back to our case: "Those who died by drowning or by capital punishment or by illness or unexpectedly serve as an example."[25] Even from this passage, it is possible to draw forth the statement that the condemned to death normally ran the risk of being unable to confess or communicate. It is therefore worthwhile to review

---

[23] Luther, "Temporal Authority," 678–83.

[24] Asso, *Erasmo*, 456; and Erasmus, *Praeparatio ad mortem*.

[25] Asso, *Erasmo*, 466.

the judicial and historical precedents of this matter.

The Augustinian Brother Luigi da Barga noted above used arguments from a counciliar canon that he had poorly understood. If he had explored more deeply the texts that comprised canon law, he would have found other and more fitting examples. For example, the synod of Reims in 630 had approved a canon that imposed the breaking of communion with a murderer who had killed without the extenuating circumstance of legitimate defense. Nevertheless, the canon allowed that this same murderer could be given the Eucharist if he repented before execution.[26] In reality, this last example of a reprieve must not have been instituted immediately because in diocesan statutes promulgated later in that same year by Bishop Sonnatius of Reims, there is a sorrowful protest against the practice of denying sacraments to the condemned. The bishop declared it a grave practice because it removed the hope and help necessary to face death. Bishop Sonnatius judged ecclesiastical authorities far more culpable because their silence ensured that the new canonical norms would be ignored.[27]

Thus not only was a criminal denied the sacrament of communion, but this was done with the connivance of the churchmen. By breaking ecclesiastical communion with the condemned and withdrawing the priest from the gallows, the church shared in the general execration of the criminal. Something similar emerged from the canons of an important synod of German bishops in Mainz in 847. The clerics discussed the fate of the bodies of those condemned to death. Could they be buried in churches? And beside the bodies, there were the souls. Was it possible to celebrate a requiem mass and make offerings for their souls? The two questions were connected. The canon the bishops arrived at affirmed that both burial and masses were possible, but it includes a long and complex explanation that reveals how intense the arguments had been, and how difficult it had been to convince those who were opposed or unsure. The case of those condemned to death is compared to that of those who were dying and who received absolution for their sins and communion. If it was permissible to offer communion to someone who confessed at the point of death, why not concede it also to those whose death was a judicial punishment for a crime? The canon

---

[26] "Si quis homicidium sponte commiserit, et non violentiae resistens, sed vim faciens impetu hoc fecerit, cum isto penitus non communicandum: sic tamen ut si penitentiam egerit, in exitu ei communionis viaticum non negetur." *Statuta synodalia Ecclesiae Rhemensis per dominum Sonnatium* in Mansi, *Sacrorum Conciliorum*, vol. 10, cols. 592–94.

[27] "Et cur ad mortem condemnatis renuitur? cum eis maxime conducat ad spem et securamen certi decessus, et praesentis agonis? Nunc autem etiam denegatur silenti Ecclesia et veluti consentienti, non obstantibus iis canonibus qui vel nunquam recepti vel saltem per usum contrarium sunt abrogati." *Statuta synodalia Ecclesiae Rhemensis per dominum Sonnatium* in Mansi, *Sacrorum Conciliorum*, vol. 10, col. 598.

recited all of the familiar biblical passages that came up repeatedly in discussions of the problem. The promise that Christ made to the good thief on the cross was invoked to show that conversion was possible right up until the last moment.[28] It is important to note that the question arose here as part of an ongoing questioning of the general problem of whether one could assign penance to a sick person who was in danger of death. Since the dying person was not in a position to do the required penance for his guilt, the priest asked only for a sincere confession before absolving him.[29]

The fate of the body and that of the soul therefore remained problematic when dealing with those condemned to death. For ecclesiastical authorities, one thing was evident: withholding the sacrament of penance from the condemned was a sure way of removing any possibility that his soul would be saved. The canon that the bishops had approved in Mainz in 847 was reiterated in their next synod at Worms in 868, and this in itself shows that the problem had not gone away and that the bishops were intent on resolving it.[30] They acknowledged that the secular ruler had the power to condemn a criminal to death, but asked that these rulers in turn recognize the jurisdiction of the church on the future of the soul. All these texts cited as their fundamental authority a passage from Ezekiel 33:11, but they gave it a distinctive twist. Whereas in the book of the Hebrew prophet, God guaranteed life for a guilty person who had repented, the Christian church interpreted this as license to kill him so long as a way was left open for his soul to achieve eternal life. This became the fundamental point of conflict and transaction between church and state in the medieval world. The most secure way to condemn someone

[28] "Quaesitum est ab aliquibus fratribus de his qui in patibulis suspenduntur pro suis sceleribus post confessionem Deo peractam, utrum cadavera illorum ad ecclesias deferenda sint, et oblationes pro eis offerendae, et missae celebrandae, an non. Quibus respondimus: si omnibus de peccatis suis puram confessionem agentibus, et digne poenitentibus communio in fine secundum canonicum iussum danda est, cur non eis qui pro peccatis suis poenam extremam persolvunt? scriptum est enim: Non vindicat Deus bis in idipsum (Num. I, iuxta 70). Nam ipse Dominus ait: 'In quocumque dice conversus fuerit peccator, peccata eius non reputabuntur ei' (Ezech. 33). Et iterum: 'Nolo mortem peccatoris, sed ut convertatur et vivat'(ibid.). Salutem ergo homini adimit, quisquis mortis tempore poenitentiam denegat, et desperat de clementia Dei, qui eam ad subveniendum morienti sufficere vel in momento posse non credit. Perdidisset latro in cruce praemium ad Christi dexteram pendens, si illum unius horae poenitentia non iuvisset: cum esset in poena poenituit, et per unius sermonis professionem, habitaculum paradisi, Deo promittente, promeruit (Luc. 23). Vera ergo ad Deum conversio in ultimis positorum mente potius est aestimanda quam tempore, propheta hoc traditur asserente: 'Cum conversus ingemueris, tunc salvus eris' (Ezech. 33)." Concilium Moguntinum I, a. 847, canon 27, in Mansi, Sacrorum Conciliorum, vol. 14, cols. 899–912.

[29] "Per presbyteros pura inquirenda est confessio, non tamen illis imponenda quantitas poenitentiae, sed innotescenda." "De infirmis in periculo mortis constitutes," Concilium Moguntinum I, a. 847, canon 26, in Mansi, Sacrorum Conciliorum, vol. 14, cols. 898–99.

[30] Concilium Wormatiense, a. 868, canon 80, in Mansi, Sacrorum Conciliorum, vol. 15, cols. 865, 883–84.

to hell was to deny him the prayers of intercession for his soul and above all
to deny him access to the sacraments. And so a constant undercurrent in the
history of executions in Christian countries was the attempt to extend to eternal life the sentence pronounced in the here and now—sometimes a barely
perceptible theme and other times clear and distinct.

The most important case concerned the royal power of the medieval
French kings.[31] There remains a precise testimony of this in a decretal of Pope
Clement V (1305–14), the Frenchman Bertrand de Got, that was published
by his successor in 1317. In this papal document, the question is whether one
should deny criminals the sacrament of penance and the Eucharist. It was not
an abstract problem, because temporal judges at the time were in fact doing
just this. It is not clear for how long or when the practice first emerged in
France. In opposition to the practice, Clement V ordered the judges on pain
of ecclesiastical censure to permit the condemned to receive at least the sacrament of penance before capital punishment.[32] Yet the papal decretal did not
succeed in ending this traditional practice, which remained in effect. At the
end of the century, the knight Philippe de Mézières (ca. 1327–1405), an in-
defatigable preacher of the crusades who had turned counselor and confidant
of King Charles V of France, proposed in a petition that the king grant those
condemned to death permission to receive the sacraments. The opposition of
Chancellor Pierre d'Orgement caused the initiative to fail. Charles V declared
that as long as his kingdom should last, the ancient custom would remain
in effect.[33] In support of Mézières's plea, the chancellor of the University of
Paris, Jean Gerson (1363–1429), gathered a list of five arguments in a formal
petition submitted to the sovereign.[34] Gerson's arguments called on the king
to respect the truths of faith that had been examined and certified by theolo-
gians, and fundamental among all these truths was the obligation to confess
one's mortal sins. All Christians were held to this obligation after baptism,
and no earthly authority had the power to block them from it. Because of
this, Gerson judged that laws and edicts directed towards blocking repentant sinners from confession had no force and should not be observed. Any
prince or judge who used his power to impede someone from confession was
himself stained with mortal sin and condemned to the punishments of hell.

---

[31] Vincent-Cassis recently returned to the topic in "La confession," 383–401.

[32] "Plures iudices temporales condemnatis hoc denegabant, et ad suam excusationem allegabant consuetudinem."
"Decretali Clementine, IX: De paenitentiis et remissionibus," in Friedberg, Corpus iuris canonici, 1190.

[33] Iorga, *Philippe de Mézières*, 438–39.

[34] Gerson, "Requete pour les condamnés à mort," 341–43.

Therefore, Gerson argued, judges were to consider themselves warned and should be aware of the dangers to which they were exposing themselves. If the document was not sufficient to lead them to stop the practice, they should at least have the sense to consult those who knew the norms of Christian law. These harsh words to judges were followed by softer ones emphasizing mercy to the poor convicts: one should not impose further pains in addition to the ones they were already going to suffer. The condition they found themselves in could drive them to despair, and they could only be helped to die a Christian death by the exhortations of a good confessor. Finally, Gerson appealed to national pride: there were areas like Lombardy where the Christian religion was less honored than in France, but even here they did not follow a custom so "hard, unreasonable, and unjust" as the French one.

Gerson's appeal found a hearing. A society riven by wars and caught in the middle of the upheaval of the Great Schism in the Catholic Church accepted a transformation of the harsh ritual of execution in a moment of social pacification. A royal edict of 12 February 1397 conceded sacramental confession to those condemned to death. Pierre de Craon erected a stone cross beside the gallows of Paris where the religious could hold confession for the condemned.[35] This concession was nonetheless a precarious one.

The reason for the monarch's opposition to the concession of the sacraments to the condemned remains nevertheless obscure. On this, Gerson's writing opens a crack of noteworthy interest:

> And if anyone says that many misdeeds/wrongdoings come to light during final confession that otherwise would not be known, answer that this reason does not change the fact that one can neither break divine law nor impede it: and also, God does not deserve [in the sense that he deserves more] that all evils be punished in this world, for [were they to be] he would have nothing to judge in the other.[36]

---

[35] Huizinga, *Waning of the Middle Ages*, 23.

[36] "Et s'aucun dist que plusiers meffais se scevent par derniere confession qui aultrement ne se scauroient mie, response que ceste cause ne excuse pas qu'on puisse pechier la loi divine ou l'empeschier: et aussi Dieu ne vault pas que tous les maulx soient punis en ce monde car aultrement il n'auroit que jugier en l'autre." Gerson, "Requete pour les condamnés à mort," 342.

The passage is important for many reasons. State judicial confession and church sacramental confession are superimposed within it, and there is moreover a potential conflict between the two. Evidently many crimes were only solved or even discovered with the final confession or *amende honorable* when the condemned freed his conscience by publicly telling the truth from the scaffold. Sacramental confession, on the other hand, risked concealing these final revelations by whispering them into the ears of a priest, who was bound by the secrecy of the confessional. The fight for confession was therefore a struggle between secular and ecclesiastical powers for access to the secret knowledge of the condemned. A connected but distinct question involved communion. The judges' lengthy resistance to allowing the condemned to partake of it arose because they saw this as a way of ratifying with a divine sanction the judicial work they had carried out. It was clearly contradictory to readmit to the communion of the church a person who was being simultaneously expelled and radically eliminated from society.

This allows us to understand why the problem continued to complicate relations between the secular exercise of justice and the religious concept of guilt for a long time. If Gerson's arguments succeeded in lifting the general prohibition on sacramental confession at the foot of the gallows in France, there remained actual cases of condemned men who were forbidden that permission to confess. The appeal by François Villon (1431–63) to "our brothers who live after us" attests to the persistence of a fracture healed only with difficulty. In Strassburg, the famous preacher Geiler von Kaisersberg (1445–1510) adopted a humble tone, in contrast to Gerson's high and authoritative statements, when sending a plea to the town authorities that they allow the sacraments to the condemned.[37] According to the Florentine Augustinian theologian Giovanni Lorenzo Berti (1696–1766), the ancient prohibition was still in effect in France in the 1700s.[38] In Spain, too, the tendency to exclude criminals from the sacraments seemed to be strong and deep-rooted. At the end of the sixteenth century, the Louvain theologian Johannes Molanus (1533–85) recalled the opinions of his master, Ruard Tapper, and also of Domingo de Soto, against this "perverse custom" of the Spanish—a convention that had continued even into their own time.[39] In 1569 Pope Pius V ordered Philip II to suspend the prohibition on access to

---

[37] Schuster, *Eine Stadt vor Gericht*, 270n.

[38] Laurentii Berti, *Florentini fratris*, 383–85.

[39] Migne, *Theologiae cursus completus*, vol. 27, col. 455. Molanus wrote a chapter on this question in his *Theologiae practicae compendium*, fols. 134v–135r.

the sacraments by the condemned.[40] Philip conceded the point, although it is important to note that even this devoutly Catholic monarch placed limits on the concession, asking that the times of execution not be altered for religious reasons. The desire to demonstrate the rigors of royal justice evidently conflicted with the delays and complications that could result from interventions by those clerical magistrates of the soul. And given the ways that clergy and condemned in the Spanish viceroyalty of Naples were able to engineer delays in execution times by means of the sacraments, the king's concerns were not unfounded. The Neapolitans demonstrated such imagination and cunning that they turned executions into a drawn-out theatrical spectacle.[41]

Reconstructing the full history of diverse practices that developed around this point would require a much wider investigation. But one observation can be made here: there seems to be a tradition and form of Christian solidarity in medieval Italian cities that extends a boundary between the rites of execution practiced south of the Alps and those practiced in the rest of Europe. The question of the right of criminals to be admitted into the grace of the sacraments throws that tradition—and the distinction between the two areas—into sharp relief. Popes from Innocent VIII to Leo X, Paul III, Julius III, and Pius IV allowed the Italian confraternities to comfort and administer sacraments to the condemned. It is telling, in conclusion, how Prospero Lambertini, cardinal archbishop of Bologna and later Pope Benedict XIV (1740–58), recognized and dealt with the matter. Before his elevation to the papacy, Lambertini dealt with the question in the treatise *De Missae sacrificio.* Acknowledging that practices differed between France and Spain on the one hand, and Italy and Germany on the other, he counseled bishops to follow local procedure and the practice in effect in that place.[42] Yet his personal opinion was that it was more consistent with Christian piety to concede communion "to the condemned to death, even for serious crimes, when they ask

[40] Pius V's *motu proprio* was conceded 25 January 1569 after the request of Bishop Pedro Guerrero. Philip II ratified it with a royal pragmatic of 27 March 1569 that imposed precise conditions: communion would be granted the day before the execution during a mass that was celebrated in the prison. The execution of the sentence could on no condition be deferred; León, *Grandeza y miseria en Andalucia,* 268. My thanks to Michele Olivari for this reference.

[41] On the delays in execution times due to sacramental confession and ecclesiastical authorities, cf. Romeo, *Aspettando il boia.*

[42] "Noi non vogliamo censurare, o approvare l'altrui condotta." Benedict XIV, *Della Santa Messa* (Venetia presso Antonio Curti, 1792), 1:197. For the Latin edition, see *De Missae Sacrificio,* sec. 2, par. 175, col. 6, pt. 5. Lambertini here refers to Juenin, *De Sacramentis,* 4.6, and to Molanus, *De Picturis,* 7. The origins are believed to have been derived from the Illiberitan council that forbade giving communion to renegade Christians.

for it and are prepared to receive it."[43] He returned to the argument in the second edition of the treatise *De Synodo dioecesana* that was published after he had become pope. Citing Pius V's letter on the topic, he was now convinced of a different position: it was the duty of the bishops "to introduce into the dioceses the discipline of giving the Eucharist to the condemned to death, and also to insert this clause into their synodical pronouncements, and this by the authority of the great pontiff St. Pius V."[44] Before becoming pope, Prospero Lambertini had been a member of the Bolognese *conforteria* of S. Maria della Morte. When accepted into the confraternity, he had organized a solemn celebration. As pope, he gave his former confraternal brothers the favor of confirming their ancient privilege of granting liberation to one condemned person every year. This was a highly coveted privilege, one in which grace recovered its full significance beyond the division between body and soul.

The contrast between a state justice determined to radically erase the one it had condemned to death, and those religious and civil forces that hoped for the prisoner's rebirth in grace or at least for reconstructing broken links of community recurred in new forms in early modern Europe. It remained a deep and perhaps irresolvable difference of opinion. In the historical phase of that ongoing debate examined here, in the relation between the Catholic Church and the secular state there emerged a possible compromise built on a distinction between the fate of the soul and that of the earthly life. In return for giving clergy the right of access to the conscience of the condemned, the state gained theological confirmation of its power to execute. In other Christian traditions, the question has to be examined in the context of evolving criminal legislation and must be explored in close connection with analysis of the secrets of the conscience and autobiographical introspection.[45]

---

[43] "...Christianae pietati magis conforme esse, ut vivifici Sacramenti participatio iis etiam, qui ob grave delictum sententia capitali damnati sunt, petentibus, et alioquin recte dispositis, non denegetur." Benedict XIV, *De Synodo dioecesana libri tredecim*, I.1.186.

[44] "...Censemus, Episcoporum partes esse, hanc disciplinam in suis dioecesibus invehendam curare, ut delinquentibus ultimo supplicio afficiendis Eucharistia praebeatur, idque in Synodalibus constitutionibus inserere, auctore nimirum immortalis memoriae Pontifice S. Pio V." Benedict XIV, *De Synodo dioecesana libri tredecim*, I.1.186.

[45] Brooks, *Troubling Confessions*.

Works Cited

Manuscript Sources

APV   Archivio Patriarchale di Venezia
FAA   Ferrara, Archivio Arcivescovile

Printed Sources

Asso, Cecilia, ed. *Erasmo da Rotterdam: Scritti religiosi e morali.* Turin: Einaudi, 2004.

Benedict XIV. *Della Santa Messa.* Venice: Antonio Curti, 1792.

———. *De Missae Sacrificio.* Venice: Typographia Balleoniana, 1797.

———. *De Synodo dioecesana libri tredecim.* Venice: Vincentii Radici, 1775.

Brooks, Peter. *Troubling Confessions: Speaking Guilt in Law and Literature.* Chicago: University of Chicago Press, 2000.

Davis, Natalie Zemon. *Society and Culture in Early Modern France.* Stanford, CA: Stanford University Press, 1975.

"Decretali Clementine, IX: De paenitentiis et remissionibus." In *Corpus iuris canonici,* edited by Emil Friedberg. Leipzig: 1879. Reprint, 1959.

Dülmen, Richard van. *Theater des Schreckens: Gerichtspraxis und Strafrituale in der frühen Neuzeit.* Munich: Verlag CH Beck, 1988.

Erasmus, Desiderius. "Praeparatio ad mortem." In *Opera omnia,* vol. 5, edited by Adrianus Van Heck. Amsterdam: North-Holland, 1977.

Gerson, Jean. "Requete pour les condamnés à mort." In *L'oeuvre française.* Vol. 7, *Oeuvres complètes,* edited by Mons Glorieux. Paris: Desclée, 1960.

Hefele, Karl Joseph von, and Henri Leclercq. *Histoire des Conciles d'après les Documents Originaux,* 2nd ed. Paris: Letouzey et Ané, 1907.

Huizinga, Johan. *The Waning of the Middle Ages: A Study of the Forms of Life, Thought and Art in France and the Netherlands in the 14th and 15th Centuries.* Harmondsworth, UK: Penguin, 1955.

Iorga, Nicholae. *Philippe de Mézières 1327–1405 et la Croisade au XIVe siècle.* Paris: É. Bouillon, 1896. Reprint, Geneva-Paris: 1976.

Laurentii Berti, Joannis. *Florentini fratris Eremitae Augustiniani librorum de theologicis disciplinis, tomus vii in quo plura traduntur, quae ad confirmationis, Eucharistiae, et poenitentiae pertinent sacramenta.* Rome: Apud Pantheon, 1743.

León, Pedro de. *Grandeza y miseria en Andalucía: Testimonio de una encrucijada* histórica (1578–1616). Edited by Pedro Herrera Puga. Granada: Facultad de Teología, 1981.

Linebaugh, Peter. "The Tyburn Riot against the Surgeons." In *Albion's Fatal Tree: Crime and Society in Eighteenth-Century England,* edited by Douglas Hay, 65–118. London: A. Lane, 1975.

Luther, Martin. "Temporal Authority: To What Extent It Should be Obeyed." In *Martin Luther's Basic Theological Writings,* edited by Timothy F. Lull, 655–703. Minneapolis, MN: Fortress Press, 1989.

Luzio, A. "Ercole Gonzaga allo Studio di Bologna." *Giornale Storico della Letteratura Italiana* 8 (1886): 374–81.

Mansi, Giovanni Domenico. *Sacrorum Conciliorum nova et Amplissima collection.* 53 vols. Florence: Expensis Antonii Zatta Veneti, 1759–98.

Mazzi, Maria Serena. *Gente a cui si fa notte innanzi sera: Esecuzioni capitali e potere nella Ferrara estense.* Rome: Viella, 2003.

Migne, Jacques-Paul. *Theologiae cursus completus.* Lutetiae Parisiorum [Paris], 1843.

Molanus, Johannes. *Theologiae practicae compendium, per conclusiones in quinque tractatus digestum.* Cologne: Birckman for Arnoldi Lylii, 1585.

Moos, Peter von. *Consolatio: Studien zur mittellateinischen Trostliteratur.* 4 vols. Munich: W. Fink, 1971/72.

Romeo, Giovanni. *Aspettando il boia: Condannati a morte, confortatori e inquisitori nella Napoli della Controriforma.* Firenze: Sansori, 1993.

Schuster, Peter. *Eine Stadt vor Gericht: Recht und Alltag im spätmittelalterlichen Konstanz.* Paderborn-München-Wien-Zürich: Schöning, 2000.

"Sixti V Pontificis Maximi foelicissimis auspiciis." In *Conciliorum omnium tam generalium quam provincialium.* Vol. 4. Venetiis: Apud Dominicum Nicolinum, 1585.

Stürmer, Wolfgang. *Peccatum und Potestas: Der Sündenfall und die Entstehung der herrscherlichen Gewalt im mittelalterlichen Staatsdenken.* Sigmaringen: J. Thorbecke, 1987.

Vincent-Cassis, Mireille. "La confession des condamnés à mort: L'exception française du XIVe siècle." In *Vita religiosa e identità politiche: Universalità e particolarismi nell'Europa del tardo Medioevo*, edited by Sergio Gensini, 163–87. San Miniato: Fondazione Centro studi sulla civiltà del tardo Medioevo, 1998.

Chapter 6

Theory into Practice
Executions, Comforting, and Comforters in Renaissance Italy

Nicholas Terpstra

In the chill of a Saturday morning in January 1540, Giovanni Gaspari da Castagne and Giannino dalla Rochetta, two *montanari* or "mountain men" from the Apennine hills that formed a jagged and sometimes lawless boundary just south of Bologna, stepped into a cart on Bologna's Piazza Maggiore for a ride a few hundred meters south towards the church of S. Domenico. The cart made its way through crowded streets of heckling spectators before turning along the wall bordering the friars' garden and moving as far as the house of Antonio Ruini. Ruini was a prominent citizen who had twice been a member of Bologna's Council of Elders (the Anziani) and one of its oldest governing magistracies; a few days earlier, a group of men had killed him on the street outside his house. Mountain man Giovanni, found at the scene, was fingered as the murderer. The cart stopped outside the house and there on the street, as Giovanni screamed out his innocence and Giannino watched in horror, the city executioner cut him into four pieces. Giannino was then taken in the cart back through the crowd to the square in front of S. Domenico, where only a week before some thieves had desecrated the public tomb reserved for members of the Council of Elders. Against the backdrop of the ruined monument, he too was cut to pieces. Two men dead, but justice was still hungry. Less than three months later, two more mountain men, Pannino and Pietro from the town of Bozano, were also quartered in a similar manner and for the same crime. Pietro was tortured on the cart as it made its way to S. Domenico, suggesting that officials now believed he had stabbed Ruini.[1]

---

[1] The first executions of Ruini's condemned murderers were on 10 January and the second on 6 March

It wasn't only justice that was hungry: Bologna was in the midst of a fam-ine that doubled and then tripled food prices in a year. The Council of Elders had worked out a plan to expel "foreigners" in order to reduce demand on urban grain supplies, and this may explain the attacks on members and monuments, and the city's aggressive response. Yet they needn't have bothered with expulsions, for by March 1540 an epidemic of *petecchie* cut a swath through the city. The same chronicles that report the deaths of Giovanni and Giannino, and Pannino and Pietro offer long lists of the great and the good who were tipped into the grave by the epidemic. With all this unrest, the year proved to be a busy one for the ex-ecutioner. More criminals went to the scaffold in 1540 than in any other year on record in that century, with the exception of 1585 when authorities were waging a determined campaign to flush bandits out of the Apennine hills. Poverty led some of these to commit capital crimes, and put others in a situation where they could not afford the fines and commutations that would keep them off the scaffold once they had been condemned.[2] Bologna's midcentury crisis of famine, plague, and crime brought dozens to the executioner and led the city's confraternity of S. Ma-ria della Morte, known colloquially as the Compagnia della Morte (Company of Death) or the Morte, to reorganize its work with the condemned, establishing a Scuola dei Confortatori, recruiting more members, and starting to keep more systematic records of those it accompanied to the scaffold.

Comforters in Florence and Ferrara had kept these "books of the ex-ecuted" (*libri di giustiziati*) for many decades already, but in spite of being the oldest *conforteria* in Italy, Bologna's S. Maria della Morte never bothered. While the *Comforters' Manual* translated in this volume shows that the con-fraternity took its work seriously, there are actually few solid details about what it did before 1540. The books of the executed and other records it began keeping around the same time make it possible to explore the realities beyond the prescriptions of the *Comforters' Manual.* This article will focus on four different dimensions of crime, punishment, and comforting in a late Renais-sance city. First, what kinds of crimes were Bolognese authorities prosecuting through this period and how many people died on the scaffold? Second, how were executions carried out? Normal city life stopped for these exercises in justice; so where, when, and how did this very public and highly ritualized event take place? Third, turning to the *conforteria* of S. Maria della Morte,

---

1540. Ruini's two terms on the Council of Elders had been March 1531 and March 1537. For contempor-ary descriptions, see Rinieri, *Cronaca,* 74–76; and Alberti, *Historie di Bologna,* 696–97. Rinieri reports that Pannino and Pietro were executed for the murder of Pietro Casono da Cento.

[2] Dean, "Criminal Justice," 29–30.

the Scuola dei Confortatori, how did comforting shift from the ideals of the fifteenth-century *Comforters' Manual* to the realities of the sixteenth- and seventeenth-century city? What responsibilities did the comforters feel towards the criminals they helped? Finally, who were these comforters and why did they take on this physically and psychologically demanding work?

When Bologna's many chroniclers wrote about crimes, they invariably singled out the most appalling crimes or spectacular executions. In the turmoil following the collapse of the Bentivoglio signory and the implementation of direct rule by papal governors in 1506, they had a lot to write about. Justice—or vengeance—was hungry indeed. Papal authorities used their control of the judiciary, including the investigatory powers of the *podestà* and recourse to summary justice to move against partisans of the Bentivoglio. Over fifty prominent individuals were executed in short order, from a high official of the notaries hanged in his black velvet robes for distributing pro-Bentivoglio propaganda, to an abbot and ten Bentivoglio friends dispatched in one go, to four senators who accepted an invitation to dine with the papal governor only to end up throttled at midnight, beheaded at dawn, and put on display in the Piazza Maggiore by morning. It was not unlike the Medici reaction that would sweep through Florence six years later, sending Pietro Paolo Boscoli, Agostino Capponi, and many others to their deaths. In both cities, treason charges nabbed more than just the highborn: an old man was hanged after muttering, "It would be better to be a servant of the Turks than of the priests—better for Bologna to have a signory of the Bentivoglio than one of the church." In 1520 a university student was beheaded two weeks before he was to receive his doctorate because he had circulated scurrilous tracts criticizing the city's governor. As many fled to the hills to continue their resistance, the lines between treason, rebellion, and banditry blurred. The Florentine humanist Francesco Guicciardini, serving as Bologna's papal governor from 1531 to 1534, bypassed the established legal system and took justice into his own hands. In 1532, he sent three hundred soldiers to hunt down a famous bandit who was operating in the hills. When the bandit holed up in a house with fifteen of his gang, the soldiers burned the house down, killing all but one, whom they triumphantly brought back to the city for execution by Guicciardini's decree.[3]

---

[3] For the executions of Bentivoglio allies and partisans in 1507–8, see "Chronache bolognese," 129–40, BCB

Chroniclers kept alert for the most striking crimes and penalties like these, and as a result recorded only a fraction of both. Drawing on the most detailed chronicles leaves us with just under two hundred executions in the more than three decades following the collapse of the Bentivoglio signory, and fifty of those occurred in 1507 and 1508. One of the few executions not linked to partisan politics through these two years was, if anything, even more bizarre than the bloody judicial purge of the Bentivoglio. On 1 April 1508, a heretic Capuchin friar who fed unconsecrated hosts to Christians while reserving consecrated hosts for donkeys and roosters was burned in the middle of Piazza Maggiore.[4]

Looking to the more systematic records left in the books of the executed from 1540, one can see how far the chroniclers' obsession with bizarre crimes and bloody punishments had led them to ignore the far larger number of "ordinary" crimes, criminals, and executions that a city like Bologna prosecuted every year.[5] From 1540 to 1600, Bolognese authorities executed 917 people. This is more than double the rate that can be gleaned from the earlier chronicles, and the difference is made up by the host of mundane thefts, murders, and miscellaneous crimes that chroniclers out for a good story couldn't be bothered reporting. Beyond the problems of reporting, justice systems were so thoroughly politicized that prosecutions themselves rose and fell for reasons beyond simple criminality. In the troubled 1410s to 1420s, Bologna executed nine to thirteen annually, while by the more secure early 1470s, this dropped to three. Florence, which was roughly the same size, went from eleven to thirteen in the late fourteenth century to seven to eight a century later, and even fewer by the early sixteenth century.[6]

A disproportionate number of executions that chroniclers reported before 1540 arose directly out of the vicious ongoing struggle between papal authorities

---

Fondo Gozzadini ms. 280: Notaries' *corretore* Ercolesse Golotto (4 October 1507); the abbot and ten Bentivoglio allies (16 February 1508); sixty-four-year-old Giacomo di Rabuino Pellacano (26 February 1508); senators Alberto di Castello, Innocenzo Ringhiera, Salustio Guidotti, and Bartolomeo Magniani (27 June 1508). Girolamo da Bussetto was beheaded 28 February 1520 (ibid., 150–51). The servant of the bandit Camillo Sacchi was executed 10 June 1532 (ibid., 154). For a later romanticized drawing of the event, see "Chronica di Antonio di Eliseo Mamelini," BCB ms. B3642#1.

[4] Fra Raimondo da Viviano (1 April 1508); "Chronache bolognese," BCB Fondo Gozzadini mss. 280, 135. This volume was compiled by Gozzadini from the chronicles of Fileno della Tuate, Nicolo Seccadenari, Cherubino Gherardazzi, Bargellini, Griffoni, and Bernardo dalle Pugliole, and notes 190 executions from the fall of the Bentivoglio in November 1506 to January 1540 when S. Maria della Morte's *Libro dei giustiziati* began.

[5] For discussions of the politics of criminal prosecution in Bologna, see Blanshei, "Crime and Law Enforcement"; and Dean, "Criminal Justice." In preparing the tables and statistics for this study, I have employed Machiavelli's manuscript copy of the S. Maria della Morte *Libro dei Giustiziati*, which is held as the "Descrizione di tutte le giustiziati di Bologna del 1540 per tutto il 1740," BAB Aula 2a C.VII.3.

[6] Dean, "Criminal Justice," 27; and Zorzi, "Judicial System," 54.

and the Bentivoleschi—almost two-thirds of those reported fell into the inter-changeable categories of rebels, bandits, and spies (63.02 percent). After 1540, when one can rely on the more systematic books of the executed, a similar figure is given over to more quotidian murders and thefts (72.51 percent). Graph 6.1 shows how many people were executed each year, while table 6.1 breaks these down by decade and also by type. The peaks in graph 6.1 correspond largely to years when Bologna was struggling with famine. The sole exception is the mid-1580s, when papal authorities launched their campaign against banditry and prosecutions rose across the board. Among sexual crimes, sodomy was clearly the greatest concern, although the eighteen recorded executions represent a very small number when compared to either Florence or Venice. Heresy and sacrilege were clearly far more serious, though even here the number was not very large.

The S. Maria della Morte scribes did not consistently record where the crimes took place, but most occurred within the city's walls. Less than a third definitely took place in the city and only a tenth that number in the surrounding *contado*; the remaining records specify no location.[7] These statistics reverse when it comes to the criminals themselves: over half lived or originated outside the city, while only slightly more than 10 percent clearly came from the city; the origins of the remaining third cannot be traced clearly. This tension between city and countryside had been a constant in Bologna for centuries.[8] Out of the almost one thousand people who lost their lives, only thirty-four were women. In short, the ones mounting the scaffold in Bologna matched those across Europe: male "outsiders" who were often young adults, who drifted into crime as they tried to survive in an alien city, and who lacked the financial resources and personal networks that would allow them to negotiate commutation of their penalties.

In a society committed to public executions, the rituals involved in the act were paramount—even more important than determining whether the right person died. Executions were never simply about eliminating a criminal. They were

---

[7] Of the 917 capital prosecutions, 264 clearly took place in Bologna (28.78 percent) and 31 in the contado (3.38 percent); in the remaining 622 (67.82 percent), the location is either unclear or not given. "Descrizione di tutte le giustiziati di Bologna del 1540 per tutto il 1740," BAB Aula 2a C.VII.3.

[8] Of the 917 executed, 103 (11.23 percent) were clearly from Bologna, while 505 (55.07 percent) were identified as originating from outside the city (either explicitly or by patronymic), and the remaining 314 (34.24 percent) cannot be traced; "Descrizione di tutte le giustiziati di Bologna del 1540 per tutto il 1740," BAB Aula 2a C.VII.3. In the thirteenth century, foreigners were executed at a rate three times that of locally born Bolognese; Blanshei, "Crime and Law Enforcement," 123; and Dean, "Criminal Justice," 22.

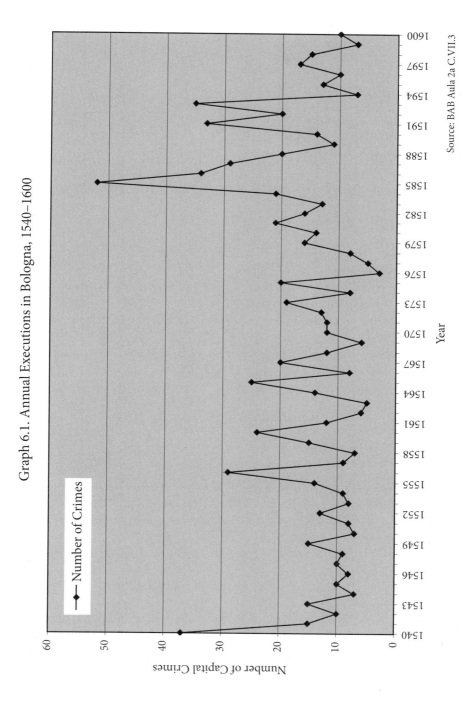

Graph 6.1. Annual Executions in Bologna, 1540–1600

Source: BAB Aula 2a C.VII.3

Table 6.1. Criminal Prosecution in Bologna 1507–1600

	Adultery	Arson	Assault	Banditry	Counter-feiting	Heresy & Sacrilege	Murder	Other	Rape	Rebel	Sodomy	Shelter Criminals	Theft	Vandalism	Witchcraft	Weapons Offense	Multiple Charges	Total
1507–09	—	—	—	—	—	1	—	—	—	50	—	—	1	—	1	—	—	53
1510–19	—	—	—	14	3	1	30	4	—	17	2	5	16	—	—	—	—	92
1520–29	—	—	—	9	—	—	2	2	—	10	—	—	2	—	—	—	—	25
1530–39	—	—	—	16	—	1	3	2	—	—	—	—	—	—	—	—	—	22
Total	0	—	—	39	3	3	35	8	0	77	2	5	19	—	1	—	—	192

Source: BCB Fondo Gozzadini 280

	Adultery	Arson	Assault	Banditry	Counter-feiting	Heresy & Sacrilege	Murder	Other	Rape	Rebel	Sodomy	Shelter Criminals	Theft	Vandalism	Witchcraft	Weapons Offense	Multiple Charges	Total
1540–49	1	2	3	1	7	9	66	8	2	0	7	1	32	2	1	1	1	143
1550–59	3	0	3	3	6	2	40	16	2	0	0	1	28	5	5	0	2	114
1560–69	0	2	0	2	8	12	42	20	0	2	5	2	43	0	0	2	5	140
1570–79	0	4	1	0	1	3	36	6	0	0	2	0	55	1	2	5	0	116
1580–89	0	0	3	6	15	8	67	5	0	17	1	1	108	1	0	5	6	237
1590–99	0	4	1	1	2	7	51	8	1	2	4	4	79	3	0	4	0	171
1600	0	0	1	0	0	0	5	0	0	0	0	0	4	0	0	0	0	10
Total	4	12	12	13	39	41	307	63	5	21	19	9	349	12	8	17	14	931

Source: BAB Aula 2a C.VII.3

theatrical lessons in public retribution and social order, and like any staged presentation, the drama had to be didactic, cathartic, and compensatory—it had to teach lessons, release tensions, and pay the debt created by the crime. Punishment had to fit both the crime and the criminal, both in its form and in its location. Many of the rituals aimed deliberately at expanding the crowd of witnesses, since it was important that justice was seen to be done. At the same time, the drama of the execution ritual had to conceal the tragicomedy of some prosecutions, for it was well known that justice was anything but blind. Apart from partisan judicial vendettas, the ones who mounted the scaffold were a fraction of those condemned to do so, and an even smaller fraction of those who had committed crimes worthy of execution. State rituals aimed to create an aura of judicial power and legitimacy, while religious rituals aimed to shift attention from the criminal's actions and prosecution to his eternal fate.

There were four basic forms of execution carried out in Bologna. Hanging was the most common—certainly statistically, but also in that it was what common people could expect for common crimes like theft, murder, or assault (figs. 4 and 18). Hanging could be humiliating, drawn out, and painful, particularly since the common practice of shoving the criminal off a ladder braced against a gallows crossbar (fig. 2) did not always give the momentum or drop that could snap the neck or kill instantly. It was also the form most likely to go grotesquely wrong if the hangman miscalculated. On rare occasions, this worked to a prisoner's benefit—in April 1505 a robust young man Pietro was hanged for theft, but when it came time to bury him, Pietro revived and was rushed to the hospital of S. Maria della Morte. In his final desperate moments before execution, Pietro had vowed to become a friar if saved, and the Augustinian friars of S. Giacomo with their confraternity in tow now came to the hospital to claim him. Friars and *confratelli* led Pietro, his noose around his neck, around Piazza Maggiore and on to S. Giacomo where they gave him a friar's robes and the name Niccola in honor of the Augustinian saint Niccola da Tolentino, to whom he had cried out his vow. Fra Niccola's celebrity and religious community couldn't keep him from older habits. Eight years later he was caught again in theft, and this time the executioner did his job more carefully.[9]

Those of better social standing could expect beheading, particularly if their crime had a more distinctly political dimension like treason or the assassination of one of their peers. These were the heads of society, and to betray

[9] "Chronache bolognese," 126, 145, BCB Fondo Gozzadini ms. 280.

that headship through a political crime was to forfeit both head and headship alike. Some Italian executioners stood behind their kneeling prisoner
to swing a sword at his neck, while a miniature in a Ferrarese *Book of the
Executed* shows an executioner winding up to swing an axe at a prisoner who
is standing. In either case, a slight error in the height or arc of the swing could
have horrific consequences, and this led some Italian cities to adopt the more
precise guillotinelike instrument called a *mannaia* (fig. 1). As the prisoner
kneeled or lay on the ground, two upright braces on either side of his neck
held a small blade in place just above his neck. The executioner delivered
the final blow with a mallet directly on the back of the blade. The *mannaia*
could also be adapted to sever a criminal's hand before hanging (fig. 18). As
Montaigne saw in the execution of some Roman murderers, the hand that
had held the knife might be sliced off before hanging, but the arm was then
quickly bandaged or staunched with a freshly butchered chicken, so that the
murderer did not bleed to death before reaching the gallows. The Bolognese
took the *mannaia* a step further with a wooden brace or yoke called a *tagliadura* whose upper and lower halves clasped tightly around the kneeling
prisoner's neck. The prisoner had to lean forward to rest the heavy brace on
a block, and this rendered him effectively immobile. The executioner then
slipped a blade into a slot positioned directly over the prisoner's neck on the
top half of the brace and then, as with the *mannaia*, used a heavy mallet to
complete the execution.

Perhaps the most brutal form of all was quartering, reserved largely
for those who threatened public order as bandits, hired assassins, or rebels.
Crimes like these could tear city or countryside apart, and so this same effect
was projected onto the rebel's body with the executioner's sword, as depicted
in some marginal drawings in the chronicle of the notary Eliseo Mamelini.[10]

Finally, Christian Europe employed burning, the ancient Roman penalty for treason, for those crimes like heresy or sacrilege that constituted treason against God. Burning both foreshadowed the flames of hell and also had
the more prosaic advantage of eliminating any relics that a heretic's followers
might steal for veneration—after Florentine authorities burned Savonarola,
they gathered up his ashes and tossed them in the Arno for precisely this
purpose (fig. 19).

The overwhelming majority of those executed in Bologna in the period of this study—777, or 84.73 percent—died by hanging. Only a tenth that

---

[10] "Cronaca di Eliseo Mamelini," fols. 51v, 77v, BCB ms. B1155. See also Ferretti, "Pitture per condannati," 101.

number (78, or 8.5 percent) suffered beheading, which was the next most common form of execution. Relatively few prisoners were either quartered or burned. The various forms are laid out in table 6.2, and the books of the executed take us behind these bare numbers to lay out more of the ritual that turned an act of judicial killing into a spectacle of public justice.

Table 6.2. Forms of Punishment and Execution in Bologna, 1507–1600

	Punishment							Total Executed	Multiple Punishments
	Not stated	Burning	Decapitation	Hanging	Mutilation	Other	Quartering		
1507–09	52	1	—	—	—	—	—	53	—
1510–19	—	1	19	69	—	—	3	92	—
1520–29	—	—	3	21	—	—	1	25	—
1530–39	—	—	1	17	—	—	4	22	—
Total	52	2	23	107	—	—	8	192	—

Source: BCB Fondo Gozzadini 280

	Not stated	Burning	Decapitation	Hanging	Mutilation	Other	Quartering	Total Executed	Multiple Punishments
1540–49	—	4	33	95	1	2	12	147	5
1550–59	0	13	10	90	0	3	12	128	16
1560–69	2	10	7	118	2	3	2	144	9
1570–79	1	8	5	103	0	1	5	123	7
1580–89	0	3	14	211	1	1	18	248	17
1590–99	5	5	9	152	1	0	8	180	9
1600	—	—	—	8	—	—	5	13	3
Total	8	43	78	777	5	10	62	983	66

Source: BAB Aula 2a C.VII.3

The ritual of execution began and sometimes ended in the very center of Bologna at the Palazzo del Podestà, residence of the city's chief judicial official. Rebuilt in the fifteenth century and outfitted with underground prisons, it framed the north side of Piazza Maggiore, facing the civic basilica of San Petronio and the Palazzo dei Notai to the south side of the square, and flanked by the fortresslike Palazzo Comunale, which held the criminal prison of the Torrone to the west. On the morning of the execution, soldiers escorted their prisoner from the Palazzo Comunale to the Palazzo del Podestà where, from an open second-floor loggia facing the square and called the *ringhiera*, scribes read the sentence in a loud voice to the crowds gathered in the *piazza* below (fig. 3). The prisoner himself stood to one side, served by the comforters who with prayers, songs, and *tavoletta* tried to turn his attention from the hundreds or thousands gathered just below him and the fate that lay just ahead (fig. 20). Some met that fate immediately as the executioner led his charge to stand up on the balustrade, tied the noose to a pillar of the loggia, and then pushed the condemned over the edge. It made little sense to hang a common thief or murderer in this way, but when dealing with a traitor, a rebel, an assassin, a public bandit, or a counterfeit, the sight of the body dangling against the very wall of the judge's palace was a powerful and universal sign of public vengeance. Florentines had used the windows of the Palazzo della Signoria to execute some members of the 1478 Pazzi conspiracy against the Medici (fig. 18), and had hanged Antonio Rinaldeschi, charged with violating a public shrine to the Virgin Mary, from the windows of the Bargello prison (fig. 4).[11]

Conducting hangings and beheadings from the safety of the Podestà's loggia on the Piazza Maggiore allowed authorities to avoid what was otherwise the next stage in the ritual—conveying the criminal to a more distant place for execution, usually a hillside that locals called the Montagnola or the Mercato del Monte. The hill was located between a public market and the city walls at the northern edge of Bologna, and it was while en route there that angry mobs might seize a hated prisoner and tear him limb from limb, or that armed allies might overwhelm the guards and spirit their friend to safety. An eighteenth-century source claims that the closed loggia overlooking the Piazza replaced the open Mercato as the site of hangings only in 1507. While this would make perfect sense given the harsh reprisals against Bentivoglio partisans that began that year, the books of the executed demonstrate nothing quite so consistent.[12] Nervous officials certainly executed almost all the Bentivoleschi from the security of the Podestà's loggia, but they also continued using the older Mercato location if they feared no public disruptions. The way north through from Piazza Maggiore to the Mercato followed a street known, as in Florence, as the via dei Malcontenti

[11] Martines, *April Blood*, 197–213; and Connell and Constable, *Sacrilege and Redemption*.
[12] *Libro dei giustiziati*, proemio, BCB Fondo Ospedale ms. 65.

(Street of the Wretched).[13] A longer string of men, women, and children lining the route could see justice on parade in the form of a procession of soldiers, officials, comforters, and criminal (fig. 5). The procession got ever longer as these spectators became participants and followed along to witness the execution. Hard by the hillside stood the S. Maria della Morte's church dedicated to St. John the Baptist, S. Giovanni Decollato, where the criminal had his final rites. On exiting, he walked a few steps to the raised scaffold prepared with the gallows, block, or pyre. While Tuscan cities like Florence and Siena preferred to locate their gallows outside the city walls, many Italian cities like Bologna, Venice, and Rome kept the city's justice within the city's bounds.

Officials were not limited to using the Piazza and Mercato. They erected scaffolds in Piazza Maggiore and other major squares. Any part of the city could serve as a scaffold if authorities wanted to bring justice to the site of the crime. In 1542, three assassins charged with murdering a member of the Lambertini family were beheaded and the pieces displayed on gallows at the Lambertini palace (4 March 1542). Two men charged with attempting a popular uprising after throwing stones and yelling outside the house of the *gonfaloniere di giustizia* Signore Giovanni Alfonso Legnami were brought back to that house for their hanging (7 August 1599). This seems to have happened most frequently with those who dared assault highborn Bolognese, but not exclusively. Two men caught robbing offices of the Monte di Pietà pawn-bank that served the poor were executed on the same day, but at separate gallows erected in front of the two different offices they had robbed (19 July 1592). A few years later a pilgrim headed to the Jubilee in Rome killed his companion on the road; he was brought to Bologna to be tried, hanged, and quartered for the crime, but the pieces were then returned to the scene of the crime to be displayed there (8 April 1600). In a reversal of this code, the site of the crime could also be brought to the site of justice—even justice after death. When an arsonist died in the conflagration of a house he had torched, the scorched timbers were salvaged and constructed into a gallows for the display of the body at the Mercato (8 October 1547).

Burning and quartering were the most violent and dramatic forms of execution, though as Montaigne reported in his account of his voyage to Rome, Italians frequently hanged a criminal before carrying out these gruesome punishments.[14]

---

[13] Some authorities claim that Bologna's via dei Malcontenti took its name not from unhappy prisoners but from a family that once lived there; Guidicini, *Cose notabili*, 3:73–83; and Fanti, *Gli schizzi topografici*, 56, 98.

[14] Montaigne, *Complete Works*, 941.

Yet while some of those who had violated Catholic spaces, clergy, rituals, or ideas were given the mercy of hanging before burning, others were not. Those who had broken into churches, raped nuns, misused the sacraments, impersonated priests, and committed sacrilege or even witchcraft were hanged first so long as they confessed the Catholic faith in their final hours. On the other hand, *luterani,* the catchall indiscriminate term for Protestants, could more often expect to be burned alive either singly or in groups, because they, unlike the others, had refused to recant and return to Catholicism. Sodomites and those convicted of incest faced similar uncompromising treatment at the stake.[15] When it came to quartering, paid killers who acted brazenly in public—*assassini da strada*—might well be hanged before their bodies were ripped apart, though much depended on who they had killed. If, like the mountain men Giovanni and Gianni introduced above, they killed a highborn man, cleric, or prominent public official, then they could expect not only quartering alive, but often some mutilation beforehand like the severing of the hand that had held the knife or gun.[16]

The drama of executions intensified when two, three, or more prisoners died on a single day. The sweep against the Bentivoglio had frequently resulted in mass executions, and outside of politically tense times, it was most likely to happen when authorities rounded up the coconspirators to an assassination, the members of a cell of Protestants, the collaborators in a major theft, or the bandits bonded together in a gang that controlled part of the Apennine hinterland—that is, it was a group crime rather than administrative efficiency that led to these kinds of intensified judicial spectacles. As table 6.3 shows, through much of the latter part of the century, one-half to two-thirds or more of all prisoners were executed in this way, with the largest being a group of twelve rebels dispatched 31 January 1587. Each received his own comforters and, as seen with the mountain men Giovanni and Giannino, each was dispatched individually.

---

[15] Crimes of the thirty-three who were hanged before burning were arson (3), counterfeiting (2), incest (1), *luterani* (9), murder (4), violation of religious objects or clergy (5), witchcraft (7), and unrecorded (2). The execution of one *luterano* was delayed for three days to give him time to repent (2 April 1583); at least one *luterano* and eight sodomites were simply hanged without burning. Crimes of the fourteen burned alive were incest (2), *luterani* (7), sodomy (4), and one murderer who butchered his wife and forced his children to eat the organs (6 December 1557). "Descrizione di tutte le giustiziati di Bologna del 1540 per tutto il 1740," BAB Aula 2a C.VII.3.

[16] Crimes of the thirty-five who were hanged before quartering were assassins (10), murder (8), murder of a public official or cleric (6), theft (7), vandalism (2), and other (2). Crimes of the twenty-seven quartered alive were assassins (6), bandit (1), murder (2), murder of a public official or cleric (11), sacrilege (2), sodomy (1), and theft (4). "Descrizione di tutte le giustiziati di Bologna del 1540 per tutto il 1740," BAB Aula 2a C.VII.3

Table 6.3. Multiple Executions in Bologna, 1540–1600

	Number of instances of multiple executions										Total number executed	% of total executed in multiple executions
	1	2	3	4	5	6	7	8	9	≥10		
1540–49	64	28	6	1	0	0	0	0	0	0	142	54.92
1550–59	38	18	7	3	1	0	0	0	0	0	112	66.07
1560–69	54	24	6	0	3	0	0	0	0	0	135	60.00
1570–79	45	12	6	1	2	1	0	0	1	0	116	61.20
1580–89	70	24	12	4	3	0	0	2	0	3	231	69.69
1590–99	71	13	5	4	0	2	2	1	1	0	171	58.47
1600	2	2	0	1	0	0	0	0	0	0	10	80.00
Total											917	61.89

Source: BAB Aula 2a C.VII.3

The path from crime scene through court to prison and scaffold had so many potential detours, shortcuts, and escapes that only a fraction of criminals were ever prosecuted to the full limit of the law. Many of those facing execution rightly felt that they did not deserve this death. Many comforters agreed. Yet comforters across Italy entered into the rituals of execution not to advocate for the criminal, but to get him or her to accept the sentence. In short, they advocated for the system. Both books 1 and 2 of the *Comforters' Manual* addressed this explicitly, with the latter emphasizing that a comforter who agreed with a protesting prisoner and took up his cause would only sow confusion and make things worse.

> Steel yourself and show in your speech that one should pay no heed to the body…if you began to feel sorry for him and indulged him, you would be courting the danger of softening yourself. The result would be that instead of comforting him, you would make him un-comfortable; and when you should be relieving him of this pain, you would make it overwhelm him. On the contrary, avoid using pitiful words and compassion as much as you can.[17]

By refusing to hear complaints, denying the prisoner a chance to respond to the public reading of the sentence, and deliberately impeding his view and hearing while en route to the scaffold, comforters aimed to render the prisoner quiet and acquiescent. Their most powerful tool was the religious message that

[17] *Comforters' Manual*, bk. 2, chap. 12; see also bk. 1, chap. 15.

the condemned could still enter heaven regardless of whether they had committed the most heinous crime or no crime at all. The promise was firm, but conditional: Christ would welcome only the one who put up no resistance to the sentence, who forgave his enemies, his judge, and his executioner, and who accepted the spiritually inverted logic that an unjust sentence and an unfair execution were *more* and not *less* meritorious because that was precisely how Christian martyrs had died. Comforters were deeply committed to securing salvation for thieves, assassins, counterfeits, and heretics, but they were as deeply committed to securing peace in the city.

The *Comforters' Manual* prescribes actions that fifteenth-century Bolognese considered effective in leading a criminal to repent and acquiesce. While it spread widely and was copied with few changes into the eighteenth century, comforting did not always follow these Renaissance prescriptions. The practical aspects of comforting changed over time and from one place to another. Individual comforters developed a personal style based on their own experience and on shifting spiritual and social values. Different crimes and criminals would also have demanded a different response—in Luca della Robbia's account, Pietro Paolo Boscoli seeks comfort from his friends and from the values of learned classical and Christian culture. A deeply pious follower of the radical friar Savonarola, Boscoli regards the comforters of Florence's Company of the Blacks as annoyances, and so barely talks to them. Finally, the justice system itself did not always make space for comforting when there were those whom authorities wished to rush quickly or quietly to the scaffold. Circumstances often militated against quiet comforting, particularly with the steady push towards multiple executions that placed three or four people on the scaffold at a time, and that led the *conforteria* to protest that it didn't have enough masters and disciples to meet the demand. And it is not known whether Bolognese authorities would have allowed rabbis to take the place of the *conforteria* when the one headed to the scaffold was a Jew. Ferrara certainly did, as G. C. Croce's ballad *Lament and death of Manas the Jew* indicates, but none of those listed in S. Maria della Morte's cinquecento books of the dead or of the executed are identified as Jewish.

The *Comforters' Manual* certainly allows for different situations, and acknowledges that a skilled comforter must read the person and the situation and adapt his approach accordingly. Offering many and varied prayers, songs, and "authorities" gave the comforter the resources he needed to be flexible and responsive to individual prisoners. Other records show further ways that

Bologna's comforters took comforting beyond the prescriptions of their *Comforters' Manual*, reshaping the prison system itself, rethinking their assumptions about how they related to the prisoner, and expanding their idea of how to serve both the prisoner and the city. Many of these changes responded to new political and religious developments of the sixteenth century that altered the contexts for comforting and that drew in a new class of comforters.

The *conforteria* was the core of S. Maria della Morte, which was one of Bologna's largest and most influential confraternities. It first emerged in 1335 as a gathering of the followers of a controversial Dominican friar, Venturino da Bergamo, who had inspired his disciples to get into the prisons to feed the poor and comfort those condemned to die. While friars, priests, and laity had long carried out this kind of charitable work as a Christian duty, S. Maria della Morte marked a departure as the first formally organized lay *conforteria* in Italy, and it spawned a host of imitators up and down the peninsula over the next couple of centuries.[18] Its members soon supplemented their work with prisoners by opening a hospital dedicated to medical care. In 1433 the confraternity also took on custodianship of the image and shrine of the Madonna di San Luca on the Guardia Hill just south of the city, and then organized the processions that regularly brought the image into the city to plead for God's mercy in famine, plague, or war; to thank him in peace and prosperity; to secure his blessing on fields and people; or to celebrate a major public occasion like a military victory or a wedding in the ruling family. When differences grew between the brothers in the 1430s about how S. Maria della Morte ought to balance its charitable and devotional activities, they narrowly avoided splitting apart their confraternity by subdividing into two groups, one institutional-charitable (the Larga) and the other devotional-penitential (the Stretta). Other local confraternities soon followed the Morte's pioneering example as a means of keeping under one roof both those brothers who emphasized charity and those who emphasized spiritual disciplines like frequent confession and communion and even flagellation.

The ranks of its members swelled and became more exclusive as S. Maria della Morte's duties and influence expanded through the fifteenth and sixteenth centuries.[19] It created the position of prior as the official entrusted with overseeing all of the confraternity's spiritual work: its worship life, cultic obligations,

---

[18] Black, *Italian Confraternities*, 217–23; Fanti, "S. Maria della Morte"; Terpstra, "Confraternal Prison Charity"; and Terpstra, "Piety and Punishment."

[19] For the texts of the privileges in the prison system and over the Madonna di San Luca granted to the Morte by various popes and papal governors, see "I privilegi di S. Maria della Morte," BCB Fondo Ospedale ms. 60. See also Fanti and Roversi, *La Madonna*.

and the comforting of prisoners by its Scuola dei Confortatori. Priors served terms of six months long, and one can turn to a late sixteenth-century hand-book prepared to instruct incoming priors in their duties to see how the confra-ternity shaped a series of administrative supports around comforting, and how the practice itself had evolved since comforters had first penned their *Comfort-ers' Manual* over a century before.[20]

Guidelines on comforting were the first thing a new prior would see on opening his handbook. The day before an execution, he received word from ju-dicial officials that a particular prisoner was to be executed the following morn-ing. The prior sent the *conforteria*'s messenger to alert that week's serving master, the man whose name had been pulled from an urn containing the names of all eligible masters at the previous Sunday morning's meeting at the Ospedale di S. Maria della Morte. This master could choose whatever disciple he wished from those currently registered with the Scuola dei Confortatori, and then the two of them headed to the Ospedale to meet with the prior. If for some reason the week's master was unable to attend, the prior had to find another who could fill in. Simi-larly, if two, three, or more prisoners were slated for execution, the prior called up whichever masters he deemed fit. As evening deepened into night, the group met at the *conforteria*'s room in the hospital to put on their uniforms—a black cape of office for the prior, and white head-to-toe flagellant's robes for the two comforters (figs. 3 and 6)—and then headed to the chapel to pray at the Altar of the Holy Sac-rament. The prior offered the usual prayers, read a brief set of instructions written on a tablet stored in the closet, passed on some of the painted *tavolette* used to in-struct and comfort the prisoners, reminded them of how important their spiritual work is, and joined them as they set out for the prison.

The group called over the hospital chaplain and exited the building. Re-citing the "Misere mei" (Psalm 51) together in a low voice, they turned right and followed the portico of the hospital and adjoining buildings as it skirted the east side of Piazza Maggiore where the sentence would be read the fol-lowing morning and where workmen might be putting the finishing touches on the scaffold. Still whispering the psalm, they turned left into the covered passageway behind the Palazza del Podestà and stopped at the outdoor shrine of the Madonna del Popolo, where they knelt and asked Mary to protect the soul of the poor prisoner. They then moved across to the prison entrance at

---

[20] The Morte's prior automatically held the position of *principe*, which was the highest position within the *confor-teria*. What follows is drawn from the chapter entitled "Del modo et ordine del andare in conforteria" in "Memorie riguardanti l'uffizio di Priore," fols. 1v–3r, BCB Fondo Ospedale ms. 43; and also the 1556 *Conforteria* Statutes, fols. 9–10, BAB Aula 2a CVII.19. On S. Maria della Morte generally, see Terpstra, *Lay Confraternities*, 24–27.

the Palazzo Comunale and consulted with the warden before going up to the private room of the Scuola dei Confortatori to wait until the prisoner was brought to them. While waiting for him to arrive, they got the room ready by preparing the altar and lighting a fire if it was winter and the room was cold.

When the condemned prisoner came to the passageway leading to the *conforteria*'s private room, the hospital chaplain waited at the head of the stairs and greeted him warmly, hugging him and leading him into the confraternity chapel where they knelt together while the chaplain said three Our Fathers and three Hail Marys. The prior then helped the prisoner up and greeted him, encouraging him to embrace the will of God with patience, letting him know that the two men standing there in the robes of S. Maria della Morte would be his companions through the night, and reminding him how great the mercy of the Lord God was and how he could acquire God's grace. With the prisoner standing by, the prior formally charged the comforters not to abandon him until the end of his life. The master then offered a prayer, and the prior left for the night.

Executions took place first thing in the morning, and two hours before this the prior returned to the prison room to see whether the comforters or prisoner needed anything. He accompanied the prisoner and comforters to the place of execution, remaining until the prisoner had died. In one of the manuscript illustrations, it is the prior in the black cape of his office who holds the *tavoletta* before the prisoner's face on this final journey, while the two comforters in their white robes and hoods walk beside him singing *laude* or reciting prayers (fig. 3; fig. 20 depicts two comforters only). Since bodies were always left to hang for a time both to ensure that the prisoner was dead and also to ensure that the onlookers had an opportunity to see, the prior and comforters left the scaffold. After a few hours—the handbook specifies "after breakfast" (dopo pranzo)—the prior returned to the hospital to gather some of the staff, who then returned with him to the scaffold to lift down the corpse and bring it back to the hospital for burial. The *auditore* of the Torrone, chief administrator of the justice system in the local government, had to give written license before the comforters could bury the corpse anywhere else or before they could pass it on to the university medical school for its weeklong public courses in anatomy.[21]

[21] In 1561, Pius IV ordered construction of a new *palazzo* for the university, one of the first purpose-built university buildings in Italy, next to the Hospital of S. Maria della Morte; spectacular public anatomy theatres followed in 1595 and 1637. The two institutions maintained close links with each other, with the university providing a medical student who served as an intern in the hospital, and the hospital providing bodies for public anatomy lessons from the ranks of executed criminals or, if necessary, those who had died in the hospital. Anatomists paid a fee of four lire, which went to special masses said for the soul of the dead one.

In fact, the burial records of the Scuola dei Confortatori show that burials
at the hospital had almost entirely ceased by the time the prior's handbook was
written, replaced largely by burial at the church of S. Giovanni Decollato. Table
6.4 shows that the switch had taken place in the 1560s, and that almost all prisoners were now buried at that confraternal church by the Mercato. This was not
unusual. Cities across Europe were moving burials out of their crowded centers
for health reasons and, as will be seen below, S. Maria della Morte's situation was
even more pressing than other Italian *conforterias* because, beyond prisoners
and those who died in the hospital, it also buried a large number of Bolognese
citizens for honor and a fee. It needed options. From 1579, S. Maria della Morte
routinely brought the bodies of Bolognese who had died in the hospital to their
own parishes for burial. A handful of prisoners also won the right to be buried
in their parish, and a small number of heretics were consigned to unconsecrated ground outside the city walls. Transfers from the gallows to the anatomists
for dissections were at a low level and erratic—all but one of those noted for the
1570s took place between 1571 and 1574—suggesting that the Morte may have
passed on cadavers from the hospital as well.[22]

Table 6.4. Burial of Executed Prisoners in Bologna, 1540–1600

	Anatomy	S. Giovanni Decollato	Not specified	Ospedale	Parish mendicant	Outside city	Total
1540–49	1	20	7	86	24	4	142
1550–59	0	12	5	83	12	0	112
1560–69	4	73	2	48	8	0	135
1570–79	10	86	10	3	7	0	116
1580–89	3	178	1	28	20	1	231
1590–99	3	153	0	2	13	0	171
1600	—	10	—	—	—	—	10
Total	21	532	25	250	84	5	917

Source: BAB Aula 2a C.VII.3

"Memorie riguardanti l'uffizio di Priore," fol. 3r, BCB Fondo Ospedale ms. 43; Grendler, *Universities,* 340; and
Ferrari, "Public Anatomy Lessons."

[22] While the main public course of anatomy took place during Carnival in January or February, transfers
from the *conforteria* to the anatomists occurred from fall through spring: September (1), October (1),
November (3), December (1), January (6), February (3), March (3), April (1). Apart from one beheaded
prisoner (8 January 1561) all had been hanged; all but one were male (25 January 1592); "Descrizione di
tutte le giustiziati di Bologna del 1540 per tutto il 1740," BAB Aula 2a C.VII.3. On burials from the hospital,
see "Memorie riguardanti l'uffizio di Priore," fol. 25r, BCB Fondo Ospedale ms. 43.

Proper burial was one of the strongest pastoral assurances and psycho-logical lures that comforters could offer to prisoners as they aimed to persuade them to repent and accept their fate—his body might be in pieces and his family far away, but he could be confident that the *conforteria* would gather it all together and see to a proper burial and a requiem mass. This had always been a charitable work of confraternities and in an age when people feared deeply that improper burial would curse them for eternity, it held a very pow-erful pull. Some also worried about the families they left behind. While the *Comforters' Manual* suggested that prisoners should not be worrying about wills and heirs, in fact comforters stood ready to help prisoners prepare a will and sometimes even ensured that legacies entrusted to them found their way back to families far away. One surviving will of 1530, scrawled out in the prison cell, dispersed the wealth of Francesco de Nanni di Francesco from Monghidoro, the remote border town on the main road between Bologna and Florence. Francesco's comforter was a silk merchant Pier Giacomo Ruggiero, who in a rough and uneven hand recorded a host of small alms for various churches and chapels and six dowries for sisters and nieces before securing Francesco's own signature at the bottom. The will gives no sign of Francesco's crime, though with 1,150 lire to distribute in dowries, he was clearly wealthy.[23] Once the will was registered with Bologna's notaries, the money could be dis-tributed to the women and their spouses.

A more complicated case a few decades later shows how far the com-forters would go to keep their promises to a prisoner. The prisoner Valerio was from Marosticha in Venetian territory, but married to Loretta del Rizzo of Monterchio close to Florence, and he stood convicted of sodomy. A few hours before he was to be hanged in July 1570, he pressed the contents of his purse—one gold scudo and twenty-four Roman pauli—and a small ring with a fake deep blue stone called a *turchina* into the hands of his comforters and begged them to see that they would get to his wife and daughters. The dis-ciple, Biagio Gambaro, took the money and ring, while the master, Francesco Pimazino, took down the will in a clear and steady hand. After the execution, they launched an extraordinary effort to ensure that the goods got to the right person. Suspicious perhaps whether the aging and effeminate Valerio was ac-tually married to Loretta—he was described at one point as "a man of little beard" and seemed not to know too much about his children—they wrote to

---

[23] Francesco gave 400 lire to an unmarried sister, 200 to a married sister, 100 each to two nieces, and 150 each to two girls whose relationship to him is not stated. The 1530 will allotted a total of 1150 lire to dow-ries; "Ultime volontà di Poveri Pazienti" #1 (9 October 1530), AAB SSC 1-1.

the municipal priors of Monterchio. The priors responded eighteen months later with testimonials that yes, while "Valerio the Venetian" had been effeminate and a bit weak (*debole*), the couple were indeed legitimately married. Two weeks later, Biagio Gambaro's brother Battista, a master in the Scuola dei Confortatori, passed the goods on to a man from Monterchio who gave a receipt and promised to get them to Loretta within the month, and indeed a few months after that came a final notice signed by three gentlemen of Monterchio that Loretta had received her goods.[24]

Francesco was possibly a bandit and Valerio a queen—given the mixed currency in his purse, he may even have been a male prostitute. Neither offered any alms to S. Maria della Morte. Yet the comforters took down their testaments and took seriously their own promises to see that these last wills were enforced.[25] They took seriously the claim, which the *Comforters' Manual* advised they repeat to the prisoner and his family, that in his last hours the prisoner became a brother of comforters. The *Comforters' Manual* was explicit and exclusive, advising that comforters tell family that this man is no longer *your* brother, but has become *our* brother.[26]

Claiming the prisoner as a confraternal brother was an extension of the imitative piety that was at the heart of Renaissance spirituality. As the prisoner imitated martyrs and the comforters imitated Christ, they became brothers and sisters of each other and so reflected the spiritual kinship of heaven. This powerful ethos animated confraternities and guilds, who invariably organized themselves around the family model. The abstraction took physical form in the confraternity's books of the dead (*Libri dei morti*) that recorded all those taken to their graves by the brothers of S. Maria della Morte. This began with *confratelli* who had joined the confraternity, paid their dues, worshipped together, and taken their turn in charitable work and administrative offices. It extended to include patients from towns across Italy and Europe who had died in the confraternity's hospital, prisoners both local and "foreign" who had been comforted and buried by the

---

[24] Valerio, "un umomo di poca barba" was about fifty years old when executed 19 July 1570, and seemed to have left his wife some time before; he offered the name of a witness who could vouch for his claim of having two daughters, Franceschina and Costantia. The two testimonials (*fede*) from Monterchio were dated 10 January 1571, though given the Florentine dating convention of starting the new year on 25 March, this is likely 1572. The receipt given by Benedetto di Matthio Gorhenchi from Monterchio (noting items and cash totaling 11.16.4 lire and one gold scudo) was dated 28 January 1572, while the final testimonial that Loretta had received the funds was dated 6 April 1572; "Ultime volontà di Poveri Pazienti" #3, AAB SSC 1–1.

[25] From 1597 it kept a register of all the wills that comforters recorded in the cells; "Memorie riguordanti l'uffizio di Priore," fol. 43, BCB Fondo Ospedale ms. 43; and "Ultime volontà di Poveri Pazienti," AAB SSC 1–1.

[26] *Comforters' Manual*, bk. 2, chap. 2.

conforteria (together with the names of the comforters who had assisted them), and the significant number of highborn Bolognese citizens who considered it a signal honor to be buried by S. Maria della Morte and gave generous alms to the brothers to secure it. Prior Giovani Antonio Bertaro began the day-by-day tallying of the *morti* in the books of the dead in 1540, though he noted in his preface that the brothers had been demanding them for some time before.[27] Turning their pages summons up images of popular contemporary woodcuts of the Dance of Death with a skeleton leading a ragtag troupe of queens and paupers, merchants and knights, priests and prostitutes hand-in-hand around the graveyard. Death obliterated all social distinctions and reversed all hierarchies. While the wealth of the rich did not circulate beyond the grave, the prayers of the poor were a powerful currency in the salvation exchange. Being listed together with redeemed thieves, arsonists, rapists, and heretics who had reconciled with God and died like the martyrs could do more for the soul of a sleek patrician than his own riches ever had (though the books of the dead also began gradually to record the amounts that the latter left for torches, wax, and alms). Of the eighty-one burials Prior Bertaro recorded in his six-month term, only twenty-one were of executed prisoners, while the rest included those patients and patricians hit by the plague ravaging Bologna that year.[28]

Bertaro explicitly invoked this traditional spirituality based on humble imitation of Christ and association with the poor, but these very traditions were already fading by the mid-sixteenth century. S. Maria della Morte's *Book of the Dead* soon reflected this evolution in the ethos too. In 1588 the prior was "The Most Illustrious Signore" Camillo Ghisilieri, and the rector was "The Magnificent and Illustrious Signore" Carollo Ruina, and these two launched a reform. Their head-turning titles show how much the social climate had shifted in Bologna generally and in the confraternity in particular. Arguing that it was shameful that Bologna's worthy citizens be recorded together with the dregs of society, they pulled the prisoners out of the books of the dead and consigned them to a new separate series of books of the executed (*Libri dei giustiziati*).[29]

---

[27] "Libro dei Morti dell'Arciconfraternita di S. Maria della Morte e dei giustiziati da essi assistiti," fol. 1r, BCB Fondo Ospedale ms. 53.

[28] For Bertaro's term, see "Libro dei Morti dell'Arciconfraternita di S. Maria della Morte e dei giustiziati da essi assistiti," fols.1r–3v, BCB Fondo Ospedale ms. 53. The number of torches and candles was first recorded in April 1541, from 1544 their value was noted in monetary terms in regular inventories at each turnover of the priorate, from 1547 the record included the cost of the funeral banner (*palio*), and by the 1550s there are complete financial records of the costs of the funerals; ibid., fols. 24r–68r.

[29] There had been two volumes of books of the dead produced from 1540, the first (BCB Fondo Ospedale ms. 53) extending to 1567 and the second ("Libro dei morti accompagnati alla sepoltura dall'Arciconfraternita di

The poor criminal was no longer a spiritual brother with power to help those who associated with him, but a contagious carrier of shame and dishonor.[30]

Who were the comforters? Why did they do this work, and how did it—and they—fit into the justice system generally? There is almost no reliable information on individual comforters in Bologna before the sixteenth century.[31] The *Comforters' Manual* itself—in both its text and its extant copies—sends a decidedly mixed message about who they were. The text is rich in the metaphors of merchant, artisinal, and professional life: the devil preys on us as thieves prey on traveling merchants; our wealth is a poor investment in the heavenly marketplace, but our good deeds are the friends who will present our case before the Lord our judge; Christ is our patron and protector, but like any patron we need to ensure he sees us regularly in his court if we want him to remember and listen to us; to save a prisoner's soul is to be a "merchant of heaven" acquiring new merchandise for God.[32] The author coaches comforters to deflect awkward theological questions from prisoners who, for instance, may want to know just what the soul is, by responding, "This is out of the ordinary and weighs on me heavily…it requires a very learned theologian to respond to it…[and] I am a cloth merchant without formal education" (io che sono uno strazarolo senza scientia). A few copies of the *Comforters'*

---

s. Maria della Morte," BCB Fondo Ospedale ms. 54) from 1568 to 1588 when entries stopped with over eighty blank pages left, though these were later cut out and the volume rebound (see description on fol. 1r). Ghisilieri and Ruini clearly thought differently about associating rich and poor in a single volume. The new *Book of the Dead* covered 1588 to 1599 (BCB Fondo Ospedale ms. 55), and in 1644 the confraternity produced an alphabetical guide to the highborn Bolognese that it had buried over the previous two centuries ("Libro dei morti sepolti accompagnati dall'arciconfraternita di S. Maria della Morte," BCB Fondo Ospedale ms. 57).

[30] Beyond that, funerals were becoming a serious and profitable business for Bologna's charities. In 1566 the Morte had gone to court against another confraternity in order to protect what we might call its "brand," winning a punitive settlement against the Compagnia di S. Giobbe, administrator of the city's infirmary for syphilitics, that prohibited the latter from marching in its funeral processions wearing robes that looked like those of the Morte. The settlement issued by the vicar general on 10 June 1566 threatened S. Giobbe with a fine of 200 gold scudo for each later violation, and included a drawing of the design that S. Giobbe's robes could have; "Libro dei Morti dell'Arciconfraternita di S. Maria della Morte e dei giustiziati da essa assistiti," fols. 159r–160v, BCB Fondo Ospedale ms. 53. The vicar general at that point was Cristoforo Pensabene, an important member of the Morte and its *conforteria* (see below).

[31] The eighteenth-century scribe and company historian Carlo Antonio Machiavelli claimed that an ancestor, Luigi di Leonardo Machiavelli, had joined the *conforteria* in 1483 and wrote many of its early texts, including the *Comforters' Manual*; Mario Fanti has demonstrated that this part of Machiavelli's otherwise reliable company history is fraudulent. See Carlo Antonio Machiavelli, "Descrizione di CXIV Maestri Ordinari," BAB Aula 2a C.VI.8 #1; and Fanti, "Confraternita di S. Maria della Morte," 126–31. A Machiavelli ancestor, Alessandro di Carlo, did serve as a disciple from 1563 to 1571; "Catalogo delli autori," BAB Aula 2a C.VI.3.

[32] *Comforters' Manual*, bk. 1, prologue, fols. 41v–42r, 44v–46v, PML ms. 188.

Manual shift this to "weaver" (tessitore), "saddler" (selaro), or simply "artisan" (artexano), suggesting that comforters came from the class of artisans and masters.[33] Yet the same author immediately adds, "As our Cato says, 'Mitte archana dei celumque inquirere quid sit,' that is, leave alone the secret mysteries of our Lord God Almighty."[34] Few unlettered artisans would speak of "our" Cato.[35] Few would be able to assemble the list of classical, patristic, and biblical "authorities" included in some manuscripts or follow the rhetorical strategy that the author advises a few pages earlier: "As you well know, a wise man who is learned wants a different kind of conversation than a rustic or a woman."[36] Certainly many extant manuscript copies of the *Comforters' Manual* dating to the later fifteenth and early sixteenth centuries were commissioned by highborn families and marked with their coats of arms, pointing to owners who were educated, wealthy, and influential.

When Prior Giovani Antonio Bertaro began keeping the books of the dead in 1540, he carefully recorded the names of the masters and disciples who served at each execution. By compiling and sorting through all the statistics, one can piece together a picture of who these comforters were, how often they served, and how their social profile changed over the course of the sixteenth century.[37] From 1540 to 1603, forty-three men became masters in the Scuola dei Confortatori, and all but the first eight had first served as disciples. Through those years, a further 162 men served as disciples without ever becoming masters. Among the whole group of disciples, about a quarter (forty-one) never served more than once, but the median for the whole group was three.[38] Masters served an average of just under fourteen years, and in

---

[33] *Comforters' Manual*, fol. 21v, BUB ms. 702 ("selaro"); and *Comforters' Manual*, fol. 137r, BUB ms. 157, ("artexano").

[34] *Comforters' Manual*, bk. 2, chap. 13, fols. 47v–48r, PML ms. 188.

[35] From the collection of moralizing couplets known as distichs by Dionysius Cato, a third- or fourth-century author of the text *Dionysii Catonis Disticha de Moribus ad Filium* commonly used in Latin education, and attributed in the early medieval period to Cato the Elder. This particular one is *Disticha Catonis* 1.2:

> Mitte archana dei caelumque inquirere quid sit;
> Cum sis mortalis, quae sunt mortalia cura.

> [Avoid asking what are the secret things of God or heaven;
> Since you are human, worry about human things.]

[36] *Comforters' Manual*, fols. 40v–41r, PML ms. 188.

[37] Statistics for this section are drawn from "Catalogo delli autori," BAB Aula 2a C.VI.3; and Machiavelli, "Descrizione di CXIV Maestri Ordinari," BAB Aula 2a C.VI.8.

[38] Of the 196 disciples for whom we have statistics, years of service are: one year (41), two (37), three (33), four (22), five (13), six (8), seven (11), eight (6), nine (4), ten (2), eleven to nineteen (15), twenty to twenty-three (4). The median was three years, and the average 4.62. Disciples served from under one year to over thirty, with an average of 5.7 and a median of 3 years; "Descrizione di tutte le giustiziati di Bologna del 1540 per tutto il 1740," BAB Aula 2a C.VII.3.

that time were called into service an average of just over twenty-three times, or almost twice annually. Disciples served an average of just over five years, and in this time they were called into service an average of between four and five times, or approximately once annually.[39]

Yet these are overall averages and give only a very general picture of a group of men who were serious about and committed to making regular visits to the prison and scaffold. Looking more closely at the records turns up patterns of recruitment of masters and disciples that tell a more distinctive story about the S. Maria della Morte *conforteria* and its connections to Bolognese politics and civil religion. The body of masters chose when and whether to add to their number and they almost always added colleagues in groups of two or three. It is possible to identity three distinct cohorts who led three distinct stages of the Scuola dei Confortatori's maturing within Bolognese politics. A first cohort of eight joined between 1538 and 1540, a second of ten between 1555 and 1557, and a third of eleven between 1599 and 1603.[40] Masters normally served a life term, but there seems something more deliberate in the turnover of the three cohorts here. With one exception, all of the first cohort of 1538 to 1540 were gone within a year of the second cohort of 1555 to 1557 joining (three before and four after, with one remaining to 1572), and again most of this second cohort left the *conforteria* in a relatively short period of time in the late 1590s. Since most members of the first two cohorts carried on to within a year of their deaths, this represents a coming together of generational exchange and periodic reform and expansion of the Scuola dei Confortatori.[41]

The first cohort of 1538 to 1540 seems to have revived the work after a period of minimal or suspended activity. It is with them that we can see the loosely organized *conforteria* reshaped as the formal Scuola dei Confortatori

---

[39] Masters served between four and forty-one years, with an average of 13.86 and a median of 14. They served from two to seventy-five times, with an average of 23.1 and a median of 18. Disciples served from one to thirteen years, with an average of 5.7 and a median of 3. They served from one to twenty-three times, with an average of 4.62 and a median of 3; "Descrizione di tutte le giustiziati di Bologna del 1540 per tutto il 1740," BAB Aula 2a C.VII.3.

[40] Dates for the first cohort of eight (two on 6 March 1538 and four on 12 June 1538, two on 2 January 1540); the second cohort of ten (five on 24 June 1555, two on 6 January 1556, one on 14 June 1556, one on 31 January 1557); the third cohort of eleven (seven on 17 November 1599 and four on 25 March 1603). Fourteen men were appointed masters from the 1560s through the 1580s; "Descrizione di CXIV Maestri Ordinari," BAB Aula 2a C.VI.8.

[41] All but fourteen of the forty-two masters joining between 1538 and 1608 died within a year of their last exercise of comforting; "Descrizione di tutte le giustiziati di Bologna del 1540 per tutto il 1740," BAB Aula 2a C.VII.3; and "Descrizione di CXIV Maestri Ordinari," BAB Aula 2a C.VI.8.

within the confraternity of S. Maria della Morte. The savage reprisals against the Bentivoglio faction had diminished by this point, and it could be that the widespread arrests and summary justice carried out by papal authorities in those decades had made the work of comforting both impolitic and unpopular, and had caused the *conforteria* to decline. Yet private chroniclers in Bologna fail to note any changes in the public rituals of execution in 1538 to 1540, so it is unlikely that lay comforting had disappeared entirely in that decade prior to that revival. All the same, the fact that within four years, S. Maria della Morte started a comforters' membership list, began keeping detailed books of the dead, and then gave the Scuola dei Confortatori its own room in the confraternity's hospital points to a deliberate effort to organize or at least reorganize the work.[42] Famine and plague whipped Bologna at the beginning and end of the 1540s, and the spike in thefts, murders, and factional violence speaks to desperation and widespread upheaval that the authorities now struggled to control by sending more people to the scaffold.[43]

Of all three cohorts, the first was the most modest in its occupations and political involvements. None were clearly drawn from the higher guilds or professions. It appears that only two had served terms on one or another of Bologna's political councils, and these were as members of the relatively minor Tribunes of the People (Tribuni della Plebe) and the slightly more influential Council of Elders (Anziani), two governing bodies that dated to the communal period. Both bodies were, at this period, playing a greater role in combating social problems in Bologna—the Tribunes by arranging successfully for the import of grain, and the Elders by arranging unsuccessfully for the export of paupers. No comforters served on Bologna's Senate, though one was the son of a senator.[44] This first cohort of eight does not include the silk merchant Pier Giacomo Ruggiero, who is the only comforter of whom there is any record before 1538, and who was one of eighteen disciples who joined the work in or before 1540.[45]

---

[42] The *conforteria's* room had a prominent location on the second floor of the hospital, to the right at the head of the main stairway; "Origine e progressi della Sacra Scuola dei Confortatori," fol. 27, BAB Aula 2a C.VII.19.

[43] Giacomo Rinieri's *Cronaca* details the effects of famine in 1539/40 and 1548/49 (pp. 65–72), exacerbated by epidemics of typhus in 1540, 1541, and 1545 (65–72, 76–91, 132), that led to the first attempts on the part of the Council of Elders to expel the poor in 1539 and 1549 (72, 238).

[44] Paolo Boatiero served on the Tribunes (1531), and Alessandro Cattanei on the Tribunes (1539) and the Elders (1528, 1532, 1536); Cattanei's father, Baldassare, was the fourth member of the family to hold a Senate seat; "Descrizione di CXIV Maestri Ordinari," #5, #6, BAB Aula 2a C.VI.8; Alidosi, *I Signore Anziani Consoli*, 73, 77, 81; and Guidicini, "Alberi Geneologici," 41, ASB Sala di Consultazione.

[45] Ruggiero was the one who recorded the last will of the bandit Francesco de Nanni from the border town of Monghidoro in 1530. He waited almost two decades more before being promoted to the rank of master

With the second cohort, the dovetailing of religious and political concerns becomes far more definite. Members of the second cohort were reformers of a different stripe, connected more closely both to the disciplinary spiritual currents then circulating around Italy and also to the expanding power of the local Senate. They were led by a young notary, Cristoforo Pensabene, who served one year as a disciple before being promoted to master in 1556. In the months before becoming master, he wrote the first extant set of the Scuola dei Confortatori's statutes to expand administration and more tightly define its spiritual life.[46]

As we have seen, its membership of powerful elite males and its broad civic and religious functions had allowed the confraternity of S. Maria della Morte to develop into a major institution in Bologna's political and religious life. It had always been caught up in the shifting forms of what one can call Catholic Reform, though it was not firmly identified with orthodoxy. Cristoforo Pensabene was one of a small core of people who wished to change that, and he approached the challenge with the zeal of a convert. At age nineteen he had been hauled before an Inquisitorial tribunal and had formally recanted in a secret agreement. New charges recurred at least twice in later years, though they were most likely politically motivated, perhaps in an effort to undermine the changes he was spearheading.[47] We saw above that S. Maria della Morte had pioneered the creation of orthodox subgroups of penitent flagellants called Stretta within Bolognese confraternities over a century before. As lay confraternal counterparts of the Observant devotional movements that were roiling and transforming religious orders in the fifteenth century, the Stretta whipped themselves, fasted, took the sacraments frequently, confessed to each other, read devotional literature, and gained a reputation for being more spiritually rigorous than the Larga. This disciplinary current represented the cutting edge of Catholic Reform in the early to mid-fifteenth century, and it moved through book 1 of the *Comforters' Manual*. At the same time, most members of S. Maria della Morte and the *conforteria* in particular continued to identify with the Larga, which had always placed greater emphasis on charity

---

in 1556, and remained active until 1585; from 1540 to 1585, he served as disciple or master in seventy executions; "Descrizione di tutte le giustiziai di Bologna dal 1540 per tutto il 1740," BAB Aula 2a C.VII.3; and "Descrizione di CXIV Maestri Ordinari," #14, Aula 2a C.VI.8.

[46] "Origine e progressi della Sacra Scuola dei Confortatori," fols. 27–28, BAB Aula 2a C.VII.19. Pensabene was commissioned 12 January 1556, his statutes were approved 14 March and 12 April, and he was promoted to master on 14 June. S. Maria della Morte revised its general statutes in 1562, incorporating Pensabene's *conforteria* statutes without any change in details—he was, in fact, on that statute revision committee too. The revision committee of fifteen was appointed 10 December 1560; "Statuti della Compagnia dell'Ospedale della Morte," fols. 1, 6–7, 13, 18–21, BCB Fondo Ospedale ms. 42.

[47] Dall'Olio, *Eretici e Inquisitori*, 288–95.

than on either discipline or doctrine. Newer devotional currents emerging at the end of the fifteenth century picked up on this idea of putting faith into practice by helping the poor and needy, and this more practical and direct approach informed book 2 of the *Comforters' Manual*. Members of both the Stretta and the Larga joined the Scuola dei Confortatori, but the latter were more than twice as active in the work of comforting prisoners.[48]

As Catholic Reform continued evolving towards the mid-sixteenth century, these emphases on stricter personal discipline and on activist charity merged more closely together. Across Italy new confraternities like the Oratories of Divine Love, new religious orders like the Jesuits, and new institutional reforms launched by the Council of Trent established higher expectations and tighter structures for the surveillance, discipline, and education of Catholic clergy and laity alike. Cristoforo Pensabene's statutes for the Scuola dei Confortatori reflected this ethos.[49] They say almost nothing about comforting as a pastoral activity, and focus instead on organizing the work and focusing the members. They dictated firm guidelines on Catholic orthodoxy (an affirmation of the Trinity, of the Catholic Church as the arbiter of doctrine, and of frequent communion), company procedure (how and where to sit and speak in meetings, and what subjects could not be discussed), and tighter social discipline (avoid blasphemy, perjury, and bad company), and included a sliding scale of fines charged when members blasphemed against God or the saints, or even if they denigrated S. Maria della Morte itself. Masters and disciples had to flee heresy and all suspect opinions, which could be difficult in a university city like Bologna that, at that point, had a substantial Protestant underground. More importantly, the statutes created a new official, the censor, to keep an eye on members: he instructed, disciplined, and mediated between them. The censor had a place of honor at the right hand of the prior. The new statutes added a bookkeeper and a secretary to keep up with paperwork, and increased the minimum number of masters to twelve in place of the seven or eight common earlier; no one could be promoted to that level without having first served an apprenticeship as a disciple.[50]

---

[48] Of the forty-two masters recruited from 1538 to 1603, twenty-eight were of the Larga, eleven of the Stretta, and two unknown. There is no discernible shift in appointment of comforters from one or the other, but those associated with the Larga were far more active, serving an average of 28.66 prisoners (range, 3–73, and median, 22) compared with an average of 12.4 (range, 1–39, and median, 7.5) on the part of those associated with the Stretta; "Descrizione di CXIV Maestri Ordinari," BAB Aula 2a C.VI.8.

[49] "Origine e progressi della Sacra Scuola dei Confortatori," BAB Aula 2a C.VII.19.

[50] "Origine e progressi della Sacra Scuola dei Confortatori," fols. 6–7, 10–11, 19–25, BAB Aula 2a C.VII.19. The fines increased from the first through the third offense, with the fourth bringing expulsion. Fines for blaspheming against God, 1.10, 5, and 10 lire; against Mary and the saints, 1, 4, and 8; and against the Company, 1, 3, and 8.

The Roman orientation of this reforming cohort was further highlighted a few years later in 1564 when one its members negotiated an alliance with the Roman *conforteria* of S. Giovanni Decollato. Aggregations like this were like a minor form of centralization within the Catholic Church after the Council of Trent, as popes created "archconfraternities" that were richly endowed with indulgences and spiritual privileges that they could share with other confraternities so long as the latter agreed to bind themselves to the Roman model. Few members of S. Maria della Morte appreciated the symbolism of being subordinate and dictated to from Rome, and they resisted the alliance until 1571.[51] A decade and a half later, Pope Sixtus V hit on a more ingenious solution by simply reversing the relation; he appointed the Morte as an archconfraternity that could draw others into association with itself just as the Roman archconfraternities did. The move recognized and accommodated Bolognese sensitivities while still drawing the Morte more closely into the Roman orbit.[52]

Not all members of S. Maria della Morte or its Scuola dei Confortatori appreciated these expanding connections to a more disciplined *Roman* Catholicism. Beyond religious orthodoxy, the new statutes imposed tight rules on attendance, on speaking out of turn, and on procedures generally. The censor began policing members more closely and scolded those who failed to attend weekly meetings or violated the statutes. At least one master and a few experienced disciples were disciplined and expelled for being disobedient, *disturbatori*, criticizing the new statutes and the officials, lacking respect, or keeping mistresses.[53] Certainly the recruitment of disciples plummeted after this time, and in 1560, the masters decided that disciples who missed coming for three months would be automatically removed from the rolls.[54]

Ibid, fols. 19–25. The statutes also appointed a *conforteria* bookkeeper to handle fines, alms, and expenses; "Catalogo delli autori," p. 16, BAB Aula 2a C.VI.3. No master appointed after 1555 had failed to serve as a disciple, though one candidate, Giorgio di Vitale Marzari, tried in 1560, 1561, and 1567 and lost each vote; ibid., p. 19.

[51] Sebastiano Mainetti negotiated the aggregation in 1564, and the Scuola dei Confortatori sent delegations to push the pact with S. Maria della Morte's executive in 1565 and 1566 before winning approval in 1571; "Catalogo delli autori," p. 21, BAB Aula 2a C.VI.3.

[52] "Descrizione di CXIV Maestro Ordinari," #26 (4 June 1586), BAB Aula 2a C.VI.8. S. Maria della Morte was Bologna's first archconfraternity; Black, *Italian Confraternities*, 72–74.

[53] Master Francesco Pimazzini and disciple Ercole Sarasini were expelled at Pensabene's insistence in 1557, possibly for complaints they voiced in the general meeting (the *corporale*) of the Morte. Pimazzini apologized and was restored after three months, while Sarasini refused and was kept out. Others were expelled and the number of times they had served are as follows: Perazzino Perrazini (2), a cloth spinner with a mistress, in 1558; Ulisse Mariscotti (5), Annibale Baldissera (4), and Achille Marchesini (2) in 1561; and Cristofaro Sarasini (2) in 1571. "Catalogo delli autori," pp. 10–18, BAB Aula 2a C.VI.3.

[54] "Catalogo delli autori," pp. 15–18, BAB Aula 2a C.VI.3. Figures for recruitment of disciples are as follows: 1540s (30), 1550s (23), 1560s (14), 1570s (6), 1580s (14), 1590s (7). Disciples had to be members of the

Eliminating critics and restricting recruitment emphasized the character of the second cohort as a cell of committed religious activists. It is telling that the most active and dedicated masters joined the *conforteria* precisely as part of or immediately after the second cohort—that is, in the twenty-five years following Pensabene's statutes and the attendant reforms. Of the ten cinquecento masters who individually comforted over forty condemned prisoners, nine joined in this period. This was due less to the rate of executions, which actually dropped through these years, than to these masters' length of service. While exact ages are not known, it appears that the men promoted in this period were younger and so, presumably, were drawn to the work out of a combination of religious commitment and political ambition. Most served for over twenty years. Some, like Pensabene, demonstrated an intensity that generated suspicions and even charges of heresy. Through his last hours before being hanged and burned as a *luterano* on 5 September 1567, Pietro Antonio Cama was assisted by a master, Sebastiano Mainetti, who had been charged twenty years before, and a disciple, Alessandro Machiavelli, who would be charged two years later.[55]

Another feature that distinguishes this second cohort is the increased social standing of masters and even more so of the disciples.[56] Cristoforo Pensabene himself led the group in this respect: the notary served twice on Bologna's Council of Elders (1548, 1564) and once as one of the Tribunes of the People (1555), and was a doctor of civil and canon law and a canon of the civic basilica of S. Petronio. The heresy charges levied against him did not harm his rise in the ecclesiastical hierarchy, and Pensabene was one of a few in the period who moved from one side of the Inquisition's bench to the other with astonishing ease. In 1561 he became the chief financial officer of the local tribunal of the Holy Office, and five years later was appointed vicar general for Bologna's Bishop Gabrielle Paleotti, who was considered together with Carlo Borromeo of Milan to be one of the preeminent exponents of the Council of Trent. Pensabene received the position on

---

Morte, literate in the vernacular, and of solid reputation before they presented themselves for investigation, discussion, and approval by the masters; "Origine e progressi della Sacra Scuola dei Confortatori," fols. 14–16, BAB Aula 2a C.VII.19.

[55] "Descrizione di tutte le giustiziati di Bologna del 1540 per tutto il 1740" (5 September 1567), BBA Aula 2a C.VII.3. Mainetti had been denounced in 1548 as part of a group of sacramentarians associated with Lelio Sozzini and Ulisse Aldrovandi, while Machiavelli was condemned on 8 June 1569 in part due to his associations with Protestants in Lyons; Dall'Olio, *Eretici e Inquisitori*, 128, 154, 266, 349.

[56] Two masters of the second cohort and 28 percent (19 of 68) of the disciples active in the 1550s and 1560s held posts on the Council of the Elders or the Tribunes of the People; "Descrizione di CXIV Maestro Ordinari," BAB Aula 2a C.VI.8.

the recommendation of Pope Pius V, whom he had known earlier, and he served at a time when Paleotti was casting the vicar's role as one concerned chiefly with judicial matters. He installed another of the Morte comforters, Tommaso Barbiero, in his old position with the Holy Office, and was succeeded as vicar general by yet another, Antonio Peruzzi, a close friend of Paleotti who went on to an even more impressive career in the church.[57] Pensabene served at least twice as a comforter during his term as vicar general, though in spite of his earlier service with the Inquisition, he did not serve any of the three men burned as *luterani* on 19 January 1567 (Peruzzi, however, did), or any of the five men burned later that year on the same charge. While the whiff of heresy continued to hang about Pensabene, the fact remains that almost a quarter of those executed for heresy in the six decades from 1540 to 1600 (i.e., nine of thirty-eight) went to the stake in the two years when he served as vicar general (1566–68).[58]

This more influential and engaged second cohort spearheaded significant changes, but their efforts were rooted in more than just religious reform movements. Politics played a major part. The sixteenth century was a time of profound developments in Bologna's systems of government and of justice, and these extended to the roles taken by confraternities. Confraternal charities proved to be effective vehicles for local patricians who aimed to recover some of the authority over government and the justice system that they had lost to Julius II's papal governors when the Bentivoglio were expelled in 1506 and again in 1512. Julius II and Leo X devised a forty-member Senate to share power with the local papal governor or legate, and through the course of the century the Senate moved successfully to consolidate as much power into its own hands as possible. A critical stage in the process occurred in the 1550s when it reorganized its own internal administration by creating eight subordinate congregations—called Assunterie—to handle all aspects of civil administration. It began taking control over aspects of government and social welfare that had previously been carried out by older magistracies like the Tribunes of the People and the Council of Elders, such as the imprisoning of beggars and provision of grain and

[57] Peruzzi had also served in the Holy Office; Paleotti promoted him to vicar general in 1568 and consecrated him bishop of Cesarea and suffragen bishop of Bologna in 1572. He was not active as a comforter after 1570; Dall'Olio, *Eretici e inquisitori,* 291–93.

[58] Prodi, *Cardinale Gabriele Paleotti,* 50. During the 1567 heresy trial of prominent Sienese notary Diofebo Spannocchi, Pensabene was named as a spiritual guide for the notary's circle. A Sardinian student went so far as to claim that he'd gone many times to Pensabene's home and had been ushered into a secret library filled with heretical texts; with a sweep of his hand, Pensabene had said, "These you must study!"(Questi bisogna studiare!). Bologna's Inquisitor Fra Antonio Balducci and Bishop Paleotti both vouched for him, and he survived the charges. Two years later, Peruzzi and Paleotti also fell under suspicion of heresy; Dall'Olio, *Eretici e inquisitori,* 291–93, 298–301.

bread from public supplies. It also moved into the institutional charities. All of Bologna's leading institutional charities, most administered by confraternities, wrote or rewrote their governing statutes in the 1550s according to a roughly uniform model that ceded significant authority to the Senate. Each institution designated a rector as its chief official, and each decided that this six- or twelve-month post would be filled by a senator. A class of senators developed who circulated from one institution to another, and inevitably these senatorial rectors were seldom members of the confraternities they now headed. They became an informal means of controlling and coordinating the work of charitable institutions that had become vital to the city's well-being. The lines between secular and religious administration inevitably became very blurred.[59]

That blurring extended into the judicial system. Papal governors had dispensed with communally appointed judicial officials like the *podestà*, and took direct control over civil and criminal justice. The criminal justice system evolved with a new chief justice, the *auditore del Torrone*, who was appointed by and responsible to the papal legates and governors. After decades of lobbying, Bologna in 1534 regained indirect control over civil justice through creation of a Senate-nominated tribunal of five judges that comprised a new body called the Rota in 1534. Efforts to do the same with criminal justice failed, but the papacy's financial needs did eventually open an opportunity. In 1563, Pope Pius IV turned the body of notaries who worked with the *auditore del Torrone* into a venal office, which he then sold to Bologna's charitable pawn-bank for the poor, the Monte di Pietà. The Monte di Pietà nominated and paid the notaries, and they in turn received criminal denunciations, evaluated evidence, set and collected fines, and made recommendations for prosecution to the papal governors. All but one were "foreign," but that one, designated the "civil notary," acted as the eyes and ears of the Senate. The arrangement, which lasted until 1797, gave the Monte significant influence over the operation of criminal justice. Since its twelve-member confraternal board in turn represented particular social groups (one senator, four nobles, four "citizens," one professor, and two clerics), this indirectly restored a significant degree of local control within the justice system.[60]

The same blurred boundaries resulted from effort under way at the same time by the confraternity of S. Maria della Morte to expand its control over the prison system. It aimed to secure from papal officials both a guarantee and also a monopoly over its privilege of working with Bologna's prisoners, and worked

---

[59] For more on this process, see Terpstra, *Abandoned Children*, chaps. 1 and 4.
[60] Di Zio, "Il tribunale criminale."

through two of its subgroups: the Scuola dei Confortatori in the criminal prisons, and the Compagnia dei Poveri Prigionieri in the civil prisons. The Poveri
Prigionieri had, from at least the later fourteenth century, brought food and
bedding to prisoners and in some cases paid their accumulated fines and fees so
that they could actually leave prison once judicially released.

The Scuola dei Confortatori aimed to secure its monopoly over comforting by securing a monopoly over the space where this took place. Renaissance
prisons were built as large open rooms rather than private cells, and the writer
of the *Comforters' Manual* had clearly worked in this crowded and semipublic
space. He offered advice on how to deflect or direct the other prisoners and
family members who gathered around as he and his disciple worked to refocus
the prisoner's attention, and how to ensure that the onlookers demonstrated
proper respect to the Eucharist when the priest offered it to the prisoner the
following morning. The first answer to these distractions was a private space devoted to comforting, and S. Maria della Morte gained Senate approval in 1549
for construction of a separate room in the public prisons "for the use and con-
venience of those who go to console and confirm in religion those condemned
to death...commonly called Confortatori."[61] The room, finished two years later,
could not be used for any other purpose, and with the key to one of its two locks
held by the prior of S. Maria della Morte, it couldn't be used by another group
either. With the support of the Senate, the Scuola dei Confortatori moved to
formally forbid access to the room by all but its own comforters in 1575, but the
action seems to have been a red flag to the papal legate.[62]

When Sigismondo Sugari, a Ferrarese nobleman turned bandit captain,
was slated for execution in December 1586, Bologna's papal legate Cardinal
Enrico Gaetani ordered that the only ones who could go into the prison to
comfort him were two Capuchin friars.[63] Capuchins were becoming more
active as comforters elsewhere in Italy, and Gaetani clearly aimed to end the
Morte's monopoly. But the Morte reacted immediately to this challenge. Prior

---

[61] ASB Senato Partiti 6 (1549–55), fol. 9r. The Senate offered a subsidy of only forty lire for construction,
suggesting that S. Maria della Morte use its own funds to construct the room. The effort to create this
space suggests that the small fourteenth-century chapel behind the Palazzo del Podestà where prisoners
had been brought the night before execution for comforting had fallen into disuse before the *Comforters'
Manual* was written; "Descrizione di tutte le giustiziati di Bologna nel 1540 per tutto il 1740" (1540), BAB
Aula 2a C.VII.3.

[62] In 1558, the *conforteria* appointed Pensabene and Battista Gambari to work on a room in the prison, suggesting either that the one approved by the Senate in 1549 and completed by 1551 was no longer considered
adequate; "Catalogo delli autori," p. 16, BAB Aula 2a C.VI.3.

[63] A later company history claims that this happened when Antonio Maria Salviati was cardinal legate, but he had
been replaced three months earlier by Gaetani; Pasquali and Ferretti, "Cronotassi critica dei legati," 138–39.

Filippo Fava, whose family was deeply involved in the Scuola dei Confortatori and who had himself served at one execution as a disciple a few years before, raced around meeting with Legate Gaetani, his vice legate, and the *auditore della Torrone* and arguing for S. Maria della Morte's privilege in comforting; other comforters and disciples no doubt also lobbied hard. Gaetani eventually relented and allowed two members of the Scuola dei Confortatori to accompany Sugari as he was hanged and quartered in Piazza Maggiore, but he was unwilling to cede ultimate control of the process.[64] Within weeks he issued a formal decree forbidding the prison warden from allowing anyone "of any grade or condition" other than those holding a written license from the *auditore* of the Torrone to assist prisoners facing execution, either in the room of the Scuola dei Confortatori or anywhere else. Little more than a year later the vice legate issued a duplicate decree forbidding admission to any but those who held a written license from *him*.[65]

Neither decree mentions the Compagnia di S. Maria della Morte. The legate and vice legate were aiming to reassert their own ultimate authority over comforting, but joint action by the Morte, the Senate, and Pope Clement VIII would soon undermine this effort. The Senate issued a decree publicly supporting S. Maria della Morte's work in comforting, while the Morte itself worked through its Poveri Prigionieri subgroup. Two men designated "captains" ran this operation, which like the Scuola dei Confortatori was subject to the overall authority of the Morte and its rector.[66] It had undergone its own reformation in the 1510s and '20s, spearheaded by a patrician who was closely allied to the new papal regime, and it had slowly expanded its administrative authority in the civil prisons ever since. The Prigionieri captains were even better connected socially and politically than Confortatori comforters.[67] All came from powerful families who were well represented in the Senate, and this made the Poveri Prigionieri a convenient vehicle for restoring local authority within the prison systems. A number of the captains had family links

---

[64] "Descrizione di tutte le giustiziati di Bologna del 1540 per tutto il 1740" (6 July1586), BBA Aula 2a C.VII.3. Giovanni Berti and Francesco dal Pero were the comforters; *Memorie riguardanti l'uffizio di Priore* (1572–1604), fol. 27v, BCB Fondo Ospedale ms. 43.

[65] Cardinal Legate Enrigo Caetano issued the first *bando* 2 January 1587; ASB Fondo Boschi ms. 543, fol. 159 (2 January 1587). See Zanardi, *Bononia manifesta* #1770. Vice Legate Anselmo Dandino issued the second *bando* 17 February 1588; ASB Fondo Boschi ms. 544, fol. 25. See Zanardi, *Bononia Manifesta* #1896 (17 February 1588).

[66] For expanded treatment of what follows, see Terpstra, "Confraternal Prison Charity"; and Black, *Italian Confraternities*, 217–23.

[67] This was Cristoforo Angelleli, and his reform work with the Poveri Prigionieri is remarkably similar to that of Cristoforo Pensabene with the Scuola dei Confortatori; Terpstra, "Confraternal Prison Charity," 217–30.

to the Confortatori, and one of them, Giulio Cesare Lambertini, served as a
confortaria disciple and then a master while still a Poveri Prigionieri captain in
the 1590s. Their opportunity came in 1592 when Pope Clement VIII launched
a wide-ranging reform of prisons within the Papal States. Wanting to reduce
corruption and increase revenue, the pope suppressed the bankrupt authority
based in Rome and empowered local bishops to sell the venal office of "prefecture of the prisons" to local confraternities. There was no surprise when the
Morte got the nod in Bologna; it had experience and connections—and had
been negotiating over a price for months.[68] The Morte now controlled the office of prison warden, and hence access to the prisons. It immediately turned
around and sold the rights to the office for an annual fee, setting the stage for
the bizarre situation in which wardens appointed by the Morte levied fines
and fees against prisoners for food, bedding, and freedom, while the Morte's
still-active captains of the Poveri Prigionieri offered charity and alms to the
same prisoners in order to offset precisely these charges.[69]

Blurring the lines between prison administration and prison charity ob-
scured the Scuola dei Confortatori's purpose and complicated its work. In 1576,
Pope Gregory XIII, the Bolognese Ugo Buoncompagni, revived an ancient practice of celebrating particular feast days by releasing a prisoner destined for execution. He chose the day of the Beheading of John the Baptist (29 August) as
the time for this liberation, and designated S. Maria della Morte as the body that
would choose whom to liberate, a power political governors usually exercised. A
year later he added permission to liberate a second prisoner on the Baptist's feast
day of 24 June. This immediately changed the dynamic around comforting. It
had been built around the idea of moving the prisoner's attention beyond execution to a new identity as a martyr, and so comforters were to refuse to discuss the
justice of the sentence or the possibility of clemency. Now they became the very

---

[68] "Deliberazione del Rettore ed Ufficiali dell'Arciconfraternita di S. Maria della Morte intorno alla Compagnia
della Carita per la Visita dei Carcerati, 1588–1613," fols. 1r–10v, BCB Fondo Ospedale ms. 70. Suppressing
the Prefetto generale delle carceri dello stato ecclesiastico allowed the pope to turn its 15,000 scudo debt into
an investment fund called the Monte della Carità. Annual remittances like the 327 scudi paid by the Morte
for the Bolognese prefecture created income for shareholders in the fund and would, in time, eliminate the
debt. See S. Maria della Morte, XI/5, XI/16, fols. 10–12, ASB Fondo Ospedale; "Origine e progressi della Sacra
Scuola dei Confortatori," fols. 16, 21–25, BAB Aula 2a C.VII.19; and di Zio, "Il tribunale criminale."
[69] The Compagnia dei Poveri Prigionieri was retitled the Compagnia della Carità dei Carcerati di Bologna.
It charged the first warden 360 scudi for the office, leaving it only 33 scudi once it had paid its own annual
fee to Rome; these fees dropped steadily (to 288 scudi in 1659, 144 scudi in 1689, and 20 scudi in 1777),
increasing the Morte's profit from the prisons; ASB Fondo Ospedale, S. Maria della Morte ms. XI/16, fols.
11–12. See also the first financial ledgers, the daybook (ms. XI/32) and the account book (ms. XI/33). The
pope created the office of "advocate of the poor" in order to safeguard the rights of poor prisoners in the
wake of these changes, but then appointed one of the highborn comforters of the Morte to the position.

arbiters of that clemency, and in that role soon were subjected to intense lobbying from individuals, families, and even the vice legate.[70] This distinctly early modern privilege—granting a group power to interrupt justice for no reason apart from an arbitrary favor granted by a higher authority—was often exercised responsibily and with mercy. The comforters pardoned a relatively large number of women, and do not seem to have turned this privilege into a money-making opportunity as Milan's S. Croce e Pietà unabashedly did. An elaborate public procession, paralleling a criminal's trip to the scaffold but usually culminating in a mass at the Ospedale della Morte, marked the occasion and highlighted the Morte's power. Yet it also identified the Scuola dei Confortatori more definitely as a body aimed at upholding, administering, and defending the judicial system.[71]

The increasingly blurred lines between administration and charity in the judicial and penal systems contributed to some curious social dynamics through the decades dominated by the second cohort. The growing powers of S. Maria della Morte drew more powerful and ambitious men to the Scuola dei Confortatori. After Pensabene, more clergy joined. Most were headed towards the upper clergy, and so unlike lay comforters who considered the work a life's task, they tended to pursue their careers beyond Bologna and left the group to take up distant posts well before they died. This was a profound departure for a brotherhood that had always been aggressively lay-oriented.[72] More significantly still, as patricians gravitated to the Scuola dei Confortatori they found the ranks of the masters full and effectively closed, and so served lengthy terms as disciples. People like Count Antonio Isolani and Senator Giulio Cesare Lambertini thus entered the prisons as the official subordinates but social superiors of the masters they were assisting.

Both Isolani and Lambertini made it into the ranks of the masters as members of the third cohort, and it is in moving towards this third cohort in 1599 through 1603 that one sees the politicization of the *conforteria* more fully achieved: this cohort included two senators, three university professors, members who had served on the Council of the Elders or Tribunes of the People two, three, or four times, a Roman baron, a Cavaliere di Malta, three clerics, and two

---

[70] "Memorie riguardanti l'uffizio di Priore," fols. 24v, 30r–v, 41v–45r, 64r, BCB Fondo Ospedale ms. 43.

[71] Gregory XIII first granted the privilege on 1 June 1576, and amplified it on 15 May 1577. See "Catalogo delli autori," p. 23, BAB Aula 2a II.C.VI.3; and "Descrizione di CXIV Maestri Ordinari," BAB Aula 2a C.VI.8, #19, #24. Milan's Compagnia di S. Croce e della Pietà argued that the money raised could go to the liberation of others incarcerated in the debtors' prison; Black, *Italian Confraternities*, 220–23.

[72] Of the nine clerics raised to master status after Pensabene, five left to take bishoprics or other positions elsewhere in Europe (Giovanni Francesco Calvi, Giacomo Campeggi, Lodovico Folchi, Angelo Peruzzi, Alesandro Scappi).

counts.[73] Isolani and Lambertini were not the only ones to have first joined in the 1560s, '70s, or '80s as disciples, and the direct intervention of powerful disciples and masters helped secure the steady expansion of powers by the Scuola dei Confortatori and the Poveri Prigionieri in the 1580s and 1590s.

Comforting had changed by the late sixteenth century as the Bolognese gradually adapted to some fundamental changes in their political system and to new currents of religious reform. Confraternities took significant administrative roles in Bologna's penal justice and prison systems through a process coordinated by the Senate and executed in collaboration with some individually cooperative popes. Control over these charities restored to the Bolognese elite that power over the judicial system that they had lost with the fall of the Bentivoglio. The growing prestige of S. Maria della Morte and the Monte di Pietà was consolidated in the later sixteenth century, above all when their responsibility over the prison system expanded. The Monte ran the courts and the Morte ran the prisons, and both took fees from the poor prisoners they were pledged to assist.[74]

In 1665, Cardinal Legate Carolo Carafa issued a decree complaining that the number of people crowding into the chapel of the Scuola dei Confortatori was interfering with the work of the comforters and distracting the condemned prisoners. What was this space now like? An illustration in one fifteenth-century copy of the *Comforters' Manual* shows a prisoner with two comforters in a small space (fig. 9), while another shows three comforters (fig. 3). The Morte's statutes warned against the problems of letting too many people in the room, and the later sixteenth-century handbook for the Morte prior notes at least four who could be there, while authorizing him to admit more if he wished.[75]

The company had always complained that the room was too small. A 1575 decree against crowds of onlookers had been issued the day after the Scuola dei Confortatori had to manage help for nine criminals, and one can well imagine how chaotic a scene that would have been. It spent its own money to expand the room once in midcentury and then again once its monopoly was secured in

[73] The Morte also decided in 1586 that masters should be honored with a special office upon their deaths; "Descrizione di CXIV Maestri Ordinari," BAB Aula 2a C.VI.8, #16.

[74] Prodi, *Sovrano pontefice*. On the growing prestige of S. Maria della Morte, see Terpstra, "The Qualità of Mercy."

[75] "Statuti della Compagnia dell'Ospedale della Morte," p. 20, BCB Fondo Ospedale ms. 42; and "Memorie riguardanti l'uffizio di Priore," fols. 1v–3r, BCB Fondo Ospedale ms. 43.

1588.[76] But Carafa's 1665 decree suggested that there was more here than simply the volume of prisoners. It limited admission to those wearing the cape of S. Maria della Morte and armed with a commission from the prior, together with a chaplain, priest, various named officials and their servants—possibly eight people and all of them confraternity members on official business. Issued by the legate and approved by the Elders, the Consuls of the Guilds, the Standard-bearer of Justice, and the Senate, the decree applied to all people, "regardless of grade or condition" and, for good measure, ordered them to leave their weapons at the door on pain of a 100-scudo fine and three pulls of the strappado.[77]

Carafa's decree suggests that the comforters' room was filling up with all sorts of highborn onlookers, and this in turn suggests that the Morte itself was turning its charitable work with prisoners into a public spectacle that attracted the kind of well-meaning charity tourists who would in future centuries take their Sunday strolls in lunatic asylums like London's Bedlam. Reading between the lines, the legate's decree gains a paradoxical and an almost comic opera quality: the ones most likely to pull rank and bring in weapons were precisely the highborn patricians—the Illustrissimi and Magnifici—on those very government bodies that had approved the decree. These were also the ones who increasingly sought membership in the Morte and its Scuola dei Confortatori. And they were the ones who wanted the criminals pushed out of the Morte's books of the dead for fear of the "contagion" of a criminal's dishonor. A Morte prior might have difficulty turning them down when they asked him permission to watch the comforting of a famous bandit or notorious murderer, either because they were his superiors or because they were his friends. Getting these same governing bodies to cosign the decree then becomes a diplomatic attempt to have these patricians police themselves, something not unheard of in the social politics of local charity.[78]

The *Comforters' Manual* reflects the spiritual ethos of the fifteenth century: by imitating Christ, a thief or murderer could become a martyr. By claiming the criminal as a brother, comforters steered him to Christ and believed that this new brother's prayers in turn would steer their own souls to heaven. As different devotional currents, political realities, and social values dovetailed

[76] The 1575 decree was issued 29 August 1575. The Scuola dei Confortatori appointed committees to investigate and improve the room in 1558, 1566, 1576, and 1588, was compensated by the Senate for costs in 1588, and invested a further 400 lire in 1590; "Catalogo delli autori," pp. 21–25, BAB Aula 2a C.VI.3.

[77] *Bando* of Cardinal Legate Carlo Carafa (18 September 1665), p. 45, BCB B 3624, #13.

[78] For a similar dynamic at work in roughly the same period between confraternal administrators and patrician women involved in Bologna's public beggars' shelter and workhouse, see Terpstra, "Showing the Poor a Good Time."

in the sixteenth and seventeenth centuries, comforting changed in subtle but significant ways. The separate room and separate listing of the dead; patrician spectators and the increasingly patrician comforters; the Morte taking prison management in hand and prisoners' fees in pocket: it is hard to avoid the conclusion that with greater powers for the Scuola dei Confortatori there came greater distance from the prisoners. At the same time, ballads like Croce's *Caso Compassionevole* and accounts like della Robbia's *Recitazione* recast at least some criminals from the old model of scaffold-saints into more secular terms as doomed lovers or noble political martyrs. With this the theatre of execution was shifting from its earlier spiritual-didactic mode into that of romantic tragedy, another reason perhaps why the highborn were so eager to crowd into the cells as spectators in an early modern version of a reality show.[79]

While the more hierarchical values and power politics of the ancien régime changed the Scuola dei Confortatori, they did not eliminate immediate realities within the prison. However radically the conditions and context of comforting changed, comforters still reached for the old *Comforters' Manual* when preparing themselves for their work in the cell, chapel, and scaffold. Not so much book 1, with its more abstract catechism penned by a cleric, which they freely condensed or tossed out. But certainly book 2, where a lay author had shown how to be a brother to a man facing a violent death. And certainly della Robbia's moving account of the final hours of Boscoli and Capponi, which demonstrated that same brotherhood; this was the time when manuscripts bearing that account multiplied in Florence. Each city's own particular history reflected the political and social adaptations of the many cities that were adapting to the ancien régime—seeing what happened here allows one to see how the religious models of the Renaissance shifted to meet the new realities of the early modern age.

Works Cited

Archives

AAB Archivio Arcivescovile, Bologna
ASB Archivio di Stato, Bologna
BAB Biblioteca Arcivescovile, Bologna
BCB Biblioteca Comunale, Bologna
BUB Biblioteca Universitaria, Bologna
PML Pierpont Morgan Library, New York

---

[79] The romanticizing of criminals became far more common by the eighteenth century; Prosperi, *Dare l'anima*, 307.

Printed Sources

Alberti, Leandro. *Historie di Bologna*, 1479–1543. Edited by Armando Antonelli and Maria Rosaria Musti. Bologna: Costa Editore, 2006.

Alidosi, Giovanni Niccolò Pasquali. *I Signori Anziani Consoli e Gonfalonieri di Giustizia della città di Bologna dall'Anno 1454 al 1640 distinti in due parti.* Bologna: Manolessi, 1640.

Black, Christopher F. *Italian Confraternities in the Sixteenth Century.* Cambridge: Cambridge University Press, 1989.

Blanshei, Sarah Rubin. "Crime and Law Enforcement in Medieval Bologna." *Journal of Social History* 16, no. 1 (1982): 121–38.

Connell, William J., and Giles Constable. *Sacrilege and Redemption in Renaissance Florence: The Case of Antonio Rinaldeschi.* Toronto: Centre for Reformation and Renaissance Studies, 2006.

Dall'Olio, Guido. *Eretici e Inquisitori nella Bologna del Cinquecento.* Bologna: Istituto per la storia di Bologna, 1999.

Dean, Trevor. "Criminal Justice in Mid-fifteenth Century Bologna." In *Crime, Society, and the Law in Renaissance Italy*, edited by Trevor Dean & K. J. P. Lowe, 16–39. Cambridge: Cambridge University Press, 1994.

Di Zio, Titzia "Il tribunale criminale di Bologna nel sec. XVI." *Archivi per la storia* 1–2 (1991): 125–35.

Fanti, Mario, ed. "La Confraternita di S. Maria della Morte e la Conforteria dei condannati in Bologna nei secoli XIV e XV." In *Confraternite e città a Bologna nel medioevo e nell'età moderna*, 120–74. Rome: Herder Editrice, 2001.

———, ed. *Gli schizzi topografici originali di Giuseppe Guidicini per le Cose Notabili della città di Bologna.* Bologna: Arnaldo Forni, 2000.

———, and Giancarlo Roversi, eds. *La Madonna di San Luca in Bologna.* Bologna: Silvana Editoriale, 1993.

Ferrari, Giovanna. "Public Anatomy Lessons and the Carnival: The Anatomy Theatre of Bologna." *Past and Present* 117 (Nov. 1987): 50–106.

Ferretti, Massimo, "Pitture per condannati." In *Misericordie: Conversioni sotto il patibolo tra Medioevo ed eta moderna*, edited by Adriano Prosperi, 85–151. Pisa: Edizione della Normale, 2007.

Grendler, Paul F. *The Universities of the Italian Renaissance.* Baltimore: Johns Hopkins University Press, 2002.

Guidicini, Giuseppe. *Cose notabili della città di Bologna ossia storia cronologica de suoi stabili sacri, pubblici e privati.* 3 vols. Bologna: Società Tipografica dei Compositori, 1870.

Machiavelli, Carlo Antonio. *Catologo delli autori, e delle materie spettanti alla conforteria.* Bologna: Lelio dalle Volpe, 1729.

Martines, Lauro. *April Blood: Florence and the Plot Against the Medici.* Oxford: Oxford University Press, 2003.

Montaigne, Michel de. *The Complete Works of Montaigne: Essays, Travel Journal, Letters.* Translated by Donald M. Frame. Stanford, CA: Stanford University Press, 1948.

Pasquali, Marilena, and Mario Ferretti. "Cronotassi critica dei legati, vicelegati e governatori di Bologna dal sec. XVI al XVII." *Atti e memorie di storia patria per le province di Romagna.* 23 (1972): 138–39.

Prodi, Paolo. *Il Cardinale Gabriele Paleotti (1522–1597).* Vol. 2. Rome: Edizioni di storia e letteratura, 1967.

———. *Il sovrano pontefice, un corpo e due anime: La monarchia papale nella prima età moderna.* Bologna: Il Molino, 1982.

Prosperi, Adriano. *Dare l'anima: Storia di un infanticidio*. Torino: Einaudi, 2005.

Rinieri, Giacomo. *Cronaca di Giacomo Rinieri 1535–1549*. Edited by Armando Antonelli and Riccardo Pedrini. Bologna: Costa Editore, 1998.

Terpstra, Nicholas. *Abandoned Children of the Italian Renaissance: Orphan Care in Florence and Bologna*. Baltimore: Johns Hopkins University Press, 2005.

———. "Confraternal Prison Charity and Political Consolidation in Sixteenth Century Bologna." *Journal of Modern History* 66, no. 2 (1994): 217–48.

———. *Lay Confraternities and Civic Religion in Renaissance Bologna*. Cambridge: Cambridge University Press, 1995.

———. "Piety and Punishment: The Lay *Conforteria* and Civic Justice in Sixteenth Century Bologna." *Sixteenth Century Journal* 22 (1991): 679–94.

———. "The *Qualità* of Mercy: (Re)building Confraternal Charity in Early Modern Bologna." In *Ritual, Spectacle, Image. Confraternities and the Visual Arts in the Italian Renaissance*, edited by B. Wisch & D. C. Ahl, 117–45. Cambridge: Cambridge University Press, 2000.

———. "Showing the Poor a Good Time: Caring for Body and Spirit in Bologna's Civic Charities." *Journal of the History of Religion* 28/1 (2004): 19–34.

Zanardi, Zita. *Bononia manifesta: Catalogo dei bandi, editti, constituzione, e provvedimenti diversi, stampati nel XVI secolo per Bologna e il suo territorio*. Florence: L. S. Olschki, 1996.

Zorzi, A. "The Judicial System of Florence in the Fourteenth and Fifteenth Centuries." In *Crime, Society, and the Law in Renaissance Italy*, edited by Trevor Dean & K. J. P. Lowe, 40–58. Cambridge: Cambridge University Press, 1994.

Fig. 1. Anonymous, *Execution of John the Baptist,* ca. 1522. Woodcuts from a manuscript reproduced in *La Passione di Revello: Sacra rappresentazione quattrocentesca di ignoto piemontese,* edited by Anna Cornagliotti, 126. Torino: Centro Studi Piemontesi, 1976.

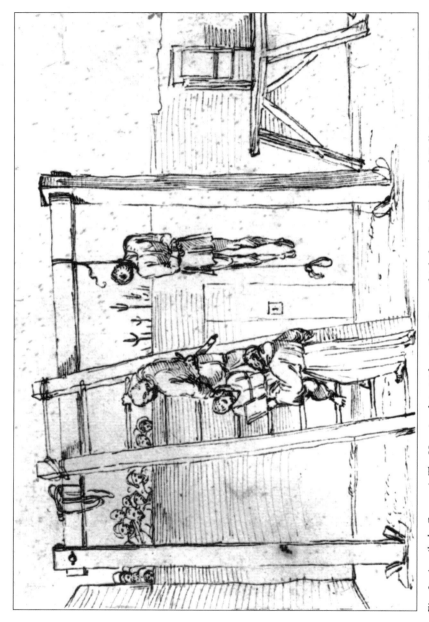

Fig. 2. Annibale Carracci, *The Hanging*, late 16th century. Pen and ink drawing, The Royal Collection © 2008, Her Majesty Queen Elizabeth II. Reproduced by permission.

Fig. 3. Miniatures demonstrating the stages of comforting, ca. 1480. Illuminated manuscript, Compagnia del spedale de la morte, Bologna, Italy. The Pierpont Morgan Library, New York. Gift of J. P. Morgan (1867–1943), 1924. Ms. M 188, fol. 5r. Reproduced by permission.

Fig. 4. Filippo Dolciati, *Execution of Antonio Rinaldeschi*, 1502. Painting on panel, Museo Stibbert, Florence, Italy. Reproduced by permission from Nicolo Orsi Battaglini/ Art Resource, NY.

Fig. 5. Giulio Morina, *The Death of the Prisoner Converted by the Saint*, ca. 1594. Wood-cut from Giulio Belvederi, *La vita della "Santa" illustrata da Guido Morina (secolo XVI)*, 72. Bologna: Tipografia Garagnani, 1912.

Fig. 6. *Madonna of Mercy with Brothers of the Confraternity of S. Maria della Morte*, 1562. Illuminated title folio from *Statuti della Compagnia dell'Ospedale della Morte* [1562], Biblioteca Comunale dell'Archiginnasio, Fondo Ospedale, ms. 42, fol. 1r. Reproduced by permission.

Fig. 7. Francesco da Rimini, *St. Mary Magdalen with Sts. Jacob, Margherita, Francis, Dominic, Petronio, and Christopher*, ca. 1335. Painting on panel, Galleria Nazionale dell'Umbria. Reproduced by permission.

Fig. 8. Francesco da Rimini, *Crucifixion*, ca. 1335. Painting on panel, Kunst-haus, Zurich. Reproduced by permission.

Fig. 9 *Two Comforters with a Prisoner*, late 15th century. Illustration from manuscript copy of the Bolognese *Comforters' Manual*, AAB ACCU IX.B.1, fol. 2v. Reproduced by permission of Archivio Arcivescovile, Bologna.

Fig. 10. "Dalmasio," *Madonna and Child with Two Condemned*, ca. 1336. Painting on panel, Musée des Beaux-Arts, Tours. Reproduced by permission.

Fig. 11. "Dalmasio," *Crucifixion with Martyrdoms of Sts. Catherine and John the Baptist*, ca. 1336. Painting on panel, Musée des Beaux-Arts, Tours. Reproduced by permission.

Fig. 12. Cristoforo da Jacopo, *Madonna and Child with Sts. Anthony Abbot, James, Catherine, John the Baptist, and Two Condemned*, ca. 1395. Painting on panel, Staatsgalerie Stuttgart. Reproduced by permission.

Fig. 13. Cristoforo da Jacopo, *Flagellation, Crucifixion, and Martyrdoms of Sts. Lorenzo and Biagio,* ca. 1395. Painting on panel, Staatsgalerie Stuttgart. Reproduced by permission.

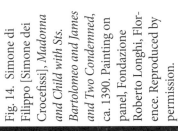

Fig. 14. Simone di Filippo [Simone dei Crocefissi], *Madonna and Child with Sts. Bartolomeo and James and Two Condemned*, ca. 1390. Painting on panel, Fondazione Roberto Longhi, Florence. Reproduced by permission.

Fig. 15. Simone di Filippo [Simone dei Crocefissi], *Decapitation of St. John the Baptist with St. Anthony of Abbot of Egypt*, ca. 1390. Painting on panel, Fondazione Roberto Longhi, Florence. Reproduced by permission of Scala/Art Resource, NY.

Fig. 16 (A, this page, and B, facing page). Bernardo Daddi, Portable Double-sided Cross, ca. 1335. Museo Poldi Pezzoli (inv. 3195), Milan, Italy. Reproduced by permission.

Fig. 17. Leonardo da Vinci, "Sketch of a hanged man," 1478. Drawing on paper, Musée Bonnat, Bayonne, France. Reproduced by permission from Scala/Art Resource, NY.

Fig. 18. Alessandro Magnanza, *Mutilation of St. Adrian of Nicomedia*, 16th century. Painting on panel, Pinacoteca Nazionale, Ferrara. Reproduced by permission.

Fig. 19. Anonymous, *The Martyrdom of Savonarola*, late 15th century. Painting on panel, Musée di S. Marco, Florence, Italy. Reproduced by permission from Scala/ Art Resource, NY.

Fig. 20. *Ippolito e Dianora*, late 15th century. Woodcut from Leon Battista Alberti, *Storia di Ippolito Buondelmonti e Dianora Bardi*. Florence: n.d. Reproduced by permission of the Centre for Reformation and Renaissance Studies, Toronto.

The Art of Executing Well
Contemporary Texts

Chapter 7

The Bologna *Comforters' Manual*
Comforting by the Books: Editorial Notes on the
Bologna *Comforters' Manual*

Nicholas Terpstra

Many of the articles in this volume refer to the manual produced in Bologna to train comforters of the Compagnia di S. Maria della Morte for their work with those condemned to execution. The translation of the *Comforters' Manual* given below aims to deliver a readable version that retains some of the characteristic awkwardness of the original texts, offering dynamic equivalence more than strictly literal readings, and modernizing both sentence and paragraph structures. Based on modern Italian critical editions, it does not itself aim to reproduce their full apparatus of citations, or offer the sophisticated stylistic and source analysis that they present, and notes have been kept to a minimum.[1] Some general comments here will clarify how the manual was brought together, adapted, and used in Renaissance Italy.

> When you have clothed yourself in the robe, kneeling then before the image of the crucified Christ, with devotion say three Pater Nosters and three Ave Marias and then the prayer of the Holy Spirit. Pray that they would illumine your intellect and expedite your tongue. When your rituals are all done, take the *tavoletta* from your prior's hand as usual. Exit from the Ospedale with silence and fear of God saying secretly "Misere mei deus." Enter into the prison making the sign of the cross and invoking divine favor on yourself. And then with a happy face [viso allegro] and quiet words [parlare modesto] greet all those

[1] Nobile, *Il libro della vita beata*, offers an edition of book 1. For books 1 and 2, see Troiano, "Il Manuale Quattrocentesco." For the *laudario*, see Troiano "Il laudario di S. Maria della Morte." For further critical context and a comparison of manuscripts, see Fanti, "S. Maria della Morte."

who are standing around in that prison. When they know who you are, take the poor one who is to be executed to yourself in a humane way [umanamente], demonstrating the sign of cordial love and having him sit in the middle of us. Then the one who has the *tavoletta* begins softly [dolcemente] to comfort him, explaining everything that is written in the following and first chapter of this our book, following then the instructions to the glory and honor of the Trinity.[2]

"This our book." This brief description of comforting can be found on the first few pages of a late fifteenth-century copy of the Bolognese *Comforters' Manual* translated here. The manual opens a rare and revealing window onto lay spirituality, particularly in its step-by-step guiding through a psychologically intense work.[3] It came in four parts: two parts of narrative text offering background and guidance to the act of comforting, and two parts of supplementary aids useful to the comforter, one a collection of prayers, poems, and spiritual songs (*laude et oracione*) and the other a collection of sayings about the art of dying well drawn from biblical, patristic, and classical authors and headed "Authorities" (*Auctoritates*). The extant manuscripts vary considerably both in how many of the four parts they contain, and how thoroughly the parts are edited. Few extant manuscripts offer all four parts together, so what is offered here is more a selective compilation than a critical edition.

In spite of the fact that dozens of men were involved in the work in any one community at any particular time—creating a potential market of many hundreds if not thousands of readers in the sixteenth century alone—the *Comforters' Manual* appears never to have made it into print. All the extant copies in Bologna and in archives in Ferrara, Padua, Ravenna, and Genoa are in manuscript, with fresh copies made well into the eighteenth century. This suggests that the confraternal comforters saw their work as a mystery—not unlike the mysteries of the faith guarded by priests or the mysteries of the crafts guarded by artisans and guildsmen.

Most of the extant manuscripts are quartos, or roughly the size of a modern trade paperback. Most were clearly designed for active use, with clasps that could secure the sturdy leather-bound covers if a comforter wanted to slip the book into his pocket before heading for the prison.[4] Some have marginalia, underlining, and the Renaissance equivalent of highlighting: a small stylized

---

[2] *Comforters' Manual*, fols. 1v–2r, BUB ms. 858.

[3] What follows incorporates and expands upon a discussion offered in Terpstra, "Catechizing in Prison."

[4] Those quartos with clasps are AAB ACCU, ms. IX.B.1; BAB ms. 4880; and BUB ms. 858.

hand drawn into the margin, with a crooked finger pointing to some notable passage.[5] Almost all copies are written in a clear and legible humanist cursive hand that would have been easier to make out in a dark candlelit cell than the crabbed and abbreviated notarial hand in which many legal and commercial documents were written. Only two of the dozen or so copies currently held in Italian and North American archives were unlikely to have been pressed into active service in the cells. One, in Bologna's university archive, is copied into a thick and heavy folio volume containing a series of different religious texts: the owner was a cleric who clearly had it copied into his compendium more for its devotional or spiritual value than as a manual to carry around.[6] The other, in New York's Pierpont Morgan Library, is a thin leather-bound illuminated folio volume produced in the late fifteenth century for a member of the Castelli family. It is too large and likely too valuable to carry into the cells. The Castelli coat of arms is prominent on the manuscript's first page together with images of stages in the comforting process (see fig. 3). On many other copies of the manual these coats of arms were, at some point in the past, carefully and completely scratched out or cut away.[7] Yet a few have other details of ownership, and these allow us to trace as many as three copies to particular comforters who were active in the later sixteenth century.[8]

The first part of the *Comforters' Manual*, known to modern editors as book

---

[5] BUB ms. 528.

[6] BUB ms. 157 is a manuscript of 225 folios, with the text of both books together with many *laude* on folios 122r through 139r. It was commissioned by Antonio Francisco, a canon from Caprara, and later came into the possession of Giovanni Giacopo Amadeo, a Bolognese who was canon at S. Maria Maggiore.

[7] Those copies with coats of arms effaced are AAB ACCU ms. IX.B.1 (arms cut out); BAB ms. 4880 (scratched out); BAB 4881 (scratched out); BUB ms. 702 (scratched out); and YBL ms. 1069 (scratched out). The only other alterations to manuscripts were those carried out by Carlo Antonio Machiavelli as he aimed to establish the claim that his ancestor, Luigi di Lionardo Machiavelli, authored the manual in 1490. Machiavelli wrote the attributions directly on the manuscripts in a weak imitation of fifteenth-century hand. See, e.g., AAB ACCU, ms. IX B 1, fol. 2v; BAB 4880, fol. 1r; and Fanti, "S. Maria della Morte," 126–31.

[8] All three were fifteenth-century manuscripts, and ownership is clearly noted in only one: AAB, ACCU, ms. IX B 1 includes a note on fol. 60v that the volume had been obtained by Giovanni Francesco Cattanio and given to the *conforteria* 28 October 1571. Cattanio served at twenty-eight executions as both a disciple (1541–52) and a master (appointed 24 June 1555, active to 1575, died 7 January 1577); "Descrizione di CXIV Maestri Ordiari," BAB Aula 2a.C.VI.8, #13. The evidence in two others is more indirect: the title page of YBL ms. 1069 includes an illumination with the initials A. L. and the note that it was owned by Domenico Landi (fol. 94v); an Antonio Landi served as a disciple from 1580 to 1581, serving at two executions. BUB 858 was given to Ubaldo Zanetti on 17 October 1762 by Abbot Giuseppe Manolessi, secretary of Senator Prospero Marsiglij Rossi (see note fol. 66r). The senator's ancestor Mino Rossi had been a disciple of the *conforteria* from 1549 to '55, serving at four executions (see BAB Aula 2a.C.VI.8). It is not possible to determine whether any members of the Castelli family were members of Bologna's Compagnia della Morte when they commissioned the copy now in the Morgan Library (PML ms. 188); there are no Castelli among the disciples and masters active in the sixteenth century.

1, was the longest and most abstract, and has been attributed by some sources to an Observant Augustinian Cristoforo da Bologna, who taught biblical theology in the Augustinian *studium* and preached widely.[9] It was titled "This is the mode and form that should be used to console and comfort those who are sentenced to death"; a Ferrarese manuscript adds "*rule* and mode and form." The second part of the *Comforters' Manual*, known as book 2, was written by an anonymous lay comforter who passed on practical lessons obviously drawn from extensive personal experience. It was titled "The training that is set for the use of those who put themselves to this most devout and holy mystery of comforting those who are condemned by justice to death." The language and terminology of these two titles highlights a difference that resonates through the two texts: book 1 is formal, abstract, and theological and fitting the description of a rule; book 2 is practical and less formal, and describes itself as a training manual that prepares comforters for what they can expect.[10]

In the best extant copies, book 1 is almost twice the length of book 2. It emphasizes that the comforter must bring the criminal to see that in the shadow of the gallows, the fate of the soul is more important than the fate of the body. More to the point, that dark shadow snuffs out any hope at all for saving the body, but it paradoxically brightens the chances for saving the soul. Everything rests in the prisoner's own decision to accept his execution calmly. By doing this and by forgiving all those who have a hand in securing his death—his enemies or victims, the police and guards, the judge, the executioner—the prisoner can change his very identity. No longer a criminal, he is transformed into a martyr. And like the Good Thief crucified beside Jesus on Calvary, he can anticipate that in the instant after the axe falls or the rope tightens, he will be with Christ in paradise.

[9] Cristoforo da Bologna was born in Bologna circa 1380, took minor orders with the Augustinian Hermits in 1394, was ordained in 1400, and eventually rose to become prior of the Bolognese Augustinian local house of S. Giacomo. He became *lector* (1407) and *sacra pagina professor* (1411) and was civic preacher in the basilica of S. Petronio until forced to step down in the wake of a dispute with S. Bernardino da Siena. Fanti declines to credit Cristoforo da Bologna because no manuscript before 1525 names him as author; Fanti, "S. Maria della Morte," 61–73. Bernardo Nobile acknowledges that the attribution is problematic, but notes that the text's argument and lacunae suggest an Augustinian author, and that Cristoforo da Bologna was known to have been associated with S. Maria della Morte earlier in the fifteenth century; Nobile, *Libro della vita beata*, 10–14. Other sources claim that book 1 of the manual was published in Rome as the *Libro della Vita Beata* (1565) and that Fra Cristoforo wrote a set of statutes for the *conforteria* in the early fifteenth century, but these claims cannot be verified and neither text is extant; Walsh, "Cristoforo da Bologna," 78–80.

[10] Book 1: "Questa è [la regula et] modo et forma de quello che denno usare a consolare et confortare le persone che sono iudicate a morte." Book 2: "Lo amaestramento che se pone in utilità de quelli che se pongono a questo devotissimo e sancto misterio de confortare quelli che sono condennati da la iustitia a la morte."

The tone of book 1 is quite different from that of book 2: less reflective, less personal, and less often marked by the latter's small touches of humanity that seem clearly to have arisen from personal experience. It is far more detached and delivers its message by logical argument and through lists—lists of sins, of qualities, of attributes, of saints, doctors, martyrs, and other exemplary authorities that have more to do with catechizing and sermonizing than with the finer points of doctrine. The best extant copy has thirty-four numbered chapters that fall into roughly three sections dealing in turn with the motivation and preparation of comforter and prisoner (sixteen chapters), the glories of paradise (thirteen chapters), and some particular theological and philosophical questions (five chapters). The comforter should be propelled into the work by charitable love for both the prisoner and his victims, and he must prepare himself through frequent confession and communion. If he aims for glory or for gossip from the cells, the whole exercise becomes pointless. In his approach to the prisoner, he has to emphasize how brief and painful this life is, compared to the eternal rest of heaven. The prisoner can have that rest simply by accepting his fate, forgiving all those who have harmed him, and entrusting his soul to God. In this task, the prisoner will be modeling himself on all those saints who await him in paradise: the martyrs, the patriarchs, the prophets, the confessors—this long series of chapters paints a living picture of the celestial court into which the prisoner can step if he simply follows the path of forgiveness. These chapters run through the heavenly hierarchy like a written equivalent of paintings such as Duccio's famous *Maesta* in Siena that show the celestial court of heaven gathered row upon row as witnesses and intercessors. Some *tavolette* included smaller versions of this image, which comforters could have used while talking to the prisoner in the cell. A final set of chapters deals more abstractly with philosophical and theological issues that might arise in the comforting process, with the longest one devoted to countering the arguments of those who believed that the stars controlled their destiny.

For all its abstraction, book 1 is not a scholarly text. Among the reasons Bernardo Nobile gives in support of Cristoforo da Bologna's authorship of it is precisely the fact that he does *not* employ the formal modes of Scholastic argument and never mentions either the *summae* or the confessors' manuals that multiplied in the fifteenth century. The author's discussions of angels, the Eucharist, and eschatology slide over the technical distinctions made by Aquinas, Antoninus, and others. Those were really beside the point. The lists seem instead like the rhetorical devices of a preacher, and the extensive citations of sometimes obscure biblical commentators suggest an author well steeped in this particular literature. Likewise, some of what pass for biblical citations are actually pastiches of various passages that have a general scriptural resonance but do not correspond to any particular biblical texts (e.g., bk. 1, chs. 11 and 14), and he sometimes errs when identifying biblical writers (e.g., bk. 1, ch. 17), precisely what one might expect from someone accustomed to proceeding on memory, inspiration, and a concern for immediate dramatic effect rather than a careful and precise scholar. He denounces those laypeople who presume to criticize preachers, and it is known that public preaching was a major part of Cristoforo's own work and reputation. Both books of the manual advised that comforters prepare their intellects by attending the sermons of learned preachers, and book 1 is effectively a preacher's own summary of what he might deliver from the pulpit. With its list-oriented approach, it thus exemplified the very catechizing of comforters that it recommended.

By contrast, book 2 is far less abstract and far more concerned with helping the comforter anticipate and respond to what lies ahead. The first half (the number of chapters varies in different manuscripts, though the text itself remains fundamentally the same) deals with the private side of comforting, describing the range of particular personalities, situations, and discussions that can develop from the time the comforter first arrives in the evening and on through the night. The second half guides the comforter step-by-step through the public rituals that begin with confession at dawn, move on to the public reading of the sentence, and continue to the gallows themselves where he is instructed in how to position himself for either a hanging or a beheading. Where book 1 sets out Christian doctrine like a catechism, book 2 offers comforting stories, conversational talking points, and responses to what a prisoner might say or what his family might do. It does not give warnings or threats of hellfire and brimstone, except in oblique or general terms. Instead it encourages the comforter to erode the prisoner's resistance by waiting, listening, and encouraging him to think of God's love. This marked a change from the fearful threats of judgment that public preachers had railed about and that church frescoes and sculptures had so vividly depicted a century or more before. It could well be that fourteenth-century comforters had been more firm and forbidding. Their late fifteenth- and sixteenth-century counterparts followed instead the pedagogy of humanist treatises and the early Schools of Christian Doctrine, which drew students in through persuasion rather than with punishments or fear.[11]

---

[11] Grendler, *Schooling in Renaissance Italy*, 333–62.

In bringing books 1 and 2 together, Bologna's Scuola dei Confortatori might have anticipated that lay comforters would use book 1 for background preparation and book 2 for practical advice. It seems that some, at least, did not. In the best extant copy of the Bolognese manual (and the base text for the translation below), Pierpont Morgan Library ms. 188, the vellum sheets of book 1's theological background are relatively clean and appear almost untouched while those of book 2's practical advice are well worn and stained by frequent use. In the second-best extant copy, Yale's Beinecke Library ms. 1069, book 1 has been removed altogether. Many other copies of the manuscript cut this book's thirty-four chapters down to twenty-four, sixteen, twelve, ten, or even six, and then condense those chapters yet further. The one manuscript that can reliably be placed in the hands of a particular sixteenth-century comforter, Giovanni Francesco Cattanio, is an example of this. Dating from the late fifteenth century, and possibly a century old by the time that Cattanio used it and then donated it to the Compagnia di S. Maria della Morte, this leather-bound paper copy shortens book 1 by omitting the many chapters on the contempt of the world and cutting out the descriptions of paradise with its chapters on the ranks of patriarchs and prophets, doctors and martyrs. This copy retains only ten abbreviated chapters from book 1 on how to address a handful of spiritual topics: pardon, mercy, the Eucharist, examining conscience, the relation of soul and body, astrology, and facing the shame of a dishonorable death. In Cattanio's copy, book 1 is reduced from being twice as long down to only one-third the length of book 2. Book 2 is not condensed at all—as indeed it is not condensed in *any* of the extant manuscripts.[12]

The third part of the *Comforters' Manual* changed most of all from one manuscript to another. This was the collection of prayers, poems, and vernacular religious verses called *laude* that were frequently put to popular tunes and that people of all kinds sang in confraternal oratories, mendicant churches, and in city streets and piazzas. Pamela Gravestock's article in this volume deals with 141 *laude* taken from seven manuscripts, with forty-one of these appearing in more than one manuscript.[13] As Gravestock notes, the Bolognese manual gives no explicit guidelines for how the *laude* were to be used, and one can hypothesize that they would have be helpful for comforters

---

[12] Cattanio's copy allotted five folio sheets to book 1, and fourteen to book 22, and drew on chapters 1, 9, 11, 15, and 30–34 of the former. For a description of all the full and condensed versions as these were known in 1978, see Fanti, "S. Maria della Morte," 131–36.

[13] See Gravestock's article in this volume. The appendix to her article is based on *laude* found in AAB AACU ms. IX.B.1 fols. 22r–55v; BAB ms. 4880, fols. 14r–40r; BUB ms. 702, fols. 73r–88r; BUB ms. 858, fols. 35r–42r; YBL ms. 1069, fols. 28r–80r, 88r–91r; and PML ms. 188, fol. 51rv. An additional fifty *laude* are found in BUB 157, fols. 139r–51r.

and prisoners alike at different steps in the comforting process. They could be sung or simply recited as verse prayers much like the Old Testament Psalms. Some *laude* had a more strongly educational bent and could reinforce religious lessons that comforters gave in the earlier stages of the process. Others emphasized the imitation of Christ and the martyrs and so would be useful in conjunction with the *tavolette* that comforters used as teaching tools within the prisons. *Tavolette* and *laude* worked together even more effectively when the condemned was brought out of the cells to hear the public reading of his sentence and proceed to the gallows. The *tavoletta* prevented the prisoner from seeing family, friends, and enemies while the incantational qualities of the *laude* kept him focused on salvation: looking intently at a Crucifixion scene, the prisoner sang directly to Christ and pleaded to be brought up into the Savior's arms. Beyond these specific points in the process, one can imagine that the *laude* might have functioned psychologically in somewhat the same way that gospel songs do in some prison ministries today, evoking for the prisoner memories of simpler times in youth when he had sung them together with family members or memorized them with other boys in the Sunday School classes of a local School of Christian Doctrine.[14] Renaissance writers frequently repeated the classical commonplace that music had power to move heart and soul, and these simple, moving, evocative songs would have been very effective in a comforting process that stretched through the long hours of the night.[15]

Musical tastes changed frequently, and so the songs attached to particular copies of the manuals changed frequently as well. Only one *laude*—"Misericordia o sommo eterno Dio" (Have mercy oh highest eternal God)—is found in all seven of the manuscripts Gravestock works with, and it is worth noting that it is the only one clearly attributed to a Bolognese: Gregorio da Rovorobella (1458–88), a notary and poet who was associated with the Bentivoglio court in the years when book 2 was most likely written.[16] The great variety of *laude* texts speaks to their practical utility and psychological impact, and underscores the fact that this was, after all, *popular* music. As such, it could indeed be seen as "the voice of the prisoner," and it may be that the

---

[14] Grendler notes that the Schools of Christian Doctrine did not isolate religious training from other educational work, and that "children also learned to read and write by chanting and memorizing prayers." *Laude* were treated as a pedagogical godsend; according to one contemporary rule, "children enjoy singing, which banishes boredom (341)"; Grendler, *Schooling in Renaissance Italy*, 339–62.

[15] See the articles by Falvey, Troiano, and Gravestock in this volume.

[16] Troiano, "Un laudario di S. Maria della Morte," 41.

manual says so little about how *laude* could be used because this was taken as self-evident. The nine *laude* translated here represent both commonly used and singular texts (including three by Andrea Viarani, the subject of Alfredo Troiano's article in this volume), and demonstrate the different emphases that this music expressed.

Finally, a fourth part that appears in some copies of the manual was a collection of sayings on death and dying drawn from biblical, patristic, and classical sources on death and dying.[17] Entitled "Auctoritates," this part varied from one manuscript to another even more than the *laude* and prayers, and recalled the highly personal notebooks of commonplace maxims that students compiled as they studied the *studia humanitatis* and came across compelling phrases or ideas that might be useful in their own compositions.[18] Most of the authorities cited in these collections offer variations on the *contemptus mundi*. Many maxims are given both in Latin and Italian, a sign perhaps of the wide social range of prisoners a comforter could encounter in his charitable work. A few manuscripts expand the "Authorities" to include such catechetical staples as the Ten Commandments, the seven sacraments, and lists of capital sins, of the works of mercy both spiritual and corporeal, of the theological and cardinal virtues, and of the requirements of a good confession, demonstrating once again that those who commissioned copies wanted above all to have a useful tool they could take into the prisons. The "Authorities" translated here also represent some of the most commonly encountered sayings in the manuals.

The translation presented here has been prepared by Sheila Das on the basis of critical editions of the texts prepared by Troiano, working with fourteen manuscript copies from archives in Bologna, Ferrara, Padua, Ravenna, Genoa, New Haven, and New York City; Pierpont Morgan Library manuscript 188 has served as the base text for determining which chapters from book 1 to include in this translation.[19] Biblical references have been given in square brackets where the text notes a direct citation or gives a close paraphrase. Since the citations are seldom literal, the biblical texts themselves have simply been translated directly from the Italian.

---

[17] Manuscripts containing "Authorities" are BAB ms. 4880 (Latin and Italian, fols. 64r–70r); BAB 4882; BUB ms. 702 (Latin and Italian, fols. 6v–9r, 32v–72v); BUB ms. 858 (Latin and Italian, fols. 30v–34v, 42v–65v); and YBL ms. 1069 (Latin, fols. 80v–83r).

[18] BUB ms. 702, fol. 42r; Grendler, *Schooling in Renaissance Italy*, 229–33.

[19] Manuscripts used: AAB ACCU IX.B.1; BAB mss. 4880, 4881/4882/4883 (separate texts for bks. 1, 2, and *Laude*, and gathered into a single codex), 4824; BBA B3599; BUB mss. 157, 401, 702; YBL ms. 1069; PML ms 188; BCAF ms. Cl. II,101; BCR mss. 177, 464; and BUG ms. G.III.2. See Troiano, "Manuale Quattrocentesco" for the critical edition (367–479) and the discussion of the critical apparatus (348–59).

Works Cited

Manuscript Sources

AAB	Archivio Arcivescovile, Bologna
BAB	Biblioteca Arcivescovile, Bologna
BCAF	Biblioteca Comunale Ariostea, Ferrara
BCR	Biblioteca Classense, Ravenna
BUB	Biblioteca Universitaria, Bologna
BUG	Biblioteca Universitaria, Genoa
PML	Pierpont Morgan Library, New York
YBL	Yale University, Beinecke Library, New Haven

Published Sources

Fanti, Mario. "La Confraternita di S. Maria della Morte e la Conforteria dei condannati in Bologna nei secoli XIV e XV." In Fanti, *Confraternite e città a Bologna nel medioevo e nell'età moderna*, 120–74. Rome: Herder Editrice, 2001.

Grendler, Paul. *Schooling in Renaissance Italy: Literacy and Learning, 1300–1600*. Baltimore: Johns Hopkins University Press, 1989.

Nobile, Bernardo, ed. *Il libro della vita beata attribuito a Cristoforo da Bologna*. Memorie dell'Istituto Veneto di Scienze, lettere ed arti 43.2. Venice: Instituto Veneto di scienze, lettere ed arti, 1991.

Terpstra, Nicholas "Catechizing in Prison and on the Gallows in Renaissance Italy: The Politics of Comforting the Condemned." In *The Renaissance in the Streets, Schools, & Studies,* edited by Nicholas Terpstra & Konrad Eisenbichler, 157–80. Toronto: Centre for Reformation and Renaissance Studies, 2008.

Troiano, Alfredo. "Il Manuale Quattrocentesco della Conforteria di Bologna: Il ms. Morgan 188 della Pierpont Morgan Library (New York)." In *Misericordie: Conversioni sotto il patibolo tra Medioevo ed età moderna*, edited by Adriano Prosperi, 347–480. Pisa: Edizione della Normale, 2007.

———. "Il laudario di S. Maria della Morte di Bologna. Il ms. 1069 della Yale Beinecke Library." PhD diss., Yale University, 2007.

Walsh, Kenneth. "Cristoforo da Bologna." In *Dizionario Bibliografico degli Italiani*, 31:78–80. Roma: Istituto della Enciclopedia Italiana, 1985.

Book 1

Translated by Sheila Das

This is the procedure and the way to prepare and make ready those who must go to comfort and console the people who are condemned to death.

[Prologue]

First, that those doing this work must put their heart in it and act only out of love for God, and also out of charity for and the salvation of the neighbor. And they must make a great effort to do this; otherwise it would be displeasing to God. And take note that it will not gain you anything for eternal life if it is done for any vain reasons: any aspect of glory or mundane pomp, or to be held in high esteem by the people of this world, or to avoid disrespect of your fellow man, or for any worldly gain, or to be on everyone's lips, or to be praised, or to be able to learn the secrets or the deeds of those people, or out of revenge, or out of ill will, or for faction, or for reward. But you should only do it out of reverence for God and to observe his commandment.

Second, so to earn the soul and the salvation of your neighbor. And take note again that oftentimes God would not let you carry out what you are going to do to proper effect if you were the least vain or concerned for your reputation, as is written above.

Third, that you should go with great fear of God and with much compassion for your neighbor. And you must be sorry for the wretched situation he will meet due to his human weakness.

Fourth, that you should feel more sorry about the vices and sins that were committed and perpetrated by those people than by their bodily death.

Fifth, that you must be very sober in food and drink and sleep so that the tongue, the mind, and the memory can well serve your thoughts.

Sixth, remember that by doing this act you become a merchant of heaven, that is, you gain for God, always by his grace, new merchandise—that is, the soul of your brother. And good for you if you manage this.

Seventh, see what a great mystery this is, that you join together with the angels of God in the conversion of the sinner.

Eighth, it would be a good idea to try and confess all your sins beforehand so that this will make you worthy of eternal life. For God, without fail, would sooner grant you what you desire to do if you are confessed.

Ninth, that you should go to a church, to an altar where you think and believe that the body of our Lord Jesus Christ would be. And humbly and with devotion you should lift your spirit to God so that he will bestow grace on you. Say Our Father and Hail Mary three times, and then say the prayer below, and God, without fail, would sooner grant you what you desire to do if you are confessed.

Tenth, then you must go.

Prayer

Omnipotent Lord God, benevolent and just judge, elector of all the elect and generous giver of all things. You who do not want any one of your sheep to perish, you who instead lead them to the true pasture [John 10:11–16], you who illuminated the holy patriarchs and inspired the holy prophets, you who elected and exalted the holy apostles, you who gave strength to the glorious martyrs, you who instructed the holy doctors, you who inflamed the holy confessors, you who purged the holy virgin women and men, you lover of chaste continence of the widows and widowers, you planter of chaste advice, you zealot of holy matrimony, you rector and governor and pastor of all your creatures, you who speak to the soul and the spirit—I pray to you with all my mind that at this point you must help and assist me and have pity on me your unworthy servant, and concede me this grace [Ps. 119:124–25]. May my memory be full of all your good deeds and good teachings, and my intellect be lucid, clear and illuminated by your celestial light, and my will be burning and inflamed with your love and your charity. And send me the aid of wisdom from your great and magnificent throne. Send me your only and eternal son, the true son of God, light of lights, wisdom of wisdom, true God of true God. Send me also, kind Father, your holy and perfect love, the tie and knot of burning ardor. Send me your Holy Spirit, spirit of goodness and knowledge, spirit of counsel and wisdom, spirit of comfort and clemency [Isa. 11:2]. And make my tongue serve me adroitly in every task, and make this person, who has to die, know the path of your truth and become aware of your goodness so that finally he departs from this world with your holy charity. Amen.

Chapter One
When you enter the prison you must use these words.

May the peace of God that is above all other things and the peace of all his saints come into this house and on all the people who are present here. Put in the heart of all of us the knowledge of God and the path of salvation for our souls, and give us grace at the time of our death so that we may be saved. Amen.

Brother and my dearest friend, God knows and the Virgin Mary too that my companion and I from this blessed charitable Company would have gladly come and visited you in another fashion and in another place and for another occasion than this one—and you should certainly realize this. But, since you are placed in this extreme sorrow, we are sad and sorry about it. But no one can contradict the will of God.

And this happens to you because it pleases the will of God our Lord. Not that God is happy about the violent death of anyone and especially not about the death of the soul, but he lets it happen and allows the punishment of the world to be given to the body so that the soul does not carry punishment and eternal suffering. And if the punishment of the body is not borne willingly, know for certain that it will not be worthy and God will not accept the soul to greater glory nor to the greater crown.

And therefore the end of your life lies at this point, my dearest brother, and you need to conform your will to what the present necessity requires, and be satisfied with the predestination, the providence, and the firm sentence of God. And from this, my brother, you can and must consider how great and unknown God's judgment is. Who could ever question and who could ever advise God, or truly investigate his hidden ways? [Rom. 11:33–34].

And tell me how many generations, peoples, nations, and individuals there are and have been and will be that God for good reason allows and lets go in different ways, on different paths, and on different roads and routes under the banner of various and different deaths.

Aren't you quite aware what you are encountering is encountered by those better than you, more noble, greater, and more worthy than you? And even according to what we see in the world, you are not the first, nor do I believe that you will be the last who encounters a similar fate.

And if you think about it, this fate has been encountered by great lords, great masters, great princes, great barons, counts, chevaliers, doctors, merchants, and by different generations of people, the great, the small, the young, the old, the healthy, the sick, the rich, the poor, the wise and the not-so-wise, the gentleman, the courtiers, the artisans, the foreigners, and the locals. Oh so many have been broken, died, and consumed by a more vituperative death than this one! And for that reason you must well consider what things and which things this variable and miserable world is able to give to its inhabitants.

And tell me, God help you, dear brother, how many persecutions, adversities, troubles, and difficulties does the world give? States, honors, and riches—until suddenly the wheel of fortune turns. There never was a tyrant in this world that so mistreated an enemy as this upside-down world treats men in this present life. And therefore, my brother, you must give little account and little value to this vile and sad world, seeing how many evils and troubles are placed inside it.

Chapter Two
Which deals with humility.

Looking hard, answer this: how many sins do we commit and who lives without sin? There is no one. Rather, there are so many sins that it is an abomination just to think about it. And for certain, take note of this, that given the many adversities, the many trials, the many burdens that nowadays reign in the world, and that we are always subject to and wrapped up in, the saner side is to elect to die than to always live in this misery and in this world that is so false and so unfair and so full of deceit.

It was David who said that this world is always a tempestuous, windy, and dangerous sea [Ps. 69:2, 15]. There is no longer anyone who does good, and by misadventure it seems that everyone falsifies his being and his state. And beware he who stays in so many errors and troubles.

And I remind you also that the glorious father St. Anthony saw this clearly. Once having risen in spirit, he saw the world represented before him all full of snares, and marveling at this he turned to God and said, "Lord God, who could ever defend himself from so many snares?" The Holy Spirit replied to him and said, "Anthony, only humility will defend you from all these snares."

And for that reason, my brother, you should look at this troublesome death with your spirit and your mind. Consider how infinite was the love and charity by which God the Father took human form. He sent his one and only son, who from so high decided to lower himself and humiliate himself even to the wood of the holy cross only out of a desire to redeem us wretched and fragile sinners and take us back and free us from the hand and from the power of the devil [John 3:16; Phil. 2:7–8].

Now, if he therefore who is the form and rule of all our good actions decided to humiliate himself so much at the time of his death, then you, brother, his creature, must be very patient and humble in your heart, considering that you have offended our Lord God in more ways than you know. There are more hidden sins than obvious ones and more secret ones than manifest ones. And there is no one who should remain unpunished.

And do not be amazed if God lets us be persecuted many times for our sins, and thus he lets various and unexpected things happen for the betterment of our souls, and if we were illuminated by the gift of divine grace, we would understand the divine judgment and we would be content with what Omnipotent God does and allows.

Chapter Three
Which deals with the temptation of the devil in the imagination.

Oftentimes as we are living in this present life and in this fleeting and wretched world, we sin in many various ways, and God in other ways, unpremeditated, punishes us for our misdeeds at the hour and at the time that we don't expect. Do not believe for this reason that God is cruel, unjust, or tyrannical. He does this because the kingdom of God and the dwelling place of the saints, which is the tabernacle of God, is so clean that no one can ascend above who is not perfectly clean and purged of every vice and sin.

Take note, and here you must know that God is a spirit who is completely holy, and for this reason if our soul desires to see God, both our soul and spirit should become holy. And purging is not done well if not by various punishments and in various ways of dying. And if you take this into consideration, you will feel a great easing in your soul. It will gain you merit before glorious God, and you will avoid the great punishments of hell.

And this I tell you because I know that many times the enemy of hell, that is, the devil, fights and disturbs man's imagination. He makes man see strange things and gives him various worries, showing him novel concepts that go against his salvation, especially in that time when he sees a man who has a short time to live in this world. And the first thing he puts before him is, "Why is it me who has to die? Why must I die? What did I do?" Is it this one thing that makes me die? And all of this ends up bringing the man to hate his fellow or to complain to God, or to wrench him from very good intention and grace of God, so that man's soul is yoked to the devil himself, lost and damned in eternal suffering.

And for this reason you, my brother, in order to prevail against this temptation, should be well at home and well aware of this point: if your present body dies, your soul will not be in perpetual servitude and in the perpetual power of the devil in hell. He is very subtle and very evil and will use all of his malice now and at the moment of your death, to make you lose your soul in the end. Position yourself, therefore, in this final part of your life to try and earn your soul a place before God and acquire the glory of heaven, remembering that the hand of God and his holy arms are always open and willing to kindly receive you and all the other sinners who want to go back to him.

Chapter Four
Which deals with the brevity of the life of this world.

Now, returning to the fact of this death that pains you so much and makes you sorry about leaving this sensual life: certainly your spirit and reason should lead you not to give it so much weight or thought. Because you know well that death is ordained for all men who have lived, who are living, and who will live in this mortal life. Consider that everyone of us will die, and this is a general truth for all states of mortals, from the great to the small, from these to those.

And tell me about your relatives, friends, and acquaintances that have died and passed from this life. What about them? Do you think that we are better than our ancient fathers, ancestors, and relatives had been? Now in a similar fashion, what you must encounter, so must we all. Some will die in one way and some in another, either by a natural death or by a violent death, and this is clear from experience.

Don't you well know that this life seems like it is a shadow that is passed through by all those who have died [Ps. 144:4]? Time passes like an arrow and like smoke in the wind, like vapor, and our life is hay compared to the flower [1 Pet. 1:24]. Our first stage of life appears and soon it descends into old age, and even of this we have clear experience. We know that the old man is full of many woes, nothing but boredom and tedium, rather than desire, seeing that his life is all affliction.

Oh how many are those that would like to have died in their youth seeing the epidemics, wars, plagues, and agonies, diseases, pains, adversities, problems, and dangers that never end. All day long death is called and it seems that it doesn't want to listen because the end is determined by God, and cannot be overruled.

You don't have as much to sorrow for as you think, considering that you are not deprived of this world. The time you would have lived until your natural death could have been one year or two or five or ten or fifteen or twenty or more or less, as pleases God. You are not certain. But even, let's say, if it had been a good one hundred years, you would have as much left at the end of that time and at the end of those hundred years as you have now of your past.

Chapter Five
Which deals with the pleasures of this world which are to come.

Once more I warn you that it seems that our depraved condition determines that however much more a man lives and ages, so much more does he become bad, since the nature of man is more ready to think the bad than the good. And do not say, "If I had lived, I would have entered into some religion or I would have conversed with religious people," since God knows everything. To me it seems that the more a man lives, the more he sins. The more he sins, the more he should accept God's judgment. And even the more we sin, the more our souls deserve greater punishment, in purgatory or in hell.

And above everything else, consider that the more we sin, the later we will see God, because the more and greater our sins, the longer and more purgative the punishment. And however much longer the punishment is, so much longer is the soul kept from the vision of God and from the state of blessedness. And so the soul remains wretched and sad from the moment it passes from this life.

Alas, tell me—and you should think carefully about all the time of your past—how did you spend it? In godly things or in worldly things or in the pleasures of your body? If you spent your time in godly things, you really shouldn't bemoan your death, since the devout soul, which always lives devoted to Christ, always desires to be with him. It can't be with him except through death, since you must know that while you are in mortal life you can't see God who is in blessed life.

If you have spent your time in worldly things, answer me: what did you get from them? Perhaps it was the worldly things that brought you to this point, here inciting you to revenge, there to rob, here to violate someone, to acquire stuff, or to have honor, glory, and pomp.

Now see how worldly things serve you at present! Oh, if only God would decide that they would not harm you any longer. You know very well that these temporal things are false and vain and abandon their possessors at the moment of death. And such a fate befalls everyone, not just one person. Ah corrupt world, whoever knows you well does not seek to find his ground in you, but he who plays in you always finds pain and affliction.

And for that reason you must be sorry for having loved this vain and fleeting world so much. And if you have spent your time in the pleasure and delight of your body, living like an irrational animal in your sensuality, so much more shameful and red-faced you should be in the sight of God. Confusing yourself in that way would be as though God had given you intellect and reason, so that you would live like a rational man, but you lived like an animal who does not have awareness.

Now tell me, my brother, of all of these pleasures of yours, both of the world and also of the body, have you ever had your fill on any day? Did you never experience after these moments of happiness and after these feasts of ours that some pain, sadness, or grief would come? And for this reason, the scripture cannot lie that says, "The laughter of man will be mixed with pain, and at the height of his happiness grief will fill him" [Prov. 14:13], because everything of the world is vain, pompous, and haughty, and it passes like a shadow and like sleep [Eccles. 1:2]. Everything of the world is like a flame of fire, and perishes like a cloud, and like the ice and the snow placed before the sun. The love of God, that is, to love him with all your heart, is the only thing that remains. And for that reason we can truly say: worldly love passes away like the wind, but who loves God is content.

Chapter Six
Which deals with the one who fears death and the state of the body.

Lift your mind and understand well what I want to tell you. My brother, I am well aware that as a sensual being you are now sad and feeling very sorry for yourself. But consider carefully whom you feel sorry for. It is surely not your soul, but only your body and your flesh. And tell me: What is our body and flesh if not stink and rot as you can see by looking in graves.

And for that reason I beg you to listen well to what I'm going to tell you now. Man and woman are composed of two natures and two substances, that is, the body and the soul. And our body is so vile, it is more vile than anything else. Now, think carefully about its origin and its origin [sic] and its conception and tell me: Where does the human body come from if not from mud and filth, and is it not but ashes and earth?

Look also what our body is during its life. The eyes, which are the most beautiful and most noble member there is, produce stink and dung. The ears, similarly, and the nose more than ever, so that every man is disgusted who sees it. And what's more, various ills, diseases, inflammation, and infinite curses all come from the body. The body in and of itself is nothing but a container full of dung. And what must the body be like after death if nothing but intolerable, fetid stink, a meal, food and excrement of worms? This, then, is what we have so much pity for! Therefore, my brother, don't have your heart fixed on your flesh and body at present, because it has been the cause of many sins and many ills and soon it will return to its beginning where it came from, that is, the earth.

Now, lift your spirit, intellect, and soul, because your soul will live forever and will understand more once separated from the mortal body, since the body is a jail and a prison for the soul. What's more, I tell you for certain that man sins mortally when he desires to live in this world forever, since he chooses not to be blessed and not to see God face to face.

Oh what foolishness it is to want to live either more or less than what pleases God, our good and wise master who is prudent and just. Mortal life is nothing but a continuous dying, and for that reason there is no better thing than to place your hope in God, because your hope in him will not be disappointed. Aim therefore to lift all your soul to God and put it in his hands and give little care to your body.

And for that reason, my dearest brother, you should concentrate your thoughts during the little time you have left in this life, putting all of your devotion in God and in being contrite for all your sins. Because in the past, perhaps, you have not been very devoted to God, not loving him very much and not giving much reverence to his saints. And perhaps also you have cursed them or sworn or complained about them. And it may also be that you hardly considered your past sins, which were not few but many.

Chapter Seven
Which deals with the Passion of the Lord Jesus Christ as our example.

And because it is necessary for you to lift your soul in devotion to God right now, first you must consider the Passion of our Lord Jesus Christ, who suffered, was crucified, and died without sin. He who was the lamb of God, the just lamb, the clean lamb, the pure lamb without vice and injustice, without faults, the lamb who was full of every virtue and every gift of the Holy Spirit, full of every grace and patience, full of every suffering and of constancy and of strength, he who was the lord of heaven and of the earth, of the angels and of all the blessed spirits, he whom the whole heavenly court desires to look at and see, and to delight in his glorious countenance. And still, nonetheless, he let himself be so mistreated, taken and tied, beaten and flogged, his bones broken, spit at, mocked and tormented, his face covered and muddied, his hair pulled and crowned, dressed in white torn rags, shouted at and cursed in his face, put on the cross and nailed, and above all else, despised.

Oh infinite patience, oh immense piety, oh holy kindness, oh sweetest Jesus! You who are full of every suffering, every sadness, every pallor, you master of every virtue, you doctor of every true doctrine, you good shepherd of all sheep, you true redeemer of human nature!

So therefore, sweet brother, you are one of the true sheep of Christ, afflicted and suffering on the cross so that your punishment would be much lessened and it would bring great comfort to your soul. Our glorious doctor St. Bernard teaches us this when he says, "Oh good Lord Jesus, nothing makes me more lovable and full of desire than when I take the cup of your Passion, working for our salvation, because the more I think of it the more I am inflamed in your love."

Where the apostle St. Paul said, "Let us run with the soul and with the spirit in Jesus, certain and struggling above on the wood of the cross, actor and maker of our salvation"[cf. Heb. 12:1], "because there is no one under the sun who can save us if not Jesus our Savior"[Acts 4:12], "to whom all the angels of heaven, and the men on earth and the demons in hell went down on their knees, and every tongue confessed that our Lord and Savior Jesus Christ reigns in heaven and on earth" [Philem. 2:10–11], seated at the right hand of glory of his Father [Col. 3:1].

And this you must believe with all your mind and with perfect faith. And soon you will see it with solid experience, because I think that, with the grace of God, you have already been called to that great heavenly company. And even if you carefully think about the extreme suffering the holy martyrs bore, it will be a great comfort to your soul and body, considering that they were neither more nor less than you, and like you were made of flesh, bones, and nerves. But, since they knew, they were willing to suffer many very bitter pains and terrible agonies considering the exchange,[20] the reward of the glory of eternal life.

And for that reason, learn in your heart a devotion like that of the holy martyrs, who willingly bore the pain and suffering for no fault of their own, but only because of their reverence for God. And so you also should try to bear it willingly, first for love of God, second for the fault of your sins. And for this reason, you should now lift your mind to God and contemplate the glory on high of eternal life, which is infinite, perpetual, and full of every good and can neither be lacking, nor finish or terminate. And this is the exchange and the crown of the saints. And at present, this eternal life you can freely merit by having your heart turned towards God, and by not caring about this miserable world, which is a fleeting and transitory thing and soon passes and goes away.

Chapter Eight
Which deals with the glory of the body when the soul is saved and of the pain of the body when the soul is damned, and of the three

---

[20] "mercade," lit. "merchandise."

prescriptions that one must follow.

Everyone must desire the salvation of his soul, so that once the soul is blessed, the body may participate in that blessing. Just as the lantern receives light from the lit candle, so does the body receive blessing from the soul.

Our body is like a lantern and a tool of the soul, and the soul, which is blessed, is like the candle lit with the light of everlasting glory. And just as the lantern, when you remove the candle, remains dark and in shadow, so too the body, when the soul is damned and killed by guilt and by penalty, remains dark and in shadow.

And take note that the soul, when it suffers the death of guilt and sins and the death of penalty, does not suffer a death that leads to nonbeing, because it is a spirit and immortal, according to the being of spirits. Just as the extinguished candle's wick still smolders without a flame, so too the soul, when God's grace and glory are extinguished, still remains alive as a soul. May God allow your life to be so full of woes that finally the body will find it of little use and of much punishment.

And for that reason, my brother, in order that your spirit should first be saved and then consequently your body, that is, in order that both should be saved and not just the soul or just the body, but the soul and the body together, you need now to dispose yourself to God. Do not look at the saying, "The body dies and to earth it must return," because he who created it the first time is quite capable of repairing it. So even if you were to live thousands of years in this mortal life, it could never be in as good a condition, nor in as good proportion or disposition as it will be in the resurrection. This is so because now it is animal and then it will be spiritual. Now it is mortal and then it will be immortal [1 Cor. 15:44, 53]. Now it is subject to pain and aches; then it will not be inclined to anything but happiness, and holy and perpetual gladness.

And for this reason, pay careful attention and here firm up your intellect. If you want to have the blessed life you must—and this is necessary—for this brief time that you have left, regulate your brief life with three good and perfect rules with a holy and good prescription. And by observing these rules and prescriptions, you will be able to have for certain the salvation of your soul and eternal life. And by doing this, you will bring much happiness to the angels who live eternally, who, as our Savior said in the holy gospel, "They make a greater celebration and with greater happiness for one sinner who returns repentant than for the righteous ninety-nine who do not need repentance" [Luke 15:7].

And if you do not abide by any one of these three rules and holy prescriptions, I cannot make you sure about your soul, but I believe rather and

I am firmly convinced that your soul and body will be presented to the perpetual punishment of hell. May it please you therefore to do what you must so that God is content with you.

Chapter Nine
Which deals with the first prescription: to have your sins pardoned.

The first and holy rule that you must follow so as to make your soul properly disposed is to dedicate yourself to this prescription: forgive every person every disrespect and every offense made against you from this moment back in time and until the moment of your death. For if you were to consider these offenses directly, you would have too much to think about.

And you must only have this forgiveness out of reverence for God, because you must know that the towering piety of God has commanded this, that we forgive all the offenses only to save our souls. In the holy gospel, Christ our Savior said, speaking to his apostles and disciples who represent all of us, "If you do not forgive those who have offended you from your heart, my heavenly Father will not forgive you your sins"[Matt. 18:35]. So keep in mind that the forgiveness of sins is a commandment.

Also take good note of this reason why we ought to forgive: the kingdom of eternal life is so clean and so pure that no one can go there or stay there who has not put his soul in order. You are well aware that he who does not forgive is not well in order nor tranquil nor relaxed, so that he cannot rise to heaven above, which is a temple of peace and tranquility.

Also look and see what not forgiving is useful for. First, it is not useful for the body in any way. For whether you forgive or don't forgive, you remain here. Second, this not forgiving weighs down your soul. Third, it puts your soul in danger, so that without fail, if you have the intention to not forgive, you will be damned. Fourth, this puts you in the hatred and malevolence of God. Fifth, for this you are placed under and bound to the power of the devil. Sixth, you will be held in the opprobrium and disgrace of the righteous, and you will depart from this world with a bad reputation and will give cause to righteous people who know about this not to pray on your behalf to God.

But, even if we let go every other aspect, forgive every person every offense and every ill so that you will be clean and ready to participate in the blessedness of eternal life. And the example of our patient lord and master Jesus Christ teaches us this. He prayed for those who put him on the cross and he entirely forgave them, those who gravely mistreated him with so many insults and disgraces, though he was without fault. And this he did when he was up on the wood of the holy cross. He lifted his eyes to heaven, to his heavenly Father, and said, "Oh good Father, forgive them for they know not what they do" [Luke 23:34]. And so you should do the same, imitating him, because all the actions of Christ are instructions to us.

Chapter Ten
Which deals with how we should pray to God for those who have offended us and those who will offend us.

And remember also the glorious act of that virtuous and valiant martyr St. Stephen who, while praying to God for himself, remained standing. And then when he was praying for those who were stoning him, he actually knelt down so that the prayer he was saying for them would be more vigorous, filled with more fervent love, and be more efficacious. He did so because they, having such a great sin, were in need of such a prayer. Then St. Stephen said, "Lord Jesus Christ, do not look at their sin and do not find fault with them, because they know not what they do, but rather forgive them this offense" [Acts 7:60].

And so we find the same with many holy martyrs, men and women, and many holy virgins, that when they were martyred they prayed to our glorious God for those who executed them and who gave them bitter punishments. And those glorious and holy martyrs did not have any sin in them, nor had they done anything to deserve the many injuries people were going to give them.

Now likewise you should model yourself after them, because we ought to take a good example and follow it. And for that reason, at this extreme point of your life, please try to take up this instruction from Lord Jesus Christ.

I also warn you that no good that you do or that is done for you is useful for the soul, if you do not forgive, and here is the reason. Don't you know that the tabernacle of God, the celestial house, that is, eternal life, comfort of the blessed spirit, is so well ordered and so well guarded and kept that no one who is defiled, dwelling in, or soiled with sin, no one who is troubled in their mind can enter there above?

And for that reason every rancor, every hatred, every desire for revenge, should be decisively swept out and cleaned away from your mind. Let God take care of all your revenge. He is the just judge, who properly punishes everyone for his sins.

Now tell me, when our Lord God taught us to pray the prayer Our Father, didn't he tell us that we must say, "Forgive us our debts as we forgive our debtors" [Matt. 6:12]? Oh how many condemn themselves by not wanting to forgive the offenses and the injuries received. And believe me, that those persons who do not forgive and who say this prayer, ask rather for God's wrath than his mercy, because the prayer says, "Oh Father in heaven, forgive us our trespasses as we forgive those who trespass against us." So if you don't forgive all of your enemies, then God will not forgive you [Matt. 6:15].

Chapter Eleven
Which deals with the second prescription: asking for God's mercy.

The second good and perfect rule that you need to follow to put your soul in order is that you should confess all your sins and ask our glorious God for mercy. Thus, considering all of the many serious ways you offended the divine majesty, humble your soul before God's countenance. Know that it is human nature to sin, but it is demonic to persist in your sins, as it is angelic to make amends for your sin. There is no person so just in this present life who does not fall into sin in one way or another. Now, think carefully and examine your conscience well if you have been entangled in all manner of sins. Believe me that all those sins have reached the sight of God and have always accused you before the just judge. And also Satan has written them down, and at the moment of your death he will denounce you before the judge of your soul.

And for that reason, my dear brother, if you want to erase those sins and not receive this shame before God and before his angels, ask him forgiveness. And repeat what the holy prophet said, "My dear Lord, do not look at the multitude of my sins, which are more than the sands of the sea and the stars of the sky and the drops of the rain; rather, look at your mercy and your immense pity, at your sweetness and your abundant benevolence."[21] My Lord, you are the one who said, "I do not want the death of the sinner, but I do want him to change and live forever" [Ezek. 33:11]. You are the one who forgave Mary Magdalene, the Canaanite, the Samaritan, the paralytic, the thief up on the cross. You forgave Paul who was persecuting your church. You forgave David who had committed the sins of betrayal, homicide, and adultery, because he ran back to you saying with a contrite and grieving heart, "My Lord, yes I have sinned and indeed I have offended your majesty. Forgive me, my creator" [cf. Ps. 51:4]. And you kindly forgave him, receiving him in the arms of your mercy. You forgave your people after many and great sins. You forgave that adulterous woman, just as we read in the holy gospel. You who forgave St. Peter who denied you three times, sweet master, and you consoled

---

[21] An example of the author's loose paraphrasing. There is no single text in the Bible that corresponds to this quotation, though it is resonant of many texts brought together.

him, looking at him with the eye of your mercy. You who forgave St. John Chrysostom, after the great sins he committed, namely fornication, adultery, homicide, and false sacrament. You forgave Mary of Egypt, whom your angel threw out of the temple for her sins. But by confessing all of her sins and making a proper repentance, you did forgive her. You, my Lord, who forgave St. Julian, who killed his father and mother and came back to your mercy with the worthy fruit of repentance, and you benevolently accepted it. You who forgive all sinners who come back to you, forgive Lord also me, weak and wretched sinner, for whom you appeared up on the wood of the cross with your precious blood. I am not, therefore, worthy to lift my eyes to heaven nor to appear before your majesty, because of all the infinite ways I have offended you. I would not be worthy of being called a Christian any more after all the many sins that I committed in view of your heavenly countenance, you who are the highest sweetness and highest good. I have sinned in sight, hearing, sense, taste, smell, and touch, and I have been bound to many kinds of faults. At this time now I render myself up to you, my Lord, asking forgiveness for all my sins with great confidence, because I know very well that your mercy is greater than our faults and our wretchedness.

Chapter Twelve
Which deals with the ways and the conditions of confession.

Third, regarding the sacrament of confession, you should now think my brother that, as we know from the holy doctors, confession must meet five conditions to achieve the soul's salvation.

The first condition is that it must be complete. That is, you should not leave inside you any sin, neither great nor small, because if you were to leave any there out of fear or shame or deceitfulness, confession wouldn't achieve anything for you. And take this parable for example: if someone were to have ten wounds and the doctor treated only nine of them, couldn't that tenth one be enough to kill him? And if he didn't make it, would it possibly be the doctor's fault? Of course not. Rather, it would be his own fault for having covered up and hidden that tenth wound. The same will happen to you, insofar as your soul will sink into perdition if you willfully cover up any of your sins from the priest, who is the vicar of Christ on earth. But don't be afraid in the least, because what you say to the priest in confession is said to God.

The second condition that you must have for confession is that you must be ashamed, that is, you should feel ashamed for all the sins you have committed. God gave you the grace to be able to remain without sin and you, creating your own misery, you fell into many sins, offending God and his saints. And you esteemed more the things of this world rather than the things of God, and you appreciated the things of the body over those of the soul, and you made it so that your soul, which was such a noble creature and made in the image of God, became so vile that it was subject to the service of sin.

You should also be ashamed of yourself because your soul, which should have been the temple of the Holy Spirit and the entire blessed Trinity, you have made into a dwelling place of demons. You should also be ashamed of yourself because you should have gone to listen and understand the word of God, and you should have paid attention to what it was and painted that in your soul so that it was properly decorated. Instead, you left the divine things alone and went to the spectacles of the world and to squares and to corner gatherings to see vain things, and so you painted your soul with sins and diabolical figures.

Now then be ashamed of yourself and do like the publican, who did not dare to lift his eyes to heaven and for shame did not enter in the temple, but while beating his chest and with shame he said, "Oh kind God, be merciful to me a sinner" [Luke 18:13].

The third condition of confession is that it should be made with sorrow, contrition, and repentance of all your sins. This is the principal property of confession: that you must be sorry for every sin that you have thought, said, or done. If you have sinned out of ignorance and if you were able to avoid this ignorance, then you should blame your laziness. If you could not avoid it, the sin will be remitted. Or if actually you have sinned out of your own maliciousness, it is necessary that you look at it carefully and recognize that it was wrong and yet nevertheless you committed it. This sin cannot be remitted, and is a great sin before God and is called "irremissible" because it cannot be remitted without a lot of sorrow and tears. Or actually you sinned out of human weakness, letting your body lead you to do many wrongs. Now, for every way that you have sinned, you must be sorry and repentant, contrite and ashamed.

The fourth condition that confession must have is that it must be open, that is, you must not excuse your sins yourself. Instead you must denounce them and show them, and not only your sins, but even sinful circumstance. How would it be if you had sinned in a sacred place, or if during a very solemn period, like Easter Day or Christmas Day, or Sunday of the feast day of our Lady the Virgin Mary, or during the feast days of the apostles or of other great saints, or if during the time of Lent, or the Quarter Days or commanded vigils.[22]

---

[22] Quarter Days: Annunciation (25 March), St. John the Baptist (24 June), Michaelmas (29 September),

Consider also the people you sinned with or those you injured, that is, whether they be clergy, priests, religious, monks, fathers, or mothers, and so many other kinds of people could be included. Now, in conclusion, everything that pertains to this fourth condition, as much as you are able, you must confess openly and not hold back any sin or circumstance.

The fifth and last condition of confession is that it should be yours and not another's. That is, you must confess your sins and not someone else's, and this David teaches us when he says, "I readied myself to confess all my sins to God"[cf. Ps. 32:5]. Take note that he did not say "the sins of my neighbor," but rather "my sins." And likewise the apostle St. James in his epistle said, "Confess to each other your sins"[James 5:16]. He did not say the sins of someone else, because he who confesses the sins of his neighbor is a traitor to him.

And for that reason, my brother, your confession should be complete, with sorrow, with contrition, both open and secret. And this confession, which is the sacrament of penance, is the second ship that will lead us to the shore of eternal life.

And do not say, "I have but little time to make penance." Remember the thief who was up on the cross, who had a shorter space of time than you do. God is so benevolent that he is content with the goodwill of the person when he sees that he is truly repentant of all his sins, and that he confesses them completely to the priest. And for that reason, examine your conscience carefully and look at how you have led your life and what you have fashioned in this world. Because if you have any false or bad contract, like usury or fraud, or if you were to have something of someone else's, try to give him justice every way in your power, because if not, your sin will not be forgiven. And if you have accused any person out of maliciousness or under torture, if he is without blame you must revoke your accusation. But not otherwise. And do not be ashamed to confess your sins, because you were not ashamed to commit them. And remember to say how you treated your family.

Chapter Thirteen
Which deals with the third proposal and rule regarding how one must be devout to receive the sacrament of the body of Christ.

The third rule you must follow so as to put your soul in order is to direct it towards God. You have to raise yourself in devotion for the sacrament of the precious body of our Lord Jesus Christ, and for this you have to have perfect faith, considering that this is Christ's noble sacrament instituted in the church.

Christmas (25 December).

All the other sacraments complete some particular grace of God, and are then gathered and bestowed on his creatures, and those graces that are bestowed in the other sacraments are preparations to receive this highest and most excellent sacrament of the body of Christ. Because this sacrament does not confer only one grace to the devout soul, but is the origin of all the graces that come to live in the soul of him who makes himself worthy to gain it and take it in peace.

Take careful note that regarding this sacrament you must understand two aspects: the first is what this sacrament is, and the second is how much reverence you must have in receiving it. Concerning the first aspect, you must firmly believe that this sacrament is the true body and blood of Christ, who was taken from the Virgin Mary, and then was put on the cross and shed all his blood for out salvation. He then, by divine power, on the third day rose from death to life and ascended into heaven, and is seated at the right hand of his Father, and on the last day he will come to judge the living and the dead.

Consider also that in this sacrament, the soul of Christ is also divine and full of every treasure of knowledge. This is the soul that was so tormented during his Passion. This is the soul that was placed in the tomb for the redemption of Christ's sheep; there is no greater testimony of the quality of his soul. This is that bread that is the perfect manna and contains in itself every sweet flavor. This is that perfect bread that strengthens the soul to climb up the mount of the blessed vision. In this precious sacrament divine generosity is conferred to the Christian people, and there was never a generation that was able to unite with God as much as we Christians through this sacrament. This is the spiritual banquet to which the eternal God has invited us all, the banquet in which Christ, who is the true God, is prepared.

Oh banquet full of every sweetness, in which the Creator amazingly puts himself in his creation, and where the one performing the sacrifice is also the sacrifice and the giver, the gift. Oh marvelous sacrament, where God is the perfect and true man and truly a sacrifice. Under the visible form of bread and wine, one actually receives invisible things, that is, the true body of Christ and his true blood, which is our redemption. And see what an incredible thing this is, that it invisibly enters your soul and fills your mind, not your body, but certainly your devout heart.

And believe me, this sacrament is not done alone nor without company. And know that at the sound of the priest's voice the heavens immediately open and the Holy Trinity descends, Father, Son, and Holy Spirit, one God and one substance, one lord of the heaven and of the earth, over visible and invisible things.

And the Virgin Mary comes directly after them, descending with her

Son, because wherever God is, the Virgin Mary should be, and it is the same with the whole heavenly court. And so here present are all of the angels of heaven and all of the blessed souls. And they all see if the person is properly disposed to receive this highest sacrament.

And for that reason, my brother, in order that you are not condemned in the sight of such an honorable company, nor sentenced to punishment by any of them, you must understand the second aspect that is necessary for this sacrament. And take careful note.

Chapter Fourteen
Which deals with the merit the man receives who devoutly takes the Eucharist.

The second aspect that you must understand concerning this sacrament in relation to your soul is this: you must examine your conscience very carefully and say, "Alas, wretched, unhappy one, with how much devotion and contrition of my sins do I receive this sacrament? How much reverence and honor do I bring and have towards this sacrament?" And the apostle Paul said, "Who receives it in an unworthy manner, will receive judgment on his soul" [1 Cor. 11:29], not staining the body of Christ. St. Augustine said, "Whom does your stomach belong to? Prepare your soul, if you want to receive this sacrament in a worthy manner: *crede et manducabis*." Prove yourself if you want to eat of this bread. Many receive the sacrament, but do not receive the effect of the sacrament. For that reason, they are called weak and ignorant (*infirmi et imbeciles*). It would be better for their souls to let it be, because this sacrament is ordained to sanctify the soul, considering that it is the food and life of the soul. Christ spoke about this in the holy gospel: "My flesh is the true food, my blood is the true drink, and whoever eats this bread will live forever" [John 6:54–55]. With that we see that this bread descended from heaven and brought life to the chaste, so they will not perish on Judgment Day, but rather they will be resurrected on the new day.

And for that reason, my brother, I beg you for the love of God that you lift your mind away from earthly things and put it in the things of God. And let go all the injuries and all revenge and return to Christ, the spouse of your soul, and you will be good to yourself. And put your hope in the benevolent God who will have you participate in the kingdom of heaven. And you will be able to say what the holy prophet David said: "I will take your sacrifice, oh Lord, and I will confess in your holy name. For you are the highest good" [Ps. 54:6]. Because he wrote, "Happy is the man who believes in God and lets go of the world" [Ps. 112:1]. And also you can sing with David in another psalm, saying, "You, my sweet Lord, unbind all my sins and then bind me to my soul. And for you I will take the holy sacrifice of the host, full of salvation, calling on your name always. And so, sacrificing myself, I will take your chalice, the peace-giving host of my living Lord" [cf. Ps. 116].

And once you have received this sacrament with devotion and with tears, you must lift your mind, commending your soul to the Lord Jesus Christ, saying these words, "Benevolent Son of God, who descended from heaven on earth to take human flesh for our sins, I pray to you to be made worthy from your suffering and that this sacrament wash away all my sins and give me strength in adversity. And that it help me against all the dangers of my soul. That it counsel me and help me to grow in good thoughts and that it guide me so that I will be in your eternal kingdom, at the time and moment that my soul will be separated from my body. And into your arms and hands, my sweet Lord, I commend my soul and spirit [Luke 23:6; Ps. 31:5]. Amen."

Chapter Fifteen
Which deals with how the shame of public execution should be disparaged and why no excuses should be made.

Understand, my dearest brother, that after having observed these three perfect rules, you should hold your soul to these two instructions. The first is that you must lift your soul away from every mundane thing and from every earthly concern. You well understand that you have little time and few hours left in this life, and for that reason it would be better for you to give yourself entirely to God with all your intellect. Do not care for your body, how it must be tied nor how it must be led in sight of all the people. In these hours and at these moments, you must remember that our Lord Jesus Christ was given into the hands of sinners, and how they took him and tied him, and how they harshly led him like a thief, and how much the people of Jerusalem scorned him.

Also, you must not think about your father, nor your mother, nor your wife, nor your children, nor your brothers, nor your parents, nor your friends, nor your things, nor your standing. You also must not care about the worldly shame, that is, how the sentence will sound, or the tolling of the bells, because these thoughts are all vain and are all diabolical instigations the devil puts in your imagination to lead you to despair. And if he makes you believe that these things are truly shameful, and if he makes you understand that the world is great and it has greatly harmed you, all this he would do so as to lead you into temptation at this point. But I want to advise you that at this point you should not hold anyone as an enemy except the devil from hell, who tries in every way to devour your soul. And indeed he will try to make you see that it would be good to make some protest about what they will say against you, so that you will seem just before the world.

My brother, we know that while our Lord Jesus Christ was being led to his death, many things were said against him and he was innocent of all of them. And nevertheless he never made any protest. And worse was said about him before Annas, Caiaphas, and Pilate than was ever said about anybody, him who was always like the gentle lamb and the innocent sheep.

And likewise, we know that the holy martyrs, while being led to their death, did not protest. First, you know that the sentence has already been given, and that it cannot be commuted. Second, neither you nor anyone has ever seen someone escape by protesting at this point. Besides, you must know, you and everyone else, that if a protest be sufficient, very many would go free. Don't you think that God knows if your protests are true or not? If they are not true, why do you want to make them? This is nothing but adding sin to sin and provoking God's wrath. So he will not be merciful towards you, seeing that to avoid death of the body you are not afraid of the death of your soul. If your protests are actually true, you know very well that they will not be helpful at that time and in that moment, because they didn't help you before the judge. Still, if your excuse was actually true, leave it in the hand of God and this should be enough. It will also be of great worth to you to gain eternal life.

Now then, lift your intellect and your soul from these earthly things and from all worldly concerns, and consider the things of God. And do not move yourself from him, but do as the holy martyrs, who did not care for the life of the body nor for any worldly things, but said like the blessed psalmist David, "I mean to guard my ways so that I do no lack in speaking with my tongue. I put my mouth under control, as I instead want to be quiet and humble" [Ps. 39:2–3] before God rather than speak and be held just before the world. And in another passage the prophet David makes the prediction, "Those who search for my ruin speak of vain things and they imagine to defame me and to bring me much sorrow. But I am like the deaf who do not hear, and like the mute, I do not open my mouth. And as I am like a man who cannot hear and does not open his mouth in excuses, with this I place my hope in you, my Lord God, and you will excuse me in my humility" [Ps. 38:13–15].

My dearest brother, do not hold this world nor the men of this life in esteem, because there do not exist such righteous people that you should hold them in high account.

Chapter Sixteen
Which deals with the miseries of the world which we leave when we
depart from this mortal life.

In order to show you how you ought to think of people in this world, my dearest brother, consider carefully how men are made still today: ungrateful and
oblivious to all the good that our Lord God gives. It is he who always helps us
and we always revert back to bad things. People of little intellect, men of little
reverence, of little charity for their neighbor, and of little love for God. Men
poorly behaved towards God, towards ourselves, and towards our neighbors,
ready to deceive and betray one another. And who is better to his companion
is held to be good and valiant. My brother, see the people you are abandon-
ing, people full of every iniquity, that is, malice, fornication, adultery, people
full of a life of the flesh who live like beasts and brute animals, people of little
intellect and reason. Now, consider briefly the people that you leave in this
sad life: very greedy men, usurers, swindlers, robbers, men who always try
to undo everyone and overwhelm the near and the distant, arrogant people,
full of disputes and affronts, full of grudges, and envious of their neighbor's
possession, people full of murders, and blood-spilling, people full of all kinds
of revenge and spite, full of every malice, whisperers, gossipers of the people,
detractors of the righteous and those who would like to live in peace, blas-
phemers of God who are not worthy to mention him, vilifiers of saints—it's a
miracle that God does not cut out their tongue!—people and men who hate
God, his feast and holy days, those who dislike God, men who find all the
evils worse than murderers, since the murderer wrongs you openly, but they
wrong you and they use your possessions, person, children, and friends, and
you do not know whom you must guard against. Foolish and unwise people,
barely revering their father and mother. And would that God willed that this
be the worst evil they committed. Men who mock the old, and youths and
good-for-nothings who turn their backs on those who give them good advice. People who hardly honor the religious, priests, and ministers of God,
who dare to judge the preachers, the confessors, and the officials of the holy
church, people full of spiritual and temporal errors, usurpers of ecclesiastical
benefices, pompous men, vaunting what they are not, men full of fangs and
swellings, men that are full of so little good and little virtue that they ought
to despise themselves and instead they despise their companions, wanting to
find the smallest fault in their companions and not looking at their own faults.
Cruel people, without mercy, without faith, and without charity. And if things
were getting better, there might be some small reason why death would give

us sorrow, but according to my judgment things are getting worse. And look at this example: that young boys nowadays are more malicious than twenty-five-year-old men.

Now, my dear brother, this is the company that you leave behind and that you abandon. Now, lift your spirit and your soul away from this company and away from these extremely vile and sad people. And turn your mind to consider and see the noble company that, with the grace of God, you will find. What a comparison between this one and the one you leave behind. And so you will be able to see and understand that it is rather the one who dies who is blessed.

Chapter Seventeen
Which deals with how we will find the Holy Trinity when we depart from this life and will go to the life everlasting in glory.

First, once your spirit is gathered with God in the mansion on high, you will find the divine majesty, the unlimited, infinite, and never-ending light, the everlasting light, lucid and clear, the light and dawn that penetrates every heart, spreading the rays of its brilliance inside the purged and cleansed minds, light of wisdom and counsel, light of knowledge and intellect, light of glory and perfect love, light of truth, and shining splendor, light of charity and fervent love, light of every abundance, measure of every eloquence, illumination of every good conscience. This omnipotent God is most excellent and of immense beauty. You will see him sitting on the throne of his divinity, raised and magnificently placed above every other thing, full of the highest prudence, decorated with divine justice, expert in providence. He is the one who sees everything, rules over and governs everything. Of which a prudent man said, speaking sweetly to God, "Oh you who govern the world with eternal reason, you are the creator of heaven and earth. You who command time that is rather beyond time, you who are stable, fixed, and permanent, you whose will everything obeys." The Father with the great power, the Son with great wisdom, and the Holy Spirit with kind mercy are one God, spanning from the east to the west, arranging all things. The Power created all things, the Wisdom arranged all things, the Mercy kept all things. And these three first persons, that is, the Father, Son, and Holy Spirit, are one God, one uncreated and eternal Lord. And the Father is fully God in and of himself, and the Son, coming from the Father, is fully God in and of himself, and the Holy Spirit, proceeding from the Father and the Word, is fully God in and of himself. And these three persons are equal in nature, substance, power, knowledge, and are present in everything. Their majesty had no beginning and will have no end. They are the beginning and end of every creature. "All wisdom comes from God and is always with him and will never come to an end. Is there anyone who can count and measure the height of the heavens, the breadth of the earth, the depth of the abyss below, the sands of the sea, the drops of the rain, and the stars of the sky?" [Ecclus. 1:2–3]. Only he is the one who can investigate all these things, count and measure them, who drew the limits around heaven, and penetrated the depths of the abyss with his great ability. A disciple of God spoke about this, saying, "Oh you who count the stars and call them all by name, the constellations of heaven and the power of the planets, the movements, flows, and times, you alone understand them" [cf. Ps. 147:4; Isa. 40:26]. Where the apostle Peter [sic], being inspired by the Holy Spirit, marveled at this ability and said, "Oh the depth of the riches, wisdom, and knowledge of God. How incomprehensible are his judgments and inscrutable are his ways. For who can know the mind of the Lord or truly give him counsel?" [Rom. 11:33–34, citing Isa. 40:13]. So that he is the highest wisdom and highest virtue and contains all good things. Every grace comes from him and through him and in him is every goodness, every delight, and every perfect gift.

And for that reason, he, the Father of light, and his Word—the fountain of wisdom, the brilliance of the eternal light, and the immaculate form, the expression of the first goodness—and the Paraclete Spirit, gift and ardor and immense love, these three persons in one unchanging God, have every honor and glory and virtue and divinity and wisdom, strength and grace, blessing and salvation, clarity and praise and perfection, now and forever and *in secula seculorum*. Amen.

Chapter Eighteen
Which deals with how we will find our Lady, the Virgin Mary in the glory of eternal life.

And then, descending according to the hierarchy of the blessed spirits, once you have been led into the everlasting glory that is communicated to all the blessed, you will certainly find up in the first created choir, up above the seat decorated and shining with divine light, that incorruptible Virgin, Holy Mother of the Son of God, the sweetest Virgin Mary, mother and virgin, immaculate, untouched and uncontaminated mother, integrity and vase of every precious stone, temple of God the Father, tabernacle of God the Son, sanctuary of the Holy Spirit, house of divinity, palace of the Trinity, and example of chastity.

Queen of heaven, lady of the angels, empress of the blessed, fountain of piety, sheltering tree of mercy, star of the sea, door of heaven, full of hope for sinners, above all blessed women, full of grace, full of mercy, full of the Holy

Spirit, whose life illuminates the churches and casts out heresy.

She is the ship that leads to the safe harbor of salvation, to the harbor of comfort, to the harbor of contentment. She is the rod of the root of Yahweh who gave birth to precious Jesus Christ, true God and man, through whom original sin was taken away. She is the ark of the Old Testament that carried us the manna from heaven, comfort of the spiritual mind. She is Noah's ark that delivered us all from the infernal flood, from the flood of sins, guilt, and punishment. She is the one who more than any other creature pleased God. She is the banner of glory. She is the one in whom God dwelt when he descended from heaven to come and live in her virginal womb. She is the one who cared so much for Christ, our Lord. She is the one who bore so much pain during the Passion of Christ. She is the mistress of the apostles, illumination of the evangelists, fortress of the martyrs, hope of the confessors, beauty of the virgins, steadfastness of the widows, gladness of wives. She is the one placed at the right hand of God, clothed in gold and surrounded by sun, and mortal things she holds under her feet. And crowned by the twelfth star, she is so close to God that no one can distinguish between her and God, and she is placed so close to God that she can see more closely and contemplate the wheels of the sun of the divinity of Christ her son, and of the omnipotent God the Father. She is the ladder of Jacob on which ascended and descended the angels of God and that brings the souls of God to the kingdom on high. She is the advocate of us all before her only begotten son, and every grace she asks from him she gladly obtains. She is so full of pity and clemency for us children of sad Eve, driven out of the heavenly kingdom and trapped in this valley of tears and wretchedness. She is the one who brings deep compassion to all the troubled and unfortunate. He who goes to her, devoutly invoking her, she does not let perish nor go to perdition.

Chapter Nineteen
Which deals with how the hierarchy is arranged and the orders of angels that we find in the glory of everlasting life.

After this, your soul, lifting its intellect (that is, the spirit) will see those angelic spirits that are so distinct and organized by the divine and infinite wisdom of God. That most holy choir of angels is the first distinct group in the three hierarchies, or multitudes, each of which sees God in a distinct way, and each of which contains in itself three ranked orders, according to the will of God.

In the first hierarchy, which is the closest to God, is the order of the seraphim and the order of the cherubim and the order of the thrones. The

seraphim are burning and inflamed with the love of God, of which David
said, "God who makes his spiritual angels and his ministers flames of fire" [Ps.
104:3]. The second order is that of the cherubim, which are full of lucidity and
knowledge, and so closer are they to God that they are able to see his divine
nature. The third order is the one of the thrones, who are so full of grace because God sits in their minds.

The second hierarchy, the one that is in the middle, contains in itself three
orders: the first is dominations, the second is virtues, and the third is powers.
The dominations command to the inferior angels what God wills to be done in
this world. The second, which are the virtues, have to constrain the devils and
take away the obstacles that would impede fulfillment of God's command. The
third order, which are the powers, have to bring God's command to execution.

The third hierarchy is the lowest, and it contains three other orders: the
first is the principalities, the second is the archangels, and the third is the angels. The principalities have to procure the salvation of the whole world, pro-
tecting it from the devil's harm. The archangels have to perform miracles and
reveal the secret of the omnipotent God. The final order, which is the angels,
have to procure the salvation of every person.

And take note that of these angels one is assigned to each man and
woman, to illuminate and direct the creature along the way of God, and this
angel is always ready to make us act well. But we are so bad that we do not
want to consent to what he secretly advises us. And this angel has to lead our
soul to paradise if it departs with the grace and love of God and our neighbor,
but not otherwise. So, my dearest brother, in order that the angel that you
have as guardian would lead you in his company and happiness, you should
forgive the offenses done to you so that angel forgives you the injuries that you
have done to him.

Chapter Twenty
Which deals with how we will find the holy patriarchs with God.

You will also see that other honorable company created by God in the first age at
the beginning of the world. First you will find Adam, the first man, and Eve, the
first woman. You will see Seth, Enoch brought over to earthly paradise, Methu-
selah, Lamech with all his descendants who were all elected to life everlasting.

In the second age, you will find Noah, who made the ark of the Flood,
and his sons, Shem, Ham, and Japheth, and all the others who are recorded in
the book of life by divine providence.

In the third age, you will find the college of the holy patriarchs, Abraham,

Isaac, and Jacob, with his twelve sons and one of his nephews; Judah, with twelve thousand marked from his tribe, and so you will find each one. And take note that the twelfth son of Jacob, who was Dan, was not placed in the number because the false Antichrist would be born from him, and for that reason, Manasseh was put in his place.

My brother, this is a noble company, because they all are men of high regard, religious men in their life and jealous of their faith in the great Messiah. These were decorated with justice and were magnanimous in hope, obedient to God's commandments, and along with the angels they see God face to face. These were prudent in their counsel, virtuous in battle, ruling with great wisdom the affairs of the world. They justly maintained their rule, which never left their hand until that time when Christ was born from their stock, that is, from the body of the glorious Virgin Mary. Then Christ was given power over heaven and earth, as true God and perfect man.

We should never lose the memory of them and they should live forever because they are worthy of God and his very sweet company. And for that reason, whoever wants to arrive securely, my brother, has to follow this noble college.

Chapter Twenty-one
Which deals with how we will find the holy prophets with God.

Following the order begun, my dearest brother, with your soul lifted from earthly love and led to the heavenly company, you will see in the fourth age the triumphant company of holy prophets. First, you will find Moses, the leader of God's people, who spoke to God face to face and to whom God gave the tablets of the Law. You will see Aaron, Joshua, Gideon, and Jephte, who killed his daughter in sacrifice to the omnipotent God. You will find David, the great prophet with the cittern[23] and the Psalter, singing and playing in the house of the Lord. You will see Job, master of patience, Tobias almsgiving, Ezra with his elevated gaze, Isaiah with his saw, Jeremiah stoned, and so you will find all the prophets, each one in his rank.

Now, note carefully that God spoke to all those with his intellect, show-ing them his secrets and the things to come. These are the announcers of Christ, inflamed with the Holy Spirit, predicting things about the future, announcing and teaching the people about the true Messiah. Some of them were sanctified in their mother's womb, and some received the Holy Spirit as children, some in their youth, some in their old age. They were men of great

---

[23] A cittern is a sixteenth-century guitar with a pear-shaped body.

sanctity and great abstinence and they were persecuted, faithful and devout, until the end. They were men who were continuously contemplating God and they were not afraid of death. They converted tyrants with their words and preaching, hounding the sacrilegious and those who went against the Law.

My brother, take comfort, because this is one of the companies that you will find, and you would not find such a company in this world. It seems that we all are afraid to say the truth and we seem to have become mute and silent about the salvation of our neighbor.

Chapter Twenty-two
Which deals with how we will find St. John the Baptist with God.

As your soul raises your eyes on high, you will see near the omnipotent God two very holy men, that is, the glorious John the Baptist and together in his company the glorious John the Evangelist. Remember well that this man the Baptist has many more honors than the other prophets. The first is that he was prophesied by another prophet. The second honor is that he was announced by the angel Gabriel, who announced Christ. The third is that he was holy before he was born. The fourth was that he knew the Savior and he celebrated him in the presence of the Virgin Mary, as he was in the body of his mother. The fifth is that he was fourteen years old when he entered the desert to make penance. The sixth honor is that his life was wild honey and grasshoppers and he never tasted cooked food and his drink was pure water.

He was the true precursor of Christ in birth, in preaching, and in announcing the kingdom of Christ, and what's more he was worthy to baptize and touch his precious flesh and to hear the celestial voice say, "Hic est filius meus dilectus in quo mihi bene complacui" (This is my son in whom I am well pleased) [Matt. 3:17]. And he saw with his own eyes the Holy Spirit in the form of a dove descending on Christ. He indicated Christ with his finger saying, "Ecce agnus Dei. Ecce qui tollit peccata mundi" (Here is the Lamb of God. Here is the one who will take away the sins of the world) [John 1:29]. He was a prophet and more. He prophesied in his mother's womb. He announced the incarnation of Christ to the holy fathers who were in limbo. Hence, a devout man said about St. John the Baptist, speaking his praises, "John the Baptist, student of all virtue, teacher of the holy life, arms of perfect justice, model of virginity, example of chastity. John the Baptist who is the lamb of God to announce the gospel of God,[24] silence of the prophets, voice of the apostles,

---

[24] "Giohanne baptista el quale è agnello de Dio ad annunciare lo evangelio de Dio."

light of the world, trumpeter of Christ, intermediary of the Holy Trinity."[25]

Now, my brother, he who was so great before God and who was so holy and so just, was, nevertheless, beheaded and his blood spilled out of malice of evil people and not, to speak truly, for his fault. But if you must be beheaded or must die in another way for your sins, you well know that you are not as just nor have had as holy a life as St. John the Baptist. And for that reason you must accept the fortune that comes upon you now and wait to be crowned in heaven like the glorious Baptist, who triumphs in the high kingdom of life everlasting, and is crowned next to God.

Chapter Twenty-three
Which deal with how we will find St. John, Apostle and Evangelist, crowned with God.

Once God has illuminated your intellect and raised you to see the blessed spirits, you will find the glorious Evangelist John raised in blessed glory, crowned with the glorious Baptist next to God.

He was the disciple, apostle, and evangelist of the Son of God. He was chosen by God. He was called as a virgin to Christ and always lived as a virgin in his life. He was the disciple of the Blessed God, who loved Christ more than all the other disciples. With his subtle intellect and clear vision, like a triumphant eagle he vigorously took to flight in the flaming chariot, and was not blinded by the splendor. With much effort he made it to the divinity, and saw and knew clearly the mystery of the Trinity, where no other intellect was ever able to arrive. Hence a prudent, devout man has said of this evangelist, "John the Evangelist, light of wisdom, clarity of knowledge, divine source, guide of sufficiency, spiritual eagle with wide wings," who by divine virtue flew above the third heaven, and with the feathers of deep contemplation, penetrated the mystery and saw the Holy Trinity, the paradise of paradises, the secret of the eternal Word. He opened the way of the truth, and expressed his loud voice, intoning, "In principio erat Verbum et Verbu erat apud Deum et Deus erat Verbum" (In the beginning was the Word, and the Word was with God, and the Word was God) [John 1:1].

And for this reason do not be amazed if this evangelist flew so high, because during the last supper that Christ had with his apostles on Holy Thursday, resting on the breast of Christ, he received many secrets of God. He

[25] Attributed in *The Golden Legend* to St. John Chrysostom; Jacobus de Voragine, *The Golden Legend: Readings on the Saints,* trans. W. G. Ryan (Princeton: Princeton University Press, 1993), 134.

savored so many of them that his spirit could savor no more, and God filled him with wisdom and knowledge and the water of salvation. And understand well that God loved him so much that even on the cross he assigned him to his mother as her son.

So! Look well, my brother: he who was so good and so wise and so close to God was nevertheless given poison to drink and put in a burning caldron of hot oil.

Chapter Twenty-four
Which deals with how we will find the holy apostles with God.

After that the ray of divine light, penetrating the blessed minds, leads the soul to see the heavenly parties and companies. And for that reason, my brother, know that once your soul departs from your body, it will be led by the Holy Spirit and be raised in love with the grace of God and placed in paradise. You will find there the glorious college of the holy apostles and evangelists that surround the seat of the Lamb, joyful and happy in the immense glory, praising and singing sweet *laude*.

First, you will see St. Peter with the keys of authority of the church, prince of the apostles and Vicar of Christ on earth; and he was crucified upside-down for the name of Christ.

St. Paul, vessel of election, resplendent with every virtue, doctor and preacher of the truth to the whole world; and he was beheaded for his love of Christ.

St. Andrew, a just, pious man and dear to God; and he was crucified for the name of Christ.

St. James the elder, true cousin of Christ and his secretary, shed his blood for his love of Christ.

St. Thomas, who put his hand in the ribs of Christ, was butchered for the name of Christ.

St. Philip, friend of the gentiles, was crucified for the name of Christ.

St. Bartholomew, a gentile and from royalty, was flayed for the name of Christ.

St. Matthew, evangelist and apostle, a deeply devout man, was stabbed in the throat for the name of Christ.

St. Simon and St. Tadeus, blood brothers, men who were holy in their spiritual life, were cut to pieces.

St. Matthias, put in place of Judas, was stoned for the name of Christ.

St. Mark the Evangelist, a man of great patience, preacher of the holy doctrine, had a halter thrown around his neck while he was celebrating the holy mass, and he was dragged all over the city, brought to the butcher's, and was made a martyr for the name of Christ.

St. Luke the Evangelist, disciple of the Virgin Mary and a very serious doctor, was crucified for the name of Christ.

St. Bernard, a man of great constancy, was burned for the name of Christ.

And all of this beautiful company you will find crowned with God, because they were patient and constant in adversity. They were the foundation of the holy church, appointed for the entire universe, and all the earth speaks of their blessedness. They are like the true palm of Christ, his fruit which will last forever and never die.

Christ said to them, "You are the salt to season all spiritual food. You are the light of the world. You are the light to shine for all those who will enter the house of God" [cf. Matt. 5:13–16]. Christ said to them, "I have not called you servants, because a servant does not know what his lord wants to do. But I have called you friends, since all of my secrets and all those of my Father, I have revealed and shown to you" [John 15:15].

And to them were also given the keys of heaven that open and close, that bind and unbind all sins. They were promised that when Christ would judge the living and the dead they would be sitting with Christ in judgment.

So, my brother, you will find these leaders of our faith and foundation of the church of Christ with God in life everlasting. For the present, you should commend yourself devoutly and call them so that they assist your soul.

Chapter Twenty-five
That deals with how we will find the holy martyrs with God.

When you are with them, you, raised in spirit by the flaming rays of divine glory, and your soul decorated with the shining light of your mind, in repose looking with the clarity that comes from the fountain of light, you will see the pure, colored with triumphant blood, and bearing victorious palms. And you will see the college and the company of the holy martyrs, who through various kinds of punishment virtuously followed the hard and bitter suffering of Lord Jesus Christ with the glorious fruit of holy martyrdom.

And take note that with bodily delights you cannot have eternal life, and you cannot ascend up there except by great efforts. Hence, the apostle Paul said, "Only he who wins by valiant fighting will be crowned" [2 Tim. 2:5].

So, my brother, because you must fight, you should take for your fortress the example of the glorious martyrs. And consider what kind of death they had. Now consider carefully in your mind and hold on to this. You are not better than they, nor have lived a holier life than those who were martyrs, and yet nevertheless those who receive more become martyrs. Some were seized with pincers, some burned, some beheaded, some were struck so much that their flesh was all torn, and some others put like fish over fire on the grill.

Ah! My brother, think what martyrdom that is and with what acceptance they prevailed over such pains. Some of these martyrs were full of holes all over, like linen, others were sealed in a vessel full of nails and rolled on the ground. Think how they were feeling. Some others were sunk in the sea with rocks hung round their necks.

And see, my brother, that they cared little for their body—where it was thrown, whether in the sea or in pits—because they knew very well that if they didn't care about it, then all of their feeling would be directed towards the soul. Some others were flayed alive. See that worse was done to them than is done to animals, because animals are killed before they are skinned, and for them it was the opposite.

Now think carefully about how much patience and strength they had. Some of them were sentenced to perpetual imprisonment and there they suffered many injuries, both in words and deeds. Some others were deprived of their tongues so that they could not praise the name of God and defend our faith. Some of them were buried alive. See what an immense cruelty this was.

Ah! Tell me, my brother, how much you would not want to come to this. Now think carefully about what pain this must have been, that some of them were made to die of hunger and thirst. Some others were stripped and dragged.

See, my brother, that those who were so torn to shreds had no part of their body still holding together. How much cruelty do you think this was, that all of their blood would be pouring out from every part of their body. Some others had their feet and hands and their male members cut off, and they were made the scorn of the whole world. Some others had their nose and ears cut off, and their eyes and teeth dug out. Now think what a torment this was. Some other of these holy martyrs were sawn in half with a lead saw, or a wooden one, or an iron one.

And for that reason, my brother, you who are so full of sins and who do not have to approach such harsh martyrdoms as these, had better resign yourself to what divine providence lets occur. Some others were sewn alive in goats' skins and worms were born inside them. Now think carefully about how they began to stink. Some others were stripped nude and were strung up with their hands and feet tied and they were put out in the sun. Now think carefully about how they felt and how afflicted they were. This was certainly a cruel death, if you think about it. Some others were tied to the stake like a target, and they were shot with arrows in the ribs.

St. Christopher, among all of the giants, was chosen for the victory palm of martyrdom. There is not enough time to try and tell you all the stories of the different kinds of martyrdoms and tortures. But even so, I want to remind you of one torment. Think carefully if this was immense. Rocks and oil were spread out in the palace's grand room and they were made to lie on top of the rocks, and their flesh fried like a fish in a pan. Some others were put on a spit and were roasted as if they were meat. Oh the infinite cruelty of these tyrants!

And you know, my brother, that the perverse world was not worthy enough to have these glorious martyrs. Still, consider that you do not have to go through any of these cruel tortures, but you still have to follow their example, so inflamed with the love of God that they did not feel the pains of the body, and all of their pains were transformed into sweetness. As we have the story of St. Andrew, when he was led to the cross, he greeted it saying, "May God save you, holy cross, decorated with the body of my master! I come to you willingly, and perfectly happy." We also have the story of St. Lawrence who said to the tyrant Decius, "Know that these coals chill me." And so we have the story of St. Agatha, who went to her martyrdom as if it were a wedding. And since for these martyrs the path was narrow and their lives were planted near the water of tribulation, their souls were always fixed only on the laws of their Lord. And in the presence of the men of the world, these holy martyrs suffered and bore many punishments and tortures. Nevertheless, their hope was always for eternal life. The holy martyrs gave their bodies many torments out of love for God, so that they would inherit the kingdom of heaven.

And for that reason, my dearest brother, now they are blessed and friends of God, since with so much patience they endured the torments and drew support from the solid rock of Lord Jesus Christ. And for that reason they are crowned by the hand of the Lord. The souls of these martyrs rejoice in heaven because they followed in the footsteps of the master and shed their blood. For that reason, they reign with God and are glad and joyous, and this is the exchange that Jesus Christ promised them. And they live in heaven with much honor.

And for that reason, my brother, I beg you for the love of God that you prepare your soul to try and bear patiently the death that is decreed for you. Because now is the time and the moment when you can enter into the company of these noble cavaliers of Christ. Because if you act in this way you can surely expect the crown of life everlasting. And the opposite also follows—now is the time and the moment when as you lose your body, you may also lose your soul.

And for that reason, commend yourself to these glorious holy martyrs, so that their merits are useful to you. And pray that they may secure God's grace for your soul and firm constancy until the last moment of your life, so that you may join their state of blessedness, which is eternal glory.

Chapter Twenty-six
Which deals with how we will find the holy doctors with God.

The eternal knowledge and supreme beauty spread the love of his grace in you, and will have raised your soul in the spirit of the blessed vision. When you pass from this mortal life, raising the eyes of your intellect about you, you will see shining like the sun the company of the noble college of holy doctors of the church with the holy Trinity, Father, Son, and Holy Spirit.

You will find crowned the glorious doctor St. Augustine. He was a resplendent sun in the temple of God, and like a morning star full of all the rays of knowledge. In comparison with the other doctors, he was like the light of the sun, and just as that light obtains its primacy over all other corporeal things, so Augustine obtained his primacy over all other doctors of the church. Consider the fruit that all day long was born from this tree: doctors, teachers, students, disciples, and in every generation, people who came to listen to the preaching, sermons, counsel, and teaching. If only God had willed that you would have been one of those who heard his teaching, it might not have come to this. Now, may all things praise God.

After that, you will find St. Jerome, a man of great holiness and great teaching; St. Gregory, a man full of piety, full of the Holy Spirit and the true pastor of the holy church; St. Ambrose, zealous of the honor of God and defender of the ecclesiastical orders; St. John Chrysostom; St. Leo, the pope; St. Bernard of the Virgin Mary; St. Hillary; St. Isidore; the venerable doctor Bede; St. Thomas Aquinas; and many other doctors who have written about the holy scripture, illuminated by the Holy Spirit. And all of these have illuminated people with their writing. Thus they may benefit from it, growing in virtue and bearing its fruit in holy deeds. It has enlightened souls to enable them to understand the hidden mysteries of God, counseling, teaching, and guiding the way of God, so we can receive the reward of blessed glory. And you will see all of these, by the grace of God, crowned with stars, inflamed with the intensity that proceeds from the first light.

Oh my brother, how beautiful it is to see such a noble company, their works and teaching! If we could always study, hear, and listen and thus observe their sayings, we could reach and arrive at their happy glory.

Chapter Twenty-seven
Which deals with how we will find the holy confessors with God.

Beside them you will find the college of holy confessor priests. You will find St. Paul, the first hermit; St. Anthony, chosen for the whole universe; St. Hilarion; St. Benedict; St. Dominic and St. Francis; St. Martin; St. Nicholas, St. Maurus, and many other hermit saints who, knowing how false and sad the world is, then abandon it and all its pomp, not heeding the devil or his temptations. They prevailed against the impulses of the flesh, which is no small victory, because the flesh is the enemy that always lives with us. They lived in the deserts so that their minds were more able to contemplate God. They were chaste, moderate, and calm; their food was roots and herbs, coarse and very stale bread; their drink was water or watered-down vinegar, and they would rarely drink wine.

My brother, we are not like this; rather we want good wine and good meat and of various kinds. They were pious, prudent, and honest men. They girded their loins with continence and their bodies with true cleanliness. They did harsh penance, continual orations, and were full of heavenly life. Their hands were busy with holy deeds. They aspired to heaven, bemoaning staying too long in this life, and would say like David the prophet, "Alas, how my pilgrimage is lasting too long" [Ps. 120:5]. And the apostle said, "Unhappy man that I am, who will release me from this mortal body" [Rom. 7:24]. They had put their will in God's commandments, trusting only in the Lord. And for that reason, their hope is now being rewarded in heaven, because all of them rest without a stain with Christ, and they have his crown and heavenly reward.

And you would have been fortunate, my brother, if you had sometimes understood, with proper devotion, the legends and the stories of their lives! Maybe you would have taken some examples and teaching from their lives.

Chapter Twenty-eight
Which deals with how we will find the holy company of the blessed male and female virgins with God.

May then the divine splendor of eternal light that illuminates the blessed minds, and the holy love that comes from the throne of God the Father, and that blessedly raises the soul to see God, illuminate your mind and lead it up above to the heavenly circle of the Trinity. And when your mind is made firm and stable, standing strongly on its feet and raising the eyes of the intellect and looking steadily up above to the high mount, you will see Christ Jesus above all aflame and seated on his throne in majesty. And surrounding him you will see thousands of virgins, both men and women, white and shining, clothed in precious gold with green garlands, and flowers and roses in their hair. They are all a sign of the living and true God. And all this company have in hand various kinds of instruments, playing and singing a new canticle in a solemn melody before the immaculate Lamb, and no one else can sing those *laude* and that new canticle except those who have been virgins in their minds and in their bodies.

They never knew what carnal sin nor bodily delight was, but they rather always lived with a pure mind. They are the heavenly lilies among which God breathes in their delightful songs. They are crowned with crowns of pearls, before the throne of the divine majesty, and they are the brides of the heavenly groom, and they rest under the wings of his virtue. And they are always happy, singing and dancing to sweet *laude* and melodies. And I also remind you that many of these virgins who were brides of Christ were martyred in various martyrdoms, like St. Catherine, who was scourged with iron scorpions and then placed on the wheel, spiked with nails and knives, and finally was beheaded.[26]

We also have St. Cecilia, who converted her spouse and brother-in-law to the faith of Christ and led them to the palm of martyrdom. And this young woman was stripped naked and put in a caldron of boiling oil and was struck three times with a sword on her neck and she ended her life in this way.

St. Agnes, a thirteen-year-old girl, was beheaded and was always constant during the torments. St. Agatha was strangled and they even cut off her breasts from her chest, and finally she died for the name of Christ.

St. Margaret, as a young girl, was hung by her arms and was all burned with lit torches. She was beheaded in the end, but was always constant during the torments, calling out to the sweet Christ. And so it happened to all of the other virgins, that each one had her martyrdom, each one harsher than yours, and they always were praising the name of Christ.

And tell me, my brother, if all those, who were young women, were so strong and constant through all these punishments, so much more should you be constant and firm before this death, considering that by this constancy you will earn your ascent up there, where these blessed virgins have been raised and crowned next to God.

Chapter Twenty-nine
Which deals with life in paradise.

Your soul, having been raised up towards the kingdom on high, will be placed

---

[26] The "scorpion" was a whip that had sharp iron bits woven into the individual strands.

there with the splendor of God and in the glory of the saints to hear with the ear of the intellect the sweetness and the melody of the blessed spirits. They sing sweetly and one's soul always falls in love upon hearing many songs of various and perfect melodies. It would be impossible to say how delightful are those songs with divine *laude* that those in the blessed life sing.

Hence, David the prophet said to God, "Oh omnipotent, virtuous Lord, how wonderful your dwelling place is! My soul, my heart fails me" [Ps. 84:2] to think of the magnitude of the delights and joys that are in your chambers, and "blessed are those who live in your house, Lord, praising you *in secula seculorum*"[Ps. 84:4].

My brother, those songs up there are not like ours. Today we sing and tomorrow we cry them, today we dance and tomorrow we fight to them. The pleasures of life everlasting are not made like this, because the todays are beautiful and the tomorrows even more so. The todays are gentle and the to-morrows are even more so; thus it is written, "Whoever drinks at the fountain of God, will always be more thirsty, and whoever eats the heavenly food, will always hunger" [Ecclus. 24:29]. Up above there is desire without need. Up above there is the stretching of time, because up above, the day does not know what is night, rather there is always light. Above there is the fullness of true glory and eternal truth.

Oh true happiness and perfect glory, oh holy banquet and sumptuous table, oh joyful glory of the eternal Father looking at the Word, your sweet child, with the kind Holy Spirit and his pious mother with the blessed spirits who sing the gentle song, raising their voices, all the while uttering, "Holy, holy, holy." They continue saying, "Oh great sun and great meridian light, oh mild spring, oh beautiful summer, oh paradisal dwelling place where there is the sweet food and drink of the souls united to God." Up above there is youth without age, happiness without sorrow.

My brother, think what sounds of life everlasting God has commanded to play in the court of paradise. If we could hear them, we would never tire of listening to them. About this we read that a holy father was making impressive orations to God that declare the highest glory and the smallest happiness that the souls enjoy in paradise. When God heard him, he sent a little bird, as beauti-ful as imaginable, and that little bird led the holy father into the desert and there he began to sing so sweetly that this holy father didn't know if he was alive or dead, because it was so sweet. And thinking back on it, he believed that he had stayed there three or four hours. And, while they were leaving, the little bird began to fly up into the sky and the holy father was left disconsolate. And seeing himself alone, he began to return towards the monastery. And when he arrived at the monastery, he found there a new community[27] with new buildings, and amazed by this he thought he must have gone insane. And so, with much humility, he went to speak with the prior of the monastery, saying, "Isn't this the monastery I left this morning when I went out?" The prior said, "What is the name of this monastery?" The holy father said, "Its name is such and such." The prior said, "That's well said." The holy father said, "How can it be that in such a short time the entire community is changed and that there are so many new structures?" Upon seeing the purity of this holy father, the prior and the monks asked in what year he had left the monastery where he had been. And they found out that he had been listening to that little bird singing in the desert for five hundred years. Now you can see therefore what the sounds of everlasting life must be like, when this song was the least and most inferior of them.

And take note and consider carefully that if human industry knew how to find so many instruments to bring pleasure to our bodies, don't you think that God, in his celestial court, has made many more instruments that bring delight to the blessed souls? Believe me, my brother, that in this world laughter is often reduced to tears, and our feasts are reduced to and end up in sadness more often than not. But the joys of everlasting life are not like that. Because up there nothing can be lacking, for God above would not allow them to encounter any scandal, woe, or pain. But rather you will find up there life without death, youth without old age, everlasting happiness. And up above you see God the Father, his one and only Son with the Holy Spirit, one God, one substance, one nature, one light, one lord, one creator. And if God grants you so much grace that you may arrive up there, you will find a thousand thousands more than what I can tell you.

Now, my brother, now is the time that you can earn the merit of seeing and hearing these things. But you should have your heart at peace, with forgiveness for all the offenses you have received and for all those that you have made to others. Ask forgiveness for your sins first from God, and then from your neighbor. And in this way you must hope in God, because he is always merciful. The fact is that the proper property of God is to have mercy on his creatures, who give themselves to him. Don't you know that the benevolence of God is greater than the evil of men?

Now, my dearest brother, I beg you for the love of God that you act so that the merit of Christ's Passion and will is not meaningless in you. But if you

[27] "famiglia."

want to know how and at what point you can earn this, you should make an effort to not be attached to the things of the world, and to forget every offense and every outrage that was ever done to you.

Therefore trust your soul only to God, if you want to reach his glory and do not care about this mortal life. And believe that you are leaving camp to go and stay with the most noble lord who is not of this world. If you are hungry, he is the bread; if you are thirsty, he is the fountain of living waters; if you are blind, he is the perfect light; if you are tired, he is rest; if you are ill, he is the perfect doctor of the soul; if you are ignorant, he is the solemn teacher.

My brother, return to God and do not wish to lose your soul. Throw yourself in his arms, because he is not cruel. Rather, he would forgive you benevolently and grant you the grace to patiently bear your suffering, and then at the end he will give you his glory.

Chapter Thirty
Which deals with the proper disposition of the soul when it will depart from this miserable life.

The second teaching that you should learn now is this. Know that the Lord God, according to his solid commandment and his invariable justice, determined and commanded this sentence to human souls when they depart from this life: their soul shall live eternally and remain with the intention and the disposition it had upon leaving the world. So if the soul departs in hatred, it will remain in hatred forever. If it departs in love and charity for God and neighbor, it will remain forever with that love and with that blessed charity.

Thus the apostle Paul said that in life everlasting the soul has neither faith nor hope because each of these virtues would have completed their purpose. But the third virtue, which is charity and divine love, will never cease; rather it will grow and become perfect [cf. 1 Cor. 13:8, 13]. And this is the reason why faith and hope will have served their purpose. Reader, note this well.

The purpose and the effect of faith is this. The intellect, which proceeds only according to the light of faith, is not itself that true and clear light that shows what one believes. Yet certainly what is clear is what is believed. But it is not due to this belief that one can plainly see that vision that faith shows you. And for that reason, St. Augustine said that faith has its own eyes with which it sees most certainly, but that faith need not see clearly that which it believes. And St. Gregory said that faith would have no merit if you saw by plain sight what you believed. And St. Paul said that faith is the shaded or veiled light, by which we see those divine things for which we should hope [1 Cor. 13:12].

And since in the blessed life, there will not be any shade or any darkness, therefore faith will not have a purpose to serve up there. There the light of glory will illuminate the soul and will lead it to see clearly that which we believe, and here is the proof. If someone has a veiled face, it is still possible to see that face very well under the shade. But one could not fully grasp it, because the view would be dark. But lift away the veil, and now the clear view will follow, and you will plainly see and grasp what that face is. It is just so in this situation, that at present we see under the shadow and under the veil of our eyes, yet we will clearly see the beatific object. Similarly with hope—in life everlasting its purpose will end, and this is the reason. Hope is the desire of the soul, since the soul desires to have that which it does not have, and with greater resolve it awaits that for which it hopes. And because the desire of the soul will be fulfilled in life everlasting, hope's purpose will no longer exist. Because then the soul would not be perfectly blessed. So these two virtues, faith and hope, do not remain in your soul once it is separated from the body. Departing with divine love,[28] the soul will seize much more and it will indeed unite with God.

So, my dearest brother, I beg you, as much as I know and can, to put aside and let go of every bad will and every hatred that you carried or that you had against your neighbor. Then these two loves will become the two wings of your soul, allowing it to fly to the glorious life of paradise. Consider carefully this matter that I am going to tell you and seal it well in your soul: you would not be able to do anything meriting life everlasting—neither you nor anyone—without this charity. If you were to have a thousand lives and you were to bear a thousand deaths without love and charity towards God and your neighbor, you could not ascend to the glory of the holy. So then make an effort, out of reverence for God, so that your soul departs from this world in grace and with true charity.

Chapter Thirty-one
Which deals with the soul's will[29] when it is separated from the body.

Regarding the free will of the soul, be aware that once it has separated from the body, it is no longer able to earn merit or to sin, since neither merit nor guilt is ascribed to it. Now, pay attention and understand well: the divine power has made three mansions, one that is above, one below, and the other in the middle.

The first mansion, which is the one below, is the punishment of hell, that

---

[28] "carità divina."
[29] "arbitrio."

infernal region, shadow of death, and valley of misery, where there is no rule, no order, but eternal horror. There the souls of the damned live. And so it is the opposite of the one above, insofar as they are beyond hope of ever leaving so many punishments. They cannot earn merit, because their hands and feet are tied, and they are in the outer darkness. The tied feet show the effect of a depraved will, the tied hands demonstrate evil deeds, the outer darkness demonstrates the blindness of the damned, who are deprived of the blessed light for eternity. And just as the saints cannot wish evil, so these cannot earn merit or sin, because to be able to earn merit or to sin, one must be able to act well or badly.

The third mansion, which is the middle one, is this present life where we live with the body and soul together. And in this last mansion, we can merit and sin as long as we are alive. If we act well, we will acquire the mansion above. And if we act badly, we will acquire the one below, that is, eternal punishment. And for that reason, the wise Solomon said in praise of the just, "He could act well and act badly: he left the evil and has done the good. He could transgress the commandments of God and he has not passed them by"[Ecclus. 31:10]. In this middle mansion, where we are now, things are arranged so that we can earn merit. So now, my dearest brother, as long as you have the time, direct yourself to try to earn merit. Do not wait for a time in another life to repent for your sins, because this would not be conceded to you or anyone.

Chapter Thirty-two
Which deals with those who say that the planets control them.

Going by what I am able to understand of what you say, it seems to me that you have fallen into a certain error that many stumble on. And the error is this: that all people who are sentenced to death are led to it by their constellation, that is, by the planet they are born under. And I think I understand from what you say that you could not die in any way other than that ordained by your planet.

Be well aware—you and every other feeling person—that this opinion is false and heretical and foolish. And I will demonstrate to you that it is false by clear and evident reasoning.

If the constellation or the planet were to lead a person to doing wrong, it would be a great iniquity caused by that planet and constellation. But the iniquity caused by the one who created the planet so unjust and so evil would be all the greater, knowing that this planet would force man to sin. And so, according to this opinion, it would follow that God, who is the creator of the planets, is evil and unjust. That this is false, this opinion of yours, everyone can clearly see.

It would also follow that the things God created were neither well-created nor

good. And this would go against the holy scripture, which says, "God saw everything he had created, and it was good" [Gen. 1:31]. So this reasoning also shows that
the planets are not bad, and that they do not have to lead someone to sin.

If the planet led you, then neither you nor anyone else should act well or
badly. You would neither gain merit nor would you sin, and thus neither blame
nor merit could be ascribed to you. Only the planet could be blamed. And thus
God would be unjust to punish you and others for the evil that the planet forced
you to do. Rather the evil planet should be punished or, truly, rewarded.

And if this opinion were true—if the planet he was born under could
only lead him to do wrong—why would God have given free will to man? It
would follow that he could not do good. If the planet led him to do good, it
would follow that he could not sin. And thus free will would be given to man
in vain, since he could not do anything but what his planet forced him to do.

It would also follow, if this opinion were true, that all those born under
one planet would have to arrive at the same end. Likewise, those born of one
birth should all be equal in everything. And so Jacob and Esau, who were
born in one birth, and under the same planet, should have been equally lucky.
And nevertheless, one was lucky and the other was unlucky; Jacob was good
and Esau bad [cf. Gen. 25:19–25].

It would also follow, if this were true, that each one who was born under
the same constellation and under the same planet, should be equally wise or
crazy, and one should die when the other one does. Everyone can easily see
that this is false. Because there could be two born under one planet, and one
of them will live a long time and the other a short time. One will be a lord and
the other a servant; one will be rich and the other poor.

Also, if this opinion were true, the human body would always share the
same inclination. And so when one's foot aches, so would the knee, and when
one's hand aches, so would the head, and so it would go for all members of the
body. One member would have the same state as another member, because all
the members of the body are born under the same planet and under the same
constellation. And experience has shown that this opinion is false.

It would also follow, if this opinion were true, that we would be controlled
by almost infinite constellations and infinite arrangements of the skies. As the
points of a celestial body pass by, the order of the stars and planets would change
as well. Since each hour is divided into four parts, and each part into many
ounces, and each ounce into many points, and each point into many atoms, and
each atom into infinite moments, and each moment changes the movement of
the sky and changes its celestial influence—therefore the new constellation is

changing and transforming continuously. So it is of little use to propose a firm plan about anything for the time to come, since we are always subject to new movements in the sky and to various constellations and various arrangements. As a result, you can see and understand that this opinion of yours is false.

It would also follow, from this false opinion, that evildoers like traitors and murderers would always be alive after a planet and constellation forced them to do wrong. And so thieves would have to go around robbing equally during the day and at night, and likewise all the other evildoers. And here is another reason that will show you that your opinion is false. You see well that heaven's order, which is good and perfect, does not contribute to this operation, but only the malice and the depraved will of the sinner contributes to it. What does it mean that the thief's nature leads him to rob at night more than he does during the day? Do you believe that the planets force him to do this? Certainly not. Rather he does it in order to have the best conditions to rob, and so as not to be seen or recognized.

And therefore do not try to blame either fortune or the stars of the sky or the arrangement of the planets. But blame instead your ignorance, or the temptation of the devil, or truly your own depraved malice. Maybe you let yourself be led by arrogance for having achieved a grand status, or maybe it was out of anger that you wanted to make vendettas, or out of avarice that you wanted to get rich with the possessions of another, or possibly it was out of greed and lust that you went out to rob, in order to eat better, or to have money to give to the whore to satisfy your lust. So, my brother, recognize and blame yourself, and ask forgiveness from God for all your sins.

Not only is this opinion false, but it is heretical and full of heresy, because it goes against the Son of God. Now, listen carefully and understand, and every good Christian take note: If the stars forced us to sin and do wrong, what need would there have been for Christ, the Son of God, to become flesh and be born into this world and live among us? This would mean that the great love that God the Father bore human nature would disappear. And then it would not have been out of need that he had Christ crucified, preach in the temple, be adored by the Magi, or brought into Egypt, or baptized by John the Baptist, and so too for the other things that happened to the person of Christ—since according to this opinion everything must be ruled by the necessity issued from the stars and constellations. Another heresy also follows: that our Lord would have gathered his apostles and performed miracles in vain, like curing the sick, clearing the sight of the blind, straightening the hunchback, resurrecting the dead, feeding five thousand men with five loaves of barley and with two fish. And so too regarding all the miracles of our Lord; it would follow that they were necessitated by the stars, and that even casting out demons was not in his power. Anyone using his mind can well understand that this is a great error and goes against our faith.

Another heresy also follows: that the doctrine of the holy gospel, given and founded by our Lord Jesus Christ, would have been ordained by the necessity of the stars. And thus both the love of God, illuminating human hearts to show the perfect way, and all the teaching of Christ, which gives the example for all of human nature, would be of little value to our salvation. According to this false opinion, we are all constrained by the command of the stars. You can clearly see for yourself, as can every faithful Christian, that this is a great heresy.

Another heresy also follows, which is this one: all the sacraments of the church, like the sacrament of baptism, confirmation, confession, communion, the holy oil of the priesthood, and matrimony, were vainly and uselessly commanded by Jesus Christ. Thus it would be of little use to our soul or our body to observe and maintain these sacraments, since everything we encounter and everything that happens occurs according to the arrangement of the planets.

Another very great heresy also follows, which is this: the Passion and the death of Christ do not bring us to eternal life, and so too his resurrection and ascension and his gift of the Holy Spirit do not have any value for our salvation. And so we would be deceived by the promise of Christ, when he said, "I give my soul for the redemption of many," and when he promises to come again as the prince and head of the universal resurrection of humankind, and when he ascended into heaven to prepare the place for all the chosen ones [John 14:3, 16–17]. So all of these things would be futile and vain, because there would be no need for them if we were forced and constrained by the constellations.

Another very great heresy also follows, which is this: final judgment would be neither just nor merciful, because it would not repay the just with goodness and it would not punish the bad. Yet this would follow from this false opinion. And for this reason, my brother, I beg you, out of reverence for God, tear out this false opinion.

It also follows that this opinion is not only false but foolish and very crazy. And this is the reason. It would follow that the ecclesiastical and worldly laws are thwarted and vain. And from *this* opinion it would follow that divine law, like that given to Moses and like the evangelical law given by Christ, would have been given for no purpose. It therefore follows that the law of Emperor Justinian and all the other laws would also have been created in vain. And the law of fear and the law of human punishment would serve no purpose.

And another craziness also follows. Neither a decree nor a decretal nor a papal constitution nor the counsel of holy men would be of any value to us in governing our lives. And so worthy men, those who are and have been for us the rule and doctrine of living well, would have labored in vain. So you can easily see what foolishness this is.

Another madness also follows. We have moral philosophy that teaches us how to live honorably with every person and in every state and in all governments, whether the government of kingdoms, of cities, of households, or of our souls. It teaches us to acquire virtue and flee vice, to be moderate in pleasure, courageous in adversity and all other moral matters. It would follow that this teaching in the instruction of children and the governing of the family would serve no purpose if we were constrained by the planets or by the stars, and if we followed their influence and not this teaching.

An extremely great madness also follows. Neither the statutes of the city nor of the countryside, nor any outside law or mutual discipline would have any value for the salvation of our souls. And therefore there would be no need for advising doctors, proposing procurators, intervening lawyers, notaries, judges, *podestas*, or rectors. And so we would live like beasts and like those who say, "Let the mightiest survive." We would be like those who rule themselves not with reason, but rather who live according to animal appetites and according to where their sensual nature leads them.

Another stupidity also would follow. It would hardly serve men, women, the rich, the poor, those great and small to go to hear sermons, masses, vespers, or other divine offices. And so too making penance, asking for alms, building churches or chapels or hospitals, making fasts, either corporeal or mental, doing good or doing wrong, or performing any other good deed. None of this would affect our worthiness to deserve the glory of the saints or to deserve to escape from a bad death. Now, my brother, I believe that if you had done these good acts I mentioned, and if you had abstained from wrong doing, you would not have come to this point.

And for that reason, my dearest brother, do not believe that this opinion is true, since it is false and heretical. Neither you nor anyone else should believe it. You should let it go, because otherwise it could be the damnation of your soul. And believe me, men's sins are oftentimes what brings one to a bad end. You should not let these vacillations, these errors, and falsities come to you right now, neither in your mind nor in your imagination. Rather you had better grasp onto something solid, which is Christ. And you should put your confidence and hope in him, and by doing this, you will attain the blessed life.

Chapter Thirty-three
Which deals with those who say that they do not want to have such
a vile death and who declare that it is not right that anyone choose
death for himself.

The divine determination and firm will of God is such that all human creatures
must discipline, rule, and govern themselves according to his will, because the
omnipotent God is such a wise lord that he cannot err, and he is so just that he
cannot do wrong. And for that reason neither you nor others should complain
about this ultimate death, which he allows to mortal persons. Accept this death
as he wills it, be it vile or not vile. You should not care about this, because corporeal death is not the one by which we are saved or damned, except by how
unwillingly or willingly we bear it.

And for that reason, take note and lift up your mind, you and anyone
who intends to see any of this. Death is divided into three kinds: the first is
corporeal death, the second is the death of sin and guilt, the third is the death
of punishment and of the fire of hell.

The first kind of death is corporeal death, that is when the soul separates
from the body. This death, in and of itself, has no merit, because it is a natural
occurrence. As the glorious St. Augustine said, "This death of the body should
not be called a bad death, whether it is done by blade or by gallows or by fire or
by water or by any way there could be." He explains more fully in the chapter
on the holy martyrs, that otherwise it would follow that the holy martyrs died a
bad death, and this would be contrary to the holy scripture that says: "Preciosa
in conspectu Domini mors sanctorum eius," that is, "The death of the saints
was precious in the eyes of God" [Ps. 116:15]. And in another place, the glorious evangelist St. John says, "Blessed is the death of those who die in the Lord"
[Rev. 14:13], that is, in God's grace. The Holy Spirit will give him rest from his
trials. So this corporeal death is the end of life, or maybe the punishment that
is given the body for the sin of the first parents, and this cannot bring about
merit or demerit. And this is the death that God spoke about to Adam, when he
ordered him, saying, "When you eat this apple, you will die" [Gen. 2:17]. That
is to say, you will die in the punishment of corporeal death. And therefore, my
dear brother, you must not care about which death you will die from, be it vile
or not in bodily terms, but you must carefully guard against dying outside the
grace of God.

Again I warn you that you would be sinning gravely if you were to seek
another death for yourself than the one God wants for you, and that worldly
law has decreed. Note that I do not say this about the friends or relatives who,

for the love of God and for the salvation of their relative or friend's soul, believe that another death would allow him to depart more happily from this life. And they could even try to change his death so that he avoids greater opprobrium from this world. And this I say assuming that they knew already for certain that he was condemned to death. They do not sin in seeking this, because one must always choose the lesser of two wrongs. And there is another reason, which is this: the wrongdoer must die in some way. He will satisfy the law and legal justice by whatever death he dies from. Having the wrongdoer die by a cruel death is done only to instill fear and awe in others, so that to ask that he die by a mild death is not a sin, but rather a work of mercy, if it contains those aspects noted above. But to do this so that the wrongdoer could escape would be against the law and against justice, and this is a sin according to worldly law.

There is still another possibility, which is this: it may be true that this wrongdoer is already condemned to death and he does not have anyone who can ask on his behalf that this death be changed. I say that he should not ask for a different kind of death, because no one should seek death for themselves. And this we know by the example that there is no martyr who ever chooses or ever asks that his corporeal death be changed. And indeed we have the moral Seneca, who being condemned to death, is considered damned because he had his death changed. St. Augustine said in his letter to the priest Victorian that God does not care about the kind of death that releases the soul for the body, be it by cord or by blade. But he pays careful attention and considers what the condition of your soul is when it leaves the body—that is, if it is in grace or not. And you, my brother, while you may be indifferent to corporeal death, you should at least, and at once, be afraid of the death of the soul.

The second kind of death is the death of sin and guilt, and this is the death of the soul. Just as corporeal death takes life away from the body, so too mortal sin takes eternal life away from the soul. For that reason it effects separation from God, who is life for the soul. Just as the soul is life for the body and it cannot live without the soul, so too God is life for the soul and the soul cannot live without God. And in the Book of Wisdom it is written about this death of the soul: "Deus non fecit mortem," or "God did not make death" [Wisd. 1:13], that is, sin. And everyone must guard himself from this death, because the soul dead in sin cannot bear fruit for God. About which Jesus said in the holy gospel, "The bad tree cannot make good fruit" nor can the dry tree bring life or produce fruit [Matt. 7:18]. And in another place he says, "Dimitte mortuos sepellire mortuos suos," that is, "let the mortals bury their dead" [Matt. 8:22] calling those dead who are in mortal sin. And see well and note that as the soul is more perfect than the body, so also the death of the soul is worse than that of the body. And about this there has already been said enough in the first chapters.

The third kind of death is the death of fire and of the punishment of hell, and this death is written about by the prophet David, "Mors peccatorum pessima" (Evil is the death of the wicked) [Ps. 34:22]. This death is bad because of the variety of punishments that are in hell, the heat, the cold, the cries, and the laments. It is worse because of the bitter and great penalty that those punishments and suffering give, but it is actually the worst because it is a perpetual and eternal punishment that will never end. This death is written about in the holy gospel, "Mortuus est dives et sepultus est in inferno" (the rich man died and was buried in hell) [Luke 16:22]. Take note that Christ did not speak of the death of the body of this rich man, because his body was buried in a beautiful sepulcher; he speaks of the death of the soul, which was buried in the punishments of hell.[30] And for that reason our Savior said to his apostles, "Nollite timere eos qui occidunt corpus et post hec non habent amplius quid faciant: timete autem eum qui potest animam et corpus mittere in Gehennam." Christ said, "Do not be afraid of those who kill the body and who cannot do more, but be afraid of him who can put the body and soul in the eternal fire" [Luke 12:4–5]. About this death, it is also written in the Apocalypse, "Blessed is he who does not participate in the second death" [Rev. 20:6].

And for that reason, my brother, pray to God that you do not taste of this death, because it is too foul and too horrible. And St. Augustine said that if the whole world were full of fire, from the east to the west, he would prefer to pass through all of this fire than to see the devil of hell. And if there were a wheel that swung from the sky to the earth and that was made entirely of razors, he would prefer to be all cut up than to feel the lightest punishment of hell.

My brother, there are two remedies for these two bad deaths, that is, the death from guilt and the death from punishment. The first remedy is to beg for charity, just as the angel Raphael and the holy man Tobias said, "Begging for charity liberates one from all sins and does not allow the soul to go into darkness" [Tob. 4:11]. Thus you may purge all your sins and find eternal life. As the prophet Daniel said to Nebuchadnezzar, "Listen to my counsel, oh king: ransom your sins with charity and mercy to the poor" [Dan. 4:24]. And

[30] Most Reformation-era and modern translations render the passage differently, such that the rich man is buried on earth and then appeals to God from the torments of hell. The Douai-Rheims version, however, gives it the sense it has here, where the rich man is buried in hell.

also our Lord Jesus Christ said in his holy gospel, "Give charity and behold everything will be cleansed for you" [Luke 11:41].

The second remedy for the two bad deaths is observing the commandments. Regarding this, God said to the prophet Ezekiel, "The son will not carry the sin of the father" [Ezek. 18:20], that is, he will not bear the punishment for the sin of the father, "if he observes justice and judgment, and keeps all of my commandments." Christ also spoke about this in his gospel saying, "If you want to avoid the punishment of hell and enter into life everlasting, observe my commandments" [Matt. 19:17].

And since I think and believe that you would have difficulty now offering physical charity, I beg you to try to offer spiritual charity for your soul. As it is written about this kind of charity, "Miserere anime tue placens Deo" (have mercy towards your soul and you will find favor with God) [Ecclus. 30:24]. And this is to say, if your life is to be pleasing to God so as to earn grace—that same life of yours that now displeases him because of your faults—you must first offer charity to yourself with the mercy that you have towards your soul. This mercy requires that you hold your sin in disdain and you are contrite about it, because just as "whoever loves sin holds his soul in disdain" [cf. Ps. 10:6], so whoever holds sin in disdain loves his soul.

So, my dearest brother, this is the act of charity you must now make towards your soul. By doing this you will find that God will be kind and merciful and thus you will die a good death. That is a death in faith, hope, justice, and love of God, and at last you find your rest with him in heavenly glory. In this kind of death, you should seek and arrange your dying by saying along with the apostle, "I have died with the body and my life is saved and risen with Christ, my God," in triumphant glory [cf. Col. 3:3–4].

Chapter Thirty-four
Which deals with those who say that they would not feel grief about this death if they rightfully deserved it.

It seems to me that this talk of yours falls into as much error as I have found in the talk of others—those who little comprehend what is good for the soul. My brother, I have listened to you talk and in what you say it seems that you complain, "If I had done something for which I deserve to die, I would not regret my death." Actually you are saying that if you had done what you are accused of doing, you would not feel grief about this death.

And for this reason, my brother, regarding what you've said, consider it and you will see that it is not wise. You should note first that there is a big difference between the punishment that one bears and the reason why one bears it. See here that it is possible that there are two people condemned to death who will die by a similar punishment, but not for similar reasons. One of them will be innocent and will be praised by this punishment; the other will be a sinner and will be cursed in the punishment. And here is an example for you. Our Lord Jesus Christ was crucified and was said to be the most just and holy of the holy, and as for the other two, they are said to have been wrongdoers and thieves. And this occurred because we distinguish the reason between one and the other. The reason for the death of Jesus Christ was solely the envy of the high priests and the scribes and Pharisees, while those two thieves were crucified for their sins.

Still, let's take another example. St. John the Baptist, St. Paul, St. James the elder, and many other holy martyrs were beheaded and even Pontius Pilate and many other evil men were beheaded. And even so the former are called saints and martyrs of Christ while the latter are called sad and evil, even though the punishment of each group was similar. But since the reason was distinguished, the former are praised and the latter are reviled. And David speaks about this relationship in the psalm: "Iudica me, Deus, et discerne causam meam de gente non sancta" (My Lord, judge my soul as you see fit, but distinguish my causes from the causes of people who are unholy) [Ps. 43:1].[31]

And likewise, my brother, you must recognize right now that if you have not done the wrong you are accused of, but nonetheless bear this punishment submissively knowing that it is God's will, you will be placed among the number who die innocently. And if you have done wrong, don't say the opposite, but instead be quiet and do not talk this way, so that you do not condemn your soul.

What's more, you should know that it is not right to say, "I wish I had done what I am accused of." Because saying this and wishing this is a mortal sin. For the soul to have a depraved or evil will is as much a sin as is the exterior act of sin. And for this reason, do not wish to be among the number of the wretched and the bad who want to have sinned more than they have. Don't you know that if you had done the wrong, your soul would suffer greater punishment? Certainly you do. And so if you did not do the wrong, you may bear this death with strength, offering it up gladly to divine justice and holding it out clean and without bitterness before the eyes of God. If you do, believe me and know for certain that it would earn great merit and it would be the reason why you will be counted among the sacred college of holy martyrs, who die without fault and without flaw.

---

[31] This is one of a number of instances where the manual gives a Latin citation followed immediately by an Italian translation that expands on and slightly modifies the sense of the Latin.

Now, since I see that there is little time remaining and that the hour when you will depart from us is rushing near, I remind you that you leave this world full of evil things, you leave people full of every kind of sorrow, and you leave evil and perverse men. And there's no guarantee that it will improve, but rather a lot to suggest that it will get worse. And also I am going to remind you that Jesus Christ, St. Stephen, St. John the Baptist, St. Lawrence, and all the other holy martyrs who were most cruelly martyred, when they reached the final point of death and saw themselves in the jaws of death, at that point they were stronger than before. They knew, as you must also know, that hostile death and even the devil are conquered by the strength of the soul. For they knew, that if the body dies the soul does not die, but is instead pulled towards heaven and the glory of paradise. There it will see God, the glorious Father, the Son, and the Holy Spirit; the glorious Virgin Mary, the mother of Jesus Christ; the holy patriarchs and prophets, the glorious apostles and holy martyrs, the glorious doctors and holy confessors, the glorious virgins and holy widows, and the whole other family and company of the omnipotent God. They are always joyful and happy, since no tear, crying, or sorrow, nor any complaint, fear, or sigh can exist up above; rather there is infinite gladness, boundless happiness, abundance, and fullness in all good things. Up above are delightful rivers, the table of the omnipotent God is set, the nuptials of Lord Christ, the immaculate lamb, the fruit trees producing every month sweet fruit, delightful and flavorful in sweetness. Oh how the kingdom of omnipotent God is glorious and abundant, where he lives with all his saints in the incorruptible glory. Let us praise therefore Jesus Christ, the son of Mary, with all the company of his saints, and put our spirit in the hand of the Father, together with Christ and the Holy Spirit. Kind Father, Son, and Holy Spirit, one God, one good, and one gift, so celebrated with delightful song, and give grace to us mortals that we may depart from this life without sin. Amen.

Therefore, my dearest brother, I warn you and remind you that, as you depart from this world, you must be devoted to God, with a true spirit, and with love for your neighbor. Thus the charity and love for God and your neighbor, which you will have at this point, will make you one of the children and family of the eternal God and of the heavenly company. And so I warn you again that your soul will eternally remain with whatever disposition and will it has when it departs from your body. And for this reason, before you depart from this life, I beg you to try to say with me this *lauda* out of honor and reverence for the glorious, kind, and omnipotent God:

Laud and Oration

Jesus, splendor of the first light
shimmering the soul with your brightness
may human peace follow in your wake
breathless for you, Creator.

Celestial height and nature immense,
God most high, triune in person
Supernal greatness and infinite measure
Prime being with boundless will,
Shining brilliance, solemn figure,
Light of glory and of shining warmth.

Blessed is the soul resplendent with intellect,
Beauty of the first substance,
Eternal Father, perfect object,
Word of God born of divine essence,
Paraclete Spirit, gift and first beloved[32]
of the Father and the Word who is the perfect love.

Contemplating the soul of this splendor,
how it is born from the first mind
of God, eternal Father,
one feels his sharp arrows
that perfectly penetrate the heart
inflamed with true fire.

Beloved Spirit issuing with peace
Proceeding from the Father, given in the Word,
Holy Spirit of charity and affection,
One with the first Person from whom it issues,
and is loved fully
with wisdom and deep fervor.

---

[32] "mança," possibly from "manza" or "amanza."

Eternal prince and immense Father,
full fountain of the first wisdom,
overflowing time with that coveted peace,
You held it out to the soul, oh Goodness,
You sent as aid your only Son,
in the guise of a sinner.

Son of God, resplendent brilliance
Clothed in flesh to bear sadness
Soul of Christ, redeeming richness,
Lucid mirror of great purity,
How just and good that such beauty
would live in a vessel so luminously white.

Mental glory for the redeemed
Who brings fervent love to Jesus
And dazed in love goes seeking
the spouse of the soul and perfect lover,
then transformed by transforming love,
languishes in loving valor.

Human effort achieves nothing
If the Word made flesh favors it little
If beloved Jesus you want to find,
You must have the purity of a spouse,
Embracing it tightly
with a forthright and longing heart.

Thanks be to God. Amen.

Glory, praise, and honor be unto You
Redeemer Christ the King. Amen.

Book 2

Translated by Sheila Das

In the name of the Father, Son, and Holy Spirit. Amen. This is the instruction manual that I offer for the use of our companions of the Company of the Hospital of Death. May the good and merciful God endow them with much grace so that they may persevere in this most devout work of comforting those who are condemned to death by the law.

Prologue

Most beloved brothers and companions of the charitable Company of the Hospital of Death of Bologna, who have assumed this charitable undertaking and compassionate work by deciding to go to the prison in order to comfort and console those poor unfortunates who are condemned to death by the laws of the commune of Bologna. I beseech you with all my heart to try your utmost to carry out this entire action in a simple way and without creating any reputation of arrogance or vainglory but to do it instead only out of love for God and your neighbor. For the whole of Christianity is directed towards this love and charity; and all the scriptures are full of these two kinds of love, without which nothing could be done that is pleasing to God.

And regarding this, the apostle St. Paul said,

> If I had prophetic powers and if I could speak with the tongues of angels so I could foretell all things to come, and if I gave my body so much punishment that I could boast, and if, for the love of God, I gave away so much of my wealth to the poor that I would not have enough to support myself, and I did not have charity, I would be like a cymbal or a bell whose sound and melodies give pleasure to others while it itself is consumed.[33]

And for this reason, my brothers, you should act promptly when this

---

[33] A paraphrase of 1 Corinthians 13:1–3.

246

charitable service is asked of you: because nothing we can do acquires God's mercy for our sins as much as adopting the mercy of Christ towards our neighbor. And by acting this way, we would keep the words of St. Paul, "Bear with one another" and you will carry out the law of Christ [Col. 3:13].

And what's more, by doing this, we participate in God's mercy and the love of neighbor out of our own necessity. Because as Christ said in the holy gospel, "It is by your own measure that you yourself will be measured" [Matt. 7:2]. So, if you use the compassion of Christ towards your neighbor, you can await mercy. And there is hardly anybody that does not need mercy since hardly anyone lives without sin. It is like St. John the Evangelist said in his canons, "If we say that we have not sinned ourselves, we deceive ourselves and the truth is not in us" [1 John 1:8].

And furthermore take note, that by performing this compassionate work you become the messenger and servant of the Lord God Almighty; that is, you seek that his good works—that he appeared in this world, talked among us, and that he decided to shed his precious blood on the wood of the Holy Cross, that roused the souls of the just—continue clean and pure and immaculate. And believe me that God will raise you up and look favorably upon all your prayers if you do this with just virtue. And he will give you so much grace that you will pass though this world without sin and then, at your death, he will give you your reward, which is eternal life. Amen.

Take note, brother and member of our Company, you who wish to perform this work, that there are many things you should do if you want to master this work; but I am only going to suggest three small measures, which are the following.

The first measure is that you should perform confession very often and this is for two reasons. The first reason is, as you well know, that if you want to accomplish some familiarity or some task with any temporal lord, you should, before entering the matter at hand, speak with him often and visit him often so that he knows you well when he sees you. And you should also try to be content with him so that you do not have to ask him for a favor that often. But since you want to familiarize him [i.e., the condemned man] with God's ways, it's less necessary that he become familiar with you than with the true confession of a contrite heart since the prophet David said that God does not despise the contrite and humbled heart [Ps. 51:17]. The second reason is that you should always keep as free from mortal sin as possible and especially when you go to perform this work. Because if you are in mortal sin and you want to reproach your neighbor whom you go to comfort for some crime, he should not be able to reproach you saying, "First you go wash yourself and then you can come to cleanse me." Thus being clean and without sin yourself, you can reproach him more strongly.

The second measure you should take is to familiarize yourself with the preaching of experienced men since in those places one sometimes often hears many beautiful things and usually very subtle arguments concerning this matter. And when you hear a nice saying or a particularly interesting argument that you like, write it down so that you can keep it in mind.

The third measure is this: you should be very simple in your diet and in your manner so that you do not have to think about anything other than what you are going to do. For I will remind you that as many times as you go to do this service will you find prisoners with different ideas and, therefore, spirits that do not share the same will. There is he who has one opinion and he who has another. And if you did not have a solid intellect and a ready mind, you would lose your way. If you do not have your heart directed towards what I'm telling you and how you should respond to it, you would risk, therefore, giving strange ideas to the one who has to die and you would risk damaging yourself and your neighbor, and you would bring shame to our Company.

[Chapter One]
The manner you must have when you enter the prison.

When you enter the prison you must use the words that are written at the beginning of this book. When you reach the man you are going to comfort, you must greet him kindly and cheerfully and say some kind words, telling him about how all the heavens are rejoicing, waiting for his soul. And take him by the hand and, like this, the conversation should begin.

And, normally, there are prisoners standing around him talking to him—some comforting him, and some listening to him—before you arrive at the prison. Because of this, when you have been in their company for the span of a half hour, then with humane words kindly ask these other prisoners to go rest and not to speak anymore. And so in this friendly way you can make them go away, because it is quite tiresome to have somebody cut in when you are speaking. And once they have left, you then make clear to the one who has to die what he has to do and instruct him about the earlier chapters as best you can.

[Chapter Two]
The manner that one must have when his relatives want to come to visit him.

It may happen, as it often does, that someone wants to come to the prison to see the one who has to die, whether it be his father or mother, brothers or sisters, wife or children, relatives or friends or companions, as is customary. If so, then before they come to him in the room where you are, say to the one who has to die,

Look, my brother, some of your relatives want to come and visit you so as to see and comfort you. And I'll be here, just outside, and I'm very happy about this, for your consolation and for theirs. Therefore I beg you, for the love of God, to try to have a good heart and to put on a good face and don't get dismayed about anything because you would cause them a lot of pain. I warn you that those who remain will feel more suffering than you who are leaving. So try to comfort them and show them that you accept all that the Lord God Almighty has you go through for the salvation of your soul.

And when you have told him this, go away and leave your companion with him. Make it a habit never to leave him alone and free to wander where he may, so that he cannot start having stray thoughts. And you then go outside to those who want to come inside and tell them this,

Look good people, your coming is a great consolation and it makes us very happy that you can come and see the relative you love, and speak and stay with him as much as you like. But I would like to ask you in all earnestness not to try to reverse what God has approved. So I advise that you do not have anything further to do with him, that is, with our brother. And if we have managed fairly well to set him on the right path and if he accepts willingly what the Lord God Almighty has him go through, then, for the love of God, try to comfort him and on no account show a troubled expression nor any sign of anxiety and suffering. But instead let him understand that he is blessed who rather passes from the trials and tribulations of this wretched world.

And when you have told them this, let them enter and let them talk and stay together as they like. And nevertheless continue comforting both parties, showing them the wretchedness of this world and how he is blessed who departs from it without a damned soul. And if they would like to talk with him about his affairs, let them talk and explain. And do not say anything further to him. Rather, let the fact that they wish to put his affairs in good order comfort him.

But if you see them talking to him about something inappropriate, for example if they complain about what he will be facing and so forth, then throw yourself in between them and, with a slightly troubled expression, break up the discussion. Redirect it appropriately, showing them compassion, since it can not be anything but the frailty of the flesh that would make him stray in his conversation.

And when they want to take their leave from him and go away, at that time you should be daring and keep speaking and don't let them draw out their departure. Rather make them all take their leave the earliest you can, before the weakness of the flesh overwhelms them, since that moment, I believe, is when one may feel the greatest torments of the flesh. And if his father or mother is there with him, then before they go, make the one who has to die ask them forgiveness on bended knee; and similarly make him give them his blessing.

[Chapter Three]
The consideration you should make when you begin your conversation with the one who has to die.

When you begin to speak with the one who has to die, you need to know and consider, among other things, his character and, secondly, his culture. This is because, as you well know, a wise man who is learned needs a different kind of conversation than a rustic or a woman. It would be a good idea to consider carefully the character of the person who has to die because in this work you will find many kinds of people: you will find very different spirits since our wills are not the same. You will sometimes find many of them who want to listen and who don't say much. And there are sometimes those who are inclined towards listening to prayers and saying them with you.

And there are among them those who are inclined to read on their own and who don't want to listen very much. And there are among them those who raise their eyebrows and don't take to heart what you are saying and who think about other things. And there are those who are immovable in the beginning and do not want to humble themselves before God, as rather you would like.

[Chapter Four]
Regarding those who are inclined to listen.

You should comfort with kind words those who are inclined to listen to your discourse and present them with good arguments that show that the life of this world is false, evil, and unjust, and that having a blessed life is happy and joyful just as it is outlined in the beginning, that is, in the earlier chapters. One should always try to speak of God's works. And regarding this, add the following two miracles, that is:

My brother, at one time there was a very holy father who was the prior of a monastery with several monks under him, many of whom were very young and very pure. This holy father ordered these monks to always talk about God's works when they were together and so God would be with them. Now it happened that one day this holy father sent all these young monks to a small vegetable garden of his so that they would have some recreation, and he reminded them that they should talk about God's works and that God would be with them. And, very pure of mind, they went to the garden and when they were in the garden they arranged themselves sitting in a circle and seated in this way they began to discuss the miracles. And talking away about this, one of these young monks said, 'Now, if our Lord must be among us, where he would sit?' And with childlike fervor, he immediately got up and took off his robe and placed it as a seat in the middle of them. Thus they went on talking and as soon as they began talking about Christ, the good and blessed Jesus Christ came among this group and sat down on the monk's robe. And he stayed there in the middle of them for as long as they were talking about his deeds. And when they began to talk about worldly things, many devils from hell appeared, in the form of pigs. Seeing this in a vision, the holy father, whose holiness let him see everything, called them over to him and asked them what kind of discussion they were having. And the young monks, not aware of what had happened, innocently told him the exact truth. Recognizing that this was a miracle, the holy father told all the monks at the monastery about it and ordered them never to talk among themselves about anything but God.

Another story also demonstrates this point that God is always with whoever speaks about God. It goes like this.

There were once two Jews who left their country and went far away to sell their goods. And having earned a lot of money they decided to return home. And so they set out on foot with all that they had earned. And while they were walking, these two Jews came upon a forest where many bandits were living. Knowing this, the two Jews did not dare enter the forest. Being afraid, one of them said, "My friend, we will be able continue on safely since I have heard it said before that whoever mentions that Jesus Christ of the Christians will always have him going alongside him and that he will not let any harm come to him." The other companion said, "I have also heard that before." And so they both went into the forest and they began speaking about the miracles of our blessed Christ. One of them said, "It was a great miracle when, at the age of twelve, he preached in the synagogue and persuaded so many Jewish teachers with his impressive arguments."

And conversing in this way, they went along talking about the deeds of Christ with each step, and God was always with them. Because of this, they made it out of the forest to safety.

Once they had reached a civilized area that seemed safe, they quit talking about God's mysteries and began talking about the money they had made. And God quickly left them. Then as these two Jews were going along, they were suddenly attacked by the bandits, who seized them and dragged them back into the forest. Once they were well hidden in the wood, the bandits asked them where the other man who had been with them had gone. The Jews answered and said, "Since we entered in this wood, we have not seen anybody but you." Upon hearing this, all the bandits became afraid and so bewildered that they asked the Jews about themselves. They replied, "We are Jews and we have come from afar to carry out our work." The bandits said, "It is a fact that we have followed you through this entire forest and we saw that there were three of you. And the other one with you was an overwhelmingly huge man with a truly terrible face. And it was because of him, who made us so afraid, that we did not dare attack you." At this point the Jews, illuminated by God, understood the truth and replied and said, "Oh, praise be to the highest God Jesus Christ who shows his compassion among all people." And they told the bandits how they hadn't felt sure about entering the forest and how they had decided to discuss the mysteries of the Christian God, hoping this would let them proceed safely until they were out of the forest. And so they went along discussing the miracles of Christ. They concluded, "There is no doubt that we firmly believe that it was Jesus Christ that you saw with us and so we promise him that if we scrape by death that we will get baptized and become Christians." Upon hearing about this obvious miracle, the bandits all became very remorseful. They converted, abandoned their wicked ways, and repented, living holy lives until the end. And the Jews got baptized and gave all their earnings and wealth to the church out of love for Jesus Christ. Thus they lived and died in great holiness.

So, my brother, you can easily see that when someone talks about the works of God, God is always with him. And thus I want to ask you that now we do the same.

[Chapter Five]
Regarding those who are inclined to listen and to say prayers with you.

You must not tire of speaking to those who are inclined to listen and pray with you. And you must not tire of getting them to reply when you make clear to them how they must perform the sacrament of confession and receive devoutly the holy body of the Lord Jesus Christ and how he must forgive the offenses and the wrongs done to him. Thus you will do two good deeds. The first is that you will teach them how to ask for God's mercy. And I tell you that nothing ignites the devotion of the heart as much as prayer. The second thing is that you will be the reason that he will not be able to think of mundane things, like possessions, children, or his father or mother, or his wife, or any other thing besides God. And it is no small accomplishment if you can relieve his soul of this difficult battle.

[Chapter Six]
Regarding those who are inclined to read.

For those who are inclined to read and so comfort themselves, and who do not care to listen much, be sure always to have with you the Hospital's *Book of the Passion* or some other book, be it the *Life of Christ* or the *Lives of the Holy Fathers* or other devout things. And let him read as much as he likes. And when he struggles reading about something beautiful or some story that you think is apt to lead him to devotion, then interrupt his reading. Make him understand the meaning of what he is reading, since I tell you that very often when he who has to die reads and looks upon a book, his heart is very far away and he thinks about other things.

[Chapter Seven]
Regarding those who are skeptical and do not take to heart what you are saying but think about other things.

You will sometimes find, almost more often than not, those who are very detached and thinking and who do not take to heart what you are saying. When you find one like this, you should be very shrewd and daring and reawaken him, mixing gentle words with firm ones.

My dearest brother, we have come here ready to spend a difficult night out of love for you and to keep you company but I can see that we're just wasting our time because it seems to me that you are not taking to heart what we have told you. This is a bad sign for your salvation since now it could be said that even though you are looking death in the face, you do not want to pay attention to

what the Holy Spirit is telling you. Keep in mind that from the present time un-
til the very moment of your death you will have two spirits that will be in your
imagination and your heart, and each will show you a road. One will be the
Holy Spirit and he will place you before the road of salvation, which we must
gain with work, with abstinence, and with tears. And this is the road that the
holy scripture speaks of when it says "The road that leads to life is very narrow."
The other spirit who will be with you will be the devil from hell and he will
place you in front of the road that leads to eternal damnation. This is the road
one travels with insolence, with laziness, and with evil thoughts. And this is the
road described in the scripture as "the very wide road that leads to hell" [cf.
Matt. 7:13]. And it seems to me that you have already begun on this road and
that you have already walked a good part of it. So I want to tell you that if you
intend to continue like this, I think it is best to let you be, rather than for us to
throw away words and time.

And nevertheless, brother of the Company, do not leave him for any reason, but rather try to rescue him from these thoughts and be compassionate
because it can only be that he is suffering in his flesh. And regarding this, we
have the example of our Lord and almighty creator, Jesus Christ who, praying
in the garden during his Passion, suffered agony in his physical nature and
sweat drops of blood. But according to his divine nature, he did not feel that
agony and was not afraid.

[Chapter Eight]
Regarding those who are hard-hearted in the beginning and do not want to be led to God.

There are those whom you will find hard-hearted in the beginning and who
do not want to hear anything you say. It seems that they do not want to hear
about God or salvation. You should be very pleasant and go after this one
with gentle words, while reminding him of God's judgment that will come
down upon him if he does not change his ways. And remind him how obsti-
nance displeases God a great deal and continue gently in this vein with kind
words. Be very careful not to unsettle him with words or harshness. Because
sometimes those who are so hardened and miserable may react quite violently
against one word they don't like, with the result that you risk never being able
to say anything that they do like, and this leads to worse. And if you see that
in spite of your words he doesn't wish to repent and remains hard-hearted, let

it be and say nothing to him. Rather, let him say what he wants. And then tell some appropriate story or some example to your companion or with whoever is around, and tell in such a way that he who is to die hears you. And when his anger subsides and he is just there not doing anything, then go and put your hand on his back and ever so gently reprove him for his folly and place him on the proper road. In this way, you pull him and guide him towards the road you want. When you have him going in this direction, do not let him think about anything except what you tell him.

[Chapter Nine]
Regarding those who want to make their will.

Sometimes there are also those who want to make their will, be it written or oral, leaving their things to whomever they like. Speak passionately to them without fear of anyone else who is present, and remind them that if they are bound to anyone by means of a debt, or even if they received anything from anyone, whether secretly or openly, then they should consult their conscience and remember that they can't make alms out of what's not theirs. And if it's the case that they do not owe anything to anyone and if they aren't bound to anyone, and they want to make a will, remind them of our Hospital of Death and recommend that they give to it.

[Chapter Ten]
Regarding those who complain that they are leaving children behind with no one to care for them and that they will end up in a bad way.

There are sometimes those who complain that their family and children will be without care and supervision. Then comfort him humbly and say,

Look, son or my brother, our Lord God made all the reasoning creatures and the animals and the birds and all things. And so he gives a way for all creatures to take care of themselves, and he feeds the animals and birds and fish who do not have a father or mother always there to care for them. You cannot believe that he would nurture beasts who lack reason and abandon in such a bitter way the creatures that he made in his likeness [cf. Matt. 6:26]. Certainly not. So you should have hope in the Creator of all things. I want to tell you a little story that will shed light on this from the Lives of the Holy Fathers. *Now listen carefully:*

There was in some part of Syria a holy father who was the chaplain of a church and who had many souls under his care. Among the people who were at his chapel, there was a poor, good man who had many children, all of them very young. And his only means to provide for them was from what he earned day to day working by the sweat of his brow. In this way, he took very good care of them. Now, it pleased God's will and he who governs all things that this good man became sick and died. His wife was left with all these little ones and was completely inconsolable as she had hardly any possessions and no support. Upon seeing this, the holy father was moved by so much compassion and deep pain that he began to complain to the Lord Almighty God, saying, "Now my Lord, why did you let this happen, that this poor man died who took such good care of his dear family. Oh my Lord, who will care for these creatures who have now become orphans, without a father or any supervision and care? And truly I do not see anything except that these creatures will barely manage to get by and will slowly starve to death." And he lamented a lot about this against the Lord God. Now our Lord who is just and who does everything justly did not want his servant to be so terribly worried and he wanted to end this complaining. He thus consoled him in this way.

While the holy father was locked in his house, thinking constantly about this matter, there was a loud knocking at the church door. The one knocking was an angel in the guise of a very poor man. The holy father went to the doorway and found this man who had knocked. Not recognizing that it was an angel, he asked him what he was doing. The angel said, "It is God's will that you come with me." At which point, the holy father bowed his head in obedience, barred the door, and followed the angel. Then the angel led him beyond the land where there was a great river clearing. And he led the holy father above a huge rock and he gave him a large iron rod and told him, "Strike this rock so hard that you break it." The holy father then struck the rock hard so that it broke in two pieces. The angel said, "Look and see if you can find any life in that rock." The holy father looked in the middle of the rock and he found a worm almost as long as his palm. Seeing this, the holy father felt a profound awe. The angel then said, "When this rock was created, this worm was created inside, and he who has for so long taken care of it inside will be quite able to take care of the children of your neighbor who is dead. So now go and do not complain to God anymore." These words uttered, the angel suddenly disappeared. And seeing this, this holy father returned back to his church and reproached himself for what he had said and done against the Lord Almighty God. And he was entirely consoled.

And so, my brother, I ask you to chase away all these thoughts and lift

*your mind towards divine contemplation and the blessed life. Let God who cre-
ated your children worry about them. He will give them the means and ways to
take care of themselves.*

[Chapter Eleven]
Regarding those who complain about dying and about leaving behind their wealth.

You should also know that at this point you will find those who do not willingly accept their death and for whom it is a very big thing. It seems that all
of their complaining stems from the fact that they have to leave their wealth
behind, and from this they suffer a lot and have no relief. To dispel this, you
must speak and comfort in the following way.

*My brother, it looks like your thoughts have taken the opposite tack than they
should have. Take into consideration that at this point you should be complaining and suffering because you have not built a fortune out of all the wealth
of eternal life. This kind of wealth is made up of prayer, charity, pilgrimages,
fasting, and other such things. And I get the idea that you kept your store quite
empty of these goods. You held it in little account and assigned it no value. Yet
it seems that you place a high value on the most vain and most worthless thing
that a person can have in this world, namely its material goods and riches.
Consider that the reasoning person does not have a greater enemy than material goods, and this is the reason. Goods are the devil's bait web and will snare
you. Just like the hook is hidden in the bait so that the fish doesn't see it until the
man decides to seize him, so too the devil hides himself in material goods until
he decides to seize a man and lead him into sin.*

*Another way material goods may be the enemy of man is the following. How
many times does a man sin and how many risks does he take to acquire wealth?
For this he betrays, robs, murders, practices usury, and kidnaps. If man were to
dedicate himself as faithfully and urgently to the works of the Lord God Almighty
to acquire eternal life, as he does to the works of the devil to acquire wealth, we
would all be saved. To show you that material goods are the worst enemy that we
have in this world, I want to tell you a story from holy scripture:*

*In the writings of the holy fathers there was once a man who had three
friends in this world. One of them seemed to be such a true friend that the man
loved him above all other things, even more than God whom he loved more than
his own soul. Another seemed like such a good friend that he loved him as much*

*as himself. The third did not seem to bother with him much at all, so that this fel-
low valued him less than anything else he had. Now it happened that this fellow
was denounced to his lord and his lord asked him to come before him. And since
he was ordered to go before his lord he became very melancholic and didn't dare
to appear before him, even seeing that he was forced to and that he had to appear
somehow or other. So he confidently went to that friend whom he loved above
all things and asked if he would go with him to appear before the lord who had
summoned him. His friend answered that he didn't want to go and that he should
go before the lord without him. Hearing such an answer, the man became very
angry but he left on good terms to go and see the friend that he loved as much
as himself. And he asked him if he would like to go with him to find out what his
lord wanted. This other friend answered and said, "I will indeed come with you
until the door of the palace but I don't want to go any further." The man hearing
this second answer became extremely upset and didn't know what to do. But as
he was constrained by necessity he very ashamedly went to see the third friend,
whom he did not particularly love or think of very highly. And he told him that
his lord had sent for him and that he did not dare to go alone. Upon hearing this,
the third friend comforted him saying that he should go confidently and that he
wanted to accompany him. And so they both appeared before the lord and this
friend presented arguments that defended the man.*

    *So, my brother, be careful of people who want to make a good impression.
Know that this lord from the story above is our Lord God and the one who was
beckoned before him was mortal man. He is summoned when death comes. And
when he is called, and since he has to die and appear before the Lord in some way
or other, he goes to his faithful friend, that is, money and material possessions
—and this is the friend that he loves more than his own soul—and he says, "Oh
my coins, help me! Ohhh my riches, do not abandon me!" And even when he sees
he's dying, he wishes it were possible to bring everything with him. But neither
possessions nor coins can help him, and they abandon him. And this is the hope
that we can have in this world for the friend that we love so much.*

    *The second friend that we pay so much attention to is our relatives and
friends. And experience proves that this is true. When man is sick and especially
when he sees himself close to death, he takes greater account of his family and
friends than he does God or his own soul. And if he has thousands of relatives, he
would give them things to do and would ask them all to help him. And note what
these relatives do. Each one comforts him. And each one pays attention when he
makes his will to see if he leaves him what he wants. And watching until that last
little breath leaves his body. These are the ones who go with the friend just until*

the palace door and no further. That is, they accompany him to the door of the church, and then they return home and let their relative be carried away, and do not care about him anymore. So you cannot depend on this second friend.

And the third friend that the man paid the least attention to is the good and bad that he has done in this world. If the man has done some good, he values it so little that he doesn't remember and doesn't know how it happened. But even hoping that he may have done a little good, he runs back to it, begging it to speak well for him and not to abandon him. And this third friend comforts him and accompanies him right until the presence of God, and represents him, and helps him, and often defends him from the cruel sentence that would have otherwise come. And this is what we should value more than anything to do with possessions, money, family, or friends. And we do the exact opposite. And see of what little use is the first friend, which is possessions, and the second friend, which is one's relatives and friends.

And thus, my brother, disparage your things and think that you came naked into this world, and just as naked you will have to leave it [cf. Job 1:21]. Take account that if you did something good in the past, it will be of greater value to you when you have passed from this life than would all of the treasures of the world. Yet do not be dismayed if you haven't done anything good in the past and if you haven't honored your Creator. Dedicate even this small amount of time that you have left in wanting to spend all of it in the honor of God and in scorning this world. The good God is so merciful that for all the hours and all the time that man repents, he forgives him. And he gives him his reward. It is written in the holy gospel that Christ told a parable of those who went to work in the morning in a father's vineyard. He paid as much to those who went to work from late afternoon till evening as those who had worked a full day from morning [cf. Matt 20:1–16]. So, my brother, it makes sense that you would be one of those who would go in the evening. If you want to be paid for the whole day, turn your heart and your mind towards God and ask him for grace and mercy, and try to be pure and cleansed of all your sins. Happily forgive every creature and be perfectly disposed to willingly offer this poor body in sacrifice to God for his love [cf. Rom. 12:1].

[Chapter Twelve]
Regarding those who are young and who do not want to die yet.

Sometimes as you pursue this work you will find some young people who are condemned and who are so unwilling to die that it seems that their whole flesh fails them. And sometimes these ones put up such a fight as they can muster that very often they lose their senses. And so when you come upon some of these, you should steel yourself and show in your speech that one should pay no heed to the body. Take note that I say this only for you who go to give comfort, because if you began to feel sorry for him, and indulge him, you would be courting the danger of softening yourself. The result would be that instead of comforting him, you would make him uncomfortable; and when you should be relieving him of this pain, you would make it overwhelm him. On the contrary, avoid using pitiful words and compassion as much as you can, for the reasons stated above regarding these types. And you will find it difficult to guard yourself from the weakness of the flesh. And so when you have talked to him for a bit with harsh and unpleasant words, and seeing that he is relaxing and that the temptation has lessened a bit, then you may talk to him in this way:

Ah my brother, now what is it that I see in your deeds? I would have thought that you have a constant heart and a stronger spirit than Samson ever had, but you are rather acting like a woman. Do you think God likes this kind of cowardice? You know very well that he does not. God likes a man who is strong and constant in his passions and who knows how to fight bravely and win. As you know very well, not everyone is honored in battle, but only those who fight and win like a man. And don't you think that God welcomes the sacrifice of your body precisely because you are so young? Yes, of course he does. I'll even tell you that God is infinitely more pleased with the offering a youth makes of his life than that of an old man. And tell me: Why is God so pleased by the sacrifice of the holy virgins like St. Lucy, St. Catherine, St. Cecilia, and many other holy virgins and holy martyrs, if not for their youth? And that God is pleased by the death, or rather the sacrifice of the life of the young, he shows us with his own Son and our Lord. In the flower of his youth and in the most beautiful state that man can reasonably have, that is, when he was thirty-three years old, God wanted him to be crucified and to die for sinners. And one could similarly say that St. John the Baptist, St. Lawrence, St. Stephen, and other martyr saints willingly offered themselves as young men to torments. And thus you should follow their example in death, especially since you never did in life. And even if you want to complain that you are too young, tell me: How much time could you still live naturally? Let us suppose that you would have lived in this world still another twenty or thirty years. You would still have to die at some point, in one way or another. And it could be that at that time you would have drowned, or been cut to pieces, or you would have fallen in despair from some tower, or been crushed by something falling on you—so that you would have died without confession, and so your spirit would die with your body.

Still I want to prove to you that if someone gathered all the time that you have been on this earth, and weighed all the good and the bad that you have had in your life, you would find that if you have had one day of peace, you had three days of the opposite. So that it seems to me that this world is a purgatory. And for that reason you should truly rejoice thinking that you are putting aside the suffering of this world. And what's more, know that this world is a dwelling place given to every person and note that, once the soul has left the body, it leaves everything behind. So that we can say that these temporal possessions are the dwelling place of the body, and that the body is the dwelling place of the soul that lives in this body until it acquires an eternal dwelling place, and that [home] is the glory of eternal life.

And therefore my dearest brother, ask God for forgiveness for all your sins and pray devoutly to him that he give salvation and eternal life to your soul.

[Chapter Thirteen]
Regarding those who ask about the soul and want to know what it is.

Brother of the Company, open the ears of your intellect and consider what is it that you want to do and what authority and questions those unfortunate condemned people will sometimes bring to you. They sometimes ask you things and they don't know what they are saying. And even so, you must try everything to satisfy their questions, in part or entirely, so that they are satisfied.

Know that sometimes you will find those who will ask you what the soul is. Note well and understand that I do not address this question in your instruction manual intending to teach you how to answer it, because I would not know how to teach you what I do not know. But I really wanted to put the case before you now so that you come across it before it comes to you like a blow. You can, then, diligently try to take measures, like preparing some wise advice about this matter, so that you have a ready response when you go to the prison and the one you are going to comfort asks you about this. But even so, corrected by those who know more than I, I will give you what has happened to me and what I have found in brief about this. When I encounter someone who asks me about this, I respond to him in this way:

My dearest brother, I would be very happy if you would turn from this question of yours as it is very out of the ordinary and weighs on me heavily. You ask this, yet I don't know what you feel about facing a lot of discussion, given the many positions that there are concerning it. As for me, I can only offer you a rather poor explanation since your question requires a very learned theologian to respond to it. So consider my response: How can you want me to answer and clarify such a thing for you, I who am a cloth merchant without formal education? Therefore, I think it's better for us to stay here, happy down below, and not to try to go discover those things that we can't find or see with our senses. As our Cato said, "Mitte archana dei celumque inquirere quid sit," that is, "leave alone the secret mysteries of our Lord God Almighty."

But nonetheless, since I see that you want to know something about this, I will speak to you briefly about it according to what the holy fathers have said. Now listen carefully.

St. Augustine said that our soul is a spirit, that is, it is an invisible and intangible thing, that God created in his own image and likeness. He then placed it in our body and stationed it there so that it would remain there as long as the body lived. And know that when God made our first father Adam, he made him out of the lowly earth; and he made the body first, then the soul. This body had no senses at all, save for what human bodies have when the soul is separated from them. Therefore, all of our senses are in the soul, and here is the reason. Once the soul has left the body, the body remains like a piece of earth. And if someone were to cut it to pieces, the body wouldn't feel anything and would not bleed. And when the body is formed in the mother's womb, if God did not infuse it with the soul that body would be a dead thing and consequently it would have to separate from the mother's body because it could not stay there, lacking the soul. And by this reasoning, you can understand what the soul is.

Furthermore, one can learn about what the soul is by reading about it in the book of Genesis. For when God made Adam from the earth, he said that he breathed the breath of life into him and thus made him alive [cf. Gen. 2:7]. And this breath was the soul, so by this account we could say that the soul is the breath of God.

Furthermore, you should know that the soul is the one thing that is differentiated by its names, that is, it has many names according to its roles. The first is called "soul," and this is its name because it is always living. It is called "spirit," and this because you cannot see it nor touch it, being inside the body. It is called "sense," and this in that it senses. It is called "intellect," and this in that it knows. It is called "mind," and this because it understands. It is called "reason," and this in that it makes distinctions. It is called "memory," and this in that it remembers. It is called "will," and this in that it decides. And understand that although all these names are quite different in how they sound, they are not different in substance. Because all these names are one soul and its properties are many, but its essence is only one. And so, my dearest brother, I want to ask you to be satisfied with what I have told you about the nature of the soul, because I assure you that the more you look at it, the less you will understand it. This is because you cannot say anything about it, not about its size, nor its color, nor that it has this flavor, nor this odor. Thus all our senses fail when we try to look for it. But do you know who can see, who can see the soul? All those blessed in heaven. So, therefore, strive to be like this as long as you are alive, so that you can arrive at seeing through experience what you desire to know by description. And try to be content with the most knowable things and try not to search for the subtle and hidden, because Christ said in the holy gospel, "Blessed are the simple; they shall die pure of heart."[34]

[Chapter Fourteen]
The manner you should have when the light comes in the morning, that is, when daylight comes.

When morning has come and you see that the day is dawning, then, if the one who has to die is sleeping, call him and wake him up with some prayer. And when you think his heart is open to listening, then go over what you have already instructed him from the beginning, namely, to try to forgive those who have sinned against him and to ask mercy from God. And above all, remind him about confession, and that he shouldn't keep anything unsaid from the priest. And similarly, if he remembers that he owes someone something, that he wills that it would be restored. And if he harbors hatred against someone and it's possible for you to get them to talk together, do it. This would be a very good thing. And remind him to think carefully about all these things, so that when the priest arrives with the body of Christ, he should tell the priest everything, omitting nothing because of shame or fear. And in this way, keep him occupied with these ideas and prayers, until you hear the bell that goes before the body of Christ. And never abandon him, so that he won't have a chance to think about other things, because, at this point, he will begin to feel

[34] An adaptation of the beatitudes from the Sermon on the Mount: Matt. 5:3–11.

the struggle of the flesh. This occurs now because people start coming and going and also because he feels that the hour of death is approaching.

[Chapter Fifteen]
What you must say when you hear the priest arrive with the body of Christ.

As soon as you hear the bell ringing in the distance, the bell that rings before the body of Christ, you then talk fervently but very simply to the one who has to die and tell him this:

My brother, you can hear that our Lord Jesus Christ is coming to visit you even in this place. Consider for a moment what moves him to deign to come to this place and among so many sinners. First, what is this, that is, who is it that comes? He is Christ Jesus, the Son of the true and living God, who was born of the virgin body of the glorious Virgin Mary and who came to live among us lowly sinners for thirty-three years. He is the one who suffered death and Passion, and who shed his precious blood on the wood of the cross. He is the one who was placed in a tomb and who remained in the sepulcher with his most sacred body, his soul, and his divinity for three days. It is his own soul that descended into hell and raised up the holy company of saints from the Old Testament, who had been waiting for him. He is the one who on Judgment Day will come with the highest authority and judge the living and the dead. He is the one who will give eternal life to the good and give eternal fire to the wicked. He who comes is the king of eternal life and with him come the glorious Virgin Mary his mother and all the heavenly kingdom. So understand well who it is that comes to visit you.

Secondly, let us see what such a Lord, accompanied by such honorable company, comes to do. I tell you that he comes for you only, to stay with you and so you with him eternally, and to lead you into his company. But understand well the goodness and the humility of this Lord, that he deigns to come unto you and in such a place, in prison. What does he come to say? "[What a] place of wretchedness?" And what does he come to do? Does he come to eat with you, or really to consume you? Of course not, rather he comes to you so that you may eat him. Oh blessed goodness, oh divine majesty, what things do I hear said about you, love and hope for all sinners? Truly there is not one person who should not cry out to God and give him infinite praise for all the kindness that he has bestowed upon humanity.

And so, my brother, for the love of such a true Lord, study your conscience well. If even a speck of sin remains there, do not be ashamed or shrewd and withhold it. Instead, confess it to the priest with all your heart. He is the vicar of Christ, so that once you have said it to him, you will have said it to God. Furthermore, let's take this example: if there were a temporal lord, or some great gentleman who wanted to come live with you in your home, think about how you would try to honor him and how you would decorate and clean your house in order to please him and make him happy. So much more should you try to clean the home of your soul and sweep out all the vices and decorate it with all the virtues, considering that it is in this house that the King of kings, the Lord of lords, wants to come live. He is God and perfect man who comes to live with you with his soul, body, and divinity, not to leave you in this wretchedness, but rather to take you with him and his company to the glory of paradise.

[Chapter Sixteen]
What you have to do when the priest enters the prison where you are, bringing the body of Christ with him.

When the priest enters the prison where you are and when you see the tabernacle where the body of our Lord Jesus Christ is, throw yourself to the ground on your knees and make the one who has to die go on his knees beside you. And make him piously entrust his soul to that Lord who has deigned to come visit him. And then, if he remembers any sin, make him confess to the priest. And when he wants to make his confession, pull yourself behind them, and don't let anyone else come so close to them that they may hear what he confesses, and make all the prisoners go down on the ground so that not one of them is above the body of Christ. And when the priest has confessed him and has given him absolution, as soon as he opens the tabernacle, get down on your knees beside the one who has to die, and make him humbly say this prayer.

[Chapter Seventeen]
Prayer

Omnipotent Lord, Eternal Father, God. I, most vile and unworthy sinner, come to take the sacrament of the precious body and blood of our Lord and Savior, our dearest Jesus Christ. For certain, I come ill to the doctor of life, naked to the king of glory, envious to the fountain of mercy, blind to the light of eternal brightness. I pray, therefore, to your ever abundant mercy and kindness, that you

deign to treat my illness, to clothe my nudity, to enrich my poverty, and to illumi-
nate my blindness so that I may receive this angelic bread and heavenly manna,
this sweetest food and the full replenishment of just souls. I pray to you with so
much devotion and contrition, with such faith and purity, and with such resolu-
tion and humility that I may receive this [bread] that works for the salvation of
my soul. Oh Lord God, omnipotent Father, I ask you to give me grace that, along
with the sacrament of the most precious body of your Son, I would receive the
virtue[35] *of the sacrament and that my soul would taste and savor its divine and*
invisible grace. Oh most gentle God, give me grace so that I may truly receive that
body of Christ, born of the glorious Virgin Mary, so that I would be worthy of be-
ing incorporated into the mystical body of the Catholic Church, his lovely spouse,
and worthy to be counted among her righteous and most beautiful members. Oh
dearest Jesus, let this your body bring harmony and sweetness to my soul, salva-
tion and evenness in every temptation, peace and joy in every trial, light and
virtue in each word and trial and deed, salvation and assurance in death, as you
live and reign forever and ever. Amen.

When you have offered this prayer, let the priest perform his office, which
is to give communion. Do not say a word, except when one must say, "Lord, I
am not worthy," then make him ask all of those present for forgiveness. And
once he has taken communion, and the priest has put away his things, that is
to say, has closed the tabernacle, before he gets up you then gently tell the one
who has to die, "See, my brother, how much consolation there is in having the
Lord of heaven and earth inside you. But so you are not ungrateful towards
such a gift, lift your mind towards the heavenly Father and say this:

[Chapter Eighteen]
Prayer

Oh most Holy Lord, Omnipotent Father Eternal, God, I give you thanks and
praise with all of my being, that you have deigned to take me back, most vile and
unworthy sinner that I am, and to take me to the most precious blood, the blood
of your Son, our Lord and dearest Savior Jesus Christ. I pray to you that this
holy communion bring me neither sin nor punishment, but that it be instead a
saving intercession of grace and forgiveness of all my sins. May this communion
be, according to your grace, the armor of faith and a shield of goodwill. May it

---

[35] "virtù," lit. "power."

*rid me of my vices and extinguish all of my lustful and carnal desires. May it be
a true and effective growth of charity, patience, humility, obedience, and virtue.
May it be a solid defense against plots of my enemies, both visible and invisible.
May it be that which puts an end to the movements of all my vices; may it be a
single and steady approach to you and my own happy consummation. I pray
that you deign to guide me, an unworthy and wretched sinner, to that ineffable
and magnificent banquet where you are the true light, complete satiety, perfect
cheer, and eternal joy for your saints. Amen.*

Then when you have finished this prayer, have the priest give him God's
blessing and then send them away.

[Chapter Nineteen]
The manner you should have when the bell begins to toll.

When the bell of the Podestà's Palace first rings in the morning, you must
be very strong because you will find most of them become completely overwhelmed and that many grow faint. And then you must ardently comfort him
and say:

*Ah, my brother, is this all the courage that you can muster in the first attack made
when you enter the battle? My, my—and I know what I am saying here—if you
do not take measures to guide your reactions differently than what I see in this
first assault, you will be defeated by your enemies. So I want to tell you something:
You have never had, in all your life, as tough a battle as you will have in these
next two or three hours that you have left to live. Because now all of your enemies
and all of the enemies of your soul will attack you—all of them—at one go. And
who are these enemies of yours who want to crush you? Know that it is the devil,
the world, and your own flesh. And do you know what the devil will do to you?
He will put all your sins before you so that you suffer and ask God for forgiveness.
But if you don't, he will instead do it so that you become ashamed and confused,
and so you lose hope that God can or wants to forgive you, as did Judas the traitor. When he gave our Lord into the hands of the Jews, he realized his evildoing
and said that his sin was greater than God's mercy. And he took a small rope and
hanged himself by the neck. Don't you do this, and don't believe this evil beast
who wants to lead you away from the straight path so that he can devour you.
Instead, follow the example of the sinner Mary Magdalene, who, though she knew
she had many sins, never despaired. Instead, she went to the feet of our Savior full
of hope, and with her tears earned his forgiveness. Do you know what a battle the*

devil is going to give you? He will remind you of all your enemies, not, obviously, so that you forgive them, but to make you even more enraged against them. And you know what? He will plant the idea in your heart that your enemies are happy that you are being brought to this point and that they say, "See, God has given that little thief what he deserved."

Take note that this kind of talk, if you consider it well, should not cause you suffering. Rather it should comfort you when you understand it not as the devil intended, but why he intended it so.

He will show you that your enemies are happy that you are being led to death. I'm telling you that it's not true, and for two reasons.

The first reason is this. If someone wants to say that your enemy is happy because of a vendetta, know that it makes him happy because he doesn't know enough. If I wished ill on someone and if I wanted him to suffer, I would certainly not want it to be the kind of ill that was useful to him. I would want him to suffer an ill that would bring him to the worst state possible, and this is ultimate desire of revenge. Therefore your enemy is not happy that you are being brought to this point, because this death is not death, rather it is life. It is not a penalty, but something that will free you from penalty and bring you to peace and rest. And even if he does want you to die, he does not want you to die this death, because he knows very well that the soul does not leave the body in any way more secure than this. Therefore you should not be anguished that he is happy that you have come to this point, because he is happy about what is actually good for you. This happiness is a mortal sin for him, and so you should pray to God for him.

The second reason your enemy is not happy about this: know that the reasoning person always leans more to compassion than to cruelty, and therefore it cannot be that anyone rejoices in what is bad for you, if we must call this situation bad. But even if some man rejoices in his neighbor's bad times, he is not a man in that moment, because he does not have humanity. Rather, we would do well to call him diabolic, because he lets the devil lead him where he will. And to show that this is true, there is no place where we read that Christ was ever cruel or that he ever delighted in someone else's hardship. And why is this, if not only because the devil never had any power over him? Therefore do not believe in any of these temptations, and do not be defenseless before the assault of this first enemy.

The second enemy that you will battle is the world, and I warn you this won't be an easy battle. Do you know what the world will do to you? It will make you understand that these things bring you great shame and wrong you: the tolling of the bell, the reading of the condemnation, your being tied and led before the people—that these things bring enormous shame to you and to those

you leave behind. And you should know that the world despises these things because each one is a crown for your soul and here is the reason why. If the world
would like to tell you that this way of dying shames you, what they say is not
true. You can see very well that all of the saints who have died, or most of them,
have died violent deaths. And the bloodshed and death of every single one is
celebrated. See that the church makes a greater feast day for a martyr than for
a confessor. And why would this be if not for his death? So because of this you
can clearly understand that for such a death the saints are honored and not
reviled. What's more, this kind of death, more than any other, lets the body die
and makes the soul live.

You might say that the tolling of the bell brings you shame, but again
this is not true. Do you really know why the tolling of the bell is ordered? It is
ordered so that each person may hear that someone is about to be executed and
so that people are moved to compassion and pray for you. How many people do
you think there are around here who upon hearing this bell say an Our Father
for your soul, or say at least "May God forgive you." If the bell did not ring and
if word simply passed around about an execution, no one would care about it
nor say anything for it. Furthermore, I want you to know that many clerics hear
this bell, and that those who are at the altar will say a special prayer for you,
and likewise those who are in the midst of doing and saying Offices, and all the
others who are supposed to pray for the afflicted, all of these will pray God to
give you strength. Whereas if the bell did not ring, they would not do anything.
Therefore, for these reasons, the ringing of the bell is nothing if not useful. And
for that the world is not happy that it does you good.

What if the world still wants to say that having the condemnation read
and being tied or led before the people shames and hurts you? All these things
are torments that have been put in your imagination so as to prevent you from
turning your heart to other things. And this is how the world will try to beat
you. Know that your enemy will not leave you the means or the power to do
anything until he has you under his thumb and you cannot do anything but
what he wants and how he wants it.

And therefore do not let such things bother you, since if you pay them
heed, you will hear so many that they'll end up giving you more pain than
death. All these things are not but what one makes of them, so if you are given
to let them shame you, your shame will feel that much greater. And if you give
it little attention, you will not feel anything.

Your other enemy waiting to assail you is your own flesh. And that your
flesh gives you suffering, I do not ask you why. It is fragile and fights for a short

time. And for this also there is a remedy. Do you know which remedy you need to conquer the flesh? There is no better thing than to turn to prayer. And to show that this is true, we have the example of our Lord Jesus Christ, who when he was approaching death and his flesh began to fight him, at that hour he said, "My soul is afflicted until my death" and he went to say prayers right away and he did not stay thinking about what his sensual nature was saying. I know full well that your flesh is flesh and that it feels pain like the flesh of Christ. But then act like Christ: do not keep thinking about what your sensual nature will show you, but rather turn to prayer and you will delight more in that than in any other thing.

And know that I wanted to warn you about all these things, so that when they come, you will have been warned and they will not lead you astray like this first one did. Be aware that, in a short while, the cavalier will be arriving who will tie you up and will lead you to the orator's stand.[36] Your condemnation will be read there and then, finally he will put you to death. At every one of these stages I will be with you and I will remind you of what you should do. Do not take these things to heart or think about any of them so much, because otherwise when you arrive at that point, then just as time passes, so you will also pass with that thought and nothing else.

For those who you find do not lose strength at the tolling of the bell and who do not seem to care about it, never stop praying at their side nor talking about miracles. You should do this so they have nothing to think about other than remembering what you have just been telling them, that is, about how the cavalier must come and tie them up, and so forth.

[Chapter Twenty]
The manner you should have when the cavalier comes to tie his hands.

When the cavalier is in the prison and has come to take him away, do not move unless the two of you are called. Rather, act as if you do not hear him and do this so that he who has to die has no reason to think that you desire him to go away quickly. And thus always make it a habit to not get worked up about anything besides your office. That is, if the cavalier is slower or if he is delayed along the way more than he should be, don't bother about it and don't

---

[36] The *ringhiera* at the Podestà's Palace.

let it show that you get bothered about it, and do this for the reason above. And when you two are called, make the one who has to die ask forgiveness of all the prisoners and ask them to pray to God for him. And then have him leave the prison and when he comes to the place where the cavalier is, ensure that he pardons all the people, and above all the officer and his companions. And as for you, always keep beside him holding the *tavoletta* high so that he has that to see and nothing else. And if even then you see that he is faltering, comfort him directly and remind him that this is the other battle that his enemies wage against him, and that he should not take it to heart, because if he lets them win, he will have a hard time escaping their grip. And thus make him always say some prayer.

[Chapter Twenty-one]
The manner you must have when he is led out of the prison.

When he is led out of the prison, make sure that you are always level with him on the right side, and your companion on the left side. Do not leave his side for any reason, allowing whoever wants to come near to do so. And when you are at the door of the prison, make him ask forgiveness of the people near him and ask them to pray to God for the salvation of his soul. And so have him praying continually until you reach the place where the condemnation is read.

[Chapter Twenty-two]
The manner you must have when he is led out to the place of condemnation and he is read his condemnation.

When you are at the orator's stand and his condemnation is read out, then you should be very daring in your speech, and never let him be still because then he would be greatly transformed due to the multitude of people he sees. And always make sure that he looks you in the eye and at the tablet, so that he does not look around. Always make him say some prayer so that he does not think, and so that he does not listen to what is being read. And this is because if he were to hear read out some crime that he did not commit, he would get very agitated. And there are times some of them may say to the notary who is read-ing, "You are lying through your teeth," and this is very bad. Firstly, because rage flames up in his heart, and also because he ends up denying everything that is being read and ends up denying the truth. For it's not possible that the notary doesn't say or read something true. Therefore be advised to make sure, if you can, that he does not commit this sin. When the bell tolls above the steps of the Basilica of St. Petronius,[37] which signals the raising of the Lord God, then you make sure that he who has to die turns and looks to where the body of Christ is raised or should be raised, and that he removes his hood or whatever he has on his head.

When the host is raised, make him repeat after you, "Blessed host, which is the Son of the true and living God, the dearest Jesus Christ, born of the glory of the Virgin Mary, have mercy on my soul and do not look upon my sins, since I am sorry and repent, and so I say 'mea culpa, mea maxima culpa.'" And you then touch him with your hand on his chest and mouth.

When the chalice is raised, you should then begin that prayer that goes, "Oh holy blessed and just blood that comes from that holy circumcision," and continue until it's all finished, and have him repeat your every word. When the condemnation has been read, make sure this man asks the people to pray God for his soul, and that if he has wronged anyone, that he asks that one forgiveness.

[Chapter Twenty-three]
The manner you must have when you will go around the square.

When you descend from the [Podestà's] palace and when you go around the square and then on through the street, keep him straight with prayers and with some pleasant sayings. And this is necessary because many people will be there to watch and to hear what the penitent will say, and also so that he cannot pay attention to what is going on around him. Because the devil sometimes makes him see some enemy of his so that he becomes enraged and his spirit suffers. And so until you arrive at the church of St. John at the market, or to the place where he is to die, you should always make him say some prayers. And when you come close to that church, begin some beautiful prayer, the most beautiful one that you know, and say it until the body of Christ is raised. And this is necessary because in such places there are always many people who are there to see the execution, together with the flagellants. And all these ones, that is, the crowd and the flagellants, like to hear beautiful things. And by doing this you provide a great service to the one who has to die, and you

---

[37] The civic church of Bologna (as distinct from the cathedral church of St. Paul), which faced the Podestà's Palace across Piazza Maggiore.

bring honor to yourself and to our Company. When he has knelt down on the threshold of the church, remove his hood. And when the host is raised, say this, "At this time we raise the Creator Jesus Christ, our Lord, the blessed host and living flesh, fruit and flower of the womb of the Virgin Mary. I am sorry for all my sins and I admit my fault, my entire fault." And give him your hand on his chest and mouth.

When he raises the chalice, you should say this: "O holy and just blood, know me fully, that at the point of my death I would not be deaf or mute. Blood of our Savior Jesus Christ, preserve my soul in eternal life. Amen."

[Chapter Twenty-four]
What you must say when you leave the church to go to his death.

When you both leave the church and go towards the place of execution where he must die, then you must comfort him with gentle words and say,

Oh creature of God, you have devoutly taken up the arms of the blessed Lord Jesus Christ, and you are armed with them now. So now you are transformed into a valiant cavalier and fight manfully since I tell you that you are near death and do not have much time left to live. This is your cross by which you must follow the dear Christ Jesus, who will reward you with his precious blood.

And in this way you always continue to comfort him until you are on top of the hill or wherever the execution will be carried out.

[Chapter Twenty-five]
The manner you must have when he is near the place where he has to die.

When you are atop the Monte del Mercato, or indeed in another place of execution, then remind him forcefully about confession. If he had kept hidden any sin out of fear or temerity, plead with him to confess to the priest and tell him frankly,

Look, my brother, you have death on your heels. It chases you so hard and for so long that by now you do not wish to hang on to it for anything. You know that death is a fraud and liar, but you should desire by now to return to God who awaits you with open arms, to receive you if you depart pure and clean and without sin. And know that you have no more time for penance and that your salvation rests in four or five words that you still have to say. Let me remind you that the disposition with which the soul leaves the body is the one that will remain with you eternally. For this reason, therefore, for the love of God, do not try to keep back any sin and do not [aim] to bring it with you. Since the priest is here, tell him everything.

In this way make him confess to the priest.

[Chapter Twenty-six]
The words that you must adopt when he comes from confession.

When he rises from confession and goes towards the execution block, or they position him from behind, then tell him these words and ensure that he answers,

Into your hands, oh my Lord, I commend my spirit and soul. I ask you, my Father, that you have mercy on my soul at the hour and at the moment of my death. Sweet Virgin Mary, I commend to you my soul. Sweetest Virgin Mary, advocate for us sinners, fountain of mercy, stairway to heaven, doorway of paradise, joy of the saints, pray to your benevolent Son by the death and Passion that he endured on the wood of the cross, that he have mercy on my soul at the hour and at the moment of my death. Sweet Virgin Mary, I commend to you my spirit.

And if you were to see that the time is advancing, tell him that prayer that begins, "Soul of Christ, purify me, etc."

[Chapter Twenty-seven]
The manner you must have when he who has to die kneels down.

When you are at the block and he who has to die kneels down to put his head on it, you kneel down as well, using your right knee and keeping the *tavoletta* in such a way that he always has his eye on it, that is, so he always sees it. And sincerely tell him the following words, "My dearest brother, make yourself strong and steady at this step and don't have fear. And aim to offer your soul, clean and devout, to the Creator who gave it to you." Do not hesitate from saying with him these last words that Jesus Christ said on the wood of the cross: "Into your hand, Lord, I commend my spirit." Make it so that his last words would be: "Into your hands, my Lord, I commend my spirit and soul." And so always have your mind on this when they fix the *tagliadura* around his neck; make him bend to kiss the tablet. Do this so that when he bends, and his throat comes near the execution block, and the *tagliadura* secures his neck so that he cannot move it, he will be severed at the first touch.[38] If he holds his neck high, even then and often by accident, the braces shift and because of this there can be much suffering/pain. And similarly pay attention to when the executioner lifts the mallet; make sure that you never move the *tavoletta* under his face until the mallet is close to the chopping block. And make sure that you pull the tablet away at the same time as the blow, so that he who has to die does not notice. Because sometimes when the tablet is taken away too soon, he moves his neck, and thus suffers many more blows, which makes it very hard on him.

And similarly, when you go up on the ladder of the gallows with one who has to be hanged, as you climb up the ladder tell him that prayer that begins, "Soul of Christ, purify me." And be careful to finish it leaving enough time so that you can say at least two or three times, "Into your hands, my Lord, I commend my spirit and soul" [Luke 23:46], so that these are the last words you make him say. And take care always to hold the tablet in front of his face and not too low. Go as high as you can, which will make it easier for you and so that he will be better able to understand what you tell him. And do not be there in a way that would block him when he is about to swing down, so that when he is knocked off the ladder he falls freely. From the moment he is pushed, you cry out three times in his ear and tell him to remember the Passion of Christ and to call the Virgin Mary to his heart. And pray to God for his soul.

[Chapter Twenty-eight]
Prayer

Oh dearest Lord Jesus Christ, for that bitterness that you endured on the cross for me, most of all at that hour when your most noble and holy soul left your most holy body, have mercy on my soul when it leaves, oh my Lord God. Amen.

Praise be to you, Jesus Christ, who lives in the Trinity, give peace to the unfortunate and save the weak. Amen.

Thanks be to God. Amen. Amen. Amen.

---

[38] The *tagliadura* was a yokelike brace whose upper and lower halves secured around the prisoner's neck. A blade fit into a slot above the prisoner's neck, allowing the executioner to sever it cleanly with a single blow of a mallet.

Book 3: *Laude* & Prayers

Translated by Sheila Das and Nicholas Terpstra

My Christ, Give Me Strength
(Cristo mio dami fortezza)

My Christ, give me strength
You who are so full of every sweetness
So I do not lose you through any bitterness
      I, a wretched sinner.
If to you my heart does not reach
Oh Jesus Christ our Lord
Oh most high Redeemer
      Have pity on me.
Oh sweet glorious Christ
Oh beloved and gracious love
How much you are desired
By all who love you purely.
Oh blessed angel
Who is at my right side
Guard me against that evil
      So that from him I am not led away.
Charged with my care, staying at my side
May my soul in his safekeeping
Renounce the false reward;
Through your loving *cortesia*
May he not look at my folly.
Have mercy on my soul
In the hour and place of my death
      So this last breath not be ruined.

For sources see Table 2.1, *Laude* in Manuscripts of the Bolognese *Comforters' Manual*.

Oh High Queen Crowned in Stars
(O alta regina de stelle incoronata)

Oh high queen crowned in stars
Virgin chosen when the angel
In his annunciation said "Hail"!

You then turned that key
That opened heaven and rid us of war
Bringing peace to us, kind and sweet.

Ah! do not look, my lady, what is on earth
But think that he saw fit to create us
In his highest image that does not err.

Because of the fault of original sin,
With his holy wounds he made everyone worthy
To enter into his high kingdom.

You alone righted the sign to the right way,
You were the reason that the door of the highest kingdom opened.

Even short sermons and many tongues
Would wish to give
Great praises and prayers to you

Because you conquer every worldly desire.
Pure Virgin, daughter of that sun
That with his death, won so many years of life.

Oh empress of the eternal schools
Although my merit is mortal and slight
Still I am ready to say this of you.

Oh holy light, oh blessed fire!
Without you no one will find the way
To the peace of that happy place.

I rush to you, oh tender, pious mother;
Before the world strips me of worth
may I find my shelter in you.

Look how this destiny, terrible and cruel,
Led me, full of false pride,
To such ruinous rocks.

Behold, my lady, the mast and sails
All overturned and already sinking to the bottom
Where I find myself in anguish.

But you who are a sun to the world
Through the power of your Son
Shine the light of your joyful love on me.

Take a quick glance—how difficult it is for me,
My heart lost and off your path
If your divine counsel does not guide me

So I turn to you before I fall,
Since whoever asks you first for grace
Will not walk in vain

To you, oh just one, I pray
That with your scales you so direct me
That I can escape every penalty.

Beautiful Virgin, my hope is in you;
Answer my pleas, I pray, with your grace
Which moves every other good.

Remembering my damned crimes,
I would deserve more than a thousand deaths
Never having observed your just commandments

But your soft wind that carries
Safe and sound every ship

Battered by the great seas;
You bring them to sweet harbor.

None has ever equaled you in this;
No first or second in any way,
Pull me from these bitter tears.

Virgin full of every grace and praise;
Reach out in help if you once again would
Loosen every knot that is my due

So that when I remember from this hour and onward
My crimes and old offenses
As I lie cold and wretched on the ground

that in you alone I hope, that you will be mild
And to me give grace enough
To see you appear in the burning flames
and pull me up into the holy company.[39]

The end

Into your arms, Virgin Mary
(In le toe braçe Vergine Maria)

Into your arms, Virgin Mary
I commend my soul and spirit,
And if I pray, sweet pious mother,
That your grace not abandon me,
Reach out to help me in this my punishment
That little by little presses down on me
In this final moment of my life
May my soul be commended to you.

---

[39] *colegio,* which Florio (1598) translates as "a colledge, a companie, a brotherhood, a fellowship, a fraternitie, or corporation."

Succor me, my mother, and don't leave me,
In you I put my hope
Make it so that at the point of my passing
My soul you take away
And set before the sight of the one Father.
Give me strength in this my punishment
And pray for me at this my final end
So that my spirit and soul pass on well.

If your helping hand does not reach
To my tired and battered little boat
Then every effort,
that to the depths of my soul I have endured,
will be lost and in vain.

O virgin Mary,
Succor me in this gasping grief,
Because you are the mother of your son,
O Virgin Mary,
And I give you my spirit and soul.

Jesus Splendor of the First Light
(Iesu splendore della prima luce)

Jesus, splendor of the first light
shimmering the soul with your brightness
may human peace follow in your wake
breathless for you, Creator.

Celestial height and nature immense,
God most high, triune in person
Supernal greatness and infinite measure
Prime being with boundless will,
Shining brilliance, solemn figure,
Light of glory and of shining warmth.

Blessed is the soul resplendent with intellect,
Beauty of the first substance,

Eternal Father, perfect object,
Word of God born of divine essence,
Paraclete Spirit, gift and first beloved[40]
of the Father and the Word who is the perfect love.

Contemplating the soul of this splendor,
how it is born from the first mind
of God eternal Father,
One feels his sharp arrows
that perfectly penetrate the heart
inflamed with true fire.

Beloved Spirit issuing with peace
Given as the Word from the Father,
Holy Spirit of charity and affection,
And of the first from whom the arrows pressed[41]
and you loved them fully
with knowledge and a deep fervor.

Eternal prince and immense Father,
Full fountain of the first wisdom,
Overflowing time with that coveted peace,
You held it out to the soul, oh Goodness,
You sent as aid your only Son,
In the guise of a sinner.

Son of God, resplendent brilliance
Clothed in flesh to bear sadness
Soul of Christ, redeeming richness,
Lucid mirror of great purity,
How just and good that such beauty
would live in a vessel so luminously white.

Mental glory for the redeemed
Who brings fervent love to Jesus

---

[40] "mança," possibly from *manza* or *amanza*.
[41] The manuscript reads "atristi."

And dazed in love goes seeking
the spouse of the soul and perfect lover,
then transformed by transforming love,
languishes in loving valor.

Human effort achieves nothing
If the word made flesh favors it little
If beloved Jesus you want to find,
You must have the purity of a spouse,
Embracing it tightly
with a forthright and longing heart.

Have Mercy, Oh God Most High
(Misericordia o alto Dio Soprano)

Have mercy, oh God most High
With heart and mouth I call you,
To help me at this dread time.

Have mercy! Oh my sweet Lord
By your grace and pity
Reaching out to me at this awful time.

Have mercy! I call to your godhead
By the mystery of your incarnation
By the glory of your birth.

Have mercy! By your suffering
That you bore on that wood for me
That was our deliverance and salvation.

Have mercy! For that high kingdom;
Promising years in the heavenly court
With favored saints, oh good Lord.

Have mercy! Through that bitter fate
Of martyrs, constant and blessed,
Who died, each one, for you.

Have mercy! I call you
Take my spirit in your hands
Not looking at my faults.

Have mercy! Oh eternal God most high
True Father, Son, and Holy Spirit
Always merciful and compassionate.

Have mercy! With great compassion
Defend me from this bitter pass
Where the evil enemy stands ready at my side.

Have mercy, Lord, not to delay
Have mercy divine majesty
Have mercy blessed martyrs

Have mercy trembling soul
Have mercy saintly spirits
Have mercy my benevolent Lord

Have mercy even though I am not worthy
Have mercy oh Virgin Mary
Have mercy oh Mother of the Lord

Have mercy oh my advocate
Have mercy oh lady of valor
Have mercy towards my due punishment

Have mercy—on me a sinner
Have mercy—I cry out loud!
Have mercy—venerated one! pure one!

Have mercy for I'm in my last hour
And then I say, into your hands, my Lord,
I commit my soul and my spirit

Have mercy, omnipotent Lord
Have mercy; ingrate that I've been

towards You, kind and wise Lord.

Mercy on my grave sins
Mercy to keep me from hell
I need you to help me now
And to give me the whole of eternal paradise.

The end.

Have Mercy, Oh Highest Eternal God
(Misericordia, o, sumo eterno Idio)

Have mercy, oh highest eternal God
Merciful and just and full of compassion
Creator of the universe, oh my Father.

I rush to your great and immense goodness
So that you assist my soul, my weary spirit
Brought to the wretched end of my days.

Here I am at this final pass
Dear Lord, who judges every mortal
In the thieving, sighing, and lowly world,

Do not look at my wrongs.
A sinner I have been, and I confess it
I deserve the fire, eternal and infernal.

In you, Lord, I trust
That by your generous grace
you will grant pardon,
having been, for me, placed and fixed on the cross.

For me, then, you gave such a gift
With your blood you ransomed me
So my heart I place in your will.

Since for me you bore
So much dishonor and harsh abuse
From those Jews,
Who so much honor had gained by you.

To you I repent my grave errors
Filled with tears and great sorrow
Crying, I think of your mortal suffering.

And I pray that your compassion
does not want to abandon me on this final day
But in deliverance will gather my spirit.

Be pleased to forgive my failings;
In thousands of ways I feel I have offended you
And not observed your commandments.

Ah Lord, inflame my heart
So through your passion
I can bear this burden with strength.

You forgave that thief on the cross
Who, crucified with you, on your right
Turned to you with devotion

Forgive me too, since I have lived wrongly
full of sins; defend my soul
from the great enemy and deep abyss.

Defend me with your grace above
Accompany me at this bitter point
And with your hand, take my spirit

See that I am wholeheartedly contrite
A true Christian and your creature
And I hope, at the end, to be united with you

Don't leave me, Lord, in fear
Of my harsh enemy at this final moment
But keep faith in you strong in my heart.

So that I hope in you alone, highest and supreme
God, true and generous creator
Whom I love, revere and fear.

Ah! Do not look at my perverse error
If ungrateful and unmindful I have been
But look at your mercy, which is greater.

Now oh Lord, my heart make strong
So, as I hope, victory follows
Over the cruel and wicked enemy, the serpent

So that, like a good warrior, I may
Ascend to you, and seek refuge
The promised gift of your worthy empire.

For thousands of years I seemed to belong
To this dark, false world
That I now must leave,
To find myself in heaven pure

Where I, oh Lord, may be worthy, with desire
To enjoy the sweet and glorious songs
Of the angels who are honoring you.

Ah! lift me up my Lord, from these tears
And take me to see that sweet face
You show the martyrs and saints.

And may I never be apart from you
Once my soul from my body melts away
Then from you a paradise comes

Making every other wish seem clearly foolish,
The searching for pleasure in this world vain,
Since everyone dies, never to return.

And therefore, Lord, with your will in me
I am content to endure this penalty
And accept it for your love and for salvation.

See my mind, completely full
Of soulful strength and steadfast faith
that makes the troubled soul serene.

He who hopes in your grace and mercy
Asks and is never disappointed; and
He who believes is always provided for.

Thus my Lord listen to these sweet words
With your dignity and great mercy
Since every moment away from you pains me

See my life, already beginning
To take comfort in coming to such an end
To leave this mud and suffering.

My soul has come to the boundary
Crying out loud for your divine succor
that destines it to join the other blessed

See the bitter bile, see the hard bridle
That Peter with the great Paul and the others
Have suffered and endured for love of you.

You gave the lesson while still down here among us
With the highest example of your holy cross
To give to some salvation and reward, then

Up there where is sung in your glory
The peace everlasting and sweet
By all the faithful whom you have made strong.

The end.

Book 4: Authorities

Nicholas Terpstra

Not all manuscripts of the Bologna manual include these collections of sayings, or "Auctoritates." Most that do draw the bulk of their sayings from the Bible, followed by the church fathers, chiefly Augustine. Others will include a few sayings drawn from ancient Greek or Roman authors. Comforters may have memorized these lines in order to have something to say quickly if a prisoner broke down, or perhaps if he proved absolutely resistant to the formulas set out in the rest of the manual. In many cases, a single saying will be given in both Latin and Italian, either one after the other or on different pages. This suggests that comforters wanted to be ready to speak to a prisoner on his own cultural level. In these cases, the Latin sayings frequently come as pithy aphorisms, while their Italian counterparts have the slightly longer and looser form of oral wisdom.

Thus, for example, at one point the Beinecke manuscript first gives in Latin: "The simple and unlearned occupy the kingdom of heaven; and we with our letters are destined for hell," and identifies it immediately as a saying of Augustine.[42] On the folio sheet facing this quotation is found a more elaborate version in Italian: "The simple and good and unlearned plainly have place in the kingdom of heaven, and we with our letters and our sciences are going to the house of the devil," although this comes without any attribution to Augustine.[43] Similarly, the Beinecke manuscript offers first in Latin: "It is human to sin, diabolical to persevere, angelic to emend," and attributes the saying to Isidore of Seville. Across the page, and again without attribution, this becomes in Italian "The human thing is to sin, and it is diabolical to persevere, but the one thing good and angelic is to correct yourself of your sins."[44]

---

[42] "Simplices et indocti regnu[m] celorum capiu[n]t : et nos cum / litteris nostris ad infernum destendimus: Augustinus." YBL ms. 1069, fol. 81v.

[43] "Li simplici et boni et senza scientia piano el loco de regno de celo / et nui co[n] le lettere et scientie nostre andiamo a casa de diabolo." YBL ms. 1069, fol. 82r.

[44] "Humanum est peccare: diabolicum perseuerare et angelicu[m] / emendare: —Hisidorus." YBL ms. 1069, fol. 82v. "Le humana cosa el peccate: et e cosa diabolim el perseuerare: / ma le una cosa bona et angelica

Since comforters chose sayings that they could memorize, the lines frequently have a rhyme that easily gets lost in English translation. "He who does not want the blessing of God in this world, will have his curse in this world and the next," conveys the Italian saying's meaning but not its alliteration of "benedictione/maladitione." At the same time, translating this as "He who does not want the good word of God in this world will have the bad word of God in this and the next" leaves us with something awkward.[45] Here as in the texts of the manual itself, biblical sayings are more often loosely paraphrased than carefully cited, and the copyist frequently adapted and embellished them to better fit the situation a comforter would find himself in.

In spite of the rubric "auctoritates" given in most manuscripts, the "authorities" behind these sayings are named more often in some manuscripts than in others. The first manuscript noted below (BBU ms. 702) gives attributions consistently, while the second (YBL ms. 1069) does so only infrequently; in this latter manuscript, the Latin sayings more frequently come with attributions, and the Italian sayings more frequently without. This distinction has been preserved in the selections given below.

The sayings range from simple moralizing to more sophisticated statements about the soul. They advise accepting without complaint any penalty, humiliation, and injustice. This is what Jesus and the saints modeled, and it is God wants from you. God upholds justice on one hand, and sees through injustice on the other, and he will reward those who accept their fate with patience and humility.

From Bologna, Biblioteca Universitaria, ms. 702

Solomon also says: "The fear of God is holy religion. The fear of God is good discipline. The fear of God is the crown of wisdom. The fear of God guards the soul from death. He who fears God and observes his commandments will have patience to the end" [fol. 6v].

Solomon says: "My son, love God and guard yourself from sin, and take nothing from the poor, and give alms happily, because alms are the grandest sign of faith before God" [fol. 6v].

St. Benedict says: Those who have patience do the will of God. And those who suffer and carry patiently the persecution of malicious men and who hum-

---

mendarse de li soi peccatij" [no attribution]. YBL ms. 1069, fol. 83r.

[45] "Qvllui ch[e] no[n] uole la b[e]n[e]dictione de dio in quisto mondo: in questo / e in laltro abia la sua maladitione." YBL ms. 1069, fol. 81v.

bly render thanks to Jesus Christ will be pardoned of their sins" [fol. 7v].

Augustine says: "Consider how much, for whom, and what grace the friends of Jesus Christ have, who are equal to the holy angels and who always see God" [fol. 8r].

Longinus says: "If the humble one is not patient, the grace of the Holy Spirit is not in him" [fol. 8v].

St. Basil says: "The humble man is always humble in his clothing, his life, and his speech. The proud man always seems attractive in all his works on the outside, and is always vile in all his works on the inside" [fol. 9r].

Augustine: "The soul is a certain participating substance given so that there can be a governing of the body. It has three virtues: it is vegetal, by which the body can be alive. Sensible, through which come the senses. Rational, by which comes intention" [fol. 33r].

Pythagorus: "The soul is eternal and receives merit and penalty" [fol. 34v].

Paul in Galatians: "Brothers, if we would follow the law of Christ, we must visit and console one another" [fol. 34v].

Aristotle: "Happy is the soul that is not infected with evil, and that is oriented to its creator and that returns to its place. Bad the soul that does evil, which does not have the intention of its creator" [fol. 35r].

Ambrose says: "Penance is weeping for past evil, and not making evil any more" [fol. 55v].

Augustine says: "Do not be afraid of anyone while still in this life. There is only the crime of despair which cannot be healed" [fol. 42r].

Jerome says: "Whoever wishes at the point of death to be sure of God's pardon, should while being healthy do penance and weep for the sins committed" [fol. 58v].

From Yale University, Beinecke Library, ms. 1069, fols. 80v–83r

There comes to us the day of penitence for the repenting of sin and the saving of the soul: Pope Gregory the Great [fol. 80v].

Doubting in faith is unfaithfulness [fol. 80v].

I am the way and truth and life of men, and who believes in me has life eternal and the Glory of paradise [fol. 81r].

Do not fear those who are armed with the power to kill the body, because the soul cannot be killed [fol.81r].

Do not wish to judge and you will not be judged. Leave aside injuries and you will be pardoned. [fol. 81r].

Render that which is Caesar's to Caesar's, and that which is God's to God: Christ [fol. 82r].

Time flies as fast as it can, and our life is brief [fol. 82r].

Why is the sinner ashamed to reveal his sins? Because to God and the angels, and also to all the souls, all will be revealed. Confession liberates the soul from death [fol. 83r].

This people with their lips honor me, but their heart is far from me [fol. 83r].

If I speak with the tongues of all men and with those of the angels, and have not charity, for me it will earn nothing [fol. 83r].

Luca della Robbia's Narrative on the Execution of Pietro Paolo Boscoli and Agostino Capponi

Alison Knowles Frazier

In late August of 1512, the Florentine citizen militia was defeated by Spanish regulars at Prato. Within days, the republican government headed by Pietro Soderini fell, and the Medici returned to govern Florence. The family's situation was precarious. Especially in the first, transitional months, as elite factions regrouped, vigilance was good policy. Among the casualties of this early Medici nervousness were two patricians: Pietro Paolo Boscoli, then thirty-five, and Agostino Capponi, aged forty-three.[1] They were suspected of plotting to assassinate Cardinal Giovanni de' Medici, soon to be elevated to the papacy as Leo X, his brother Giuliano, and their cousin Giulio.

It is not clear that Boscoli and Capponi actually posed a threat. Today, most historians agree with Roberto Ridolfi's assessment that the plot was "one of the usual conspiracies" of that time, "more literary than bloodthirsty."[2] Contemporaries were less sure of this distinction, at least as far as their own safety was concerned.[3] The material evidence for the plot was, at any rate, flimsy and possibly fabricated. An incriminating list of conspirators was passed to the Otto di Guardia, the Florentine magistracy in charge of criminal justice, and came to the knowledge of Giuliano and Giovanni de' Medici.[4] The pro-Medici Otto, after interrogating Boscoli and Capponi under torture, rendered a guilty verdict.

The remainder of the story is described in a precious and moving eyewitness

---

[1] Polidori, "Notizie," 283n2, gives the men's ages. See also Pincin, "Boscoli"; and Lazzaretti, "Capponi."

[2] Ridolfi, *Life of Niccolò Machiavelli*, 135–36.

[3] See, for example, comments by Niccolò Valori (1464–1530) in the family *ricordi*, quoted and discussed in Jurdjevic, *Guardians of Republicanism*, chap. 4. I am grateful to Professor Jurdjevic for allowing me to read his chapter in advance of publication.

[4] Pincin, "Boscoli," 219a.

account, the *Recitazione*, which is translated below. As Boscoli and Capponi waited, shackled, in a chapel of Florence's government building, the Bargello, their death sentence was announced. Both men fell into a kind of shock. Barely eight hours remained to prepare for death, and the noisy, crowded chapel—which had been made into a holding cell—was a difficult setting for that intimate work. The rituals of comforting, however, transformed the chaos into glimpses of self-knowledge and acceptance. Guided by friends and confessors, and accompanied by members of the Confraternity of the Blacks, each of the condemned made his way to some spiritual peace. In the early morning darkness of Wednesday, 23 February 1513, first Pietro Paolo Boscoli and then Agostino Capponi met death by beheading.

Luca della Robbia (1484–ca. 1519), the young author of the *Recitazione*, was a highly educated editor of classical texts and a devout follower of the Savonarolan movement.[5] The second aspect of his persona seems most to govern the *Recitazione*, both because it is written in his Tuscan vernacular rather than his professional Latin, and because it promotes the evangelical message of the Dominican friar Girolamo Savonarola (1452–1498).[6] The author himself foregrounds his own piety as a guarantee of his candor. The *Recitazione* is "a thing truly told" (*Rec.* 3), della Robbia explains, because nothing more requires his honesty than the matters of Christian conscience and salvation raised by his dear friend Boscoli's final passage.

Della Robbia twice—once in the preface and once in the epilogue (*Rec.* 3 and 47)—identifies his narrative quite simply as a *ricordo*, an informal recollection. It is an atypical *ricordo*, however, even for that elastic genre. Contemporary readers would have perceived elements of ritual and testament. The subject of exemplary death suggested Christian martyrology, and an elite few may have recalled Plato's *Phaedo* on the death of Socrates or Poliziano's letter on the death of Lorenzo de' Medici.[7] The question and answer format, along with della Robbia's managerial role, brought to mind the priest's catechism, while Boscoli's yearning search for God denotes what today would be called a spiritual biography, a form that contemporaries knew as *vitae sanctorum*, lives of saints.[8] The title, *Recitazione*, declares a historical narrative clearly enough,

---

[5] On della Robbia, a relative of the famous artist, see Fragnito, "della Robbia." Also important is Lazzerini, *Nessuno è innocente,* recapitulating the *Recitazione* at 147–56.

[6] Dall'Aglio, *Savonarola,* introduces the extensive bibliography.

[7] Bacchelli (*Morte*, 42) proposes the model of Socrates' death. For Poliziano's letter, see Poliziano, *Letters* vol. 1, bk. 4, letter 2, and the analysis by Godman, *From Poliziano to Machiavelli,* chap. 1.

[8] For more straightforwardly managerial instructions on consolation, see Paglia, *"La pietà dei carcerati,"*

and in conjunction with the closing thoughts on tyranny (*Rec.* 48–49), intimates a veiled form of political history.[9] The *Recitazione* is included here, however, as a model comforting text: it represents the material details, the conversational directives, and the emotional currents of the *conforteria* (*consolateria* for the classicizing Florentines) by the book, so to speak.[10] On one hand, this close fit is hardly surprising—indeed is almost tautological—for the *Recitazione* is, alongside St. Catherine of Siena's famous letter to Raymond of Capua about the death of Niccolò da Toldo (1375), one of the comforting tradition's foundational documents. But on the other hand, the fit is somewhat disconcerting, for della Robbia was neither a San Marco friar nor a member of the Confraternity of the Blacks (towards whom he is somewhat reserved; e.g., *Rec.* 32).[11] But he had clearly absorbed the practices of the *consolateria* and the related format of the Savonarolan "art of dying well."

Or rather, the *Recitazione* proves he had absorbed those practices if we are in fact dealing with a text that has not been manipulated by later readers to express them. For della Robbia's *ricordo* demands caution on two counts: not only because it is such an emotionally wrought fusion of narrative forms, but also because the twelve manuscripts so far identified must be dated at least a century after the event.[12] For some readers, this late manuscript tradition will irreparably damage the *Recitazione*'s authority. Other readers will point out aspects of language and content to argue that the manuscripts are unlikely to have been substantially manipulated; they will treat the *Recitazione* as difficult but not impossible evidence for the events and sentiments it purports to represent.

But the late date of the *Recitazione* manuscripts is only the first problem. Readers confront a second methodological decision regarding its interpretation. At one extreme, those who approach the *Recitazione* as a straightforward document will discover a historical account that is relatively unadorned, transparent, and true to the author's statement of intention (*Rec.* 1–3)—all in all, a

---

254–58, which transcribes a Jesuit document from 1550 Rome.

[9] On the republican politics of the *Recitazione,* see Marchi, *Testi cinquecenteschi,* 11–14; and in depth, Jurdjevic, *Guardians of Republicanism,* chap. 4.

[10] For Trexler (*Public Life,* 197–205), the *Recitazione* reliably demonstrates the socially integrative work of the ritual. Compare more literary readings, cautious about della Robbia's representation of Boscoli's passage through the ritual, by Weinstein, "The Art of Dying Well"; and Falvey, "Scaffold and Stage" in this volume.

[11] Verde ("La congregazione di S. Marco," 183n13) establishes that della Robbia was not a San Marco friar, although two cousins of his were.

[12] For a list of these manuscripts, see page 324 below. For more on them and attention to their variants, see Frazier, *Death of Pietro Paolo Boscoli.*

reliable reflection of its Savonarolan context. The traditional approach to the *Recitazione* favors this documentary reading. Filippo Luigi Polidori, for example, assumed that della Robbia set down his experiences and impressions of the events immediately and without calculation, while Ricardo Bacchelli remarked that the humanist wrote with an "art that [he] did not consider art."[13] At the other extreme (rather familiar after the linguistic turn) are those readers who cast the *Recitazione* as literature. They discover a translucent and complexly motivated narrative, one that is riven rather than stabilized by its Savonarolan subtext and its ostensible documentary status. Arsenio Frugoni and Katherine Falvey have proposed that we bear in mind the analogy of theater as we approach the comforting process.[14] As the play's director, author della Robbia is neither naive nor unambitious.[15] That possibility invites at least an elementary distinction between that author and "della Robbia," the first-person narrator who arrives at the Bargello chapel to observe, to comfort, and to record. The author profits from readers' failure to make this distinction (indeed, from their quite fascinating desire not to make it), since that failure secures the truth-effect of the narrative. But the narrator's part may be crafted—just as crafted as the personae of the two condemned men: the putative hero and his antitype.[16] We see the same crafting in the "good" and "bad" confessors, Fra Cipriano and Fra Iacopo, and in the group persona of the Confraternity of the Blacks—well-meaning and devout, but spiritually and emotionally clumsy.

Three different aspects of the *Recitazione*—the depiction of friendship, the direct and indirect references to Savonarola, and the humanist language and models used in composition—clarify what is at stake in these disagreements about reading and interpreting the text, and also serve to introduce readers to its historical context.

---

[13] Bacchelli, *Morte,* 42–43. Pincin ("Boscoli," 219b) observes, "In realtà non possediamo elementi per datare lo scritto."

[14] Frugoni, "Morte di Pietro Paolo Boscoli," 94; and Falvey, "Scaffold and Stage" in this volume.

[15] Pincin ("Boscoli," 220a), addressing "[l]a natura squisitamente letteraria del testo," notes that della Robbia admits exercising a principle of selection (*Rec.* 3).

[16] Capponi and Boscoli are presented quite differently (Frugoni, "Morte di Pietro Paolo Boscoli," 95), but scholars disagree on the nature of the difference. For Lazzerini (*Nessuno,* 5), Boscoli's "insofferenza" contrasts unfavorably with Capponi's "serenità"; for Trexler (*Public Life,* 202) and Lazzaretti ("Capponi," 6b–7a), Capponi is restless and discontent. Compare Capponi's chatter and noisy commendations (e.g., *Rec.* 38, 48) not just to Boscoli's managed conversation and movingly recited prayers, but also to Savonarola's directions on prayer. Note also the men's contrasting relationships to money and to the writing of their bequests (e.g. *Rec.* 11, 17, 31), as well as della Robbia's report on the set of Capponi's face after execution (*Rec.* 47). As the word "sincerità" occurs only here, when it seems to be delicately in question, one gathers that the *Recitazione* was written to establish Boscoli's sincerity.

Managing friendship

Della Robbia was no mere observer of Boscoli's passage: the emotional force of the *Recitazione* arises from the fact that he was a fully engaged participant. He had, for example, experienced imprisonment and interrogation himself, and was on close terms with other victims of this Medici campaign against the republicans.[17] His engagement is most powerfully grounded, however, in the deep friendship that bound the comforter and the condemned. Luca della Robbia loved Pietro Paolo Boscoli.[18] Nothing more is known about their relationship than the claims of the *Recitazione* itself (e.g., *Rec.* 1, 5, 8, 23, etc.), but a portrait of friendship is one undeniable achievement of the narrative. It emerges most simply in how della Robbia eases Boscoli's last hours by comforting, praying, reading, expounding, and advising. At Boscoli's own request, della Robbia undertakes some practical duties of friendship: promising to deliver coins, to observe a vow, and to care for Boscoli's mother (*Rec.* 11, 17, 33). Della Robbia reports on the beheaded men's facial expressions, finding in Boscoli's a peacefulness that suggests his soul is safe, and then carries Boscoli's coffin to burial (*Rec.* 47), explictly joining friendship to patriotism.

The men's closeness appears not only in the *Recitazione*'s content, but also in its syntax, as the broken vernacular suggests sincerity. Now intimate, now formal, the shifting registers encourage the deduction that della Robbia wrote in haste, beset by emotion, anxious to honor Boscoli and to set the public record straight about his friend's character (*Rec.* 29). The epilogue, reporting a conversation with Boscoli's confessor three months later, cites Aquinas to dismiss the criminal charges that had led to Boscoli's imprisonment and execution in the first place (*Rec.* 29, 48–49). The confessor certifies Boscoli's innocence, sanctifying the traitor as a martyr. Thus, with the *Recitazione*, della Robbia performs the friend's final office by enshrining Boscoli among the just. By struggling through to this verdict of political innocence, however, della Robbia manages to cancel the point of the *consolateria*, which was to bring the condemned to accept without complaint the justice of the secular sentence. He himself, in the persona of the narrator, had pointed out to Agostino Capponi that such efforts at self-justification were forbidden (*Rec.* 31).

---

[17] Della Robbia's imprisonment occurred in April 1498, following Savonarola's execution; see Villari, *Storia di Girolamo Savonarola*, 2:ccxxxix–ccxlii, from ASF, Signori, Carteggi, Minutari n. 16, fols. 161r–162v (corrected collocation from Verde, "La congregazione," 183n13).

[18] Cf. Savonarola, *Compendium philosophiae naturalis*, 6.25–41, on *amicitia*. See also Kent, *Friendship, Love and Trust*.

Imitating Savonarola

Scholarly readings of the *Recitazione* have paid close attention to the Savonarolan aspects of the text.[19] These aspects were frankly seditious, under renewed Medici rule. Thus it matters that they are not just verbal, as when the narrator della Robbia paraphrases Savonarolan exegesis to strengthen Boscoli's Christian resolve (e.g., *Rec.* 24). Della Robbia also courts danger by offering his friend the physical model of Savonarola's passage to death (*Rec.* 27). Awaiting execution, Savonarola trusted God's mercy and so received forgiveness; Boscoli should do the same. What needs forgiving, at this point in the narrative, are not the political crimes dismissed in the epilogue—if that were the case, the *Recitazione* would not be a famously representative text of the comforting tradition. Rather, divine mercy is called down to forgive original sin (*Rec.* 25, 31) and sinful acts like the betrayal of others under torture (*Rec.* 13, 27). Della Robbia follows Savonarola in citing the great "traitor" Peter, who secured Christ's forgiveness in spite of having denied him three times. By attending the death of a young, gifted humanist, guiding him to salvation, della Robbia himself follows the example of Savonarola's attendance on Pico della Mirandola.

Della Robbia thus commemorates the friar in at least three ways. He offers Savonarola's words and holds up Savonarola's model to Boscoli, and then, in his own body, he inhabits Savonarola's guiding role to manage his friend's passage. The loving comforter simply must achieve the prisoner's conversion, for the success of Savonarola's posthumous reputation and thus the politics of his supporters, the *piagnone,* hangs on it.

Writing the humanist vernacular

Since only late manuscripts of the *Recitazione* remain, we do not have an accurate representation of della Robbia's vernacular. Nonetheless, scholars have long appreciated linguistic aspects of his narrative: Polidori's 1842 edition, for example, concludes with an index of notable usages (that list is, in fact, one way to counter the suspicion of textual manipulation). Moreover, contemporary models abound that provide a sense of della Robbia's Tuscan. That he would write in the vernacular seems obvious enough. The formats and functions of

---

[19] Most recently, Jurdjevic (*Guardians of Republicanism,* chap. 4) analyzes della Robbia's *Recitazione,* his *Vita di Bartolommeo Valori,* and Niccolò Valori's contribution to the family *ricordanze* to demonstrate the Valori family's Savonarolan sympathies. For an older, complementary approach, see Cantimori, "Il caso del Boscoli."

ricordo, ars moriendi, and *consolateria* demanded the mother tongue, even if models from Seneca, Plato, and Boethius, not to mention the range of humanist experiments with consolatory literature, moral-philosophical dialogue, and saints' lives, might have suggested other possibilities.

Della Robbia's Tuscan was not, however, the artless vernacular of a man unlearned in Latin. While still in his early twenties, della Robbia edited four volumes of classical texts for the Florentine publisher Filippo Giunti.[20] It was serious work, not only because Giunti imitated Venetian Aldus Manutius by producing octavo volumes in italic font (and often by mimicking Aldus's choice of titles), but also because della Robbia's prefatory letters were ambitious and suggestive. He chose elite dedicatees, marking their importance with fulsome praise of history and philosophy as sources of virtue; "civic humanism" predominates.[21] First came two biographical-historical works. Quintus Curtius Rufus's *Historia magni Alexandri* (December 1507) was dedicated to another Alessandro, the son of Donato Acciaiuoli, who had translated the *Nicomachean Ethics*; *Caesar's Commentaries* (April 1508) went to the more platonically inclined Niccolò Valori, who would suffer for his part in the Boscoli-Capponi plot. Then followed two volumes of Ciceronian moral philosophy: *De Officiis, De Amicitia, De Senectute,* and *Somnium scipionis* (June 1508), dedicated to Pierfrancesco de' Medici (June 1508); and the *Tusculan Disputations* (September 1508), dedicated to Neoplatonist and Savonarolan Girolamo Benivieni. After this yearlong flurry of editorial activity came an almost five-year silence. During this time, the Medici returned to Florence, Boscoli was executed, Machiavelli composed *The Prince, and* della Robbia presumably wrote the subversive *Recitazione* while working hard to convince the Medici that he was not a threat—and succeeding, to judge from later political appointments.[22] Finally, in 1514, twenty months after Boscoli's execution, della Robbia appeared a fifth and final time as editor of a Ciceronian rhetorical collection—*De Oratore, Brutus, Topica, Oratoriae partitiones,* and *De Optimo genere oratorum* (October 1514)—dedicated to Lorenzo Segni.

With this dedicatee, della Robbia brushes disturbingly close to the matter of the *Recitazione.* Lorenzo's relative Antonio Segni had died following torture on suspicion of involvement in the Boscoli-Capponi plot; in the *Recitazione*

---

[20] Ceresa, "Giunti"; and Bandini, *Iuntarum,* 1:127–29.

[21] Baron, *Crisis*; Hankins, *Renaissance Civic Humanism*; and Jurdjevic, "Virtue, Commerce." I am grateful to Professor Jurdjevic for his thoughts on the current underappreciated status of the Baron thesis (personal communication).

[22] In 1517 and 1519; Fragnito, "della Robbia," 293a.

itself, Lorenzo's name appears twice (*Rec.* 23, 31). The dedication thus takes
on the profundity of its context, even when della Robbia simply repeats com-
monplaces: "We are born not just for ourselves; rather, our friends, our relatives, and our city each claim a part of our origins." But his former idealism has
cooled: della Robbia no longer draws his exhortations from exemplary history
or counsels the curative effects of classical philosophy. Rather, the citizen serves
by "correcting and emending codices" of rhetoric. The epistles thus enact a conversion to political quietism: civic virtue comes to rest in rhetoric's resigned
abstractions. Like his friend Benivieni, della Robbia too would "never take up
arms against the state in his hopes for a republic, but hoped that liberty would
be conceded."[23]

The contrast between della Robbia's intellectual position before and after the Boscoli affair is underscored by comparing the 1513 *Recitazione* with
della Robbia's aggressively republican, panegyrical, and classicizing Latin *vita*
of Bartolomeo Valori the Elder (d. 1477).[24] In the *Vita*, written well before the
1512 return of the Medici, Bartolomeo Valori's citizenly service is explicit,
uncomplicated, and triumphantly patriotic, just as one would expect in a humanist's secular and Latin biography. In the *Recitazione*, by contrast, written
in the shadow of the Savonarolan rupture, Boscoli's public service is implicit,
secret, subversive, and tragic. Both exemplary figures, Valori and Boscoli, are
Christian. But the tenor of the *Vita Bartholomaee*, intent as it is on the *vita
activa* of urban politics, is a classicizing filial *pietas*, expressed in a controlled
Senecan uprightness and modeled after the Roman historians Suetonius and
Plutarch. Bartolomeo operates at the highest levels of power: he serves as ambassador to popes, emperors, and cities; he is elected repeatedly to Florence's
ruling councils; his words change the course of European events. At the same
time, his *caritas* reaches down to benefit even Florence's poorest citizens. The
Recitazione, in contrast, intent on death and eternal salvation, acknowledges
the relationships that sustained the power of Florence's oligarchs only to set
those earthly ties aside. It acknowledges wealth only to shrug off its import.
What emerges is not quite a *vita contemplativa*, for Boscoli is too pressed for
time and must, according to the Savonarolan script, suffer a heroic death on
the active, martyrological model. If Valori's stoic *apatheia* is celebrated when
he tearlessly accepts the deaths of son and wife, Boscoli's last burning wish is
to escape stoicism. He is not afraid to die (*Rec.* 34), he is afraid to die without

[23] Polizzotto, *Elect Nation*, 249; and Roush, "Dante as Piagnone Prophet."

[24] Jurdjevic, *Guardians of Republicanism*, chap. 4, discusses the circumstances of composition.

God. And he cannot think of any other way to be sure of his closeness to God than hot tears and mystic absorption.

In this last respect, at least, the *Recitazione* reveals a humanist yearning after late medieval women's spirituality—that affective and corporeal piety that joined God's transcendence and immanence, just as Boscoli wanted.[25] Like those medieval women, for whom the vernacular was also the necessary idiom, so too the men who strove after such signs of sanctity became suspect, for the institutional church could apprehend and control the internal life—so valued by Savonarola—only indirectly. The beauty of the *Recitazione* is that it opens two men's brave spiritual lives to us still.

---

[25] On the affective and somatic qualities of late medieval women's spirituality, and male interest in it, see for example Coakley, *Women, Men*; and the classic Bynum, *Holy Feast*.

Narrative of the Death of Pietro Paolo Boscoli and of Agostino Capponi

Preface[26]

1. I recall how, on the 22nd of February in 1513, a Tuesday afternoon during Lent, Agostino di Bernardo Capponi and Pietro Paolo di Giachinotto Boscoli were condemned to die as conspirators against the house of Medici, for having wanted to free the city and to kill Giuliano and Lorenzo and Messer Giulio, as the truth came out at their interrogation.[27] They were held four days from the 18th, which was a Friday night, up to that Tuesday. On Tuesday evening, I, Luca di Simone di Marco della Robbia, knowing that they had to die, was drawn by great compassion to console (as much as I could) Pietro Paolo, to whom I was very close. I wanted to know also if he was indeed the man that I and many of his friends had judged him to be, gifted with a great soul and with not less prudence and Christian faith. I was present at the Bargello the whole night, from about 8 all the way up to the time of his death, which was at about 4 in the morning.[28]

2. Because I knew that he was a man of singular intellect and well educated, and that he spoke with great vigor, I noted diligently all his words, both questions and replies, and kept them in my memory. And so that such a great and well-formed example of strength and spiritedness would not be lost after the condemnation of such a good, noble, and generous citizen—a young man of about thirty-two years, "blonde and handsome and noble to behold,"[29] but

---

[26] This is a simplified version of della Robbia's text. Frazier, *Death of Pietro Paolo Boscoli*, includes full commentary with full introduction. Paragraphing and speech indentations have been added for ease of consultation, and do not occur in the manuscripts.

[27] Della Robbia gives the year as 1512 according to the traditional Florentine calendar, which began the new year at the Feast of the Annunciation (25 March).

[28] The Bargello was the seat of the *podestà* and the Otto. Della Robbia's traditional approximate timekeeping is silently modernized throughout (he counts from evening prayers at sunset in February in Florence); Bacchelli, "Morte di Pietro Paolo Boscoli," 63n.

[29] Thus ("biondo e bello e di gentile aspetto") Dante describes Manfredi, son of Emperor Frederick II and Bianca Lana of Sicily; *Purgatorio* 3.107, cf. 108.

shortsighted—so, I say, that memory of him would not be lost, I wrote down the things that he said on that night, faithfully writing the truth, neither cutting nor adding (and of this I call to witness God, and the Confraternity of the Blacks and many others who were bystanders), to recite all his words. From these words can be grasped his magnanimity, his outstanding devotion to his hometown, his mother, and brothers, and his singular kindness towards his friends, but above all, his patience, humility, faith, hope, and charity, and finally the perfect conformity of his will with that of God.

3. And in order to write more truly, I will also put down the words of others, such as those of the confessor, and of the above-mentioned Agostino Capponi, and of others. So that the narration may be perfect, I will begin from the beginning, following all the way to the end, leaving aside, however, his least words and those from which no lesson, but only bits of information, can be deduced—they were very few. But before I begin, let everyone who will read this present recollection know that he can trust it as a thing told truly and without passion, for it would disturb my conscience more than a little to write lies, especially on such a subject which, if I am not mistaken, pertains strongly to the Christian faith.

The blessing

4. And so, in the name of Jesus Christ and of the Blessed Mary and of the holy apostles and especially of Peter and Paul after whom he had been named, let this be the beginning.

The narrative

5. At about 8 o'clock, having had his supper, Boscoli was brought with his legs in irons to the chapel where the Confraternity of the Blacks waited with others. And when he arrived there he was told that he had to die by someone there from the household of the *capitano* who spoke rather poorly, like a man who barely knew the vernacular, and who finished off his task in a couple of words, in such a way that few were aware of it.

Yet Pietro Paolo cried out, "Oh Pietro Paolo, oh poor Pietro Paolo! What has become of you!"

Then I, moved by the greatest compassion, seeing my beloved friend in such great distress, went first to him as lovingly as I could, with a gesture full of mercy, and greeted him like this: "God save you, dearest friend. 'Do not fear those who kill the body, for they cannot kill the soul'" [Matt. 10:28].

And he, as though he had not recognized me, did not respond to me at all, but said, "I want Fra Zanobi Acciaiuoli, for I told the *signory* of the Otto that, having to die, I wanted to stay four hours with the confessor, and they promised me that.[30] See that I get it." And I, comforting him, told him that he would be consoled.

6. Soon a man came to tell us that Fra Zanobi was not in Florence, but at Rome. Then he said, "See that I get someone from there, because I need a man who is learned and good."[31]

"Don't worry," I replied, "you will be consoled."

"I have little time, and I am too loaded down with food, and I have eaten salty things, so that I don't feel able to join my spirit to God." And suddenly he cried out, "God have mercy on me, that these men have weighed me down with food! Oh, thoughtlessness! If they had told me before dinner, I would have eaten just a little and that would have been enough."

7. Then in came Agostino Capponi with his legs in irons too, and perceiving that Pietro Paolo was lamenting, he spoke as if to reprove and comfort him: "Oh, Pietro Paolo, Pietro Paolo, do you not die willingly? What are you doing?"

"Oh, Agostino, I die willingly. But I regret two things. First, that Antonio Serristori and Piero Ridolfi fed me this morning with hope for life, and somehow I clamped onto it.[32] The other, that they gave me too much to eat. How can I turn my spirit towards God?"

"Don't be afraid. Just let us die willingly."

8. Sitting down, Boscoli turned to me saying, "You see, Luca."

"Yes, dear friend." I added, "For some time, Pietro Paolo, I have been persuaded by an idea, and if you too believe it deeply, I do not doubt that you will take this step, which is a great one, with little effort. And it is this, that not

[30] The humanist poet, translator, and librarian Zanobi Acciaiuoli (1461–1519) experienced political imprisonment in 1494, and subsequently joined the Dominicans. He took the habit from Savonarola himself and lived for some time at San Marco, managing the temporary placement of the Medici library there. His last months were spent as Vatican Librarian to Leo X.

[31] When Boscoli asks for someone "from there," he means someone from the Dominican convent of San Marco. This Florentine convent passed in 1435 from the Benedictine order to the Dominican Observance. From 1490, San Marco was firmly associated with Savonarola.

[32] Antonio Serristori and Piero Ridolfi were members of the pro-Medici Otto di Guardia.

one leaf falls from a tree unless God wills it."[33]

He replied, "I believe it surely. But see to it, Luca, that I have that confessor, for the time is very short. I have a big burden: the truth is that I don't have any restitution to make."

"That's pretty good."

"Oh, Luca! I have always been ungrateful to God, and have offended him in every way. Still, I hope in his mercy."

"That is what is important. 'Why then is your soul sad, and why are you distressed? Hope in God, for when you will have confessed to him, you will see him face to face'" [Ps. 42:5].

9. He said, "On with it." And rising from his seat to lie on the mattress with his feet in fetters, he spoke thus: "Since it pleases God that we be the first to be made an example to this people, let us be at it." And taking a position lying down in the usual way, he turned to me and said, "Luca, this confessor?"

I replied, "Okay, but you have to understand that I don't know if you can have a friar from San Marco, because you know they are under suspicion, so that I doubt they will want to come here. Isn't there someone at the abbey you like?"[34]

"Who is there?"

"There is the abbot, who is Don Giovanni Battista Sacchetti, and some others, who are considered good confessors."[35]

"I need one who can stir my emotion. See if I can have one from there."

10. And as he spoke these words, there came Stefano, the illuminator of letters, and he offered to go to San Marco to try to get him consolation.[36] And then there came another man and he said, "Messer Iacopo Manelli is here. He can take him."[37]

"I don't want Messer Iacopo," Pietro Paolo responded with a loud and free voice. Turning to the aforementioned Stefano, he said, "Go to San Marco, and bring the one from Lucca" (meaning Fra Santi, but he did not know that

---

[33] Cf. Matt. 10:29, echoed in a popular rhyming Italian proverb: "non cade foglia che Dio non voglia."

[34] San Marco was under suspicion as a hotbed of Savonarolan anti-Mediceanism. The abbey referred to here was the Benedictine Badia Fiorentina di S. Maria, near the Bargello. It was founded in the tenth century and in 1437 it entered the reforming Congregation of S. Giustina.

[35] Giovanni Battista Niccoli Sacchetti professed at the Badia on 15 June 1488 and served as abbot from 1511 to 1512; he died at Rome the following year while abbot of S. Paolo.

[36] This Stefano may be the person mentioned in Vasari's Vite (Florence: Giunti, 1568), pt. 3, 471–73, as a student of the well-known Gherardo miniatore (1446–97); Polidori, "Notizie," 287n11.

[37] Manelli was known to be a Medici partisan; Bacchelli, "Morte di Pietro Paolo Boscoli," 75n.

name, which he did not use in San Marco).[38]

"If he can't come," I said, "get Fra Serafino" (a friar, in my opinion, quite suitable to Boscoli's nature).[39]

11. In the middle of this, turning to those standing around, he said, "Ah! Be still! Don't bother me!"—because they came up to him one after another. "Luca here is enough for me; he knows my nature. If I want anything, I'll tell him. You others pray to God for me." And pulling from his sleeve a memorandum [*ricordo*] written in his own hand while in prison, addressed to his brothers, he told me to give it to them, and he said, "Here is written all my business and my will. I leave no obligations at all, except that they sometimes pray to God for me." And he gave me a separate instruction about his brothers and asked my opinion and I approved his arrangement. He said, "Anyway, Luca, read this memorandum."

And so I did, before and after his death, and I took from it great consolation, for it contained spirited passages and great devotion towards his mother and his brothers; from which he took great comfort in being able to console his mother, saying always that he died willingly. I gave the memorandum to his brother Francesco and it is in their house. A memorandum, indeed, to read willingly.[40]

12. He started in on his mother, saying, "Who will console her in such great tribulation? Poor woman! She's done for!"

I replied, "Pietro Paolo, I have spoken with her."

"Really?"

"From Sunday on, I have been there every day, and she, although her feelings are troubled, still her reason is comforted by God, because you know that she is a good person and does not lack for comforters. The nuns were there from Faenza and they comforted her greatly." [41]

"She is indeed a good person."

"So that you might believe that I have been there, you sent today for a

---

[38] The reference may be to S. Pagnini of Lucca (1470–1536), whom Vincenzo Quirini had unsuccessfully invited to join the Camaldulensian order in 1512; Polizzotto, *Elect Nation,* 157n96. Within the next decade, after moving to Lyons, Pagnini would complete the first full new translation of the Hebrew Bible; Centi, "L'attività letteraria di Santi Pagnini."

[39] Perhaps Frater Serafinus Pauli de Bellandinis of Florence (1477–1535), named in Creytens, "Les actes de la congrégation," 217, entry 78, as an excellent preacher.

[40] Or "I remember, indeed, that I read it willingly" (Ricordo, certo, da leggerlo volentieri).

[41] The Faenza nuns came from the Vallumbrosan convent founded by the mystic St. Umiltà (1226–1310, can. 1948).

pair of socks, that I was there."

"Yes, I sent for those socks as a sign of leave-taking from my mother and of the love that I have always felt for her."[42]

13. Then he started in on the interrogation, telling me certain things about Niccolò Valori, since he appeared to think he was dead.[43] And he charged me to say to Ser Zanobi, one of the Eight, that he should remove certain words, and so it was done.[44] In the same way also he began to talk to me about Agostino Capponi, lamenting that he [Capponi] had been a little hasty in drawing up that conspiracy, and nevertheless that in the interrogation he [Boscoli] had burdened him with it somewhat. And he said to me, "Does he think that I will ask his forgiveness now?"

"Confess first to God, and then ask his forgiveness," I replied.

"Okay, that's what I will do" (again, as I described, they were things of little importance).

14. Then he said again, "Ah, Luca, see that no one else comes here. I don't want to be disturbed."

"Don't worry, no one else will come here," I replied. "Wouldn't you be happy if that relative of yours from the Giugni family (who was Antonio di Francesco) were here with us?"[45]

"I like him." Then he said, "Ah, Luca, pull Brutus from my head, so that I can make this passage entirely as a Christian."[46]

"That's not hard, since you wish to die a Christian. Anyway, you know that those things about the Romans are not written simply, but with cunning."

"And even if they were true, what does it matter to me, since they didn't know the true goal."

"Look, you yourself have cured yourself."

"Luca, don't praise me."

---

[42] Bacchelli suggests that the wool socks may symbolize Boscoli's final journey ("Morti di Pietro Paolo Boscoli," 78). No scholar has otherwise accounted for these socks ("calcetti"; also slippers or leggings) as homely proof of Luca della Robbia's visit to Boscoli's mother.

[43] On Niccolò Valori, see Jurdjevic, *Guardians of Republicanism*. Boscoli feared that his deposition had led to Valori's execution; Bacchelli, "Morte di Pietro Paolo Boscoli," 79n.

[44] Without the removal of these words, Niccolò Valori might have suffered more than the two years' imprisonment at Volterra and the lifetime exile to Città di Castello that was imposed upon him; Polidori, "Notizie," 289n15. Ser Zanobi di Tommaso di Puccio Pucci was *proveditore* to Balía appointees of 22 September 1512.

[45] The Latin form of the family name Giugni is Junius (see note 46).

[46] Marcus Junius Brutus, assassin of Julius Caesar, was placed by Dante alongside Judas Iscariot in the lowest circle of hell (*Inf.* 9.34); see Lazzerini, *Nessuno è innocente*, 33–41. Della Robbia may refer also to Lucius Brutus, avenger of Lucretia and opponent of kings (Livy, 1.59).

"No, far be it from me. I am here to help you. Just tell me what you need. Then I will be strong, with God's help, to console you, or rather, you will console me."

15. And he said, "My intellect believes the faith and wishes to die Christian, but it seems to be forcing me. And I seem to have a hard heart. I don't know if I can explain my perception."

"I have understood it. You want to have a sweet love for God, with tears and sighs, and you want your intellect to consent spontaneously to the faith."

"Yes, that's it."

"Pietro Paolo, the second thing is not necessary for salvation, but it is good if we have the first. It's to your credit that you force your intellect and submit it to the faith, although I think that soon it will not seem to you forced, and so also you will have tears, because you are going to have some help, that is, confession, communion, indulgences, and the prayers of the bystanders. Don't waver, just aim to have all your desire fixed on God, for he says, 'Son, give me your heart' [Prov. 23:26]. Give him your heart, and let him take care of things."

"If only that were enough! Is it enough? I do it." And he added, "Lord, I am yours. Do with me what you will, so that I may please you."

16. Then one of the bystanders said to me, "Let him see the *tavoluccia*."[47]

"No need for the *tavoluccia*," he replied. "I'll be in a bad way, if I don't recognize him without the *tavoluccia*." And as though he were somewhat distracted, he said to me, "Oh, Luca! You should have written me off when you heard that I was taken."

"You know that I recognized the danger. I prayed to God for you, and cried and cried. Then I said to myself, 'I know that if Pietro Paolo saw me, he would rebuke me, saying that friendship ought not to be soft and effeminate.'"

"You know well that death does not trouble me," he said, "because we must all die, but my mother comes to my mind. Can't I at least see my brothers?"

"Your mother and your brothers are Christ, according to the gospel." Then Anton Giugni, who was still there, recited to him the exact words of Christ, when the disciple asked him, "And are these your relatives?" etc., and Christ's response [Matt. 12:46–48]. And he replied, "Well said."

17. And turning to me, he said, "Has my family prayed for my life?"[48]

---

[47] On the *tavoluccia*, or *tavoletta*, see the article by Ferretti in this volume.

[48] "Prayer" is meant in perhaps the broadest sense, since Venetian chronicler Marin Sanuto reports that the

"Yes," I said, "everything has been done, and your mother and the others have given you to God, and take great consolation hoping that God will not abandon you."

"So be it." Then pulling out some coins, which were few, from his handkerchief, he gave them to me so that I would take them to his house, and then he said to me, "I was wrong earlier when I replied loudly that I did not want Messer Iacopo, since he was present. I know I was bad."

"No," I replied, "you didn't do it to offend him, but because it didn't seem to suit your needs to confess to him."

"That's how we excuse ourselves."

18. Then, "Luca, I have little time. I would need to be with the good friars for a month. I think I could become completely spiritual. But I hope in God that in this night he will help me." And suddenly he asked for water to drink. "So that," he said, "I can get rid of some of this salty food." And thus he drank a flask of water with great civility. Then, turning to me, he said, "Luca, they gave me eight drops of the rope, and from that I realized that they wanted to finish me off.[49] Nevertheless, thanks to God, I do not feel in myself the least glimmer of hate towards any citizen. And I know that Antonio Serristori and Piero Ridolfi like me, because before this incident they were pleasant and kind to me, and I don't feel bad about having to die, for after all, they take from me twenty-five years of life, and I, as you know, have never done well in this world, nor do I know if I would have, because the whole world could not suffice to content me.[50] But I feel bad about the short time that they have given me to recognize my goal, which is God."

19. "Luca, this food is impeding me, so that I cannot unite myself with God as I would like. And still I seem to have a hard heart, and many images come into my mind, and it seems to be taking the confessor a thousand years to get here."

"He should be here soon. Pietro Paolo, don't let this food bother you, who have nothing more to do with men, but with God, whose mercy is infinite and whose generosity has no measure. He doesn't look at food, but rather at your heart. Make yourself be full of love for him." And briefly I told him Christ's parable from the Gospel of St. Luke about the two debtors, where it is concluded that he who loves more, finds more mercy from God. "Many sins

---

family attempted to intercede for Boscoli with the Medici and with the Otto; Bacchelli, "Morte di Pietro Paolo Boscoli," 86n.

[49] Boscoli here refers to torture by strappado.

[50] Boscoli, aged thirty-five, assumes that the natural term of his life would be sixty years.

will be forgiven him, for he loves much," Christ says there [Luke 7:47].

20. And he said, "If it's enough that I have a ready desire to please God, with grief for my sins, that I do have. But I don't yet feel a certain sweetness as I would like."

"That desire is enough, and the sweetness is not necessary, nor are tears. But I hope that you will have them."

And he, with great effect, said "'Have mercy on me, God, according to your great mercy' [Ps. 51:3], not according to the mercy that men have, but according to yours, which is great."[51]

"Shall we say some psalms?"

"Luca, I can only say Paternosters and Ave Marias," wishing to say that he did not know the psalms by heart, and he said this with grief.

"That is the best prayer that can be said. If you want, go ahead and say the Paternoster by yourself." And so he did, silently, with great devotion.

21. Then I said to him, "Pietro Paolo, don't you think that God has worked this grace, by bringing you to a place where you may recognize yourself, and so may recognize him, too?"

"I understand it that way, and may God be thanked forever."

"Let us speak the truth. Hadn't you lost your goal up till now, or at least misplaced it?"

"Lost, lost. Only let me recover it in so short a time."

"The thief had less time and so did many others. Just have faith."

"Read me the creed of St. Athanasius."

And as I found it to read it, he said to me, "It would be better if I read it."

I replied, "I would like that." And he, having taken, with his sleeves, the little booklet, read about twelve lines with such feeling that it made the bystanders weep.[52]

22. Then he said, "Enough." And turning to me, he said, "Luca, tell our friends that they should study sacred scripture, that a man continues with the habits contracted in this life even in death, and I have lost a lot of time." And seeing that I was crying, he said, "Luca, don't do that. Help me for the rest of this time, and after my death, pray to God for me."

---

[51] Contemporary readers would have thought immediately of Savonarola's Latin meditation on Psalm 50/51, "Miserere me Deus," written while he was in prison and frequently printed both in Latin and vernacular. For the English text, see Donnelly, *Girolamo Savonarola*; for the modern Italian text, see Centi, *Girolamo Savonarola*.

[52] To hold an honored book with one's sleeves or with a cloth, rather than bare hands, is a traditional gesture of respect; it is often depicted in presentation pages of medieval manuscripts.

And I, repressing my tears as much as I could, said, "So I will, and when you are in blessedness, where I hope you are going, remember me."

"I will do it." And suddenly he said, "What sort of death do we have to die?"

"I don't know."

And he added, "Let it be what God wants."

23. Then he said, "Luca, I'm wanting to know when was the last time I talked to you before I was taken."

"It was Friday night about sunset, in the shop of Pier Guicciardini when Lorenzo Segni was there, that I held you for a moment by the hand, and wanted to accompany you to the Palazzo, where you wanted to go, and you did not want that.[53] About two hours from then, or earlier, according to what I heard, you were taken."

"Was it, eh? The nighttime?"

"Yes."

"True, I remember well now. Luca, don't abandon me! You are in an unpleasant situation."

"Oh, Pietro Paolo! How could I abandon you? Why did I come here? You know the love that I have always borne for you."

"It is reciprocated, and not without reason."

24. Then he said "Listen, read me, if you will, a passion."

"Okay, which one do we want?"

"As you please."

"Let's take the one by St. John."

And before I could begin to read, he said, "Luca, when some beautiful exposition occurs to you, say it."

"Pietro Paolo, that's a burden on my shoulders, for I have neither the insight nor the training in holy scriptures."

"This is no time for formalities, do what I told you, say whatever God inspires in you."

And so I began to read, and where it seemed fitting, I spoke as much as God granted, and he seemed to take great consolation from it. And at the words, "I am" [John 18:6], at which the Jews fell back, I spoke to him about the eternity of God, which *is*, strictly speaking, because other things do not

[53] Boscoli seems to have been on his way to the Signoria, or main government building, when he was arrested. Lorenzo Segni, father of the historian Bernardo Segni, was a Savonarolan sympathizer. The Guicciardini family were silk merchants and bankers; the figure mentioned in this sentence is probably Piero di Iacopo di Piero (d. 1513), father of Francesco Guicciardini, the historian.

exist except insofar as they participate in him, but there was no need to place his limit there, because there, no days exist. And therefore the prophet said, "Make known to me, God, my end, and the number of my days" [Ps. 39:4]. And these words I expounded to him according to the exposition of Fra Girolamo in the first sermon on Amos about the psalm, "I will guard my ways" [Ps. 39], although that is the exposition of St. Augustine on the psalms, but made more accessible by the Friar.[54]

25. Then he, all uplifted, said, "I can pretty well conceive [Christ's] divinity, that is, the believing in it and imagining it according to our capacity to imagine such a thing, if it can be called a thing, for we have no word for it. But I do believe it, and thinking about it, I am quite satisfied. But [his] humanity I cannot imagine so well, although I believe it, you understand."

"Say it out," I said.

With great emotion, he replied, "I wish that the humanity of Christ would offer itself to me and I want to understand it as if he were to come out of the woods and run into me."

"Who do you think he is? You are a sinful man, still a traveler, with faculties that don't allow you to distinguish clearly. Go slowly, Pietro Paolo. Make yourself humble with faith. Forget this 'woods,' which may be a trick 'of our enemy the devil, who circles round like a roaring lion, seeking whom he may devour, and whom we, in faith, must resist' [1 Peter 5:8–9]. Say with David, 'Lord, my heart is not exalted, nor are my eyes lifted up, nor did I walk in great acts and in marvels, but I sat humbly'" [Ps. 131:1–2].

And then he said, "So I wish to do. 'I will not walk in great acts and in marvels above me, Lord Jesus, but I shall sit humbly.'"

26. Then he said to me, "Keep reading."

I, continuing, told him some things literally, but more often spoke allegorically about the meanings of the gospel, as much as the Holy Spirit allowed, showing him at length how willingly Christ suffered for us, always in humble and gentle suffering, and completely intent on fulfilling the mystery of our redemption, and how he bore all for love of us. When I got to that passage where the servant of Caiaphas strikes Jesus Christ [John 18:22], I told him that I thought that that servant had been a flatterer.

He replied, "Why would you think that he was otherwise?" And he added,

---

[54] The Friar here is Savonarola. See Augustine, "Commentary on Ps. 39" [38 in Vulgate numbering], in *Ennarrationes in Psalmos,* ed. Weidmann.

"Ah, if only I could cry a little at the passion of my Lord! Turn to liquid, hard heart of mine. Do you not know that I die willingly? Come with me sweetly. It's not obedient, Luca. It's still hard. Is the desire enough for him?"

"You know well that it's enough. Don't torment yourself over not having tears and a heart all softly sweet, as you want. I think you will win greater merit in this battle. Just hold strongly to the faith and let all your desire be for God."

"So be it, Luca, keep reading."

26. And turning to someone who was closer by, he said, "When the confessor gets here, tell us. Is he coming, so far as you know?"

Then one of them responded, "A friar from San Marco will be here soon; he's on his way, to get here."

"Good. When he arrives, tell Luca here."

"Yes, take care," I added, "when he arrives, to tell me."

27. And I recommenced reading, turning back, and reading that passage when St. Peter denied Jesus Christ [John 18:16–23], wishing to show him how great God's mercy is, I stopped, and I sent the group a little distance away, and one to one I spoke to him thus: "Pietro Paolo, a brave man who also found himself in the position that you're now in, was Savonarola."

"I understand you, go ahead."

"When he was expounding the psalm 'Lord, have mercy on me' [Ps. 50/51:3], he was meditating on this denial by St. Peter. And he took from it a great trust that God would forgive him. And so should you yourself. Because he said that if St. Peter had been questioned infinite times, he would have denied Christ infinite times. Thank God, therefore, he said, that the questions ended. 'If there had been a thousand interrogations, there would have been a thousand denials.' And then he said, 'If St. Peter did thus in response to words, what would he have done in response to the rope and other tortures? And if words did these things, what if the Jews had come to blows?'[55] He says here that St. Peter would have said and done anything to get out of their hands. And nevertheless God pardoned him, and with the Holy Spirit he did not worry about difficulties, tortures, and his own life, for love of Christ. And this, because he no longer trusted in himself, as at first, but having bitterly lamented of his sin, he 'received strength from on high' [Acts 1:8]. And so, be humble, recognize your goal, and you will have a great grief. For although you have never denied Christ as St. Peter did, still you have denied him with

[55] A play on words in Savonarola's Latin: "et si haec fecerunt uerba, quod si Iudaei uenissent ad uerbera."

ingratitude and with other errors, as most of us do. And as St. Paul says, 'We confess him with words, but deny him with deeds'" [Titus 1:16].

28. He said, "Fools that we are! Lord, have mercy on me, for I want to follow you this night, as I am able. Oh, Luca, this exposition suits me. Fra Girolamo was a great man. In this he distinguished himself. But I can't do the same."

"The point is not distinction. Just have faith, hope, and charity. He was always busy with doctrine in the convent, skilled in scripture, and it's not surprising that in death he distinguished himself. For you, it's enough that God give you sufficient grace that you make this passage in his honor, that is, for love of him, remitting to him your sins."

"I want nothing else. 'Forgive us our debts, as we forgive our debtors, and lead us not into temptation, but deliver us from evil. In Christ our Lord, amen.'" He said these words with such great effect and feeling that it could not be told.

29. And then I was called, for the confessor had arrived and was there in the room. So rising from Pietro Paolo, I went there. It was Fra Cipriano from Pont' a Sieve, a friar from San Marco, in that year prior of San Domenico at Fiesole, who had come that evening to San Marco for other business.[56] Perhaps he was sent by the blessed God for this task, for truthfully Boscoli could not have a man more fitting, because that friar was skilled in confessing, learned, and full of warmth, quite energetic, practical, and a good administrator, very friendly and polite. To him I secretly spoke thus: "Fra Cipriano, here you have a speculative intellect to manage, a learned young man, my dear friend. I recommend him to you as strongly as I know and can. He awaits you with great desire."

Then Fra Cipriano said, "Does he believe the faith?" For already there had gone out a false rumor that he did not believe.

"You know well that he believes the faith," I replied. "Wait until you're dealing with him. You will be amazed to see such great resolution both in the faith and towards the death that he must undergo. But it is quite true that he knows he needs help. He will speak to you freely about his doubts, and I hope in God that you will console him. And before you go to him, I want to recall a notion that I have heard, not read, that St. Thomas [Aquinas] says that these conspiracies are not licit."

And he confirmed it, that St. Thomas had said it.

---

[56] The S. Marco convent chronicle identifies him as "Frater Cyprianus Petri de Cancellis ultra Pontem ad Sevem, sacerdos, obiit die 3 Julii 1513…"; Polidori, "Notizie," 298n22.

"Ah well, let him know that, so that he will not by chance be deluded about it."

And Fra Cipriano, "So I will do."

"I want to tell him that you have arrived and who you are."

"Yes, good. In the meantime I will pray here a little."

30. And I said, coming into Pietro Paolo's presence, "The confessor has arrived, a good man."

"Who is he?"

"He is," I said, "a man named Fra Cipriano, son of a peasant from Pont' a Sieve, but learned and good. God has sent him to you. I do not doubt that he will satisfy you."

"Thanks be to God. Have him come in."

And so called, Fra Cipriano came into the presence of Boscoli, by whom he was seen with all reverence, for, lying on the mattress, with his feet in fetters and manacles on his wrists, he rose a bit as best he could, and with both hands bared his head, replying to Fra Cipriano, who had said, "God save you, dearest brother."

"And you too, my father. Welcome."

And turning to me, he said, "Go away for a little. For it may be better for him if you can." And so it was done. And then I and the others went away so that he could confess very secretly.

31. As he confessed, I spoke with Agostino, who had been confessed by Messer Iacopo Manelli and had made a few bequests, written out by Messer Iacopo. I asked him if he recognized me, in order to ascertain his state of mind. Then he, quite happy but still more spirited, said, "Of course I recognize you. Recommend me to Lorenzo Segni, my godfather, that he may pray to God for me. I have to give him twenty-five ducats, which I leave here for him. Recommend me to him, for he is a good citizen and wishes to do good. You, too, pray to God for me. I die willingly although innocent."

"Oh, Agostino!" I said. "Only Jesus Christ died innocent. Let go of all ideas of justification and recommend yourself to Jesus Christ who forgives you your sins and gives you a true penitence, so that you can save your soul."

"You're right. What innocence can I have, who have always offended you, my Lord? You sent me sickness and made my friends tell me to confess, and I said, 'No need, I'll get better.' Now I recognize my ingratitude and I thank you, Lord, that you have brought me to a place where I must settle my account diligently tonight. Ah, good Lord, this is a sure sign that through the merits of your passion you wish to save me. I give myself to you, I want to be yours, I feel myself completely consoled, and even this is given to me by you."

And so fervently, with a loud voice, he spoke good words always, very bravely bearing death. And in speaking he said that he had suffered two drops of the rope, but that his sins merited much worse.

32. At this time the Confraternity of the Blacks, as was customary, began to sing the penitential psalms, or rather, to read them. Then Pietro Paolo spoke up energetically, "Fathers and brothers, I don't need this noise in my ears, it bothers me a lot. I have little time, please be quiet so that I can confess. This singing of yours doesn't please me. If you want quietly, by yourselves, to pray to God for me, I beg that of you, and will be indebted to you."

Fra Cipriano added, "Yes, each of you speak like that, silently, which will be the same, and won't bother us." And so it was done. All those men got busy praying silently to God for them, because to tell the truth the first way was rather indiscreet, although well meant.

33. Anyone who looked at Boscoli would see that he confessed with great intention and emotion, for he was very firm and still, so much so that although the time and the circumstance required it, still such firmness and stillness in such affliction consoled me somewhat. For it appeared to me that he made his confession so well and with such peace that I marveled not a little. Agostino meanwhile never ceased recommending himself [to God], almost shouting. He was so close by, that I think his manner of praying may have bothered Boscoli as he confessed.

During the confession, Pietro Paolo had me called several times, and recalled to me his deeds, and once he said, "Luca, when I was very little, I made a vow to go on foot to Santa Maria Impruneta, and I never fulfilled it.[57] Please will you take up this obligation for me? I put it upon you by right of friendship."

"By the same power I take up the obligation," I replied.

Another time, calling me, he said to me, "Luca, I recommend to you my mother, to be to her a third son. Console her as you can, which she needs, and go often to be with her while she is still alive, because I know that she will come quickly behind me. You pass by there frequently from your house. Talk with her, encourage her in her suffering, and tell her that I die willingly, that she should sometimes pray God for me."

---

[57] Santa Maria Impruneta, near Florence, was the site of a miracle-working image of the Virgin. For associated processions and miracles, see Trexler, "Florentine Religious Experience."

And I, not without tears, promised all.

34. I asked Fra Cipriano if he had given absolution, so as to be able to stay there together with them. And the friar replied not and said, "I'm absolving him now."

And after the absolution, I drew near. Fra Cipriano valiantly comforted him, encouraging him to bear death.

Then Boscoli said, "Father, don't waste time on that, because for that, the philosophers are sufficient.[58] Just help me so that I can undergo this death out of love of Christ. I want to go boldly to death, with such faith that my senses are drowned. I feel in myself a great battle, which troubles me more than death, because I am resolved to die."

Then the friar spoke to him thus, "Look, my brother. This battle that you feel, you will have to have it up to the final moment, and no Christian, saint though he may be, can free himself from it. Not that it is necessary to win, because even Jesus Christ had this contradiction between feeling and reason, and in that consists our victory. But so that you may be armed, I want you to be accompanied on this great passage by three women.[59] The first is, that I want you to believe what Jesus Christ and Holy Mother Church command. The second is, that you have a lively hope in the remission of your sins through the passion of Christ. The third is, that I want you to make this death for love of Christ and not for another reason. Just hold in your mind that your sins merit this and worse."

35. Then he replied, "You're right. I need to have three things." And thus, with other words, he repeated what the friar had said. And for the first, he spoke thus:

"I must believe what Christ commands."

"Yes, and what the church commands," Fra Cipriano added.

"What God commands."

"And the church, which is the same thing."

"Okay. I do. Second," said Boscoli, "I must have a firm hope in my salvation through the merits of the passion of Christ, and that too I have. The third is, that I must suffer this death for love of him and not for any other vanity, and also that I have, but not in the way that I would like, that is, with great emotion and warmth."

Then Fra Cipriano said, "This warmth lies in the will. Are you not content to suffer this death for love of Christ? And also to recognize that your sins

[58] This rejoinder is usually said to be a reference to della Robbia's edition of Cicero's *Tusculans*.
[59] This sort of personification would have seemed familiar to contemporaries on account of Dante's canzone "Tre donne intorno al cor mi son venute" and *Inferno*, canto 2; Bacchelli, "Morte di Pietro Paolo Boscoli," 122.

would merit this and worse?"

"Yes. But I would like more warmth of spirit. 'God, come to my aid. Lord, hasten to help me'" [Ps. 70:1].

36. Then Fra Cipriano, "That's good. Say that verse with all your feeling."

And he, again, repeated it with such force that he seemed to pull down all heaven to his aid. And he added, "'In you, Lord, have I hoped. Let me never be confounded. In your justice, deliver me'" [Ps. 31:1]. And then he said, "I feel rather comforted."

And seeing that an order was being given that they should receive the Eucharist, he turned to Fra Cipriano and said, "The sacrament that I am going to take, won't it give me great strength?"

"You know well that it will. 'You will walk in the strength of this food to Horeb, the mountain of God'" [1 Kings 19:8].

"So I hope." And turning to me, he said, "Luca, take that *tavoluccia* and hold it like this in front of me, because I don't want to be distracted by seeing anyone." And so I did.

37. And suddenly he said, "Luca, if any of our friends are here who want to talk to me, it would be good if they came now, because later at the time of communion I don't want to be bothered, and also afterwards."

Fra Cipriano said, "Yes, he's right."

"I'll see if there is anyone," I replied.

"This is not a very important matter," Fra Cipriano added.

"That's right," Boscoli said. "Let it be, Luca. The friends are God, for he is everything." And suddenly he added, "Come on! Let's pay attention! The time is drawing near." And he said, "I believe in one God, the Father Almighty, maker of heaven and earth." And thus, with great emotion, he said the whole creed. But when he was near the end, he began the little creed, and we put him back on track to say the big one and he did it again from the beginning, so that he said it entirely.[60] Then came the most holy sacrament. When it had arrived, he said, "Oh, infinite goodness! Oh, immense love! Oh, salvation of the world! Have mercy upon me!" And he began to cry with such devotion and decorum that he seemed a little girl.

38. And Messer Iacopo Manelli, who had the sacrament in his hand, had someone ask Agostino if he wished to speak to Pietro Paolo. Then Agostino

---

[60] The "little creed" is the Apostles' Creed; the "big" one Boscoli was reciting is the Nicene; Polidori, "Notizie," 303n42.

turning to Boscoli spoke, comforting him and encouraging him, and asked his pardon for those things in which he might have offended him. And warming up to his talk, he wasn't finishing. Pietro Paolo once or twice wished to reply, but Agostino, continuing in a louder voice, didn't allow him, so that one of the bystanders said, "Agostino, that's enough."

Then Pietro Paolo spoke like this: "Agostino, the time is short and all the words that we say are wasted, but I will speak briefly. I beg your pardon for anything I have done to offend against you in this life, and especially that I offended against you in the interrogation. I thank you for comforting and encouraging me in this passage, and again I comfort you, that with all your heart you ask God's pardon, praying to him that he will make you strong at the final moment, and if you have time, pray to God for me."

39. Then Messer Iacopo, having finished the confession, devoutly communicated them, not without tears from both. And then he read them the indulgence, according to that allowed to those of the Confraternity of the Blacks. Then Pietro Paolo, full of fervor, said the Paternoster many times, and when he came to those words, "Forgive us our debts" etc., with great emotion he repeated them, adding always at the end, "through Christ our Lord." He said the Magnificat, the Salve Regina, with Fra Cipriano and me together.

Then there came to him, to greet him, Domenico di Cante, comforting him in suffering. To him he said, "Domenico, it's nothing," and he kissed him on the face. "Pray to God for me, and tell our friends that I die willingly."

Then there came Angelo the paper seller, to whom he said, "Oh my Angelo! Give me a kiss."[61] And Angelo, with warm words, comforted him.

40. He responded, "Angelo, I am resolved on death, but I would like to abstract myself completely in God and I cannot. I am not satisfied. I would like to go to this death boldly. I would like to join myself with the intellect of God."

Then Angelo, and Giovanni Covoni, who came there, replied, "Pietro Paolo, do not waver. You have a strong faith; do not carry on with such subtleties. The Lord is full of mercy. Give yourself to him, that is enough."[62]

"I do it." And he added, "'God, incline to my aid. Lord, hasten to help me. In you, Lord, have I hoped. Let me never be confounded.'" Then he said, turning to Giovanni, "Oh, my Giovanni! Pray to God that he make me strong,

---

[61] "Angelo cartolaio" is perhaps the stationer who worked with Filippo Giunti to produce a vernacular *Imitatione di Giesu Christo* in 1509 (either Angiolo Tucci or Agnolo di Michele di Giovanni Toni).

[62] Giovanni di Benedetto di Giovanni Covoni was one of the priors of the Florentine *signoria* for March and April 1503, and again March and April 1508; Polidori, "Notizie," 304n46.

for the time is approaching."

Giovanni replied, "Do not doubt. Just give yourself over to the Lord, for the earth is full of his mercy."

"So I wish to do. 'In you, Lord, have I hoped. Let me never be confounded. In your justice, deliver me. Have mercy on me, God, according to your great mercy.'"

41. A few times he drifted off and Fra Cipriano comforted him by briefly expounding figures from the Old Testament and verses from scripture. He savored them. But several times, turning to Fra Cipriano, he said, "In this journey I have to have three things. I have to believe the faith. I have to have firm hope that God will pardon me. And the third is that I have to suffer this death for love of Christ and not for others. Okay, I have it. Just remind me of it often. Ah! I want to translate myself completely into God, but I cannot do it as I wish. 'May your will be done, on earth as in heaven'"[Matt 6:10]. And he went on with the whole Paternoster, but repeated, "Forgive us our debts, as we forgive our debtors" [Matt. 6:12] with such force that it cannot be told.

And the friar said, "Come on, place yourself in him. You are his. Keep your mind on those three things and have a brave spirit, hoping in the help of Jesus Christ."

42. And he replied, "Don't abandon me before the final moment. Help me to finish the work. God will make it up to you for me."

"Don't worry, my brother," the friar replied,. "I will always be with you and Luca here, your dearest friend, will still help you."

"Do just so, I beg you, Luca."

I answered, "Oh! We will not be absent. But hope in God. 'Act manfully, strengthen your heart, trust in God'" [Ps. 27:14].

And as the time had come, he stood up energetically. The Confraternity of the Blacks was wishing to put the hood on him (for he was in a monk's habit), but he said, "No need for the hood." And turning to me with a gesture of leave-taking he said, "Goodbye," and nothing else.

This word nearly made me faint, such tenderness came upon me. And I did not respond, except, "Farewell. God is with you."

43. And thus, in the monk's habit, he went down and with strong words he helped himself, through God, saying, "God, incline to my aid," etc.[63] The friar encouraged him with verses of the Psalms and he sometimes drifted off, so

[63] Boscoli went down, that is, from the chapel into the courtyard of the Bargello.

that the friar said, "Do you hear?"

"Go on speaking. I hear," he replied.

Because the friar spoke verses of Psalms suited to him, Boscoli asked Fra Cipriano that he should say them again and so he said them.

And as he went down the stair, all full of love he spoke thus, turning his eyes to the *tavoletta*, "Lord, you are my love. I give you my heart. I love only you, and yet I love everything, for I love each one out of love for you. Here I am, Lord. I come willingly. Give me strength and vigor." And he spoke with such emotion, that whoever heard it wept and wept.

44. And when he was down [there], leaving the first step, he encountered the Confraternity's crucifix.

"What am I to do?" he said.

"This is your captain, who comes to arm you," the friar responded. "Greet him, honor him, ask him to make you strong."

Then he said, "Greetings, Lord Jesus. I adore you, hanging on the cross. Make me, I beg you, like to your Passion. True Lord, I ask you for peace."

And thus, going down the second step, he kept commending himself, saying, "'Into your hands, Lord, I commend my spirit. You redeemed me, Lord, God of truth.'" When he was on the little platform of the stair, he said, "Is it enough, a good preparation towards God? For I feel some battle. Recall to me those three things."

Then I, who was behind him, said, "Well you know that it is enough. Say to him, Fra Cipriano, that verse by David, 'Your ear heard the preparation of their heart, Lord'" [Ps. 10:17].

"Okay, yes." the friar replied, "Your ear heard the preparations…," and told him once again the three things.

And he answered, and said, "'Let your ear hear the preparation of my heart, Lord Jesus.'"

45. Then the executioner, because he wanted to put a kerchief over his eyes, asked his forgiveness and offered to pray to God for him.

"Go ahead and do your duty," Pietro Paolo said. "And when you have put me at the block, leave me like that for a bit and then finish me off, and that you pray God for me, I accept."

The reason why he asked for a little time at the block, was that he had all night long always desired a great joining with God and he didn't feel that he had achieved it as he desired, so that he hoped in that last moment to make a great effort and so to offer himself wholly to God. And because in that act of

being placed down, he knew, there was movement, agitation, and some dis-
turbance, he asked that, once placed, he be given a little time. So the friar had
decided and the others who had managed it.

46. Before he was placed at the block, just in front of it, bolt upright, he spoke
in this way: "I submit myself to the faith of Jesus Christ and I wish to die in
it, and although I have, an infinite number of times, offended against divine
goodness, nevertheless I hope to win salvation in the blood of Christ, and not
in anything else. And since it pleases you, my Jesus, that I bear this death, I
accept it willingly out of love of you."

And placing himself down, and the executioner, giving him the shortest time,
cleanly removed his head, which, so cut, continued to move its mouth for a time.

47. Then came Agostino, who valiantly commended himself and energetically conducted himself to that point, when the executioner in two tries removed
his head. Then those of the Blacks took Boscoli's body. It seemed the head of
a little angel, and even dead retained a certain decorum.

He was carried to the abbey in Florence to his [family's] sepulcher, and
I asked the favor to be among those who carried him and it was conceded to
me. Thus I was able to repay the debt of our friendship and perhaps, or rather,
without perhaps, to repay the debt of our city. When the body arrived at the
abbey, many monks from there were present, and with tears from all the bystanders he was piously buried.

I saw Agostino dead also. He retained on his face a certain wry expression, perhaps not distant from true sincerity. He was buried in Santo Spirito
in his sepulcher. God received them to himself.

This was the truth, and in memory of this event I made this recollection
[*ricordo*], perhaps ineptly, but truly.[64]

The epilogue

48. I record also that in the month of May when I was at Prato and was speaking with Fra Cipriano, who was there as prior of the convent, about other
things, having finished the first topic of conversation, I asked him what he
thought of Boscoli, because I had not seen him again from that night up to the
time of the Feast of the Holy Spirit, which was, as I said, in May.

[64] On 22 April, the Florentine government decided not to confiscate the two men's goods, as would normally be done; Polidori, "Notizie," 308n58.

He began to cry and said, "Oh, if only he were alive! But God gathers the fruits in their season [cf. Ps. 1:3]. I have not ever found a livelier intellect. It seems impossible that in that place, so full of noise (for you know that Agostino never left off shouting out his commendations of himself to God—how I dislike that way of doing things), that I would have been able to make a general confession, if he had not had such a unique character. It was enough just to give him a hint." And then he added, "I wept for eight days almost straight, I could not get enough of tears, such love he displayed in that night."

49. I asked him his opinion about Boscoli's soul. He answered me, "I firmly believe that he is blessed and that he did not have to suffer purgatory. And to tell you my opinion (but, he said, these are not things to talk about, for people then say, these friars always interpret things according to their desires, I do finally want to tell you, keep it to yourself), I believe that he was a martyr, without any doubt, because I found in him a good and brave intention, to such an extent that I was amazed. Let it be enough for you, Luca, that few of his sort are born. He was a young man of enormous valor and of the highest intention.

"And as for what you told me that night, that I should remind him that conspiracies are not licit, you should know that St. Thomas makes this distinction: either the tyrant is taken on by the people themselves or they rule by force, all at once, in defiance of the people. In the first manner, it is not licit to conspire against the tyrant. In the second, it is meritorious."[65]

And this I read afterwards.

A Note on the Translation.

The translation above is based on the edition by F. Polidori in *Archivio Storico Italiano*, 1st series, 1 (1842): 275–308, which is a revision of Polidori's earlier presentation of the text in "Notizie di Luca Della Robbia, latinista e storico del secolo XVI," *Viola del pensiero: Ricordo del MDCCCXL anno II* (Livorno: Vannini, 1839 for 1840), pp. 61–90. Polidori's 1842 edition was then republished

---

[65] Cf. *Rec.* 29 above. Thomas Aquinas (ca. 1225–74) does not say precisely these words; cf. *Summa Theologica* 2.2, quaest. 42, "De seditione," esp. art. 2; quaest. 69, "De peccatis contra iustitiam," esp. art. 4; and quaest. 104, "De obedientia," art. 6. Della Robbia and Fra Cipriano may be aware that *De regimine principum* (*On Government by Princes*), traditionally attributed to Aquinas, is divided in its evaluation of tyranny. While books 1–2.4.7 of the treatise support rule by one person no matter how corrupt, books 2.4.8 through 4 (by Ptolemy of Lucca, ca. 1236–1327) vigorously prefer the rule of many, at least for a free people such as the inhabitants of the northern Italian city-states. See Blythe, *Thomas Aquinas*, esp. 47–49.

by R. Bacchelli, *La Morte di Pietro Paolo Boscoli* (Florence: Felice Le Monnier, 1943), with a lengthy preface and further notes.

I have spot-checked the printed editions against twelve manuscripts in Florence, Rome, Venice, and Bologna:

Bologna, Biblioteca Universitaria
　　ms. Ital. 6, fols. 58–67
Florence, Archivio di Stato
　　Archivio Bardi, III.39, fols. 146r–158v
Florence, Biblioteca Nazionale Centrale
　　Fondo Conventi soppressi, ms. G.9.1608; 21–40
　　Fondo Gino Capponi, ms. 265, fols. 137–81; ms. 305, fols. 259r–289v;
　　ms. 237, 351–422
　　Fondo Palatini Panciatichi, ms. 117, vol. 1, pp. 398–418
Florence, Biblioteca Riccardiana
　　ms. 2312, fols. 32–46
　　ms. 1500, fols. 31v–40r
Rome, Biblioteca Angelica
　　ms. 2230, fols. 122r–135r
　　Rome, Biblioteca Casanatense
　　ms. 3610, fols. 2r–15v
Venice, Biblioteca Marciana
　　ms. It. VI 129 (5945), 31v–40r

Works Cited

Archives

ASF　　Archivio di Stato, Florence

Printed Sources

Augustine. "Commentary on Ps. 39" [38 in Vulgate numbering] *Enarrationes in Psalmos*, edited by C. Weidmann (CSEL 93). Vienna: Verlag der Oesterreichischen Akademie der Wissenschaften, 2003.

Bacchelli, Ricardo. *La Morte di Pietro Paolo Boscoli.* Florence: Felice Le Monnier, 1943.

Bandini, Angelo Maria. *Iuntarum typographiae annales.* Lucca: Bonsignori, 1791.

Baron, Hans. *The Crisis of the Early Italian Renaissance.* 2 vols. Princeton: Princeton University Press, 1955. Rev. 1 vol. ed. with epilogue, Princeton: Princeton University Press, 1966.

Bynum, Caroline Walker. *Holy Feast and Holy Fast.* Berkeley: University of California, 1987.

Cantimori, Delio. "Il caso del Boscoli e la vita del Rinascimento." *Giornale critico della filosofia italiana* 8 (1927): 241–55.

Centi, Timoteo M. "L'attività letteraria di Santi Pagnini (1470–1536) nel campo delle scienze bibliche." *Archivum fratrum praedicatorum* 15 (1945): 5–51.

———. *Girolamo Savonarola: Preghiere dal Carcere* 2nd ed. rev. Siena: Cantagalli, 1990.

Ceresa, M. "Giunti, Filippo." In *Dizionario Biografico degli Italiani,* 57:87a–89b. Rome: Istituto della Enciclopedia italiana, 2001.

Coakley, John W. *Women, Men, and Spiritual Power: Female Saints and Their Male Collaborators.* New York: Columbia University Press, 2006.

Creytens, Raymond. "Les actes de la congrégation toscano–romaine." *Archivum fratrum praedicatorum* 40 (1970): 125–230.

Dall'Aglio, Stefano. *Savonarola e il Savonarolismo.* Bari: Cacucci, 2005.

Donnelly, John Patrick. *Girolamo Savonarola. Prison Meditations on Psalms 51 and 31.* Milwaukee: Marquette University Press, 1994.

Fragnito, Gigliola. "della Robbia, Luca." In *Dizionario Biografico degli Italiani,* 37:291a–293b. Rome: Istituto della Enciclopedia italiana, 1989.

Frazier, Alison Knowles. *The Death of Pietro Paolo Boscoli* (tentative title). Toronto: Centre for Reformation and Renaissance Studies, forthcoming.

Frugoni, Arsenio. "La morte di Pietro Paolo Boscoli." In *Incontri nel rinascimento: Pagine di erudizione e di critica,* edited by Arsenio Frugoni, 93–100. Brescia: La Scuola, 1954.

Godman, Peter. *From Poliziano to Machiavelli: Florentine Humanism in the High Renaissance.* Princeton: Princeton University Press, 1998.

Hankins, James. *Renaissance Civic Humanism: Reappraisals and Reflections.* New York: Cambridge University, 2000.

Jurdjevic, Mark. *Guardians of Republicanism: The Valori Family in the Florentine Renaissance.* New York: Oxford University Press, 2007.

———. "Virtue, Commerce, and the Enduring Florentine Republican Moment: Reintegrating Italy into the Atlantic Republican Debate." *Journal of the History of Ideas* 62 (2001): 721–43.

Kent, Dale. *Friendship, Love and Trust in Renaissance Florence.* Cambridge, MA: Harvard University Press, 2008.

Lazzaretti, A. "Capponi, Agostino." In *Dizionario Biografico degli Italiani,* 19:6a–7b. Rome: Istituto della Enciclopedia italiana, 1976.

Lazzerini, L. *Nessuno è innocente: Le tre morti di Pietro Pagolo Boscoli.* Florence: Olschki, 2002.

Marchi, Gian Paolo. *Testi cinquecenteschi sulla ribellione politica.* 1978. Reprint, Verona: Fiorini, 2005.

Paglia, Vincenzo. *"La pietà dei carcerati": Confraternite e società a Roma nei secoli XVI–XVIII.* Rome: Edizioni di storia e letteratura, 1980.

Pincin, Carlo. "Boscoli, Pietro Paolo." In *Dizionario Biografico degli Italiani,* 13:219a–220b. Rome: Istituto della Enciclopedia italiana, 1971.

Polidori, Filippo Luigi. "Notizie di Luca Della Robbia, latinista e storico del secolo XVI." *Archivio Storico Italiano* 1st series, no. 1 (1842): 275–308.

Poliziano, Angelo. *Letters.* Vol. 1. Edited, annotated, and translated by Shane Butler. I Tatti Renaissance Library 21. Cambridge, MA: Harvard University Press, 2006.

Polizzotto, Lorenzo. *The Elect Nation: The Savonarolan Movement in Florence, 1494–1545.* Oxford: Clarendon Press, 1994.

Ptolemy [Bartholomew] of Lucca, with portions attributed to Thomas Aquinas. *On the Government of Rulers: De Regimine Principum.* Translated by James Morgan Blythe. Philadelphia: University of Pennsylvania Press, 1997.

Ridolfi, Roberto. *The Life of Niccolò Machiavelli.* Translated by Cecil Grayson. Chicago: University of Chicago Press, 1963.

Rousch, Sherry. "Dante as Piagnone Prophet: Girolamo Benivieni's 'Cantico in laudedi Dante' (1506)." Renaissance Quarterly 55, no. 1 (2002: 49–80.

Savonarola, Girolamo. *Compendium philosophiae naturalis.* In *Girolamo Savonarola: Scriti filosofici,* edited by G. Garfagnini and E. Garin, 305–477. Rome: Belardetti, 1982.

Trexler, Richard. "Florentine Religious Experience: The Sacred Image." *Studies in the Renaissance* 19 (1972): 7–41.

———. *Public Life in Renaissance Florence.* New York: Academic Press, 1980.

Verde, Armando Felice. "La congregazione di S. Marco dell' ordine dei frati Predicatori: Il 'reale' della predicazione savonaroliana." *Memorie domenicane anno 100,* n.s. 4 (1983): 151–238.

Villari, Pasquale. *La storia di Girolamo Savonarola e de' suoi tempi.* Florence: Le Monnier, 1930.

Weinstein, Donald. "The Art of Dying Well and Popular Piety in the Preaching and Thought of Girolamo Savonarola." In *Life and Death in Fifteenth-Century Florence,* edited by Marcel Tetel, Ronald G. Witt, and Rona Goffen, 88–104. Durham, NC: Duke University Press, 1989.

Chapter 9

Public Execution in Popular Verse
The Poems of Giulio Cesare Croce

Meryl Bailey

The son of a blacksmith, Giulio Cesare Croce (1550–1609) was a self-taught poet and writer who claimed to have dedicated his life to verse after reading an old volume of Ovid.[1] Best known for his satirical stories about the peasants Bertoldo and Bertoldino, he also produced comedies, burlesque poems, and dialogues. Much of Croce's verse was popular poetry in its most literal sense. His works were meant to be sung or read in the public squares of Bologna and other cities, where he also sold printed pamphlets of his compositions. Many of these were republished posthumously, suggesting a continued interest in his works.

Working in the city squares as a traveling minstrel, Croce is likely to have witnessed many public executions, and he memorialized several of these events in verse.[2] One such poem, *Caso compassionevole*, describes executions carried out in Bologna's Piazza Maggiore on 3 January 1587.[3] The spectacle was unusual in several respects.[4] Two of the condemned were well-born members of local

[1] Much of what is known about Croce's life comes from his own autobiography; *Descrittione della vita del Croce*, 5–23. An 1879 monograph on Croce by Olindo Guerrini (*Vita e opera di Croce*), provides extensive bibliographical information, historical context, and an invaluable appendix of Croce's publications. In many cases, Guerrini's entry on a given work includes research on its underlying historical circumstances.

[2] Two of these poems are translated here. A third, *Lamento quale ha fato il Carotta e suoi compagni* (Modena: Paolo Gadalino, n.d.), concerns the hanging of a Florentine called "Carotta" and a group of his fellow malefactors in Bologna on 31 January 1587. The poem is discussed in Guerrini, *Vita e opera di Croce*, 445–46.

[3] Croce, *Caso compassioneuole e lacrimoso lamento di due infelici amanti condannati alla giustitia in Bologna, alli 3. Genaro 1587*. The poem was published in at least six editions. The present translation is based on the 1623 edition, which includes a brief dialogue between the lovers, a lament by Ippolita, and verses not found in earlier editions. Croce also wrote an account of the story in Bergamasque dialect, suggesting that the appetite for such tales extended beyond the city directly impacted by the crime.

4 The facts of the case derive from Guerrini, *Vita e opera di Croce*, 363–65, which in turn draws on two primary historical sources: *Libro dei giustiziati*, S. Maria della Morte, BUB mss. 916; and Ghiselli, *Cronache*, BUB

Bolognese families, and one of these was female. Ippolita Pensarotti and her lover, Ludovico Landinelli, were convicted of having poisoned Ippolita's father.[5] Their social status was affirmed by the execution ritual, for both were decapitated rather than hung, and both were buried in their home parishes. A third accomplice, the servant Giovanni Antonio dal Tolle, was executed by hanging and buried in the mass grave in S. Giovanni del Mercato. All three were assisted by lay comforters from S. Maria della Morte.[6]

Thoroughly integrating the traditions and expectations surrounding capital punishment in Bologna into his description of the event, Croce portrays the deaths of Ippolita and Ludovico as an ideal exercise in the ritual of public execution. Both, he claims, died willingly, putting their faith in God and focusing on salvation. The executioner's aim is mercifully precise, and each dies from a single blow. But it is Ippolita's behavior that is described in the most extraordinary terms. She is gracious, dignified, and content. Comforting her comforters from the confraternity of S. Maria della Morte, she speaks the words that typically would be theirs and moves them from tears to joyful acceptance of her fate. Aware that the battle for her soul will be fierce even in her final moments, Ippolita dies steadfast, fully repentant, and with a prayer on her lips. Despite her crime, the poem suggests that her nature is not inherently criminal. All external signs, her beauty, her words, and her decorum, mark an internal strength of character and her "honest blood." Her purity and honor are also suggested by the nuptial metaphors that appear repeatedly in Croce's description of her actions. Her good death and eventual salvation are affirmed by the gentle smile on her face even as her bloodied head lies upon the execution platform. The vast crowds that have gathered to witness the execution weep at the sight, and all rush to attend the funerals of the two unfortunate lovers. While the prisoners' willingness to die may have contributed to the crowd's response, one suspects that their youth and social status were equally important in evoking this display of compassion. By contrast, the hanging of their accomplice, the servant Giovanne Antonio dal Tolle, goes completely unmentioned.

Croce offers a very different poetic response to a pair of executions that

---

ms. XVIII. The execution is also recorded in a copy of "Descrizione di tutte le giustiziati di Bologna nel 1540 per tutto il 1740," BAB, Aula 2a C.VII.3, 3 Gennaio 1587.

[5] Ghiselli specifies that the poison added to Girolamo's medicine was an arsenic compound used in women's makeup; Guerrini, *Vita e opera di Croce,* 365.

[6] "Descrizione di tutte le giustiziati di Bologna nel 1540 per tutto il 1740," BAB, Aula 2a C.VII.3, 3 Gennaio 1587.

occurred in Ferrara on 30 April 1590. On that day, Madonna Lavinia Bendadei was decapitated for the murder of her elderly brother-in-law. The records kept by the Ferrarese *conforteria* describe the incident as follows:

> The wicked woman had conspired with a traitorous Jew named Manasso. Since it was Carnival, the assassin wore a mask.... As you know, the lady paid with her head. The Jew was put on a wagon, surrounded by rabbis who comforted him. He was led to the Fassolo neighborhood where he had committed the crime, and where [the victim and Madonna Lavinia] had lived. After he was tortured with pincers, they cut off his hand. Then, having returned to the square, the site of the execution, he was hung by the neck.[7]

Recounted in a singsong rhythm adapted to public performance, Croce's *Lamento et morte di Manas hebreo* focuses only on the guilt and fate of Manasso and makes only vague references to the involvement of another individual in the crime.[8] The tone is mocking, and the brutal details of the execution—the cutting off of a hand, the prisoner's legs kicking the air in his final moments—suggest a certain vengeful satisfaction on the part of the poet.

Both the *Lamento di Manas* and the *Caso compassionevole* are meant on one level to be didactic. In the latter, the public, and especially women, are encouraged to learn from the example of the Bolognese lovers. However, the *Caso compassionevole* is written in *terza rima*, placing the poet within the tradition of Dante, and it soon becomes clear that its real subject is love rather than justice. Croce gives the couple little responsibility for their crime. Referring to them as Pyramis and Thisbe, star-crossed lovers of myth, he hints that they were motivated by love and parental interference rather than avarice. Indeed, he explicitly assigns blame to love itself, that "disloyal traitor" who drives people to irrational acts of passion.

The contrast between these two poems speaks to a hierarchy among the biases and societal taboos of Croce's time. As both a child who killed a parent and a woman who killed a man, Ippolita's transgression could easily have been cast as an unforgivable inversion of the social order. Instead, invoking a

---

[7] This information derives from records from a Ferrarese book of the condemned, transcribed in Guerrini, *Vita e opera di Croce*, 444–45. The archival source is the *Libro delle giustizie seguite in Ferrara dall'anno 1441 sino al presente, favoritomi dall'Illmo. e Revmo. sig. dogg. Girol. Arciprete Baruffaldi, uno dei sig. della Sacra Scuola dei Confortatori di essa citta,' e da me Ubaldo Zanetti trasuntato litteralmente dal predetto originale, l'anno 1736*, BUB ms. 917. Manas, or Manasso, is an Italianized form of the biblical name Manasseh.

[8] Croce, *Lamento et morte di Manas hebreo*.

series of mythological and historical figures who followed love to a cruel end, Croce transforms her story into a tragedy of classical proportions. For his part, Manas was a Jew who killed a Christian, perhaps motivated by a carnal relationship with his accomplice. As such, his crime reinforced one of this society's profound anxieties—the fear of sexual interaction between Christian women and Jewish men—and his brutal execution seems to have evoked little sympathy.

The poet's differing treatment of the two events is also advertised by the imagery on the respective pamphlet covers. Printed copies of the *Lamento di Manas* are prefaced by a woodblock print of a man hanging unceremoniously from a tree. Instead, the print on the cover of the 1623 edition of the *Caso compassionevole* shows a gently smiling woman holding a chain and being led forward by a lavishly dressed man in a feathered beret. Though simple, this woodcut generates several levels of meaning. If the chain represents the love that joins Ippolita and Ludovico, it is worth noting that neither is bound: although he leads, she follows of her own accord. At the same time, the chain presages their ultimate end. As Ludovico looks back at Ippolita and gestures ahead, his call to love is also an invitation to death. Their voluntary grasp of the chain as they stride forward to meet their fate demonstrates their willingness to die, reinforcing the poem's presentation of the event as both a tragedy and an exemplary model of the enactment of justice.

The piteous case and tearful lament of two unhappy lovers condemned to death in Bologna on January 3, 1587.

Giulio Cesare Croce

I will tell of a new case, the twisted fate of two unhappy and unfortunate lovers and their sad end—harsh death. Since it happened, surely I should tell of it. Impetuous youths, don't refuse to listen to my song. Rather, learn from their example. For after the fact, then, it is no use to say "I did" or "I said," because you did not believe that justice is inescapable. He who wants to satisfy the whim of his every unbridled desire offends first nature, and then God, and finally himself, just as today Lodovico and Hippolita (who loved each other so much during the time they were given) clearly show. With their heads filled with song and with such a burning love, they clung together in sweet embraces, and now all their joys end in tears.

Already I hear tearful words all around. Already I see every heart melt, and I hear a thousand laments for them. Everyone pines with love and their breasts are filled with sadness that such a beautiful couple suffers today. But if God's laws are disdained and children take up arms against their parents, then may those great laws be fulfilled.

Because Hippolita loved too much, she devoted her wiles to bringing death to her family. And in the end Lodovico did it, but he soon regretted her counsel. In what should have been the medicine of her father, mother, and brother, he put hidden poison to bring them ruin. And so it is right that together these followers of unwholesome love should suffer death for their wicked act.

But it was love that caused these effects, oh cruel and blind love that kills man and infects everyone. Disloyal and treacherous love, those who follow you become fodder for the crowds, and so often lose their lives and

This poem was published in at least five editions between 1610 and 1640. The present translation is based on the 1623 edition (Bologna: Heredi di Cochi, 1623), which is the most complete edition of those available. I am grateful to Dr. Lisa Erdberg for her assistance with this translation.

their honor besides. Surely it has been clearly seen (not once but thousands of times) that those who yield to you are miserable. The Trojan shepherd knows it, and Pyrrhus, and Achilles, and the suffering wife of Sychaeus, Hero, Leander, Myrrha, Byblis, and Phyllis, Jason, Hercules, Hippolytus, and Theseus, Medea, Phaedra, Ariadne, and so many others, that not even the gifted Orpheus could recount them all.[9] But whether what is said of them be true or false, this is the most striking story, the clearest case that has ever happened among us. This woeful chronicle, full of bitter tears, will never be forgotten for eternity. So that this strong and fierce pain does not exhaust me, I will tell the brief story and lay bare its clearest cause.

When they knew they were to die, they were overcome, but they came to their senses quickly, for courage shut the doors on fear. And it was clear that both died more than willingly and that they put everything in God's hands. They directed all their hopes and thoughts towards contemplating that other life, as all prisoners trust in faith. And realizing how they had strayed from the path that carries man to salvation, they prayed to God that he help them at this harrowing point. They felt great contrition and gave many alms, so that heaven would grant them remission.

Think not that the lady was crying. Rather, she went with a happy and beautiful countenance, restraining her joy, and when she heard the bolt of the prison door opening, smiling and content, she approached the warden. And speaking joyfully with him she said, "Has my hour arrived? I am ready. Let us go happily." And then she prepared and bathed herself as if she were going to her wedding, unconcerned for cruel death.

Finally, when the hour of torment arrived, both were led to be comforted for the good of their souls. But soon they collapsed into bitter tears, such that their comforters wept with them instead of talking. And she said, "Weep not, noble sirs, for I care nothing for this death. It is enough that my soul be beyond suffering. I deserve worse, because once the body is dead, it feels neither pain nor pleasure. It is the soul's turn to pay. Please pray to the King of heaven that he may want to forgive my every sin. Invoking him at this point—that's what counts. And a thousand times and more I confess my sins, for I have offended my Lord in so many ways, and only this grief strips and exhausts me. In my breast I feel such fervor, and in my heart such boldness, that I do not fear death's great fury. I pray only that the Redeemer give me

---

[9] In these two tercets, the poet lists individuals, known from classical texts such as Ovid's *Metamorphoses* and Virgil's *Aeneid*, who were harmed or led astray by love.

such steadfastness and strength now that the devil cannot possess me."

Thus spoke the lady, and she seemed to feel such sweetness that those who were nearby rejoiced happily with her. The other prisoner also gave such a speech, and meanwhile daylight appeared, and the piazza filled with people who wanted to see such a dreadful place. Above a high platform were the mallet and blade to finish the savage party and make the chopping block wallow in their blood.

On the third of January 1587, downcast, their heads were cut from their bodies. First came the lady. And she here kneels on the platform, with her arms and hands tightly bound. After she had said a devout prayer and committed herself fervently to God, everyone wept. Then, bowing her head piously, she joyfully placed her white neck on the chopping block. Oh bitter blow, ruthless and wicked! The blade fell and cut off her head in a single blow, and her rosy face turned white, and she collapsed. And that mouth remained smiling, perhaps to show that she was out of the pain that had held her heart captive. For when a man is truly certain of death, passion and fear last only for as long as he lives, and they die with him. Wearing a black mourning dress, with veils and bands, like a dignified lady who was born of honest blood, the lovely lady died saying Hail Mary. And the executioner grabbed her head and quickly set it beside its body. Then he laid her out at one side of the platform and covered her with a cloth so that the other one could not see her so clearly.

Moments later, her dear beloved offered himself on the platform, completely defeated, his face pale and his strength gone. In his head, both eyes were so hollow that he seemed dead, and he didn't hide the pain that afflicted his heart. He ascends the platform tearfully. Once there, he finds himself at a point so momentous that it strikes terror in every living breast. And casting his eyes downwards, he sees the other body beneath the blanket, pale and lifeless. Then he is stricken with twice the pain. He grieves for he recognizes his lover, whence he seems to feel two deaths in a single hour.

And had he had a longer time to speak, Lord, what he would have said, or wailed, over that body. Perhaps he would have said "Oh lady, you suffered such a bitter death for my love, for I was the cause of your woes. If I can lessen your pain with my own, if the thought of the good that one gets in the afterlife still awaits us, I will always love you, because one who loves must love, and you have always loved me, oh, alas, in this short life. I thank you, and I will put my body beside yours to follow you soon for I am about to draw my last breath."

And if she could have spoken she would have answered him, "Come, my dear, come be near me. And even though this death separates the soul from the body, it doesn't diminish or erase a great love. Rather, it restores and reunites it here; since we suffer the same fate, our affection remains complete, and never ends. And since time is short, come quickly, for I await you, and together we will go to the heavenly court. This heart and this breast, which were yours before, are yours still. In the end, this is the spirit that took shelter with yours."

Each would have said these words, and many more, to the other on this occasion, but there was no time for speeches. For soon the executioner, as he always does, makes him kneel and loosens his collar, and urges him towards his death, and he suffers. Then, his prayer finished, he bows his head. The sharp blade falls, cuts off his head, and ends his life in an instant.

So the cruel battle of these two unhappy lovers came to an end. Thus ends the misery that troubles these souls. Both died in a single hour; both left their lives on a high scaffold, still in the spring of their youth. And as if it were a nuptial bed, she lay like Thisbe next to her Pyramus on that tragic funeral platform.[10] Can anyone in Bologna remember having seen a thing so incredible, an event so momentous, as this spectacle?

And when the next day arrived, they were both given honest burial in their family tombs, as it should have been. So many people rushed to ogle their disgrace that it was remarkable beyond measure. The streets were full of carriages, and there was no one, adult or child, who didn't reflect with pity that day. He was wearing a beret, and she wore white, with beautiful flowers. He rests at the Servi, and she in San Martino.[11]

There it is, the tragedy revealed. Learn from her, ladies and maidens, and don't shake your heads at my words. If God has made you good and beautiful, try to conserve such a treasure, and do not be impious or rebellious towards him. Instead, try to emulate those who, coming into possession of a graceful and lovely work by some excellent painter, richly and nobly adorn it in gold and silver in order to double its worth. This is how you should behave. And inside, you should be as you are on the surface, honest and virtuous. This complements beauty. Do not be so curious and trusting, especially in questions of honor, but always be modest and timid. Be temperate in love, and let not your heads be turned towards lascivious thoughts or malign humors. May Hippolita and Lodovico be a mirror for you today, for they became the executioner's victims because they knew not how to control themselves. I beg

---

[10] Pyramus and Thisbe (Hyginus, *Fabulae*, 242; and Ovid, *Metamorphoses*, 4) were ill-fated lovers who were kept apart by their parents, and who killed themselves after an attempt to meet clandestinely went awry. Much like Romeo and Juliet today, their story would have been widely known in this period.

[11] The Servi is S. Maria dei Servi, Ludovico's home parish. San Martino was Hippolita's home parish.

you, try to avoid diabolical and evil temptations, and let yourself not be carried away by emotion.

And this is also written for those men who are taken by a beautiful face. Their love should come to an honest end. Do not try to use a woman for material gain, since women are bent easily and maidens are tricked even more easily. Treat everyone with civility. Do not let avarice lead you to do something evil and fraudulent. Do not take advantage of illness, nor let an evil plan turn you to evil deeds.

Fear God's supreme justice, for happy is he who keeps the end in mind.

Dialogue of Lodovico and Hippolita

Lod.:   Are you not that Hippolita who promised while alive to love me until death? And who, led today to a frightful death, is about to lay down her life for my love?

Hip.:   Yes, I am she; and if I loved you in this life, I am ready to love you still after death; and death would be dear and welcome to me if you lived on after me.

Lod.:   Me live and you endure death? Let heaven not be pleased but that this life vanish. And if not to this death, then to an even more pitiless one.

Hip.:   So if we lose our lives for love, let us die, my sweet darling, because this death is no death—this life is death.

Hippolita's Lament

How much better it would have been had my mother suffocated me, piteous, in swaddling clothes, or if I had been killed, ripped apart by wolves as soon as she brought me forth. This wretched body and this soul, before it could sin, would have been returned to their maker. Oh, how my soul was spurred towards evil council, and wickedness unleashed my appetite. Would that then I had been given as prey to pillagers, put in shackles, burned alive, as the tyrants did to the saints. Soul, why were you not timid then, why did you not take flight, why did not you direct your wings towards God, who gives life to everything?

Lament and death of Manas the Jew, who was put on a wagon and tortured with pincers, whose hand was cut off, and who was then hung for murder and other great and terrible crimes. An event which took place in the magnificent city of Ferrara on the last day of April, 1590.

Giulio Cesare Croce

Oh Manas, traitor, what have you done, shameless one? You have been impious and ruthless in committing such a misdeed. Oh Manas, traitor.

Merciless and cursed one, what did you think you were doing by so crude and horrifying an act? Oh Manas, traitor.

You scoundrel, who convinced you to commit such a crime? Who planted this savage and strange thought in your mind? Oh Manas, traitor.

Wretched is he who believes that sins can stay hidden, for in the end all abuses are made manifest to the Prime Mover. Oh Manas, traitor.

I thought that I had committed this excess secretly, and that I would go on happily without punishment or pain. Oh Manas, traitor.

But my usual iniquity gave me away, so now the Minister of Justice will scratch my itch. Oh Manas, traitor.

Now learn from my example, all you rabbis! Ignore my babblings, and do not march to the beat of my drum. Oh Manas, traitor.

This translation is based on the 1623 edition: Bologna: Heredi di Cochi al Pozzo Rosso da San Damiano, 1623.

How much better it would have been had I not done such dreadful things, devoting myself to making *gemelle*[12] and to the baker's craft. Oh Manas, traitor.

I wanted to insinuate myself and mingle with the flocks of others, so I ignored the laws of my people and came to be a killer. Oh Manas, traitor.

Come on, for now the deed is done! I realize that my error leads me, cold and trembling, to this dance. Oh Manas, traitor.

Now that I am on the cart and the irons are in the fire, it no longer seems so jolly to feel such searing heat. Oh Manas, traitor.

Alas, this is the greatest torment! By God, look away, Mordechai, and do not weep to see me in such weakness. Oh Manas, traitor.

Oh Jacob, my dear friend, help me, dearest brother. Run up there to the palace to speak with the authorities. Oh Manas, traitor.

Alas, I ask for help in vain, for the sentence has already been decided, and I deserve neither mercy, nor aid, nor favor. Oh Manas, traitor.

Be strong, Manas, because you need to be. Alas, the reproachful executioner wants to show me his worth. Oh Manas, traitor.

By God, if I thought that I would end up in this forlorn state I would not have committed the crime, and I would have left love alone. Oh Manas, traitor.

Come on! Now I am hurried and jerked along, tormented, burned, and beaten—what shame and dishonor! Oh Manas, traitor.

And so, on the last day of April, the first day of the week, I was brought to the final hour, as I frankly deserved. Oh Manas, traitor.

They cut off my hand at the Fagiolo[13] (oh, a painful thing!) and displayed it on a wall amidst the din and uproar. Oh Manas, traitor.

[12] A local name for a type of baked confection.
[13] That is, the neighborhood where the crime occurred.

But soon I was rushed away from the Jews, who had not wanted me to suffer such abuse, for they loved me fervently. Oh Manas, traitor.

All the children shouted at the top of their lungs that morning, and their screams made such a commotion that everyone was shocked. Oh Manas, traitor.

Never again will I make *gemelle* because they cut off one of my hands, then tortured me with pincers and drained me of all strength. Oh Manas, traitor.

By God, as they say, look not at me, for I am finished. Already I am dead and gone, no longer here to make an uproar. Oh Manas, traitor.

Rest in peace, Benjamin. Aaron, I am at your service. Please tell Solomon how I died with great honor. Oh Manas, traitor.

And you can be sure that I am brought to this torment, to savor this terrible flavor, because of the service I did for another. Oh Manas, traitor.

They wanted to kill me on the Sabbath, but I made such a fuss that they chose Monday instead. Oh Manas, traitor.

And since I find myself at the place where everything comes to an end, even if I seem afflicted and sad, I feel brave and heartened. Oh Manas, traitor.

And in these final breaths I want to give advice to everyone, adults and children, and I say these things fervently. Oh Manas, traitor.

Oh, Jacob, my dear friend, everyone should remember that they too will soon end up a lifeless form. Oh Manas, traitor.

Pay attention to God, I can say no more than this, since I am already feeling the approach of the final terror. Oh Manas, traitor.

Now that I am strung up here and I kick the wind once or twice, I will end my lament, for my last breath escapes me. Oh Manas, traitor.

Works Cited

Archives

BAB Biblioteca Arcivescovile di Bologna
BUB Biblioteca Universitaria di Bologna

Printed Sources

Croce, Giulio Cesare. *Caso compassioneuole e lacrimoso lamento di due infelici amanti condannati alla giustitia in Bologna, alli 3. Genaro 1587.* Composta da Giulio Cesare Croce. Bologna: Gli Heredi del Cochi. Al Pozzo Rosso, da San Damiano, 1623.

———. *Descrittione della vita del Croce; con una esortatione fatta ad esso, da varij animali ne' lor linguaggi, à dover lasciare da parte la poesia. E dui indici, l'uno dell'opere fatte stampare da lui fin' ad hora; l'altro di quelle che vi sono da stampare. Ed altre opere curiose, e belle.* Bologna: Appresso Bortolomeo Cochi, al Pozzo Rosso: 1608.

———. *Lamento et morte di Manas hebreo, qual fu tenagliato sopra un carro, & gli tagliorno una mano, e fu poi appiccato per homicidio, & altri delitti enormi, & obbrobrioso. Caso successo nella Magnifica citta di Ferrara il di ultimo d'Aprile 1590.* Bologna: Gli Heredi di Cochi al Pozzo Rosso da San Damiano, 1623.

Guerrini, Olindo. *La vita e le opere di Giulio Cesare Croce.* Bologna: Nicola Zanichelli, 1879.

Contributors

Meryl Bailey (University of California, Berkeley) is a doctoral candidate in the history of art, specializing in the Italian Renaissance. She also holds degrees in anthropology and law. Her dissertation explores the imagery and ritual associated with capital punishment in Venice, and focuses on the comforting confraternity known as the Scuola di San Fantin. Her research draws upon art history, anthropology, law, and theology to broadly consider how imagery, private ceremony, and public spectacle help cultures to deal with state-sanctioned violence.

Sheila Das (Vanier College, Montreal) is a scholar of late Renaissance rhetoric who has published a number of articles on Venetian literature, including "Sarpi's Portraits in the *Istoria del concilio tridentino*," in *Studi Veneziani* (2004) and "The Disappearance of the Trojan Legend in the Historiography of Venice" in *Fantasies of Troy: Classical Tales and the Social Imaginary in Medieval and Early Modern Europe,* edited by Alan Shepard and Stephen D. Powell (2004).

Kathleen Falvey (University of Hawaii, Manoa) is a scholar of late medieval and literary drama who has conducted research on the public plays produced by the confraternities of northern and central Italy. Among her publications in this area are "The First Perugian Passion Play: Aspects of Structure," *Comparative Drama* 11/2 (1977); "The Italian Saint Play: The Example of Perugia" in *The Saint Play in Europe,* edited by C. Davidson (1986); and "An Investigation into the Imaginative and Dramatic Context of the Italian *Conforteria*," *Fifteenth Century Studies* 13 (1988).

Massimo Ferretti (Scuola Normale Superiore, Pisa) is an art historian and conservation expert who taught at the universities of Bologna and Milan and was director of the civic collections of art in Bologna (where he oversaw the reopening of two long-closed museums) before becoming professor of art history and director of the Laboratory of Visual Arts at the Scuola Normale

Superiore in Pisa. He is the author of numerous studies dealing both with art conservation and with late medieval artists, including "Un nuovo momento bolognese di Jacopo della Quercia," in *Arte a Bologna: Bolletino dei musei civici d'arte antica* V (1999); and *Fonte Gaia di Jacopo della Quercia* (2001).

Alison Frazier (University of Texas, Austin) is a historian who writes on the intersection of humanism and religion in the Renaissance, with an emphasis on the humanist reconstruction and rewriting of sacred history. Her 2005 book, *Possible Lives: Authors and Saints in Renaissance Italy,* was awarded the Phyllis Goodheart Gordon Book Prize of the Renaissance Society of America. She has held fellowships from Villa I Tatti and the Guggenheim Foundation.

Pamela Gravestock (University of Toronto) is a research associate at the Centre for Reformation and Renaissance Studies who works on issues related to death and memorialization and also on dimensions of the early modern imagination. She is the author of *Expectations and Experience: The World of the Medieval and Renaissance Traveler* (2002); and "Did Imaginary Animals Exist?" in *The Mark of the Beast: The Medieval Bestiary in Art, Life, and Literature,* edited by Debra Hassig (1999).

Adriano Prosperi (Scuola Normale Superiore, Pisa) is the leading international authority on sixteenth-century Italian religious history, and holds the Chair in Reformation and Counter-Reformation History at its most prestigious university. His work ranges over the fields of popular culture, social discipline, history, and anthropology, and he has conducted advanced seminars on the *conforterie*. Prosperi has published eleven books and over fifty articles, including most notably *Storia di un infanticidio* (2005) and *Tribunali della coscienza. Inquisitori, confessori, missionari* (1996).

Nicholas Terpstra (University of Toronto) is a historian of early modern social history in Italy whose work has focused on the intersection of religion and politics, and particularly confraternities, charitable institutions, and the networks of care available to marginal populations. He has written many articles and is the author of *Abandoned Children of the Italian Renaissance: Orphan Care in Florence and Bologna* (2005) and *Lay Confraternities and Civic Religion in Renaissance Bologna* (1995), which was awarded the Howard Marraro Prize of the Society for Italian Historical Studies.

Alfredo Troiano (Yale University) is a literary scholar who has conducted research on various themes in late medieval and Renaissance Italian poetry and songs, and in particular on literature produced in relation to death. Among his publications are "'Sozzo, malvascio corpo, lussurïoso e 'ngordo': La visione del corpo nel *contemptus mundi* di Iacopone da Todi" in *Yale Italian Poetry* VIII (2005); and "Un laudario per condannati a morte: Il ms. 1069 della Yale Beinecke Library di Yale," in *Studi e problemi di critica testuale* (2005).

Index

prayers (continued)
    at tolling of the bell, 269
    upon awakening the condemned, 263
    upon receiving communion, 266–67
preaching, as resource for comforters, 248
priests, 207, 263–65
prisons
    controlled by confraternity, 149–50
    and privacy, 150, 154–55
    reform/secularization of, in Papal States,
        152
processions
    at executions, 18, 27–28, 128–29, 131
    for God's mercy, 133
    laude singing at, 33
prophets, in paradise, 219–20
Prosperi, Adriano, 63, 66
Pseudo-Dalmasio. *See* Dalmasio
punishment theories, 107–12
Pythagorus, 291

Raphael, angel, 240
Rave, B., 89
Raymond of Capua, 23, 52
reason, as soul, 262–63
religion *vs.* astrology, 237
Revello, *Book of St. John the Baptist,* 18–23
revenge, as ungodly, 205
Ridolfi, Piero, 309
Ridolfi, Roberto, 293, 304n
Rimini, Francesco da
    The Crucifixion, 86–87, *166*
    St. Mary Magdelen with Saints, 84, 87, *165*
Rinaldeschi, Antonio, 128, *162*
rites and rituals. *See also* processions
    in Croce's poetry, 328
    of execution, 127–32, 328
    outlined in book 2, 188
    purposes of, 7–8, 125
    and urban setting of, 81
Robbia, Luca della. *See* della Robbia, Luca
Rovorobella, Gregorio da, 32, 190
Rufus, Quintus Curtius, *Historia magni
        Aleandri,* 299

Sacchetti, Giovanni Battista, 305
sacraments
    confession, 207–9
    denied to criminals, 111
    Eucharist, 209–12
    and judicial *vs.* sacramental justice, 113
    penance, 209

validity of, for the condemned, 104–5, 108
    vs. astrology, 236
saints
    in heaven, 222
    invoked in *laude,* 38
    mentioned, 66, 89, 100–101, 205, 207,
        220–23, 225–28, 238, 243, 247,
        260, 289, 291, 314, 323
salvation
    of body and soul, 202–3
    for the condemned, 187, 308, 317–18, 332
    forgiveness as prerequisite for, 204–5
    and ways of confession, 207–9
San Marco, 304n–305n
Savonarola, Girolamo
    burning of, 126
    followers of, 296, 298, 311n
    martyrdom of, *178,* 313–14
    as model, for Boscoli, 313–14
    and San Marco, 304n
    viewed as heretic, 298
Scuola dei Confortori, 134–40, 144–54
Segni, Antonio, 299
Segni, Lorenzo, 299–300, 311n, 315
sense, as soul, 262
Serafino, Fra, 306
sermons, and *lauda,* 33n
Serristori, Antonio, 304n, 309
shame, 207–8, 212, 268–69
Siena, 23–26
sin
    and conditions of confession, 207–8
    crime distinguished from, 106
    despair, as unpardonable, 62–63, 212–13
    forgiveness of God, 206–7
    as hindrance to comforters, 247
    as human nature, 214–15
    mortal, to protest innocence, 242
    secret *vs.* manifest, 197
singing, as disruptive to confession, 316
social status
    and burial, 139, 328
    of comforters, 7–8, 147–56
    and execution, 328–30
Solomon, 233, 290
songs. *See laude* (devotional songs)
Soto, Domingo de, 113
soul
    as corrupted, 207–8
    death of, 225, 239–40
    defined/described, 262–63
    as eternal, 213, 231–32, 261, 334
    and forgiveness, 204–5

Biblical Index